Values Education for Dynamic Societies

CERC Studies in Comparative Education

1. Mark Bray & W.O. Lee (eds.) (2001): *Education and Political Transition: Themes and Experiences in East Asia*. Second edition. ISBN 962-8093-84-3. 228pp. HK$200 / US$32.

2. Mark Bray & W.O. Lee (eds.) (1997): *Education and Political Transition: Implications of Hong Kong's Change of Sovereignty*. ISBN 962-8093-90-8. 169pp. HK$100 / US$20.

3. Philip G. Altbach (1998): *Comparative Higher Education: Knowledge, the University, and Development*. ISBN 962-8093-88-6. 312pp. HK$180 / US$30.

4. Zhang Weiyuan (1998): *Young People and Careers: A Comparative Study of Careers Guidance in Hong Kong, Shanghai and Edinburgh*. ISBN 962-8093-89-4. 160pp. HK$180 / US$30.

5. Harold Noah & Max A. Eckstein (1998): *Doing Comparative Education: Three Decades of Collaboration*. ISBN 962-8093-87-8. 356pp. HK$250 / US$38.

6. T. Neville Postlethwaite (1999): *International Studies of Educational Achievement: Methodological Issues*. ISBN 962-8093-86-X. 86pp. HK$100 / US$20.

7. Mark Bray & Ramsey Koo (eds.) (1999): *Education and Society in Hong Kong and Macau: Comparative Perspectives on Continuity and Change*. ISBN 962-8093-82-7. 286pp. HK$200 / US$32.

8. Thomas Clayton (2000): *Education and the Politics of Language: Hegemony and Pragmatism in Cambodia, 1979-1989*. ISBN 962-8093-83-5. 243pp. HK$200 / US$32.

9. Gu Mingyuan (2001): *Education in China and Abroad: Perspectives from a Lifetime in Comparative Education*. ISBN 962-8093-70-3. 252pp. HK$200 / US$32.

10. Williams K. Cummings, Maria Teresa Tatto & John Hawkins (eds.) (2001): *Values Education for Dynamic Societies: Individualism or Collectivism*. ISBN 962-8093-71-1. 260pp. HK$200 / US$32.

11. Ruth Hayhoe & Julia Pan (eds.) (2001): *Knowledge Across Cultures: A Contribution to Dialogue Among Civilizations*. ISBN 962-8093-73-8. 391pp. HK$250 / US$38.

Other books published by CERC

1. Mark Bray & R. Murray Thomas (eds.) (1998): *Financing of Education in Indonesia*. ISBN 971-561-172-9. 133pp. HK$140 / US$20.

2. David A. Watkins & John B. Biggs (eds.) (1996, reprinted 1999): *The Chinese Learner: Cultural, Psychological and Contextual Influences*. ISBN 0-86431-182-6. 285pp. HK$200 / US$32.

3. Ruth Hayhoe (1999): *China's Universities 1895-1995: A Century of Cultural Conflict*. ISBN 962-8093-81-9. 299pp. HK$200 / US$32.

4. David A. Watkins & John B. Biggs (eds.) (2001): *Teaching the Chinese Learner: Psychological and Pedagogical Perspectives*. ISBN 962-8093-72-X. 306pp. HK$200 / US$32.

Order through bookstores or from:

Comparative Education Research Centre
The University of Hong Kong
Pokfulam Road, Hong Kong, China

Fax: (852) 2517 4737   E-mail: cerc@hkusub.hku.hk   Website: www.hku.hk/cerc

The list prices above are applicable for order from CERC, and include sea mail postage; add US$5 per copy for air mail.

Values Education
for
Dynamic Societies

Individualism or Collectivism

Edited by

William K. Cummings
Maria Teresa Tatto
John Hawkins

Comparative Education Research Centre
The University of Hong Kong

First published 2001
Comparative Education Research Centre
The University of Hong Kong
Pokfulam Road, Hong Kong, China

© Comparative Education Research Centre 2001

ISBN 962 8093 71 1

Contents

List of Tables and Figures

Preface

This study has provided a rewarding experience of collaboration to researchers in 20 settings across the Pacific Basin. In addition to the authors of the several chapters, a number of co-workers and over 800 educational elites generously shared their time to elaborate their best thinking on the nature and importance of values education and its future development. All who worked in preparing the papers for this book have profited immensely from the common experience, and we hope in the pages that follow we will be able to convey some of those riches to the readers.

The study was made possible by a grant from the Pacific Basin Research Center, which is affiliated with Soka University of America. We wish to express our deep appreciation to John Montgomery, Director of the Center for his intellectual and moral support, and we hope this product will be a useful addition to the valuable work of the Center. Our appreciation is also extended to Jay Heffron who took a deep interest in the study, and to Mark Bray who provided many thoughtful suggestions.

CHAPTER 1

THE REVIVAL OF VALUES EDUCATION
IN THE PACIFIC BASIN

William K. Cummings
John Hawkins
Maria Teresa Tatto

Introduction

The pace of social change picked up in the last quarter of the twentieth century, and nowhere is this more evident than in the societies situated in the Pacific Basin. Several of these societies have experienced exceptionally rapid economic growth, and despite recent setbacks have moved into that small circle of highly industrialized nations with annual per capita incomes in excess of US$10,000. The new affluence has unleashed a quest for ever greater material success, seemingly eroding traditional conceptions of moderation and virtue.

Nearly all of the Pacific Basin societies have strengthened their commitment to democratic forms of government; and especially in the cases of Russia, South Korea, and Indonesia this has been accompanied by major political change. Authoritarian and centralized regimes have been replaced by more participatory and decentralized governments. In some areas of the Pacific Basin, separatist movements have emerged to challenge former conceptions of "national" identity. Underlying all of these changes is the new autonomous citizen seeking greater opportunities for self-expression and exhibiting skepticism when faced with traditional social constraints

The rapid and often radical changes experienced by the societies of the Pacific Basin have led to much debate about societal goals and about the responsibilities of individual citizens. In virtually every society, these debates have pointed to the need for major adjustments in the process of educating young people. Especially notable has been the quest by national leaders for a reform and strengthening of values education. Whereas a collectivist bias characterizes the mainstream image both of Pacific Basin societies and of the purpose of values education, a surprising new theme in the recent values education discussions has been the determination to foster autonomous personalities so that each member of the respective societies has the strength to make wise decisions.

The objective of this book is to describe these recent developments and debates and to outline the new directions they suggest for values education. There are a number of reasons for focusing on the Pacific Basin and the values perspectives of its leaders.

- First, the region is rapidly rising in importance in the new international order and hence it is important to gain a better understanding of developments there.
- Secondly, the region is exceptionally diverse in terms of its traditions and history, and the implications of this diversity deserve sensitive analysis.

- Thirdly, in many Pacific Basin settings past traditions are undergoing inten-sive review. The outcomes of these reviews are likely to have a profound im-pact on the future direction of history.
- Fourthly, much of our understanding of the region comes from research on macro issues and processes with less attention to the views of leaders, either past or contemporary.
- Finally, values education is a prominent part of education in most of the Pa-cific Basin countries, and there may be lessons to learn.

In this introductory chapter, we introduce the setting for the study, the methodo-logy, and some of the findings. The twelve chapters that follow will go into the details of particular settings. In the final chapter, we will return to some of the issues raised as we strive to interpret the significance of the study.

The Importance of the Pacific Basin

The Pacific Basin, comprising all societies that touch the Pacific Ocean or its re-lated seas, includes several of the largest nations in the world: China, the U.S., Indone-sia, Russia, Japan and Mexico. In the Basin, there are also many smaller societies, such as the numerous small islands of Micronesia and the Pacific Ocean, including Hawai'i and the affluent city-states of Hong Kong and Singapore.

Several of the earliest civilizations of human history were located in the Pacific Basin: China and the Confucian offshoots in Korea and Japan, the Mayan kingdom, the Incas. Through at least the first half of the last millennium, the Pacific Basin was the most affluent area in the world, and there was considerable interaction in certain areas. For example, there was extensive commerce and cultural exchange in East Asia as well as in Central America. Thus the cultural development of most Pacific Basin settings long precedes that of Western Europe, but it was Western Europe that emerged as the major force in world history from the fifteenth century.

As Western Europe reached out to the world to expand its commercial and cul-tural influence, most of the Pacific Basin was colonized. The three areas escaping this fate were Russia, Japan, and Thailand. The American colonies were able at a relatively early stage to shed the bondage of colonialism followed in the early nineteenth century by the various nations of South America. China with its open-door policy avoided an intensive form of colonial domination. But most of the Asian nations of the Pacific Basin continued under colonialism until the mid-twentieth century. A major impact of colonialism was to orient the economies and official cultures of these settings to West-ern Europe rather than to each other.

The Eurocentric direction of Pacific Basin interaction was accompanied by a plethora of caricatures of "Asian" values as contrasted to Western values.[1] Some were demeaning, such as Northrop's (1946) contrast of Eastern and Western traits, or Wittfogel's (1957) thesis of Oriental Despotism. Hajime Nakamura in his thoughtful analysis of the *Ways of Thinking of Eastern Peoples* (1964) sought to debunk these simplistic arguments and highlight the complexity of Pacific Basin cultures.

---

[1] Edward Said (1978) in *Orientalism* has provided the most provocative analysis of these cul-tural caricatures.

Table 1.1 The Cultural Heritage of Selected Pacific Basin Settings

	Civilization	Religion	Colonial Experience	Neo-Colonial Experience	Political Economy
Thailand	Indigenous/ China	Buddhist	—	U.S./Japan	Capitalist
Malaysia	Indigenous/ Europe/ Islam	Islam/Hindu/ Buddhist	British	Japanese	Capitalist
Singapore	China/ Europe	Buddhist	British	British/ Japanese	Capitalist
Hong Kong	China/ Europe	Buddhist/ Christian	British	—	Capitalist
China	China	Buddhist/ Confucian	Europe/ Japanese	Russia	Socialist
Taiwan	China	Buddhist	Japanese	U.S.	Capitalist
Korea	China	Confucian/ Christian	Japanese	U.S.	Corporatist
Japan	China	Confucian/ Shinto/ Buddhist	—	U.S.	Corporatist
Russia*	Europe	Orthodox Christian	—	—	Socialist/ Capitalist
USA**	Europe	Protestant	British	—	Capitalist
Hawai'i	Indigenous/ Europe	Buddhist/ Protestant	U.S.	U.S.	Capitalist
Mexico***	Mayan/Europe	Catholic	Spanish	U.S.	Capitalist

*   This study includes elites from Moscow, Kemerovo, and Vladivostok
**   This study includes elites from New York, Michigan, California, and Hawai'i
*** This study includes elites from six Mexican states

The vast area of the Pacific Basin and the long history of development have enabled many distinct socio-cultural societies to develop. Within the area are represented most of the salient dimensions of diversity now influencing global interactions:

- In terms of civilizational origins, the societies of the Pacific Basin encompass the Western European, Mayan, Chinese, Polynesian and Islamic groupings.
- In terms of religion, they include the Western Judeo-Christian tradition, Islam, Confucianism, Buddhism, Shintoism, and many local religions.
- In terms of colonial experience, different societies were exposed to the yoke of all of the major colonial powers: Great Britain, France, Spain, Portugal, the Netherlands, the United States, Japan, and the Soviet Union.
- In the post World War II period, especially significant has been the neocolonial influence of the United States, first through its occupation of Japan and Korea, then its involvement in the Vietnam War, and through its role in trade and commerce. Similarly, the economic presence of Japan has been enormous.

- The economic systems of the region range from the laissez faire capitalist extreme of the U.S. through the Asian corporatist models of Japan and Singapore, to the socialist predilection of the People's Republic of China.
- Several of the Pacific Basin societies are in a process of "transition" between two sets of ideological and normative principles with profound impact on every facet of life including the debates on values education.
- Also within each society, there is much diversity.

Many of the Pacific Basin societies currently have political independence while others such as Hawai'i and Hong Kong are politically incorporated in larger mega-states. Given the relative autonomy of certain of the Pacific Basin societies in larger mega-states, we have decided in the following account to minimize attention to formal political boundaries and focus more on distinctive societal entities which we will call settings. Most of the chapters focus on particular settings, with the exception of the chapters on the U.S., Russia, and Mexico that cover several settings. Altogether, this study covers twenty distinct settings in the Pacific Basin. Table 1.1 above identifies the settings included in the study, and notes some of their special characteristics.

So long as the societies of the Pacific Basin were under colonialism, the overall level of socio-political and economic development was suppressed. The United States, the first Pacific Basin society to become liberated, took advantage of its independence to become a major economic and political power by the turn of the twentieth century. Japan and Russia followed suit. But most of the other Pacific Basin societies were constrained in their development through the mid-twentieth century. It was only following liberation from colonialism that the Pacific Basin began to emerge as a major force in world affairs.

The initial emergence of the Pacific Basin from colonial dominance was by the sword. Japan took on the Allied Powers in World War II, followed by Communist China's struggle against the same alliance in the Korean War, and the conflict to liberate Vietnam of the sixties. The intra-regional imperial role of Japan as dominator of Korea and elsewhere, as well as the presence of China in Tibet, are additional elements of the Pacific Basin drama. Through these sustained struggles with external dominators, the societies of the Pacific Basin were able to remove many of the shackles of colonialism and neocolonialism and regain confidence in their efficacy. Success in these struggles was followed by a commitment to economic growth, with a strong emphasis on expanding exports throughout the world.

Even as conflicts were taking place in certain areas of the Pacific Basin, other areas were experiencing rapid growth. In the United States, the western states of California, Washington, and Oregon came to be the fastest growing areas. Japan from the mid-fifties began to stabilize its economy and enter into an extraordinary period of economic growth that resulted in its economy becoming the second largest in the world and vaulted its per capita income past that of most Western European nations. Other Pacific Basin nations also began to experience prosperity.

With the growth of commerce in the region and the decline of international political conflict, the interaction between Pacific Basin nations began to accelerate relative to the interaction of these nations with Western Europe. For example, whereas in the fifties approximately three-fourths of the trade of the U.S. was with Western Europe, by the mid-nineties approximately three-fourths was with other Pacific Basin countries (Task Force for Transnational Competence, 1997, p. 33).

Given the magnitude of recent economic change, it is remarkable that the political boundaries separating the various Pacific Basin states have remained essentially unchanged. There have been relatively few border disputes or instances of political consolidation through the use of force. Only in the case of the break-up of the Soviet Union and Indonesia have these transitions led to the emergence of new political entities. While the legal boundaries have been remarkably constant, the ideals and aspirations guiding the behavior within the established boundaries have undergone great ferment. In cases such as Korea and Russia, this ferment has strong geographic and social underpinnings, whereas in the United States it seems primarily anchored in social and religious affiliations that transcend geographic area.[2] In many instances, this ferment has become manifest in the form of new constitutions, the formation of new political parties, and the legislation of new practice concerning civil, social, and economic rights.

The Decline in Value Consensus Due to Rapid Social Change

In times of relative tranquility, there is likely to be a high level of value consistency both between the leaders of different segments of a society and between leaders of different generations. But in times of rapid change, this consistency may break down.

Rarely has humanity witnessed such an extraordinary pace of ideological, geopolitical, and economic change as in the past quarter century. The world's population has doubled, and its productivity has tripled. With new discoveries in communications, media, and computers, the possibility for the global transmission of information and images has radically improved. The cold war has passed, and the strength of most nation-states has weakened due to financial difficulties and the centrifugal pull of both local and transnational forces.

While the incidence of these changes is worldwide, it can be argued that the pace of change has been particularly intense in the Pacific Basin. Over the past quarter century, several Pacific Basin nations have experienced the highest rates of sustained economic growth ever witnessed in human history, rising from the ashes of World War II to build industrial societies and significantly improve the material standards of their citizens (World Bank, 1993). And over the past few years several Pacific Basin nations have experienced dramatic and hopefully temporary reversals in their economic fortunes. The political repercussions of these economic slumps are still unraveling, especially in Indonesia, Malaysia, Thailand, and Russia.

The rapid pace of social change in the Pacific Basin has been accompanied by a sharp rise in value dissensus, heightening uncertainty about future directions. This dissensus is evident in the political sphere with the emergence of new political parties

---

[2] For example, in South Korea's most recent presidential election there were sharp differences in the voting patterns of the South (Chulan area) and elsewhere. The major cleavages in the U.S. appear to be class, race, and religious commitment with geography operating as a secondary factor.

as well as in other areas: new music and lifestyles, increasing rates of crime and juvenile delinquency, rising rates of divorce and childbirth out of wedlock.

The current value dissensus in the Pacific Basin provides the rationale for this study. Recognizing the role of leaders in shaping the future direction of values, the study seeks to find out what values the leaders believe have the greatest promise for the future, and what are the specific approaches the leaders believe will be most conducive for conveying the salient values.

Selecting Settings and Sampling Leaders

Given the complexity and size of the Pacific Basin, it was impossible to include all of the settings in the region. So it was decided to include all of the large societies and to choose a sufficient range of smaller societies so as to cover the major dimensions of cultural variation highlighted in Table 1.1. The twenty settings in the study capture most of the salient dimensions of diversity in the region, except for the failure to complete fieldwork in Indonesia and an under-sampling of settings influenced by French colonialism. It should be noted that several settings were included in the large societies of China, the U.S., Russia, and Mexico in recognition of the internal diversity within each.

Within each setting, our concern was to interview a "representative" sample of at least thirty *leaders with a record of accomplishment in the field of values education.* To carry out the interviews, expert teams were formed for each setting composed minimally of one senior and one junior researcher; where practical, one of the team members was an "outsider" so as to enhance the objectivity of the field-based decision-making. Each team sought to select appropriate leaders from a diversity of previously identified positions: central educational authorities, leading educational intellectuals, religious leaders, leaders of related NGOs, politicians, people in educational institutes, academic leaders (e.g., deans of education schools and prominent professors), curriculum designers in moral education, and/or values/moral education specialists. No more than one-third were to be front-line educators. In view of the diverse positions of respondents, consisting both of decision-makers and critics, in the remainder of the book they will be referred to interchangeably as leaders and elites.

Recognizing the impossibility of developing a meaningful definition of leaders that would fit the various countries and settings under consideration, no effort was made to choose a random sample. Rather each team was expected to choose those leaders that best reflected their setting, keeping in mind the common commitment to diversity. By social position, 6 percent of the sample are political leaders, 17 percent are central educational authorities, 5 percent are religious leaders, 11 percent are from related NGOs, 17 percent are intellectual leaders, 12 percent are academics, 18 percent are local school leaders, and 20 percent are curriculum designers or teachers of values education; 21 percent are women. This distribution was more or less similar for each setting, though the full details for the setting samples can be found in the respective chapters. In total, responses were obtained from 834 leaders.

Values, Social Development, and Social Capital

Perhaps the most controversial theme in the contemporary values debate is the relative primacy of collective as contrasted to individualistic values. A major thrust of values education in most Pacific Basin settings (the U.S. may be the principle exception) has been to foster collective values and to de-emphasize individual values (Cummings, Gopinathan, and Tomoda, 1988). These collective values have encouraged the accumulation of large stocks of social capital[3] through supporting strength in the collective entities of the family, the community, and the state. But at the same time, some argue that these collective values have handicapped the struggle for modernization of the Asian societies of the region such as Japan and China.

Mainstream Western thinking about modernization has stressed the primacy of individual over collective values. This is the essence of Durkheim's (1933) discussion of the shift from mechanical to organic solidarity, or Toennies (1957) contrast of *gemeinschaft* and *gessellschaft*. Individualistic values are said to be favorable to entrepreneurship (Weber,1958), scientific and technical innovation (Barber, 1952), aesthetic creativity (Boorstin, 1992), critical and responsible participation in democratic politics (Almond and Verba, 1963), and also are conducive to a more efficient labor market (Polyani, 1957) and industrial labor force (Inkeles and Smith, 1974). These arguments have been used to account for the greater success of Europe and North America in bringing about the industrial revolution and achieving international dominance since the time of the Reformation relative to the former great empires of Asia. While Marxist perspectives stress the role of collective solidarity in realizing the class struggle to overcome the despotic capitalist ruling class that triumphed in the industrial revolution, Marx himself was very skeptical of the qualities of most non-European societies, making allusions for example to Asian despotism. Max Weber in his comparative study of religions was also pessimistic about the potential of Confucianism and Buddhism for promoting social change.

Indeed, most Western theories whether liberal or Marxist have viewed Asian collective values as impediments to change. This same line of reasoning has shaped the work of Western area specialists who have studied Asian societies. For example, Bellah (1957) argued that Tokugawa religion, while favoring loyalty to feudal lords and later to the leaders of the Meiji state, stood in the way of the emergence of vibrant capitalism and a civic society in the early modern period. Levy (1955) and others (e.g. Redding, 1988) have argued that the Chinese value system favored family-owned businesses that were limited in growth prospects because the family-owners were unwilling to trust outsiders with major management responsibilities. Similarly, it has been argued that the collectivist bias has limited the capacity for scientific and technical creativity or industrial innovation (Bartocha and Okamura, 1985; Nakayama, 1991, p. 46 ff).

While these pessimistic arguments have persisted, certain areas of Asia defied the experts. Japan led the Asian flock in the sixties with an extraordinary economic resurgence. Since then the Four Asian tigers of Taiwan, Korea, Hong Kong and Singapore have followed Japan's lead. And other Asian societies have been nominated as strong candidates for entering the ranks of the Newly Industrializing Societies.

---

[3] See Portes (1998) and Woolcock (1998) for a definition and discussion of social capital.

The rapid advances of Asian societies have been accompanied by a revisionist perspective on the nature of collective values. For example, collective values are said to facilitate the team-work and bottom-up decision-making essential to the effective functioning of the large organizations common to advanced capitalism (Vogel, 1975; Miyanaga, 1991). Collective values are also said to favor a strong achievement-oriented work ethic and the type of family support that motivates young people to aspire for educational success as well as to accept the meritocratic norms that shape job recruitment and promotions (Berger and Hsiao, 1988, p. 5). And collective values are said to be compatible with pro-growth public policies including pro-business attitudes, limited government intervention in business operations, and restraint in the provision of social welfare (Lodge and Vogel, 1987).

Distinct from the relation of collective/individual values to fostering technical and economic change is their role in supporting the quality of life in families, the community, and the polity (Tu, 1991). Also, it has been observed that collective values lead to high levels of voter turnout in elections in many Pacific Basin countries. But critics note that the typical voter tends to vote according to the dictates of political machines that dominate in their communities, and fail to exercise independent judgement to select candidates that best reflect their personal interests (Curtis, 1988).

In sum, there is extensive debate about the relative efficacy of collective and individual values. Assuming that collective values foster the accumulation of social capital, does this necessarily mean that individualistic values favor a decline in social capital? While Western formulations of cultural systems tend to place collective and individual values in opposition, several of the studies that follow present the contrary view that the strengthening of individual values may enable the more effective functioning of modern collective entities such as high-tech corporations and truly representative party politics. Indeed there may be a need to reassess the relation of various social values to the prospects for social capital in the Pacific Basin.

The studies that follow give considerable attention to these debates, with special focus on the orientations of Pacific Basin leaders: which values do they consider important and why? Is there a discernable shift in their value preferences? The studies point to a great irony, which we will stress in the concluding chapter. *At the very time that leaders in North America and Western Europe, influenced by the revisionist arguments, are developing a new interest in communitarian values, leaders on the Asian side of the Pacific Basin are developing a more favorable attitude to more individualistic values.* The Asian leaders have come to believe that these individualistic values are an essential foundation for the future modernization of their societies.

Leaders and Values

Research on social and cultural capital has pointed out that the values a culture holds as important are strong forces that help shape societies and influence such aspects as form of government, schooling, productivity and social well being (Putnam, 1993; Coleman, 1994; Bourdieu, 1977; Bourdieu and Passeron, 1977; Inglehart, 1997). These studies also observe that important societal changes are often preceded—and accompanied—by dramatic changes in values and cultural beliefs (Diamond and Plattner, 1996; Inglehart, 1997). Societies that have moved from authoritarian to more democratic forms of government see this change reflected not only in the organization

of their government and in the school curriculum, but also in the media and in the relationships individuals have with one another.

Some values focus on "ends" such as increased economic productivity or improvements in culture or the quality of life. Others focus on "means" such as the enhancement of civic mindedness so that governments are more responsive. A different
example is the value of freedom from social constraints so that individuals can enjoy
greater autonomy to realize personal goals.[4]

Talcott Parsons and Edward Shils in *Towards a General Theory of Action* (1951,
p. 53) assert that human behavior is:

> Oriented to the attainment of ends in situation, by means of the normatively
> regulated expenditure of energy. There are four points to be noted in this
> conceptualization of behavior: (1) Behavior is oriented to the attainment of
> ends or goals or other anticipated states of affairs. (2) It takes place in
> situations. (3) It is normatively regulated. (4) It involves expenditure of en-
> ergy or effort in "motivation" (which may be more or less organized inde-
> pendently of its involvement in action).

This formulation takes the point of view of individual actors. Parsons and Shils
then proceed to consider the interaction of actors in roles and organizations. The parallel components are values, norms, organized roles, and situational facilities. According to Neil Smelser (1963, p. 32) values are the core components of social systems with the characteristics of the other components logically shaped by and hierar-
chically derived from the core values.

The above theoretical formulation, often referred to as structural-functionalism,
tends to assert that social values are "shared" by the members of a social system. Other
social theories, most notably conflict and critical theory (Gouldner, 1971; Collins,
1971; Apple, 1982), while agreeing on the categorization of the components of behavior, dispute the contentions that values are truly shared and that they are core components. These theories argue that particular actors who enjoy dominant positions seek
to bias the content of social values so as to advance their interests; thus the interests of
the particular groups, sometimes called the ruling class, are the core components. The
interested parties introduce their bias through obtaining influential positions in the
agencies of values education such as the media, voluntary organizations and schools
(Bowles and Gintis, 1976). Thus, these critics, do not deny the impact of values on
behavior; however, they insist that the members of society are influenced by distorted
values, a "false consciousness", fostered by the ruling class and/or particular vested
interests.

It is certainly the case, as illustrated in the case studies that follow, that the leaders
of societies devote much time to defining and clarifying values. The values that leaders
stress tend to reflect both their sense of the common good and their particular interests.
Religious leaders are more likely to stress values of spirituality and abstinence,
whereas economic leaders may stress inner-worldly achievement and consumption.

---

[4] M. Rokeach in his *Nature of Human Values* (1973) makes the distinction between ends and
means values; in that all values become goals for concerted action, other theorists do not find
the ends/means distinction to be essential. For example, who is to say the quest for freedom is
a means to some other end or an end in itself (Patterson, 1991).

Leaders use their social positions to promote their values amongst the public through such channels as the media, public campaigns, religious organizations, and formal educational institutions.

In recognition of the above debate, the research that follows makes no assumptions about the commonness of the origins of social values. It only assumes that values play an important role in shaping the direction of behavior. Also in recognition of the effort by special interests to influence "common" values, the studies below intentionally sample leaders that represent a broad range of interests in the respective societies.

The Translation of New Values into Values Education

Given the considerable changes taking place in the political and economic spheres of Pacific Basin societies, there would appear to be an expanded need for debate on the new rights and responsibilities of the citizenry and for new efforts to educate citizens about the implications of the recent changes. Indeed, among the leaders of these changing societies, there has been much discussion as will be reviewed in the chapters that follow. Will future generations have a greater social consciousness, or will they be more concerned for their own private interests? Will they be more or less committed to correcting environmental injuries, to resolving social conflicts, to strengthening community life?

The outcomes of these debates concerning prospective values are certain to play a central role in shaping the quality of social capital that will be available in the twenty-first century. But, at least until the past decade, the leaders in most Pacific Basin societies were not notably effective in translating the conclusions of these debates into programs of values education that would help the new generations adjust to the changes.

In earlier times when societies were going through major shifts in their political economies, leaders articulated new values and turned to the schools to promote these through values education. The most notable such transformation occurred with the birth of the modern nation-state on the eve of the nineteenth century. Prior to the modern period, schools assumed an important role in values education with a prominent focus on religious education. The French revolution, with its stress on the values of the new Republican State, sought to draw a clear line between religious and Republican values; Robespierre, speaking in 1793 to the National Convention, declared: "I am convinced of the necessity of operating a total regeneration, and, if I may express myself in this way, of creating a new people" (quoted in Glenn, 1988, p. 20). The common school movement, as it developed first in Western Europe and later in the United States, stressed the role of the school in building a new democratic society while at the same time drawing a line between civic and social education in the schools and religious education in the homes and churches. Meiji Japan was also fascinated with the common school concept, but saw the new school as a means for promoting modernizing Western Science, on the one hand, and the Eastern moral values of respect for the Emperor and hard work, on the other hand. And with the conclusion of the Russian revolution in 1917, the new Soviet government triumphed and declared its determination to use the school to create the socialist revolution. Of course, in these first modern societies other institutions continued to engage in parallel programs of values education, but it is not stretching the point to suggest that they came to look on the school to play the predominant role in values education.

Yet over time, each of these societies also asked the school to intensify its contribution to other forms of socialization, notably a strengthening of the academic curriculum and an increasing stress on the development of vocational skills. And, at least in certain settings, this stress on additional responsibilities for the school has been accompanied by a diminution of the school's role in values education: Japan dropped moral education as a separate class following World War II. And over the past four decades, the United States has placed ever more restrictions on the teaching of religion in schools, perhaps best symbolized by the legal ban on prayer in schools. And in the socialist world of the Soviet Union and China, there is the longstanding tension between the Red versus expert curricular emphasis.

Most observers suggest that the resolution of these curricular challenges has led to a diminution of the time and attention devoted to values education. And with the shift away from values education, there has been a growing perception of a decline in the general standards of social behavior. Sociologists plot the upward trends in juvenile delinquency as well as white-collar crime in virtually every industrial society. Particularly stressful in recent years have been extreme crimes such as the mass shooting of teen-age students in Littletown, Colorado, U.S., by a former peer. Equally shocking was a recent case in Japan where a student from an ordinary middle class family killed a schoolmate and put the cut head in front of the gate of their school. Similar stories of disturbing moral behavior are in the news in all of the countries included in this study.

Interviewing Elites as a Means to Understanding the Current Values Education Debate

It is not yet clear whether the seismic cultural, political, and economic changes now occurring in the Pacific Basin will lead to a fundamental reordering of values. But incidents such as the above have certainly spurred a renewed discussion of values education throughout the Pacific Basin. One indication of the renewed interest is the sharp increase in the frequency of statements in public speeches, popular magazines, official reports of commissions, and declarations of government policy on values education (Cummings, Gopinathan, and Tomoda, 1988).

At the risk of oversimplifying, it might be said that these debates focus on four core questions—

Why should there be improvements in values education? Leaders in the different settings of the Pacific Basin have highlighted many issues including the need to become better prepared for work, the need to make better use of the fruits of work, the need to participate responsibly in democratic politics and civic society, the need to develop richer personalities that are more introspective and creative, and the need to develop a more caring attitude to the environment. Altogether, fifteen distinctive themes were identified by the research group responsible for this book. Given the large number of themes, it is useful to ask which themes are most important in which settings.

What values should receive the greatest emphasis in values education? Values education covers many areas from civic responsibility to spiritual development. Which of these should be given the most emphasis in publicly coordinated programs for values education?

Who should be the focus of values education? Parents naturally believe they have a major responsibility to convey sound values to their young children, but are there other stages in the life cycle that also should be a focus for intensive efforts of values education such as in the university or the workplace?

How should these values be developed and transmitted? While values education is often provided in schools through formal instruction, some leaders proposed other locations such as youth groups, military service, and religious organizations. Thus, a final question is the proper locus of values education, and what are the most effective pedagogical and experiential approaches for communicating and transmitting values.

While documents provided important insights on these debates, the coordinators of this book concluded that a full understanding of the current movement would be incomplete without interviews with the leaders of these debates.

The Sigma International Elite Survey of Values Education

An early decision of the combined group responsible for this book (coordinators and all team members) was to develop a research approach that would help highlight points of divergence in the thinking of elites rather than areas of agreement. The group concluded that the diverse tendencies in values education of the region were a reflection of the emerging complexity of the contemporary life. Indeed, the diversity could be thought of as a source of strength and creativity. The methodology for highlighting differences required a new survey approach, the Sigma International Elite Survey,[5] complemented by careful investigations of the sociopolitical context in each of the sites of the Elite Survey. The special features of the Sigma Survey are:

- The intentional selection of an elite sample from each setting that represents important points of variation in terms of political/ideological affiliation, social position, gender, and regional location;
- The development of questions that reflect the particular concerns of each setting;
- The use of a question format that requires respondents to clarify where they stand (e.g. rank-ordering from a list with many options; and
- Follow-up questions to selected respondents who take exceptional positions on particular responses.

Two workshops were devoted to developing the instrument for the Sigma International Elite Survey, and four drafts were field tested prior to arriving at the final instrument. This instrument (included as Appendix A) has separate sections for the Why, What, and How questions as well as sections on hot issues and on the national experiences believed to provide the most useful examples to incorporate in values education curriculums. The instrument was originally prepared in English and then translated

---

[5] The letter sigma is used by statisticians to symbolize variance. The sigma approach developed in this study seeks to highlight differences or variance. It should be contrasted with the delphi approach, which seeks to develop consensus and thereby to reduce variance.

into the respective national languages by experts who checked their work with back translations.

Organization of the Book

The chapters that follow, focusing on specific settings, begin with a review of the social and political environment and then provide interpretations of the results for the Sigma elite survey for the particular setting(s). While each author follows a common outline, there is necessarily some variation in the approaches reflecting both contextual differences and the styles of the respective authors. For example, the chapters on the larger countries tend to give some consideration to regional variation. In contrast, those on the smaller countries give more consideration to international comparisons. Also some of the chapters use relatively complex tools of analysis while others focus mainly on simpler statistics such as means and ranks.

The major finding of the study is the primacy that Pacific Basin leaders in all of the settings accord to more individualistic values; however, in terms of second tier values, there are interesting variations that can be clustered into four groups:

- Russia, where exceptional stress is placed on fostering individual autonomy and spiritual development; and
- Several settings which stress civic consciousness, democracy, and various "post-modern values"; included in this group are the several settings in North-America as well as Taiwan and Japan. In that the elites of the latter two societies indicate a concern to adopt certain "Western" values, we refer to this group as the "Far" West.
- An East Asian group that stresses the traditional values of hard work and the strengthening of national identity while also encouraging new directions;
- A Southeast Asian group that stresses a need for strengthening moral behavior and democratic values;

The final chapter of the book will go into more detail on the specific characteristics of each cluster. It is mentioned now in order to account for the order in which the several case studies are presented. Russia, which is experiencing perhaps the most profound changes of all of the societies in our sample, is taken up first, followed by a sequential view of the settings in the three other clusters. As it turns out, this ordering of cases results in a gradual westward journey from Russia through North America (including both the U.S. and Mexico) to Japan and Taiwan followed by a focus on East Asia and finally on Southeast Asia. We turn now to the setting chapters.

References

Almond, G. and Verba, S. (1963). *The Civic Culture: Attitudes to Democracy in Five Nations.* Princeton, NJ: Princeton University Press.

Appelbaum, R.P. and Henderson, J. (eds.) (1992). *States and Development in the Pacific Rim.* Newbury Park, CA: Sage Publications.

Apple, M. (1982). *Education and Power.* New York: Routledge and Kegan Paul.

Barber, B. (1952). *Science and the Social Order*. Glencoe, IL. Free Press.

Bartocha, B. and Okamura, S. (eds.) (1985). *Transforming Scientific Ideas into Innovations: Science Policies in the United States and Japan*. Tokyo: Japan Society for the Promotion of Science.

Bellah, R. (1957). *Tokugawa Religion*. Boston, MA: Beacon Press.

Berger, P.L. and Hsiao, H.M. (eds.) (1988). *In Search of an East Asian Development Model*. New Brunswick, NY: Transaction Publishers.

Boorstin, D. (1992). *The Creators*. New York: Random House.

Bourdieu, P. (1977). *Outline of a Theory of Practice*. (F. Nice, trans.). Cambridge, U.K. and New York: Cambridge University Press.

Bourdieu, P. and Passeron, J-C. (1977). *Reproduction in Education, Society, and Culture*. (F. Nice, trans.). London: Sage.

Bowles, S. and Gintis, H. (1976). *Schools in Capitalist America: Educational Reform and the Contradictions of Economic Life*. New York: Basic Books.

Coleman, J.S. (1994) "Social Capital in the Creation of Human Capital," *American Journal of Sociology*. Supplement: S105-108.

Collins, R. (1971). "Functional and Conflict Theories of Educational Stratification," *American Sociological Review* 36: 1002-1019.

Curtis, G.L. (1988). *The Japanese Way of Politics*. New York: Columbia University Press.

Cummings, W.K., Gopinathan, S. and Tomoda, Y. (eds.) (1988). *The Revival of Values Education in Asia and the West*. New York: Pergamon Press.

Diamond, L. and Plattner, M. (1996). *The Global Resurgence of Democracy*. Baltimore, MD: Johns Hopkins University Press.

Durkheim, E. (1933). *The Division of Labor in Society*. (G. Simpson, trans.). Glencoe, IL: Free Press.

Glenn, C.L. (1988). *The Myth of the Common School*. Amherst, MA: University of Massachusetts Press.

Gouldner, A.W. (1971). *The Coming Crisis of Western Sociology*. London: Heinemann.

Hagen, E.E. (1962). *On the Theory of Social Change*. Homewood, IL: The Dorsey Press.

Inglehart, R. (1997). *Modernization and Postmodernization*. Princeton, NJ: Princeton University Press.

Inkeles, A. and Smith, D.H. (1974). *Becoming Modern: Individual Change in Six Developing Countries*. Cambridge, MA: Harvard University Press.

Levy Jr., M.J. (1955). "Contrasting Factors in Modernization of Japan and China." In S. Kuznets, W.E. Moore, J.J. Spengler (eds.). *Economic Growth: Brazil, India, Japan*. Durham, NC: Duke University Press.

Lodge, G.C. and Vogel, E. (1987). *Ideology and National Competitiveness*. Boston, MA: Harvard Business School Press.

Miyanaga, K. (1991). *The Creative Edge: Emerging Individualism in Japan*. New Brunswick, NY: Transaction Publishers.

Nakamura, H. (1964). *Ways of Thinking of Eastern Peoples*. Honolulu: East-West Center Press.

Nakayama, S. (1991). *Technology and Society in Postwar Japan*. London: Kegan Paul.

Nord, W.A. (1995). *Religion and American Education*. Chapel Hill, NC: University of North Carolina Press.

Northrop, F.S.C. (1946). *The Meeting of East and West*. New York: Macmillan.

Parsons, T. and Shils, E. (1951). *Towards a General Theory of Action*. Glencoe, IL: Free Press.

Patterson, O. (1991). *Freedom: Freedom in the Making of Western Culture*. New York: Basic Books.

Polyani, K. (1957). *The Great Transformation*. Boston, MA: Beacon Press.

Portes, A. (1998). "Social Capital: Its Origins and Applications in Modern Sociology." *Annual Review of Sociology*. Vol 24: pp. 1-24.

Putnam, R.D. (1993). *Making Democracy Work: The Civic Traditions in Modern Italy*. Princeton, NJ: Princeton University Press.

Pye, L.W. (1985). *Asian Power and Politics*. Cambridge, MA: The Belknap Press.

Redding, S.G. (1988). "The Role of the Entrepreneur in the New Asian Capitalism." In P.L. Berger and Hsiao, H.M. (eds.). *In Search of an East Asian Development Model*. New Brunswick, NY: Transaction Publishers.

Rokeach, M. (1973). *Nature of Human Values*. New York: Free Press.

Smelser, N.J. (1963). *Theory of Collective Behavior*. New York: Free Press.

Said, E. (1978). *Orientalism*. New York: Pantheon Books.

Task Force for Transnational Competence (1997). *Towards Transnational Competence*. New York: Institute of International Education.

Toennies, F. (1957). *Community and Society—Gemeinschaft and Gessellschaft*. (C.D. Loomis, trans.). East Lansing, MI: Michigan State Press.

Tu, W.M. (1991). "A Confucian Perspective on Global Consciousness and Local Awareness." *International House of Japan Bulletin* 11(1): 1-5.

Vogel, E. (Ed.) (1975). *Modern Japanese Organization and Decision-Making*. Berkeley: University of California Press.

Weber, M. (1958). *The Protestant Ethic and the Spirit of Capitalism*. (T. Parsons, trans.). New York: Charles Scribner Sons, 1958.

Wittfogel, K.A. (1957). *Oriental Despotism: A Comparative Study of Total Power*. Oxford: Oxford University Press.

Woolcock, M. (1998). "Social Capital and Economic Development: Towards a Theoretical Synthesis and Policy Framework," *Theory and Society* 27: 151-208.

World Bank, The (1993). *The East Asian Miracle: Economic Growth and Public Policy*. New York: Oxford University Press.

Russia

CHAPTER 2

RUSSIA:
TOWARDS AUTONOMOUS PERSONALITIES

Olga Bain

Introduction

It can be argued that values education was one of the most contested issues in late 1990s Russia. Both the concerns about the rising deviance of behavior in the society in "transition" and the challenges of entering the new century brought values education into the center of professional educators' discussions. The purpose of this study is to frame the values education debate in Russia in a comparative perspective, taking into account the overall project's why-, what-, and how-dimensions of teaching values in schools.

These three dimensions translate into the major purposes of the present study—to interpret views of educators 1) on the impact of social change in the "transitional" society upon the role of schools in values transmission, 2) on the content of values which guide educators in their practice, 3) on the types of environments most conducive to values education, on the appropriateness of indirect vis-à-vis direct value learning, and on the relation of values learning to the age of children.

These major goals were complemented by specific research questions in the Russian study. How is the values education debate in Russia shaped by its most influential contexts —societal, political and policy-related? How does a leading group of educators and scholars in the central (federal) institutions of education respond to these environments? Is there a polarization or considerable agreement among them as to what values to teach the young?

These issues were to set up the background for conducting a sample survey from a larger pool of educational elites identified here as those capable of influencing decisions by school communities to participate in or to stand aside from pedagogical values transmission and values learning. The pool included the intellectual, policy-making and administrative core of the federal center (the city of Moscow) and the newly-born educational elites in two regional cities, totaling three settings[1]. The assumption was that not only regional authorities assume their rights in shaping their own educational policies in the increasingly decentralized context of the Russian federalism, but most importantly educational ideas and initiatives can no longer be simply downloaded from the center. Instead they are nourished and implemented by a variety of individual schools and their regional public supporters. Therefore, the analysis of

---

[1] The data analyzed in this chapter comes from the survey completed in three Russian cities: Moscow, Vladivostok, and Kemerovo. The survey was conducted in the three locales respectively by Vladimir Sobkin, director of the Moscow Center of Sociology of Education of the Russian Academy of Education, by Andrey Uroda of Far-Eastern State Technical University, and by Olga Bain of SUNY Buffalo. The author is greatly indebted to the survey conductors for their cooperative effort. In addition to the present analysis, the interpretation of the Moscow elite survey by Vladimir Sobkin is forthcoming in the Russian language.

the survey, conducted at the end of 1997 and the beginning of 1998, focuses on spotting patterns in self-reported attitudes and views. In other words, the study tests whether preferences in the elites' attitudes on values education are primarily correlated to the local setting (regional correlation), or to the elites' positions, gender, and workplace (interregional correlation).

Beyond the variation of attitudes by regional or interregional characteristics, the study explores the discernible features of the values logic through a set of parameters obtained by the procedure of factor analysis. These parameters are analyzed to illuminate the relational value of the expressed axiological attitudes, which is critical for this study as well as for the international comparisons of the larger project.

The structure of the chapter follows the logic of the project design. It opens with the theoretical framework. Then it discusses the influences of the three major contexts on the Russian values education debate and explores the response of the central elite to these challenges. It proceeds with the discussion of the methods and findings of the survey from a cross-regional perspective. Finally, it discusses implications of the semantic analysis of attitudes towards values for the international comparative study. The chapter concludes with the policy implications of the study.

Theoretical Framework

The significance of the study underscores its specific purpose: while many studies on attitudes and values target individuals and their value system, the current international project seeks to understand the differences and similarities in the way educators view the educational effect of schooling on the values of the youth. In stating these views educators emphasize values most significant socially and individually as they see them, they relate these values to the larger societal context, and they look for the most appropriate pedagogical means to support or discourage these values at school. This is the way the "why", "what", and "how" parts of the project design originated.

The additional dimensions of the Russian study in the project relate to recent trend of decentralization, i.e., whether regional identities are evolving to shape values agenda, whether they compete with other identities such as belonging to professional or new public networks. Whether they actually do not compete but compensate for the disruptions of previously functional bonds and ties. In other words, we seek an answer to whether an educational policy formulation format is possible to construct in the context shaped by the three major factors: a) newly established democratic institutions, b) the evolving self-governing structures that replace centralized planning, and c) enormous dislocations in the socio-economic and normative fabric of the nation.

To this end, we have surveyed contemporary sociological discourses for the conceptualizations used to describe the value system phenomenon in the countries undergoing rapid and fundamental change. Two concepts we find pertinent: one is "social capital", and the other is "nations in transition". Below we turn to the way these discourses inform the present study.

The recent literature has not been inattentive to the changes in value and normative systems in contemporary societies and, in particular, in new and nascent democracies. This concern is prompted by the importance of "cultural transition" for the success of the economic and socio-political reforms the countries in Central and Eastern

Europe (CEE) and Newly Independent States (NISs) of the former Soviet Union are embarked on. That is, the importance of "changing mentalities, attitudes, values, and social relations" (Birzea 1996, p. 674). The abruptness, depth, and scope of societal transformation are said to be the causes of the enormous rise of deviant behavior in general, and in the rise of suicide rate in particular (Cerych 1995). To interpret these changes some authors (e.g., Birzea 1994) resort to *anomic* theory, introduced by Emile Durkheim (1951) in his *Suicide*. While this theory has been developed to identify the triggers of deviant behavior, it does not attempt to interpret the dynamics of the transitional context itself. At best it concludes that cultural transition is a long-term project, often not synchronized with major institutional changes, and that it would require replacement of at least one generation.

Further, the application of anomic theory to the transitional countries involves some contradictions. Firstly, while the case for anomie is based on evidence of the increased prevalence of attitudes of disenchantment and affective insecurity, at the same time it is indicated that reforms in CEE and NISs are nurtured by the spontaneous initiative of individuals (Birzea 1994, Cerych 1995). These obviously contradictory statements about the role of the transitional context—in both enhancing anomie and mobilizing individual and collective consciousness for a new collective project—are referred as "a double and quasi-contradictory role of transition" (Cerych 1995, p. 426).

Secondly, the phenomenon of anomie caused by the abruptness of value system change entails recognition of value vacuum as a source of value disorientation. Though plausible theoretically, this concept backfired in formulating educational policies when values education was ousted from schools in Russia alongside with the ideological and formalized rituals of pro-communist upbringing. Soon thereafter it has been admitted that value-neutral educational policy is only an illusion.

Thirdly, the abruptness of transition implies a common and identifiable point of departure from a so-called "totalitarian system". The term in its turn is based on the assumption of a perfectly integrated and authority-centered society with no room for conflict. But, as Adam Przeworski has pointed out, ideology was not the cement that held the societies of the Eastern-bloc countries together starting from the late 1950s (Przeworski 1995, pp. 1-9). He refers to the surveys in Poland and Hungary that showed that these societies in particular were highly materialistic, atomized, and cynical. The evidence from other Eastern European countries demonstrated that communist ideology was no longer the backbone of these societies, and that, on the contrary, the very ideals that serve as the basis of their social order became a threat to it (pp. 2-3). Thus, Polish students of technical professions imbued with rationality were mostly critical about the rational state order. The working class movement in Poland brought an end to the social order, which arguably expressed its interests.

For other concepts of societal change we look into studies with an overall evolutionary approach. These theories emphasize that the behavior of individuals and organizations is not driven strictly by rational choices and incentives, because at the least the latter are always obscure and uncertain (Nelson and Winter, 1982). Therefore, while exploring "transitional" societies in particular—either their economic or sociopolitical change—the focus is both on the role of "inheritance", path dependency of institutions and on the variation of simultaneously existing forms, which under certain adverse stimuli produce innovation (see, e.g., Stark and Bruszt, 1998).

The normative aspects of change, consolidating or disintegrating forces in the societies are not disregarded in these studies. Thus, Adam Przeworski (1995, 1997), while examining factors that help or interfere with new democracies of southern and eastern Europe and Latin America sustain and consolidate, points to the weakness of civil society in new democracies. This weakness comes mainly from the weak structuration of interests to be represented. First of all, individuals can rarely be forced into interest representations by formal rules or governmental incentives; secondly, new democracies find it difficult to break away from old practices under which the authoritarian state would provide officially recognized, monopolistic forms of interest representation; thirdly, even in new democracies the organization of interest groups composed of largely dispersed actors (such as consumers, renters, women) is low relative to the interests representing compact and privileged groups (Przeworski, 1997, pp. 51-64). Adam Przeworski finds it doubtful to attribute the reasons of such weak structuration of interests to the in-flux of property relations since a similar pattern is observed in the established democracies as well. He further suggests that

> Perhaps what we are observing is not "individualism" nor "anomie" but just a tacit agreement that collective choices are so constrained by to a large extent international, economic, and political factors that little is at stake in political participation. Since politicians do not offer alternatives, people do not perceive them (p. 57).

Yet he sees the signs of normative consolidation in the fact that the legitimacy of democracy became to be judged independent of the efficacy of democratic governments. That is in spite of mistrust to politicians and "even in the middle of the economic crisis…, democracy as such was questioned only by small minorities" (p. 59). Underdeveloped interests representing networks contribute to the sense of weak moral cohesion. Profound economic crisis and sharp social inequalities aggravate this attitude, and last but not least, the erosion of public confidence in governments, which alternate between the "bitter-pill" and popular support enhancing strategies, adds to the effect. The cultural foundations for the societal cohesion are also endangered by the dividing temptation of a quick profit, and the impact of fundamentalist ideologies, such as nationalism and religious fundamentalism (pp. 61-62). As a rule, new democracies possess not only weak states but also weak civil societies.

The concept of civil society prompts a look at the larger contemporary discourse of social capital, of which it serves as a part. Thus, Michael Woolcock (1998) uses the concept of civil society in his integrated theoretical model of social capital and economic development. According to Michael Woolcock, civil society is a special form of social capital that is generated at the intersection of top-down and bottom-up societal relations. In this model weak states are the product of low inter-institutional horizontal integrity and low level of functional vertical interactions (in the form of institutions and forums) between the family and the state through which the conflicting demands can be mediated.

Indeed, in today's Russia civil society is weak since various interest groups appear relatively unstructured and not equally represented in the political arena. Russia's state also seems to be weakened – especially in the face of growing demands from regions to make the reportedly shared authorities functional. At the same time, the state has developed exclusive bonds with some representatives of business and financial circles, which are referred in domestic political discourse as oligarchy. The circle of bonding is vicious: business tycoons provide financial support for the state in return for policies leading to oligopoly, which ultimately strips the state treasury of the taxation income.

When looked at the micro-level though, the horizontal and vertical social ties in today's Russia and networks appear very imbalanced. In the situation when the rules and laws are not universally ensured, to survive in every-day life, to find employment, to start one's own business, to sell or to rent an apartment, etc., one is increasingly relying on the familial ties and close connections. Therefore, it appears extremely difficult to apply Michael Woolcock's model of social capital availability in the micro- and macro dimension, and to locate Russia in this matrix.

Another conceptualization about the societal value system comes from evolutionist writers as a core vs. periphery metaphor. While this metaphor is widely used to explain the role of legacies of the past in the "transitional societies" (i.e., related to a slow pace of change in the core of institutions and organizations rather than on the margin), it does not appear to provide account for relative weakness of civil society. On the contrary, it would entail that after dismantling the centralized channeling of interests into officially recognized forms of representation those suppressed peripheral interests would find most intensive forms of representation. However, the outcome is different as described above. Still we consider that center/periphery concept of the normative societal structure, as suggested by Edward Shils (1975), would retain its explanatory power. Especially in the case of highly centralized and territorially extensive societies that "tend to have a spatial center which aspires to be the seat of central institutional and cultural systems" (p. 39). The distance between the center and the periphery is great in terms of dignity, but periphery may retain its own relatively autonomous centers, and so the center does not enjoy the absolute domination of the periphery. According to Edward Shils such societies have little political life (in other words, participation), they remain relatively minimally integrated and represent the bureaucratic-imperial type. This model, rather than an ideal totalitarian model by Edward Shils, may be considered the closest to the pre-transitional Russia. Especially because of the increasing gap between the centrally down-loaded ideology and the relatively autonomous sets of mind in the periphery.

A question arises whether governmental decentralization would enhance diversity in regional identities. With the decreasing role of the center in societal integration, regions may either compensate for this function or enhance centrifugal tendencies. We expect that regional identity would enhance further divergence of regions when it does not compete with other identities. And on the contrary, if the regional identity is not dominant it may induce some kinds of consolidating tendencies.

In conclusion, it is evident that the theory of social and normative change in the so-called transitional nations is still evolving. It is apparent that such a theory will be highly insightful for understanding societal dynamics in nations of different level of social capital and economic development.

The Context of the Values Debate in Russia

At least three contexts of contemporary Russia are most influential for triggering and shaping the discussion of the values-reproduction role of schools. These are identified below as societal, political, and policy-related contexts. It should be noted that the influence of the global context is recognized as powerful though its influence is mediated through the innate societal challenges. After the first years of lifting up the "iron curtain" the fascination of learning first-hand about the world gave way to seeking one's own place in this world and, consequently, raised issues about the relationship between innovation and tradition. Thus, a more introverted perspective can be traced even when the global challenges are discussed.

It is not an exaggeration to say that the debate abound values education has occupied the center stage in contemporary Russian education over the past decade. The debate has drawn more and various public voices over time. That is why the review that follows is prefaced with citations from the recent sources.

Values Agenda in the Societal "Transitional" Context

We had ideals and noble goals. Nowadays children do not have anything like that, only TV thrillers, street life, and, at best, a computer... ("Uchitel'skaia Gazeta", 1998, 48).

A decade ago the nation made its choice to embark on the way of building a democratic society and a new economy which would best serve the interests of democracy. What was then called a "transitional period" of societal transformation is referred to by contemporary domestic observers a decade later as a "revolutionary explosion" that resulted in a tremendous dislocation of the societal fabric in every sphere of life—economic, socio-political, normative. Rapid and massive transformations of the economic and political life of the society have been accompanied by unprecedented deviance of behavior, crime and corruption; rapid decline of living standards for entire social groups; an increasing gap between the rich and the poor; rupture of economic, social, and human networks as a result of the dissolution of the U.S.S.R., dividing socio-economic stratification, sporadic flare-ups of ethnic grievances, and power struggle that is fueled by political figures who aspired to capitalize on these conflicts and ruptures. The social stability is jeopardized.

The overall sense of moral crisis has contributed to the already pervasive feeling of frustration, defeated expectations, and uncertainty. This resonated at the national level in the 1996 President Boris Yelstin's call for an uniting national idea, and at the school level in the call for a protective and caring school environment, free of repression and imposition of any kind. The accumulation of unresolved society's problems is overwhelming. Though these problems are not strange to any society, they, as a well-known Russian sociologist Igor S. Kon put it, "were never solved by us before, and moreover, they were not even posed as such. We have found ourselves in a minefield: wherever you go, you are bound to find an explosion of problems, because we need all the solutions, at once, and not tomorrow, but a day before yesterday" ("Pervoe Sentiabria", 1999, #18, March 13).

Schools found themselves vulnerable to the multiple influences of the larger society. The socio-economic status of schoolteachers sharply declined forcing teachers to resort to desperate measures right up to hunger strikes. Both federal and regional governments proved unable to stop physical degradation of many schools, and to liquidate chronic delays in teaching compensation. Consequently, the value of education for the society at large was questioned by many critics. Juvenile delinquency and drug-addiction continued to absorb the young people. Rapid socio-economic stratification added to the increase of school drop-outs and homeless children of school age. The differences between elite urban schools and small rural schools reached an astronomic order. Excessive consumerism and extreme individualism of mass global culture threatened to fill in the seeming "value vacuum" at Russian schools. The rigid command-driven administration continued to remain the favorite style of many educational bureaucrats and, at the same time, some schools could not help but accept the "recommendations from above" as a prescription for execution under the circumstances. The rise of ethnic sentiment by multiple ethnicities threatened to desegregate access to schooling along ethno-centric lines.

What preceded these outcomes was the early 1990s' educational reform widely supported by the Russian educational community in a bottom-up movement. The reform proved to be radical. It aimed to eliminate old ideas and theories of values education and political upbringing. However, the reform's two major accomplishments— depoliticization and deideologization—had a significant side effect: many teachers felt dismayed. At the same time the new goals of humanistic education and a child-centered approach paradoxically produced practices of early streaming and selection and consequently left out many children who did not fit certain psychological or physiological "standards". With the banning of the old system of bureaucratized ideological indoctrination, values education was left to be a family matter, and many teachers and parents were relieved to see that the goal of schooling was only to give knowledge. Some scholars argued that in the humanization of Russian education one can observe a shift to such extreme individualism that does not recognize either nearest or more remote socio-cultural influences (Daniels et al., 1995, p. 37).

From the early 1990s on, private schools started to open and different confessions patronized their own schools. At the same time, educational reformers had to defend the principle of secular public schooling when confronted with the churches' persistence to fill in the "value vacuum" and abstractness of general human values. The discussion about religious education and public education emerged again in the mid-1990s. The discussion addressed the consequences of thinking "by negation" and going to extremes: if in the old system the principle of freedom of worship was replaced by atheist propaganda, therefore presently this freedom should have been translated into freedom of religious influence. Importantly, the new state policy for secular schooling emphasized respect towards individual human rights (including the freedom of worship) as long as these rights do not contradict or impinge on other people's rights. Therefore, neither religious education nor atheism was considered suitable for public schools. However, in the renewed discussion some educators stressed that it was short-sighted to ignore the importance of teaching world religions as socio-cultural phenomena in view of their significant influence on economics, politics, families and values orientations in the societies (Garadzha, 1995). This discussion is illustrative not only in terms of the necessary fine-tuning and refining of major concepts and goals of the educational reform, but also in terms of the pervasiveness of "either-or" thinking and dogmatic implementation of ideas. This task of implementing new ideals is even more challenging because the "front-line" between old and new thinking lies, as Edward Dneprov emphasizes, within individuals themselves but not between offices, parties or camps.

The issues of values education can be viewed from an intergenerational perspective. Adults, teachers and parents alike, want to see their children different from themselves. How much different? A director of the urban education center in St. Petersburg Galina G. Kucherova administers the program of students learning about city's problems. She wants to see the young responsible, energetic and not indifferent:

> We want to bring up young people not to demand a better future for themselves, but to understand the difficulties in solving problems, and to keep striving to find a solution... When schoolchildren first come to our center, we confront their enormous indifference, which is inherited in all of us almost genetically. Our generation is used to the idea that nothing depends on each of us individually, earlier we were treated as 'parts of the larger state machine', and now we have faced such powerful processes that many remain with their hands folded. Initially children, looking to their parents, stay indifferent to everything. But this is not right! Most important to make them shake themselves and start acting. If one is doing a thing, it is moving forward, if one does not, then nothing comes out of it. We want to grow non-indifferent persons. I do not feel at ease about their future, but there is no other way. Otherwise nothing will ever move off the deadlock in our country ("Pervoe Sentiabria", 1999, #36, May 25).

The head of the rural administration in Krasnodar region Vladimir Romanenko sees effects of schooling on values and economic relations to be crucial for community development today. He advocates the program of close partnerships between schools and agricultural businesses, and he sees the young as cognitively and psychologically mature to independently generate new ideas and implement those in real life situations:

> New technologies require a different psychology from a manager and a floor worker alike. We need thinking and dynamic children, not only knowing their subject very well. We notice that economic partnerships based on contracts serve as the basis of the entrepreneurial success today, but those relations are not respected by many who are involved. We need youth as bearers of a new psychology and a new world outlook ("Pervoe Sentiabria", 1999, #23, March 30).

These opinions are illustrative of how different members of the community—teachers, local authorities, businesses and the like—come to view consensus-building in their respective locales about the priority of values education through implementing joint projects beneficial for the community. These community-oriented and consensus-building projects are largely small-scale and bottom-up in character. The data about these efforts is scarce and sporadic for the nation as a whole, and is overwhelmingly preoccupied with the consequences of the major reforms accompanied with profound economic crisis and sharp social inequalities.

Political Context of Values Education Debate

We shout that children are outside the politics and constantly use them in dubious power games ("Uchitel'skaia Gazeta", 1998, 48).

Another specific feature of the values education debate in Russia is that while education as a whole is sorely neglected in the broader political process, values education is frequently mentioned. Indeed the broader political debate between major sociopolitical ideologies shapes the debate on values education. Several educators who have taken stands on education of values find that they and their positions have been incorporated in the broader political process. The political situation is marked by rivaling ideologies and groups: nationalist, monarchist, authoritarian and religious ideas compete with economic and social liberalism. As Edward Dneprov, a prominent Russian educator and a reformer, emphasized in the interview conducted for this study, the political situation is crucial for the future of Russian democratic reforms. Politicians of various "colorings" find it both necessary and convenient to speak to the situation of moral crisis and the unprecedented emergence of deviance. Meantime there are voices among educators to free education of politics, and let teachers think and decide as professionals. It has been argued that mass pedagogical consciousness was destroyed when the old system of education fell apart and modern schools became dispersed along the large spectrum of chaotic differentiation (M. Fisher). Teachers themselves have been targeted by different groups, organizations and individuals who seek to impose their needs and values on schools.

Policy Context of Values Education: Actors and Strategies

The third specific feature of the Russian context for values education regards the "how" issue, i.e., how, in educators' view, the consensus about which values schools to teach the young is to be reached. The positions on values education have without doubt a centrist inclination—in that the key advocates wish to see their positions adopted by rival political groupings and promoted through a national political process. Several policy-making bodies have been identified:

1. President supported by a Special Educational Council (to include, according to Edward Dneprov—a prominent liberal educator,—experts, leading teachers and public representatives);
2. Ministry of General and Professional Education (a single body that merged in the fall of 1996 both the Ministry of General Education and the State Committee for Higher Education);
3. Parliament (the lower chamber—Duma—with strong representation of communist and nationalist parties and an upper chamber of the Federation Council which represents regional elite from eighty-nine republics, regions and metropolitan areas of the Russian Federation);
4. Individual schools
5. Teachers' Congress
6. Regional self-governments and local communities.

Yet for several of the current values education positions, the ultimate arbitrator of values should be the free personality—the new Russian citizen exercising his or her free conscious. So there is a logical tension in the arguments about the ultimate goals of values education proposals and the strategy of their implementation.

Values Education Debate: Between Neo-Marxism and Post-Modernism

In the mid-1990s, the values education impact of schools became intensely debated primarily by the group of the leading educators at the top of the decision-making hierarchy, both reformist and conservative. This renewed interest in values education was triggered by the influence of the major contexts discussed above. The salient features of this debate are the following:

1.   The major emphasis is on the philosophical foundations of values education, rather than on methods of pedagogical support of value orientations;
2.   Positions on values education targeting normative uncertainty are found to be engaged by politicians in their political struggle;
3.   Little or almost no research is done on values education in various regions and localities of the Russian Federation;
4.   Values in education are contested from a variety perspectives of educational studies.

Indeed, with the increasing perception of normative uncertainty in the society, the debate over values in education and education in values has penetrated all kinds of areas in educational studies. The term "education" itself is used in the Russian pedagogical tradition to embrace such distinct notions as "character education", "teaching", "learning", and also a socio-psychological concept of "personality development". Philosophers and historians of education are looking into historically specific educational goals and values (see, e.g. Ravkin 1995), into the relationship of traditional and innovative values in the situation of social change (Gleiser and Vilotievich 1997). Experts in pedagogy discuss value-based relations that develop between a teacher and a learner, among learners in class, thus focusing on the personality-oriented education (see in this regard an integrative model of humanization of education by the academician Berulava). The journal "Pedagogy" of the Russian Academy of Education conducted numerous round-table sessions on the related issues, among them are "The Russian Orthodox Church and Education", "Personality- and Value-Oriented Education". A new journal, "New Educational Values", has been established to introduce concepts and values new for Russian educators such as multiculturalism, conflict resolution, charter-schools, and others.

Most contested has become the issue of the values educational impact of schools especially during the period that followed denouncement of the ideological indoctrination of Soviet school. On the whole, the values debate centers on several large concepts: what Russia and Russian tradition is; how innovations are related to traditions; what humanism is; what liberalism is. Because of the importance of these concepts for the nation, many political actors find it convenient to use the issues of values educa-

Table 2.1. The Continuum of Attitudes to Priorities in Values Education

Values Priorities	Bolshevik Model	Socialist (with human face) (Gorbachev)	Radical Liberalism (Dneprov, Gazman)	School-based (Novikova-Selivanova - Karakovsky)	New Russian model (Nikandrov)	Nationalist	Neo-communist
Post-modernity							
1. Personality Independence	Subordination to class interests	Self-realization	Self-determination & self-development	Self-actualization	Virtue of freedom within	Subordination to the national ideas	Subordination to the communist ideal
2. Moral/ethic principles of behavior	Class morality	General human & socialist values (collectivism, value of labor, patriotism)	General human values	Common sense and socialist values	Religious values as norms of behavior	Religious values	Common sense & class morality
3. Ecology of relations to nature, oneself & others	Conquer nature	Respect, equality, tolerance	Respect, responsibility, tolerance, protectionism	Respect, responsibility, protectionism	Respect, responsibility, protectionism	-	-
3a. Sex education							
4. Attitudes to the outer world and others	No Closeness	Yes Coexistence of different systems	Yes Openness, integration, tolerance	Family education Partnership b/n equals but nationally specific	Family education Partnership b/n nationally specific	No Closeness, Russian way	No Closeness, Russian way
Modernity							
1. Economic values:							
- Planned economy	++	+	-			+	++
- Market economy	-	-	++			+	-
- Individual initiative	+	+	++	+/-	+	+	+
2. Civic/sociopolitical values:							
a) Safety net	+	++	+/-	+		+	++
b) Political freedom	-	+/-	++	+		+	+
c) Responsibility:							
- to criticize	-	+	+	+		+	+
- to participate	-	+	++	+		-	-
- to serve	++	+	+	+		+	+
3. National values: a) Respect							
- for state	++	++	+	+	+	++	++
- for Russia	+	+	+	+	++	++	++
- for locality	+/-	+	+	+	++	+	++
b) - multiculturalism	-	+	++	+	+		
- melting pot	++	-/+	-/+	-			
- religious belief	-			-	++	++	
4. Gender education	Traditional roles	Traditional roles					-

tion debate in their political agenda. A prominent liberal educator Edward Dneprov cites in this regard a similar imperative attributed to Nadezhda Krupskaya in the early 1920s: "If you want to take power, take the school". Several distinct positions on values education have been identified in this study [2]. They are outlined in Table 2.1. Because some of these positions seek to identify new values for the society at large, they tend to target adults as well as children of school age and hence do not have well-developed programs for schools per se.

The table outlines positions on values education by several political ideologies, and by their philosophical or axiological dimension. The latter ranges from post-modern, to modern, and neo-marxist discourses. The neo-marxist positions are aligned with some of the contemporary leftist political ideologies. The distinction between modern and post-modern axiological categories appears especially significant to discuss. Many observers (domestically and internationally) sense in the transitional context of Russia and CEE democracies the process of "catching up" with the modernization stage of the western established democracies. As Alex Inkeles and David H. Smith (1974) suggest in their seminal study of becoming modern, modern individual attitudes and behavior are more instrumental, because "new and more effective ways of doing things are central to the modernization process, with changes in ways of relating to other people coming largely as side effects" (p. 291). In other words, modern values reflect the functionally divided world, where the modern state has the central position and imposes expectations of instrumental one-dimensional roles on individuals—whether in economic production, political participation, national loyalty, or economically and politically expedient gender roles. One of the central concepts of becoming post-modern in Ronald Inglehart's study of forty-three societies is termed as "post-materialist" (1997), which in essence "brings people back in" the focus of the value relationships. Indeed in Russia and other transitional societies the normative uncertainty and the hardships considerably have raised materialist value on the list of priorities for many people. However, Russian educators desire to teach today's youth the post-modern values of a future non-repressive society, to use the words of Herbert Marcuse (1964). These values center on a human being and the multiplicity of his or her relations to others, to society and to the world. The concept of value appears to be

---

[2] Among the interviewees were a prominent liberal educator Edward D. Dneprov, who served in the position of a Minister of Education in 1990-1992 and now a director of the Federal Institute of Educational Planning by the Ministry of Education and also an author of two distinguished books on Russia education policies (Dneprov 1994, 1996); a Vice-President of the Russian Academy of Education Nikolai D. Nikandrov (elected as the RAE President a year after the interview) and an author of several important works on values education in Russia (e.g., Nikandrov 1997a, 1997b); members of the research group at the Institute of Personality Development of the Russian Academy of Education (director Valeria S. Mukhina); Liudmila I. Novikova and Natalia L. Selivanova (Karakovsky, Novikova, Selivanova 1996) – leaders of the research Center on Theory and Practice of Contemporary Issues of Upbringing at the Research Institute of Educational Theory and Pedagogy; principal investigators Z. I. Ravkin and Mikhail B. Boguslavsky of the Group of Methodology in Historical Pedagogical Research. Sources of the relevant data were interviews, monographs, theses of conferences on the related issues, publications in the journal of the Academy of Education "Pedagogika," "New Educational Values," "Research in Sociology," teachers' newspapers "Pervoe Sentiabria" ("The First of September") and "Uchitel'skaia Gazeta" (Teachers' Newspaper").

anthroposophic. It places the highest value on the human personality and self-development. Internalization of post-modern values is also a desired goal of educators (see, e.g., Valitskaya 1997). The educational innovation movement in Russia has produced a variety of humanistically oriented schools since the mid-1980s, such as schools of developmental education, of the dialogue of cultures, of ecological education, schools of self-determination, "schools-parks", Waldorfian and Montessori schools, and many others. Therefore, we consider it essential to define contemporary values education positions in terms of modern and post-modern categories. Some anthroposophic post-modern categories are outlined as Personality Independence and Development; Ethics and Morality Principles; Ecology of Relations to Nature and Other People; Attitudes to the World.

While it is much debated what values should be promoted at schools, there is a consensus, however, among educators as to what values should not be included. These are all the dogmatic and politicized values that Soviet schools intended to inculcate in the minds of youth. Nikolai D. Nikandrov uses the term "bolshevik model" to differentiate it from everything positive and attractive that the socialist traditions and ideals contained. According to the bolshevik model values in education should be handed down by the state. The morality was declared to be class-based and later on as societal, while "society" was equated to the state power and its avant-garde—the communist party. Education was turned into dogmatic political indoctrination through a system of formal educational events. The practice of substituting what exists with what should be increased the gap between formal schooling and life, it devalued many educational ideals, especially those articulated in the Code of the Communist Builder. Though these ideals were articulated in a very politicized form, they referred to many general human values such as equality, justice, respect to the elderly, mutual cooperation; but in contrast to the reality they sounded very hypocritical. With the launch of "perestroika" such values as "Soviet internationalism" (i.e., "molding new Soviet men and women" beyond ethnic origin or heritage) and "collectivism" (as the unconditional domination of the faceless mass over its individual members) have been sharply criticized and rejected. In the mid-1980s perestroika movement, the enormous imbalance in the relationship between the individual and the state and the need to address this tension was articulated. The ideal of socialism with a human face was declared. Practically it meant elimination of the state monopoly (destatization) in education and culture at large. Humanism, democratization, integration into the world civilization, openness and a return to general human values—these were the key concepts in people's attitudes in those days. The nation witnessed massive enthusiasm and the rise of teachers' creativity.

The ideas of the humanist "pedagogy of cooperation", liberated from formalism and indoctrination, embraced the minds of many talented and innovative educators in the 1980s. Humanist pedagogy emphasizes the goal of free education to bring up a free personality. This renaissance of the pedagogy of freedom occurred during the "perestroika" and "glasnot" period, which brought other freedoms to the society: freedom of speech and associations, freedom of political participation, freedom of private enterprise. Educators, however, were exploring the image of inner personality freedom, a kind of freedom that can not be decreed, allowed or institutionalized, but it grows somewhere from within a personality. Pedagogy of freedom is grounded in the rich Russian educational tradition starting with the humanist child-centered holistic pedagogy by Konstantin D. Ushinsky (1824-1871) and a free school established by Lev N. Tolstoy (1828-1910). It was continued at the beginning of the twentieth century by Petr F. Kapterev (1849-1922), Konstantin N. Wenzel (1857-1947), Pavel P. Blonsky (1884-1941), Lev S. Vygotsky (1896-1934); by Vasili A. Sukhomlinsky (1918-1970) in the mid-century; and most recently (1970-1990s) by talented educators such as Victor Shatalov, Sofia Lysenkova, Evald Ilienkov, Shalva Amonashvili, Vasily Davydov, and others. The principles of the 1980-1990s educational movement of pedagogy of freedom and cooperation were stated in the "Teacher's Gazette", led by Vladimir Matveyev in 1986 (Manifesto of Pedagogy of Cooperation) and by Simon Soloveichik, the editor of another teachers' newspaper, "First of September", in 1994 (Soloveichik 1994). The bottom-up teacher movement provided an enormous impetus for the reform of the entire educational sector.

Outstanding credit for pushing radical liberal reforms in education goes to Edward Dneprov, a Minister of Education in 1990-1992. Dneprov's think tank on values education was inspired by Oleg Gazman (1995) and Alexander Tubelsky (1994), who developed the concepts of a reflective and autonomous personality and self-determination based on the Russian pedagogical tradition and their own pedagogical practice. A parallel can be drawn in pedagogical thinking on values education of the 1990s and the 1920s. Both periods are marked by certain instability of value systems and the excitement of creating a renewed society. Thus, continuity in the innovative educational thought may be established. Several ideas, central to Lev Vygotsky's school of psychological pedagogy, have resonated closely with educators at the end of the century. First of all, for Lev Vygotsky "moral behavior is developed like any other behavior through social environment" (Vygotsky, 1926/1996, p. 207). The important implication from this is that people are not born with moral feeling, but develop it through interaction with each other in their social life. The primary role of an educator is then to "organize concrete and meaningful social relations that permeate children's environment"; "to educate means to organize life" (p. 221).

Lev Vygotsky rejected the principle of authority in moral education or its support by awards and punishments. He insisted on moral behavior "as a free choice of social forms of behavior" by autonomous personalities (p. 213). Yet, Vygotsky warned after Nathorp: "we do not think that people can easily turn into angels, if they are given freedom. We only know that they become devils, when they feel enslaved" (p. 220). Vygotsky drew a delicate but a very important line between freedom from authority for an individual and a truly free and autonomous individuality. This understanding has been carried by the Russian pedagogical thought through years, and it has highly enriched Russian pedagogy.

A values educational process appears to be a cooperative effort of both a teacher and a student. Because "self-experience can be the sole educator of a person" (p. 51) in a certain social situation that brings out innermost satisfaction; while a teacher serves as "an organizer of an educating social environment" (p. 52). These ideas were very close to the movement of pedagogy of cooperation in the 1990s, where personality self-development and self-determination were highlighted in educational cooperation of teachers with students.

The principle of deideologization of schools, articulated by radical reformer Edward Dneprov in the early 1990s, became somewhat of a lighting rod. The expectation that all teachers now freed from the pressure of political dogmas would develop spontaneous local responses was exaggerated especially when teachers were facing day-to-day the fight with hardship, delayed salaries and declining standards of living. The hypothesis of the "ideology vacuum" has been most discussed again of late. One extreme position stated that schools "freed" themselves of the "burden" to transmit values, focusing only on the development of the knowledge-based cognitive intelligence. Another position has warned that education is never value-neutral and that value vacuum is an illusion: in fact, schools may continue supporting old values or silently submit to the pressure of new values of consumerism and commercialization, to the ideologies of certain socio-political or religious groups.

Some educators questioned the abstract character of general human values, noting that teachers are attracted to concrete ideals and values. Nikolai D. Nikandrov, President of the Russian Academy of Education, argued in his proposal for values education in Russian schools (1997a, 1997b) for the "Russian scenario". According to him, a new Russian school should be modeled neither after Northern American nor after the dogmatic pattern of the Soviet schools. In order to bring certainty into the question what values should be listed as general human values, he suggested two possible approaches: to follow either common sense or religious values.

In his view, the former ultimately originated from the latter. According to Nikandrov, Russian Orthodoxy will provide the moral basis to unite people of different nationalities in the Russian Federation and guarantee democracy (in its original sense of "people's rule") to the Russian Federation. He refers to Tsarist Russia where the Russian Orthodox Church supported the monarchy and united people in their service to the monarchy. According to Nikandrov the basic values are human life and health, culture and education, family life and procreation, political and economic culture. Nikandrov argues that religious education is a source of virtue, conscience and conscientiousness—those moral feelings that guide behavior from within the individual. He considers these values typical of a specifically Russian mentality as expressed in culture, traditions and people consciousness that may be different from the Western mentality of individualism.

To conclude the discussion of several contemporary values education positions, it should be stressed that:

1. Values education has moved to the front of educational debates during the past several years. Indeed, the society experiences tremendous dislocation of its organization and of its normative foundations. It witnesses enormous deviation of behavior in various spheres of life. Hence there is a widely spread sense of a moral crisis and uncertainty in values orientation.

2. Values agenda in the society is increasingly used by various political groups.

3. Leading intellectuals with positions on values education find themselves inevitably involved into this political debate.

4. Similar to the political parallelism, the leading intellectuals, who expressed themselves regarding values education agenda, are polarized according to the philosophy they espouse—from the post-modern anthroposophic statements to neo-marxist positions.

Given this variety of philosophical positions on values education among the leading Russian intellectuals and the political meanings attached to them, the following questions arise:

a) whether a similar polarization divide educational elites in the regions/locales of the Russian Federation;

b) whether, under the conditions of the changing relationships between the center and regions in the Russian polity, educational elites in the center and locales demonstrate disunity of opinions on the values agenda similar to the leading intellectuals;

c) how divisions and similarities in the educational elite's attitude inform the actors about the challenges of the educational policy-making.

Priorities of Values Education in Three Locales Through the Eyes of Educational Elites

The formal debate on values education analyzed above has been induced by the rejection of the norms and values of the pre-"perestroika" society. The leading scholars and educational policy-makers do not see eye to eye with regard to a renewed agenda of values education. The most salient dimensions along which the variety of positions can be plotted are axiological and political. The diverging positions manifest, on the one hand, the history of the search for values orientations in the society in transition through the past decade, and, on the other hand, the predominance of politically engaged positions. There is, however, an important additional question about the relative acceptance of the respective positions in different sectors of the Russian educational community. If the assumption is that the primary responsibility about what values to teach the young should rest with school communities in various Russian regions, then the attitudes of the key education figures in Russian regions matter immensely. Furthermore, defining the nature of differences within regions and between regions is essential for setting up a democratic policy dialogue.

The analysis, that follows, focuses primarily on this sociopolitical question through interpretation of views of educational elites in three Russian cities, representative of major regions. Our particular concerns were to determine whether there were important differences by region (center-periphery and regional effects), position in the educational system and gender (interregional effect). Each of these sociopolitical factors is highly salient in the contemporary Russian educational context.

Survey Respondents' Profile and Method

A survey instrument created by the joint effort of the international project group was administered in three Russian cities with the specific purpose in mind described above. This specific purpose shaped an additional dimension to the cross-national comparative study. The design of the Russian part of the project aimed to compare the polarization and political nature of the previously identified values education positions with the orientations on values education by a larger group of elites identified from a functional perspective.

Method

A survey was administered to the purposeful sample of educational elites. Sixty-nine people from the elites in three cities (thirty-five in Moscow, sixteen in Kemerovo, and eighteen in Vladivostok) were surveyed, followed by selected semi-structured interviews. In order to secure answers from those elites considered representative of the three settings no survey mailing was relied upon in the two cities and only partially in the third one. Instead respondents were approached personally. That allowed the research team to engage respondents into discussions of some contradictory issues as they saw them and to encourage respondents to disclose some of the beliefs underlying their reasoning.

Eleven questions in a Likert-style (seven-point rating scale) format and seven questions in a ranking format were developed. The questions were evaluated in a pilot test to determine whether the range of forced-choice option was exhaustive; for two questions open-ended options were added. The survey was run anonymously, the contact and names were retained only for the purposes of follow-up interviews and sending the report. The background characteristics included position, workplace, years of experience in education, and gender.

The correlational statistics, statistics of central measure and frequencies were employed to compare attitudes of the elites across regions, positions and gender. The data was processed with statistical weighting in order to secure equal account to each region. The statistics were analyzed in the context of the values agenda debate and they were complemented by quantitative data from interviews. Factor analysis was run to extract major themes or patterns in the perceptions of values education. The results were tested against the contextual and quantitative data.

Definition of Elites

We define educational elites as those individuals who demonstrated the ability—due to professional or scholarly reputation, administrative position or public prominence—to influence the direction of schooling policies. Educational elites identified thus far in each of the three cities were grouped into four categories by their position in the educational system as follows:

- educational policy-makers, intellectuals and bureaucrats/administrators (including Ministry of Education, Russian bureau of UNESCO, regional and municipal departments of education, editors of selected research institutes and journals on education, sociology of youth and philosophy);
- NGO and public leaders (including Russian Children's Fund, association of innovative schools, Pedagogical Society of the Russian Federation, public commissions on juvenile delinquency), religious leaders (educational department of the Russian patriarchate), and journalists

writing for teachers' press;

- front-line educators (including innovative schools principals and teachers, teachers of the year and teachers granted other outstanding awards);
- values education and pedagogy specialists (heads of associations on methods of education, researchers at Academy of Education, chairs of pedagogy departments at universities and teacher training institutes).

Regional Sites

The three cities of Moscow, Kemerovo and Vladivostok are representative of three regions, that are separated from each other by large distances. Since public schools are no longer centrally funded, their well-being has become dependent on the taxable capacity of regions and municipalities which vary considerably through the country. For 1992-1994 per-capita educational allocations as related to the monthly minimal subsistence level were 1.61 in Moscow, 1.32 in Kemerovo, 0.72 in Vladivostok, the national average being 1.11 (Goskomstat 1996a).

Moscow lies in the historical center of Russian culture. It became the center of concentrated administrative and intellectual resources during the years of the centralized planning that encompassed all aspects of life including education. Nowadays, the proportion of Moscovites with any postsecondary education is 70.3 percent, which is 17.8 percent higher than the average for the nation (the respective statistics for the Kemerovo region and the Maritime region are 51.8 percent and 55.1 percent)[3] The number of registered unemployed was six and a half times lower than the national average in 1995. The number of Moscow schoolchildren attending schools in a second session (shift) is 14.6 percent, which is lower than the nation's average 24.8 percent and more than twice lower than Kemerovo and Vladivostok (35.4 percent and 32.4 percent respectively). In our survey Moscow respondents represent the central educational elites.

Kemerovo respondents represent local elites of a western Siberian city located in the Asian part of Russia, half way from Moscow to the Pacific, in a highly industrialized and resource rich area, which has the highest population density in the entire Siberia and Russian Far East and has a diverse ethnic representation. The city was founded in 1918. It is in effect a contemporary of the Russian revolution and an exemplar of Soviet industrialization. In the past three years the emission of polluting industrial contaminants into air was reduced by a third, however Kemerovo remains on the list of ecologically damaged cities. In the contemporary national political arena the city is located in the area known as the "red belt" according to the predominance of the political vote cast in the 1996 presidential elections.

Vladivostok represents local elites in the city-port in the Russian Far East on the Pacific Coast, the furthest south-eastern point from Moscow. It dates back to the past quarter of the nineteenth century and it grew fast in the early 1900s with the completion of the Trans-Siberian railroad. Contemporarily the city is known as one of the first proposed free trade zones with neighboring China, Korea and Japan. The crime rate

---

[3] These statistics and the following in the section are calculated or refer to Goskomstat (1996b).

per population is relatively high—it was three times higher than in Moscow and almost twice higher than in Kemerovo in 1995. Vladivostok is currently known to be heavily influenced by the local politics of the self-interested politicians who paralyze many positive developments there.

Findings

Beyond Socialist Values

We shall start with presenting the ways respondents answer the last question of the survey instrument. Respondents were asked to express their agreement on a seven-score rating scale as to the recognition or existence of several distinct values systems in the world and as to the relevance of teaching these values at Russian schools. The four groups of values named—Asian, socialist, Islamic and Latin American—are considered by experts to play an essential role in the value orientations of people in the countries participating in the international project. There is an overwhelming rejection by the Russian elite respondents of the relevance of teaching socialist values in Russian schools today (average rating is 5.17), though they are less decisive in rejecting a distinct system of socialist values (average rating is 4.16). The respondents more readily accept Islamic, Asian values, and Latin American values as such (2.61, 2.65, 3.39 average ratings respectively) than teaching these values in Russian schools (5.62, 4.19 and 5.42 respectively). From among the sets of values of all the four groups, respondents appear less categorical in deciding whether Asian values are suitable in Russian schools (average rating is 4.19). It follows from interviews that the attraction of Asian values comes from the so called "Asian miracle" of the effective combination of western-style modernization with indigenous traditions in a gradual evolutionary development. Yet our goal was not to trace the characteristics of individual perceptions of the four groups of values. It is important to state that socialist values are unanimously considered by the Russian elites as unsuitable for teaching at contemporary Russian schools. Is there a need for today's school teaching values at all? And if not socialist values then which values do educators see as most important for the Russian youth? The next two sections address these particular concerns.

What Are the Most Pressing Needs for Values Education?

Respondents were asked to rank the most urgent from the list of seventeen reasons, agreed upon by the international project experts, for calling values education a special agenda in contemporary Russian schools. In essence, the respondents were asked to relate the role of schools in promoting values to the current social changes and challenges of a national and global nature.

There appear to be a certain hierarchy in the motivation for values education as perceived by respondents. Three groups of reasons according to the degree of their relevance to values education stand out. Their relative importance (mean ranks) and a degree of respondents' agreement (standard deviations=SD) are presented in Table 2.2 below.

The first group consists of arguments which are ranked the highest (rank positions are 1-3 or 4) by the absolute majority of respondents (56 percent to 66 percent) with the highest degree of the manifested agreement. These arguments address the foundation of personality development through spiritual integrity, individual responsibility, autonomy and self-determination. Important is the stress on the link between freedom of reflective self-determination, spiritual integrity and daily behavior. A strong emphasis is also placed on intergenerational cultural continuity—whether within the family or as a respect for the national heritage. These are significant socio-cultural layers in the personality structure.

Table 2.2 Groups of Arguments which Call for a Values Education Agenda
(in decreasing importance from 1 to 17)

	Argument	Mean Rank	SD	% who marked the argument as important
I	To provide a foundation for spiritual development	1.78	2.01	65.5
	To increase the sense of individual responsibility	3.83	2.82	56.6
	To help each young person to develop a reflective and autonomous personality	3.92	3.44	65.0
	To develop appreciation for to national heritage	4.97	3.77	63.9
	To provide a guide for behavior in daily life	5.19	3.31	56.3
	To strengthen families	5.20	3.66	60.8
II	To help youth interpret values transmitted by the mass media, Internet	5.65	3.88	48.7
	To combat juvenile delinquency (bullying, gang violence, drug abuse)	5.88	3.94	60.6
	To promote world peace	5.94	3.18	28.8
	To combat ecological abuse	5.95	3.55	49.5
	To promote tolerance for ethnic, language, and racial groups	6.32	3.78	41.4
	To encourage civic consciousness and democracy	6.32	3.66	44.4
	To foster economic development (through hard work, creativity, individual competitiveness)	6.17	3.31	53.3
	To promote more orderly and caring school communities	6.63	4.44	42.8
III	To improve opportunities for girls and women	7.66	4.19	35.3
	To promote values of justice and equity	8.13	4.59	26.8
	To promote pride in local communities	12.99	5.12	14.7

*Respondents were asked to select most important arguments (totaling 17) and then rank them. Therefore, the table cites the percentage of respondents who marked the argument as important. Not surprisingly, the most often selected arguments are in the first group, and standard deviations tend to increase with the decreasing frequency of selection.

The second group includes arguments relating to concrete social challenges or problems recognized as such in contemporary Russia. This group of arguments reflects recognition by the elites of a normative uncertainty in the society. This uncertain situation develops under the impact of either newly established institutions (such as democratic and economic institutions, mass media) or societal problems exacerbated by the transitional context (such as juvenile delinquency, ecological abuse, tolerance between various groups and peaceful resolution of conflict). As distinct from the first group, the second group of arguments target specific problems in the society and relates only indirectly to the principles of pedagogical guidance or support of personality development. A number of respondents consider this group of arguments secondary or derivative to the first group in the hierarchy of importance for a values learning process. As a consequence, the number of respondents who consider this group of arguments most important for values learning is lower than those who emphasize the first group of motives, and the degree of opinion divergence about rank placement is much higher.

The third group of arguments represents relatively less important areas to be addressed in values education programs. The specific values relationship suggested in these arguments do not appear to be key in the hierarchy of values education motivation perceived by the respondents.

Overall, there is no significant divergence of opinion related to region, position or gender. However, some variation by these factors is worth discussing.

Regional Variation

Kemerovo and Vladivostok elite express less concern about opportunities for girls and women than Moscow elite, but more concern about ecological abuse. Moscow and Kemerovo elite are more concerned than Vladivostok about issues of tolerance to various ethnic, language and racial groups. Vladivostok respondents are more concerned about juvenile delinquency than elite in other locales. Moscow elites are more concerned than other elite samples about the values transmitted by mass media and Internet. Kemerovo placed more stress than elites in other samples on the development of reflective and autonomous personalities.

Variation by Position

Values education/pedagogy specialists tend to underestimate (as compared to other positional groups) the effect of mass media and Internet on individual values structures, but place a higher emphasis than other groups on keeping school communities more orderly and caring. As probably the most recent group in the educational policy arena, NGO leaders underrate (relative to other groups) the importance of helping each child to develop a reflective and autonomous personality, but see schools as more important in addressing social problems such as juvenile delinquency and promoting tolerance among ethnic, language, and racial groups. There is no opinion expressed by this group, no matter how small it is, about the relevance for school education of the issue of promoting more opportunities for girls and women and pride in local communities. Educational administrators and governmental officers emphasize more strongly than do other positional groups the role of schools in economic development through teaching of appropriate skills and values and the importance of promoting world peace. This group, together with a group of NGO leaders, see schools as

slightly more important than other professional groups the role of schools in strengthening family values and values of democracy.

Variation by Gender

The variation by gender appears to be minimal from the three patterns considered
here—even with regard to the issue of more opportunities for girls and women (the
mean rank score is 7.8 for male respondents and 7.62 by female respondents respectively). Yet, male respondents seem to attach more weight to the development of reflective and autonomous personalities, of individual responsibility, and of democratic
values than female respondents do. In comparison to the predominant male respondents' opinion, female respondents see the school's role as more important in strengthening families, developing ecological awareness, and overall spiritual foundation.

As a way of summing up at this moment, it should be pointed out, firstly, that a
certain hierarchy of motives for values education stands out, with respect to the first
question of the survey. There are distinct groups coherent in their inner logic—a group
of personality-oriented reasons and a group of motives suggestive of concrete socio-
political and economic issues in the society. We will test further whether this distinction holds with regard to specific goals of values education. Secondly, the variation in
attitudes by region is largely attributed to the specific socio-cultural situations in the
three locales concerning the intensity of common problems, such as ecological abuse,
juvenile delinquency, exposure to a variety of information channels, employment opportunities by gender, multinational population and the such. Thirdly, voices of educators appear to stress specific differences in policy dialogue according to their position in the educational system. Thus, administrators appear to draw more immediate
linkages between the nation's tasks in strengthening democracy and new economic
relations, on the one hand, and the school values education agenda, on the other. In
contrast, front-line educators and pedagogy specialists see this linkage to be indirect.
They place the highest priority among the positional groups on the need for
personality-oriented development in value teaching at schools. At the same time pedagogy specialists tend to disregard the importance of new socio-cultural factors in values transmission and to emphasize the need to restore traditional order and a caring
climate at schools. Variation by gender does not appear significant, though it may
grow into a potential problem, since the teaching profession is over-represented by
women but education policy-makers are over-represented by men.

What Values Are Important to Include in Schooling?

Given the motives that underlie a particular concern for value orientations among
young people by educational elites, the next question to be asked is which values the
survey respondents consider most important and relevant for contemporary Russian
schools to back up and promote. There are two questions in the survey that provided
data for this inquiry. The first one requested respondents to indicate the relative importance of the value themes (thirteen themes listed) as goals for the school values
education effort on a seven-score Likert scale. The second one requested opinions
about agreement or disagreement with selected statements on values education goals at
schools. Responses to the former question are summarized in Table 2.3 below.

The top five areas of value orientation, that schools need to help the young people to develop, are in the opinion of the respondents consistent across the three regions. Indeed the value ranking, common to the respondents with different positional status in three cities, reflects a considerable consensus among the Russian educational elites about priority value areas in need of pedagogical support. These values relate, first of all, to the need to reconstruct the "ethical foundations" of the societal cohesion based on the moral choices of free autonomous individuals. Secondly, they refer to the nation's task to build a "civic society", to improve standards of living through transforming the economy by way of "hard work", and to address consequences of the "ecological abuse" of the early stages of industrialization. Apart from these big national goals, perceived at the very personal level, other issues concern the elite in the survey—about protecting "family values" and strengthening one's belief in the nation and the national collective effort ("patriotism" and "nation's consolidation").

Table 2.3 Average Score of Areas of Values Education (on a 7-score scale)
(in decreasing importance)

Areas of values education	Average score on a 7 score-scale	Standard deviation
Moral Values	1.74	1.34
Personal Autonomy and Reflection	2.14	1.51
Civic Values	2.21	1.51
Ecological Awareness	2.33	1.63
Work Values	2.43	1.47
Family Values	2.87	1.82
National Identity and Patriotism	3.01	1.67
Peace and Conflict Resolution	3.06	1.79
Democracy	3.23	1.91
Global Awareness	3.50	1.73
Gender Equality	3.99	1.96
Diversity and Multiculturalism	4.28	2.01
Religious Values	5.70	1.79

A slightly higher divergence of opinion is noticeable in the ranking of such values as "peace and conflict resolution", "democracy", and "global awareness". Although the importance of these values to be promoted at schools is perceived quite high. Thus, the superior value of democracy is acknowledged when compared to other forms of polity. But more importantly it is asserted that for the knowledge and democratic skills to be functional, one has to be predisposed to use them. These dispositions are broadly known as "civic values", which allow free citizens to relate to others in the society in a non-oppressive way and through various institutions. In so doing numerous conflicting demands (between individuals, between groups, and between individuals and a collectivity) need to be conciliated. In a way, civic values (or social capital, as they are sometimes termed) are an important socio-cultural prerequisite for democracy to function and sustain. In this way, civic values encompass the values of peaceful conflict resolution and democracy.

Finally, among the values considered irrelevant to be taught at schools, "religious values" are unanimously named irrespective of region, position or gender of respondents. This is the only value area that is unanimously considered to be unimportant for schools (the score range is 4.8–6.6 on a seven-score Likert scale). The reaction of the surveyed educational elite in support of the secular character of general education schools is especially important at the time when a number of religious leaders attempt to extend the influence of the church and other religious groups over schools that provide general education to the public. There is, however, a delicate line between teaching religious values and transmitting knowledge about different religions. While unanimously committed to assisting children in developing their own values, at the same time, the educational elite espouse the widest range of opinions as to whether schools are also responsible to help every child to gain deeper understanding of their own religion. This is where educational elites face a dilemma: how far schools should support development of individual values in every child, whether these values extend over to individual religious commitments. Still, teaching and propagating religious values is not considered relevant in public schools by the overwhelming majority.

According to the average rank score, less important appear to be the values of "diversity and multiculturalism" and "gender equality". But the degree of agreement in the opinion is very low, so that the value of diversity and the value of gender equality range from "rather important" to "very unimportant" (the range is 3.28-5.29 and 3.01-4.97 respectively).

We looked for the motives of these mixed reactions in interviews that followed the survey. The motives most frequently provided are the following:

"Against":

1) "both gender equality and diversity are not perceived as issues publicly: the radical feminist ideas do not enjoy popular support; the emphasis on diversity may only contribute to already damaging centrifugal forces in the society that have sparkled ethnic tensions and separatist tendencies in the polity";

2) "fraught with new disruptions too much time and energy has been spent on celebrating diversity and demonstrating sovereignties, more important at this point is to look for national consolidation of diversities";

3) "boys, not girls, should be given more opportunities and motivation for achievement at school; the fact is that girls receive a lot of encouragement for achievement at school, but boys often calculate very early that they do not have to make too much effort and instead stay "big lazy cats" because they know that they have more opportunities than girls after graduating from schools".

"For":

1) "there is a need to support respect and tolerance for diversity, especially ethnic and religious diversity, because the history of our country has accumulated too many grievances between ethnicities";

2) "there is a need to develop public awareness and intolerance towards sexism in employment";

3) "sexism has become the part and parcel of our life, so that according to some polls, every fourth female adolescent respondent in Moscow wishes to become a model or a stripper".

These reactions reflect the complexity of the contemporary Russian social and political situation, as well as cautious statements on how school can effectively promote values of equality in the face of enormous inequalities in the society.

However, the overall agreement about the most important values to be supported at school is remarkable—especially when compared with the polarization of value positions taken by the educational scholars in central educational institutions.

The more significant variation about the priority value areas for teaching at school is related to regional affiliation of the surveyed elite, and to a less degree to their positional status or gender. Now we turn to the discussion of these differences.

Variation by Region

This mainly refers to the placement of some of the top values education themes relative to each other. Thus, Moscow elites consider ecological awareness as the least important among the top five, while the elites in the other two cities rank ecological awareness second from the top.

Table 2.4 Placement and Average Score (on a 7-score scale) of Areas of Values Education by the Respondents in Three Cities

Values Themes	Moscow	Kemerovo	Vladivostok
Moral Values	2.06 (1)	2.06 (2/3)	1.11 (1)
Personal Autonomy and Reflection	2.37 (2)	1.44 (1)	2.65 (5)
Civic Values	2.49 (3)	2.31 (4)	1.83 (3)
Ecological Awareness	3.14 (5)	2.06 (2/3)	1.76 (2)
Work Values	2.66 (4)	2.56 (5)	2.06 (4)
Family Values	2.94 (6)	2.94	2.72 (7)
National Identity and Patriotism	3.51 (7)	3.19	2.29 (6)
Peace and Conflict Resolution	3.60	2.69 (6)	2.88
Democracy	3.37	2.81 (7)	3.50
Global Awareness	4.03	3.06	3.41
Gender Equality	4.60	3.38	4.00
Diversity and Multiculturalism	4.29	3.81	4.76
Religious Values	5.71	5.67	5.71

Among the values following closely the first five, Moscow and Vladivostok elites stress family values and patriotism (national identity) higher than the other values, while Kemerovo elites give priority to peace and conflict resolution and democracy. Kemerovo regional elites felt more concerned about the importance of teaching the value of diversity and multiculturalism as compared to the elites in the other two regions. This comes as no surprise in an area with a relatively dense and ethnically diverse population in Siberia, known as well in the past for the eruptions of social unrest. Particularly massive strikes of coal miners in 1991 accounted for more than half of the nations' strikers that year. The miners' movement precipitated the political independence of the Russian Federation and the dissolution of the Soviet Union at the end of 1991.

Elites in Vladivostok feel much stronger about the importance of the value of national identity and patriotism than do elites in the other two regions. The survey instrument distinguishes between the value of national identity and patriotism, on the one hand, and nationalist sentiment, on the other. The latter is related to the question about the importance of national pride and the veneration of heroes. This aspect of nationalism was low-key for the Vladivostok elites. We propose an explanation for the relatively high emphasis on national identity and patriotism in Vladivostok as follows:

1. Edward Shils' center-periphery hypothesis of the core values that shape nation's identity may be extended to the statement that in highly hierarchical and centralized societies the core nation's values are dictated by the strong center over its peripheral subordinates, so that when the role of the center weakens there appears to be a strong need for localities to prop up the core values. This need may be especially strong at the locales most distant from the center.

2. This need is felt especially urgent by the educational elites in Vladivostok in the context of local factors: firstly, the clash between self-interested local politicians threatens to reinforce a secessionist sentiment, and, secondly, national leaders of the ultra-left nationalist party make use of this local situation and threaten to redirect searches for national identity into nationalism. These particular threats in the socio-political and cultural context of Vladivostok lead the regional educational elites to decide on a relatively high ranking for the values of patriotism and national identity.

Positional Variation

Perceptions of themes in values education vary less by position or gender of the respondents. These gaps are minimal, though some patterns may be distinguished.

**Table 2.5 Ranking of Values Education Themes by
Values Education/Pedagogy Specialists**

Important	Avg. Rank/Place	Least important	Avg. Rank/Place
Moral Values	1.22 (1)	Religious Values	5.00 (13)
Personal Autonomy	1.44 (2)		
Ecological Awareness	2.00 (3-4)		
Work Values	2.00 (3-4)		
Family Values	2.11 (5)		

Variation by position is observed in the group of values education/pedagogy specialists who place stronger emphasis on the personality-oriented values, such as moral values, personal autonomy and reflection, peace and conflict resolution, ecological point of view, and less emphasis on other values, e.g., democracy and civic values (see Table 2.5). In contrast, educational policy-makers and bureaucrats place civic values higher than moral values and personal autonomy and reflection (see Table 2.6).

Table 2.6 Ranking of Values Education Themes by
Educational Policy-Makers and Bureaucrats

Important	Avg. Rank/ Place	Least important	Avg. Rank/ Place
Civic Values	2.04 (1)	Religious Values	6.14 (13)
Moral Values	2.36 (2)	Gender Equality	4.43 (12)
Work Values	2.36 (3)	Diversity and Multiculturalism	4.29 (11)
Personal Autonomy	2.61 (4)		
Family Values	2.82 (5)		

Table 2.7 Ranking of Values Education Themes by
NGO and Religious Leaders, Journalists

Important	Avg. Rank/ Place	Least important	Avg. Rank/ Place
Moral Values	1.00 (1)	Religious Values	5.58 (13)
Ecological Awareness	1.25 (2)	Diversity and Multiculturalism	4.61 (12)
Personal Autonomy	1.50 (3-4)		
Democracy	1.50 (3-4)		
Global Awareness	2.75 (5-8)		
Family Values	3.25 (5-8)		
Civic Values	3.25 (5-8)		
Patriotism	3.25 (5-8)		

NGO leaders stress democracy, and civic values, global awareness, and ecological awareness alongside the top priority values of morality and personal autonomy (see Table 2.7).

Table 2.8 Ranking of Values Education Themes by Front-Line Educators

Important	Avg. Rank/ Place	Least important	Avg. Rank/ Place
Moral Values	1.62 (1)	Religious Values	5.68 (13)
Ecological Awareness	2.04 (2)	Diversity and Multiculturalism	4.56 (12)
Personal Autonomy	2.24 (3)	Gender Equality	4.32 (11)
Civic Values	2.42 (4)		
Work Values	2.58 (5)		

Front-line educators recognize the importance of both personality-oriented values and societal values and the importance to balance them both (see Table 2.8). This pattern indicates that front-line educators have developed a comprehensive view on the role of school and should be an inseparable part of the policy-making process.

Variation by Gender

Male respondents placed lower scores on average and, therefore, lower emphasis on all the values than female respondents did. The only exception is personal autonomy and reflection, which men scored higher than women did. The standard distribution in the attitudes by gender is similar. The female respondents are especially likely to stress such values as global awareness (by a margin of 1.15-0.99), patriotism (by a margin of 0.95), conflict resolution (by 0.91), civic values (by 0.79) and gender equality (by 0.59). Their views are most unanimous about civic values, ecological awareness and moral values (SD of 0.93, 1.21, 1.38 respectively), while male respondents mostly agree on moral values and the low importance of gender equality. Female respondents seem to be more attracted than their male counterparts to the values of gender equality, family values, patriotism, global awareness, peace and conflict resolution, and they tend to de-emphasize the value of personal autonomy relative to their male counterparts (see Table 2.9).

Table 2.9 Placement and Average Scores of Areas of Values Education
(on a scale from 1 to 7) by Gender of Respondents

Value Themes	Female	Male
Moral Values	1.77 (1)	1.84 (1)
Civic Values	1.84 (2)	2.63 (4)
Ecological Awareness	1.90 (3)	3.05 (6)
Personal Autonomy and Reflection	2.30 (4)	2.16 (2)
Work Values	2.45 (5)	2.50 (3)
National Identity and Patriotism	2.60 (6)	3.55 (8)
Democracy	3.06 (7)	3.45 (7)
Peace and Conflict Resolution	2.70 (8)	3.61 (9)
Family Values	2.84 (9)	2.92 (5)
Global Awareness	3.10 (10)	4.08 (10)
Gender Equality	3.83 (11)	4.42 (12)
Diversity and Multiculturalism	4.27 (12)	4.32 (11)
Religious Values	5.80 (13)	5.62 (13)

Teaching Values of Other Societies

The gaps in perception of importance of teaching other societies' values and cultures support the thesis that when confronted with the weakening role of the center in the generation of core values, localities increasingly take on this function. According to this hypothesis the further from the center, the stronger the emphasis placed on studies of societies of eastern Asia: China, Japan and Korea in the first tier, followed by Singapore, Indonesia, Malaysia, and Thailand.

The strongest affinity with East Asian societies is felt by the educational elites in

Vladivostok. In contrast, Kemerovo educational elites attach equal emphasis to the leading countries of the West (U.S., U.K., France) and the East (China and Japan). As compared to these two regional samples, Moscow elites rank studies of most of these societies much lower. Educational elites across all the three Russian regions give first priority to studying Russian history and culture.

How Should Values be Implemented?

In line with the long-standing pedagogical tradition of a synthetic approach to teaching and up-bringing, Russian elites emphasize that from 82 percent to 100 percent of the school curriculum on average should target at values education. Furthermore, a decided advantage is given to values education as integrated throughout curriculum (from 66 percent to 75 percent on average) rather than as a specific subject.

Interviews with some of the survey participants indicated that the extracurricular collective forms of the Soviet-style education are either entirely rejected as too formalized and ideologically oppressive for an individual, or reconsidered in attempt to separate the "grain" of socialization from the "weeds" of indoctrination. In the past decade the importance of direct cognitive learning about values was reestablished on the wave of "glasnost" (freedom of speech and pluralism of opinion). In traditional schools new subjects were introduced, such as foundations of ethics, foundations of family values (including sex education), history of religions and others. It was important to speak openly and honestly about issues that were not debatable in the past.

However, the importance of cultural education is recognized so far as it complements development of deeper interpersonal relations between adults and children based on cooperation and freedom. This is because no new methods or subjects of learning may compensate for a general climate of egotism, isolationism, or aggressiveness. And on the contrary, schools not equipped with the most recent technologies and methods may grow responsible and self-sustained personalities in an atmosphere of care, trust and respect. The principles of cooperation and freedom in pedagogy have become, as discussed above, the major concepts of Russian pedagogical thought in the last quarter of the twentieth century—as in the pedagogy of cooperation. The concepts of both cooperation and freedom are very important as well as the link between them, because a truly free and autonomous person grows one's own inner freedom to make moral choices where the only measure is one's own conscientiousness.

Positional and Gender Differences

From the elites who participated in the survey, positional differences and some gender variation in opinion stand out regarding the issues of how values education should be implemented, no regional variation is noticeable. Front-line educators and pedagogy specialists tend to emphasize integrated curriculum more strongly than other positional groups by a margin of 10 percent on average. Also women tend to place a slightly higher emphasis on the integrated curriculum than men do.[4]

---

[4] Means were compared in three modified data sets (weighted by gender, region or position distribution) with means in an unaltered data set. The qualitative data from interviews was used as an additional check-up.

While values education specialists express very decisive opposition to the differentiation of values education programs by academic ability, front-line educators are the least rigorous in their general non-acceptance of the principle. While it is widely recognized that teaching methods may vary as applied to children with different abilities and inclinations, values education, as values specialists insist, is not related to individual academic abilities. Yet front-line educators are inclined to admit that various efforts and approaches are required to teach values to children of different ability.

Central administrators give the highest percentage of values education to be taught as a specific subject (30.8 percent), while NGO leaders and related professional categories are less likely to see values education organized as specific school lessons (18.7 percent), thus leaving some role in values education for other social institutions.

The respondents from all positional groups emphasize the importance of values education starting from an early age before individuals develop their values system rather than in secondary school. So it is recognized that values education is most effective at the moment of development of individual value orientations. In other words, it is much more difficult to "overhaul" the already developed world outlook.

Table 2.10 Average Ranking of the Top Three Settings Most Relevant for Values Education and Percentage of Respondents Who Marked Settings as Important

Settings	Religious Education	Civic Education	Moral Education
During school as a class	1.82 (29.9%)	1.74 (43.3%)	1.80 (41.9%)
During school through rules of behavior	1.80 (28.0%)	1.86 (80.6%)	2.12 (77.4%)
Outside school (clubs, sports, arts)	2.41 (40.9%)	2.19 (55.8%)	2.39 (59.1%)
Internships and community service	2.19 (29.7%)	2.03 (43.5%)	2.30 (38.7%)
Camps	1.97 (25.3%)	2.23 (30.0%)	2.17 (34.3%)
Religious groups and institutions	1.70 (73.8%)	1.85 (27.9%)	2.23 (42.8%)
Military training and civil service	1.70 (19.2%)	2.19 (30.9%)	1.96 (29.5%)
Home and family	1.65 (89.6%)	1.82 (76.9%)	1.51 (97.1%)
Media	2.29 (55.9%)	2.43 (58.6%)	2.45 (64.2%)

Where Should Values Education be Taught?

The respondents were asked to rank the top three among nine settings—most effective and relevant, in their opinion, for three types of education—religious, civic, and moral. Because a number of ranking positions is small relatively to a number of settings, both the average ranking score and a percentage of elites who marked the setting as relevant were taken into consideration. The results are presented in Table 2.10 above. It is important to note that the majority of respondents considered it unsuitable to preach religious values at schools since they support the secular character of Russian general education in schools. At the same time the respondents made a point that religious education, as an impartial study of cultural history of different religions and concessions, is suitable at school for the cultural orientation of youth.

There is a significant consensus among the Russian elites, who participated in the survey, about the leading role of "home and family" in instilling moral and religious values, and to a lesser degree in supporting civic values. The role of "school" is recognized as most effective to support the development of civic and moral education. And there is an important distinction between two forms of school education. The majority of respondents strongly stress a school climate and the way schools are run as most effective for children and teenagers to learn civic values and develop a moral orientation. The school curriculum (either integrated or as a specific subject) is considered a relevant complimentary setting for learning civic and moral values at schools. Much smaller number of respondents consider school settings quite suitable for teaching about different religions, although the priority in effectiveness on the development of religious beliefs and feelings is given to the concerted effort of family and religious institutions. The effectiveness of "other institutions and social practices" on educating the youth is considered less prominent than in the leading settings. Although the appropriateness of educational effects of social life outside school, family and religious groups is accepted by a greater number of respondents for moral orientation (44.76 percent on average) and civic education (41.20 percent) than for religious education (34.20 percent).

Relatively high is the assessment by the elites role of "religious institutions and groups" not only in religious education but also in promoting civic values. This may be attributed to the activization of religious groups in the public political arena and their attempt to lead the search for national consolidation. Close to half of the respondents consider religious institutions favorable for developing the morale of the youth.

Almost the lowest is the evaluation of the adequacy of contemporary "mass media" for values education, yet from slightly over half to two thirds of respondents recognize its enormous impact on the youth's values orientations.

There are some marked differences in assessment of the adequacy of various settings for values education by elites holding different positions in the educational system. Front-line educators and pedagogy specialists tend to consider the influence of social institutions and practices outside school and family as less adequate for teaching values as compared to schools and families themselves. The group of administrators and NGO-related categories view internships, community, national and military service as having a higher degree of relevance for civic and moral education than do school elites. In general NGOs rank education through media much higher than all the other groups. Administrators and NGOs also tend to underestimate the educational effect of school climate.

In sum, it is important to indicate that an overwhelming majority of Russian educational elites stress the significant role of family in teaching moral and religious values (if any) to the young. By this it is admitted that schools are much more disadvantaged to help youngsters to develop moral integrity without a concerted family effort in the first place. The institution of family is also considered supportive of civic education provided at schools.

With regard to religious education, an important clarification is made: while schools may decide to introduce the young to the cultural history of various religions, development of religious beliefs is a family matter and a matter of church or other religious groups. This attitude is supported by the secular character of general education in Russia. This finding confirms the previously stated one.

There is a potential strenuous division between the group of front-line educators and pedagogy specialists, on the one hand, and administrators and NGO and other public or religious groups, on the other hand. With regard to the most effective setting for values education, the latter group appears to underestimate the effectiveness of the way schools are organized and run, and to over-stress the influence of other social institutions. The front-line educators, by way of contrast, have doubts about the values education provided by communities. Whether because of disrespect to the formalized and ideological forms of community involvement of the recent past or because of a sense of caution in unsafe and value-uncertain community environments, life in communities surrounding schools appear underdeveloped and mutually untrustful for its members. This presents potentially aggravating implications for the educational policy formulation and policy implementation.

Whom Should Values Education Target in the First Place?

The respondents were asked to rank the top three groups as the primary subjects of three forms of education—religious, civic, and moral. The categories included six groups of children/teenagers by age and two groups of teachers by experience (practicing teachers in in-service retraining and beginning teachers as interns or teacher learners). Both the average ranking score and a percentage of respondents who marked the groups as important to receive values education are paired in Table 2.11 below.

Table 2.11 Average Ranking of Top Three Age Groups as Target Recipients of Values Education and Percentage of Respondents Who Marked Age Groups as Target

Age group of learners	Religious Education	Civic Education	Moral Education
Young children (3-4 years old)	1.85 (32.1%)	1.78 (30.5%)	1.88 (39.1%)
Preschoolers (5 years old)	1.68 (38.8%)	1.74 (36.3%)	1.95 (51.2%)
Primary level (6-11 years old)	2.06 (51.1%)	1.79 (58.6%)	1.89 (75.6%)
Secondary level (11-14 years old)	2.13 (50.8%)	2.04 (74.3%)	2.18 (73.2%)
High school level (15-17 years old)	2.13 (56.6%)	2.23 (78.2%)	2.28 (69.0%)
University level (18 years old)	2.28 (48.4%)	2.44 (64.4%)	2.31 (49.5%)

Teachers turned out to be almost always a secondary concern (after students) for the Russian elites, and the distribution of ranking is summed up in separate tables for students and for teachers below.

Age Factor in Values Education

There appears to be a strong consensus among the elites that values education is most effective when started in early childhood before individuals develop their world outlook. The difference is observable between preschool and school age groups for these three forms of values education. It is obvious that family and possibly some institutions other than mass schooling (such as kindergartens, Sunday church schools and others) play a primary role in values education of children—not only moral and religious, but also civic. Starting with the school age and, consequently, with attendance of secular general education schools, the role of religious up-bringing drops considerably. Yet more than half of respondents (56.6 percent) consider adolescence—the time of a painstaking rediscovery of one's identity and orientation—relevant for helping teenagers to orient themselves about various religions through exposure to the history of world religions. More than three quarters of respondents (78.2 percent) consider adolescence a target age for civic education—the age marked by the personal world-view revision and by the eligibility to exercise citizen's rights. The major focus of moral education at school is at the primary level. The concern for moral education is sustained through all levels of schooling, though at later ages other concerns (civic education and education about religions) may take the lead.

Table 2.12 Average Ranking of Groups of Teachers as Target Recipients of Values Education and Percentage of Respondents Who Marked These Groups as Target

Groups of teachers by experience	Religious Education	Civic Education	Moral Education
In-service teachers	1.98 (35.0%)	1.82 (44.7%)	1.77 (37.7%)
Teacher learners	2.28 (40.8%)	2.18 (51.8%)	1.97 (43.7%)

Teacher Training

When turning to instructors as a target group for value orientation, the respondents feel a stronger need to provide teachers with special instruction on moral education than for the purposes of civic or religious education (see Table 2.12). Since moral education is recognized as most effective from as early an age as possible, the role of an adult can hardly be overestimated. According with this logic the respondents rank first teachers, followed by children of early ages, as primary groups for moral education. Moral revisions of self are something that every person goes through in his/her life, but this requirement is made much stricter to those in the teaching profession. Remarkably, front-line educators appear more demanding than other positional groups with regard to strengthening the moral visions of practicing teachers (average ranking score for this group is 1.67). Consequently, the need of exposure to civic and religious education appears in a decreasing order. Among the positional groups only pedagogy specialists give some slack to practicing teachers as compared to beginning teachers. All other groups appear more demanding to practicing teachers (through periodic re-training) than to beginning teachers. Yet, the number of respondents who chose novice teachers as a target group for various value-enhancing programs is larger on average by a margin of five to six per cent, than those who are focused on practicing teachers.

How Do the Russian Educational Elites Think About Values Education at Schools? International Comparative Perspective

For cross-national comparisons of elites' views on values education and for better understanding of the inner logic of responses of the Russian elites, factor analysis was run on Questions 3 and 4. Both questions seek responses on the overlapping content area. The first one relates to ascribing scores of importance and relevance of values education themes on a scale from 1 to 7, the latter focuses on the controversial issues within these themes. The procedure of factor analysis helped to distinguish four sig-nificant groups of attitudes among the elite respondents. The analysis of major reasons and motives for values education at school (Question 1) as well as interview data con-firm such stratification:

Personality-oriented Values

Those who stress personal autonomy, importance of developing children's own values and critical thinking also tend to place a greater emphasis on moral values; harmony, i.e., values common to all irrespective of differences by class, ethnicity or religion; family values and gender equality.

Strong linkages of the values of personal autonomy with other personality-related values and moral values illuminate a specific meaning of these values in the Russian context today. This relationship can be seen in the Russian pedagogical tradition of holistic humanist pedagogy. The Russian pedagogical thought and practice of the end of the twentieth century is consolidated into the pedagogy of free development and cooperation. The ideas of free education go back to the school established by Lev Tol-stoy in nineteenth-century Russia, and they return today in the form of John Dewey's philosophical connection between education and democracy and other innovative edu-cational methods. However, in the opinion of the Russian educational elites, the value of internalized personality freedom stands apart from the values of democracy, which is more instrumental in its character and is not so closely related to the value of moral integrity. Indeed, as Adam Przeworski stresses, democratic procession of conflict through following procedures is not necessarily moral or rational, and democracy calls for a suspension of the belief that democratic outcomes are certain in their rationality or high moral status (1997, p. 61).

If we look at other national contexts from this perspective, we would seek for the meaning of the value of personal autonomy as manifested through its links to the closely adjacent values. Thus, e.g. autonomy is closely associated with the political values of democracy and civic education in the Singapore context, with social change in the Mexican context, with the moral foundations of democracy in the Thai context. In the Malaysian context moral values are tightly linked to spiritual and religious val-ues rather than to the value of personal autonomy.

It is obvious that the specific account of values can be revealed through the relations of this value to others in the semantic structure of values of each culture. Therefore the most insightful focus of values in a comparative perspective is on their relations to other value concepts within a certain culture.

Openness of World Outlook

Another strand of thinking of Russian elites relates to global and ecological values, to the value of peace and conflict resolution, democracy, the value of understanding all political views and individual competitiveness. Thus, an emphasis is put upon such orientations as openness/receptivity, non-aggressiveness, tolerance, pluralism, interconnectedness. These orientations are seen as non-contradictory to individual competitiveness and are to be supported by democratic structures.

Larger-society-related Values

The third strand stresses civic values, patriotism, gender equality, family values, peace and conflict resolution and work values. Interestingly, family values are emphasized both as the basis for personality-oriented education and for teaching the values of the larger society. Attitudes that guide behavior both within the consolidated society (values cluster 3) and beyond the boundaries of conventional nation-states (values cluster 2) are both non-repressive and non-aggressive in character.

The fourth strand in attitudes is religious and traditionalist: those who choose religious values tend to stress the duty to help the less fortunate, girls' destiny in home-building, loyalty to government and national pride.

Most importantly, these strands of thinking among Russian elites are found not to be correlated with regional affiliation, gender or position of respondents, but to run across the whole pool of respondents. However, the prevailing perceptions represent a mixture of the first three strands of thinking. The procedure of factor analysis allows us to focus on the relational significance of the analyzed categories. And so it maintains the major semiotic assumption of drawing the meaning from the relations between symbols or categories. The four clusters of value categories identified above fit a three-dimensional semantic continuum:

1. from more open to more isolationist;
2. from more personally autonomous to more loyal to the outside authority;
3. from more progressive and instrumental (in the language of modernization) to more traditionalist.

Thus the predominant logic of the Russian educational elites' respondents is characterized as more open, more personality-oriented and more progressive rather than isolationist, loyalist and traditionalist. This conclusion is also suggested by the analysis of interview data and other survey questions. It is significant especially in the face of normative uncertainty and polarization of the educational elites in the central research and policy-making institutions.

Conclusions and Policy Implications

Given the polarization of the positions on values education among the leading intellectuals, it is notable that the educational elites in the center as well as in the three regions of the Russian Federation indicate a high level of consensus about the values they rank as most relevant and important for teaching in Russian schools today. The top-priority cluster of values is oriented towards personality autonomy, self-development, and moral integrity. A considerable consensus about these personality-oriented values was evident across the three regions. At the same time it allows variation in self-determining particular goals and values on the way of individual development and growth within a learning community of schools. The most desired values dispose individuals towards an open and progressive world-outlook.

Regional elites differ in some of their values attitudes under the pressure of specific challenges and the socio-cultural situation they are facing. Most significant however is the variation by position and to a lesser degree by gender—especially with regard to some controversial issues about values education and the pedagogical aspects of value learning. It is remarkable that professional ties continue to be strong while many social bonds have collapsed. This variation in stance by professional status and position makes a case for an equal representation of innovative principals and teachers (and other front-line educators) as well as women in the policy-making area alongside with pedagogy specialists and policy-makers and bureaucrats, who are predominantly male.

The regional variation in values perceptions may be approached as well from the perspective of a center-periphery hypothesis in the national normative consolidation. The hypothesis distinguishes between the core and peripheral values, and claims that the core values are responsible for the formation of national integration. In the context of the decentralizing (or disintegrating) polity, locales most remote from the center experience the most urgent need to support the generation of core values. Though schooling in its value orientation remains significantly Euro-centric, the more to the east from the center the lesser is the center's grip over the values and more significant is the intention to reach out to the neighboring East Asian societies.

For cross-national comparisons, fundamental is the centrality of the concept of personal autonomy and reflection. It represents the continuous Russian tradition (which was suppressed or even persecuted in certain historical periods but never forgotten or dogmatic) of a child-centered holistic pedagogy which values individual motivation, will and reflection in one's own development and "unfolding"—in the social environment free of enforcement. Thus, other fundamental personality-oriented values tend to cluster around the value of personal autonomy and reflection in the responses given by the Russian elites sample. The other two predominant value strings reflect such respondents' orientations as openness (as contrasted to isolationism) and progressiveness (as opposed to traditionalism). These particular semantic oppositions characterize the Russian sample's responses and the predominant pattern in attitudes where inclinations to be more personally autonomous and reflective, open and progressive predominate. The same relational semantic of values logic is found to be an appropriate tool for international comparison.

References

Birzea, C. (1994). *Educational Policies of the Countries in Transition*. Strasbourg: Council of Europe Press.

Birzea, C. (1996). "Education in a World of Transition: Between Post-communist and Post-modernism", *Prospects* 26(4): 673-681.

Cerych, L. (1995). "Educational Reforms in Central and Eastern Europe", *European Journal of Education* 30(4): 423-435.

Daniels H., Lucas, N., Totterdell, M. and Fomina, O. (1995). "Humanization in Russian Education: A Transition Between State Determinism and Individualism", *Educational Studies* 21(1): 29-39.

Dneprov, E.D. (1994). *Chetvertaja Shkolnaja Reforma v Rossii* [The Fourth School Reform in Russia]. Moscow: Interprax.

Dneprov, E.D. (1996). *Shkol'naya Reforma mezhdu "Vchera" i "Zavtra"* [School Reform between "Yesterday" and "Tomorrow"]. Moscow: Russian Academy of Education and the Federal Institute of Educational Planning.

Durkheim, E. (1951). *Suicide*. Glencoe, IL: Free Press.

Garadzha, V.I. (Ed.) (1995). "Kruglyj stol: Kul'tura, obrazovanie, religia" [Roundtable Discussion: Culture, Education, Religion], *Pedagogika* 5: 50-63.

Gazman, O.S. (1995). "Ot avtoritarnogo obrazovanija k pedagogike svobody" [From Authoritarian Education to the Pedagogy of Freedom], *Novyje Tsennosti Obrazovanija* [New Educational Values] 2: 16-45.

Gleiser, G. and Vilotievic, M. (Eds.) (1997). *Obrazovanie: Traditsii i Innovatsii v Uslovijakh sotsial'nykh peremen* [Education: Tradition and Innovation Under the Conditions of Social Changes]. Moscow: Russian Academy of Education.

Goskomstat (1996a). *Education in the Russian Federation*. Moscow: Goskomstat.

Goskomstat (1996b). *Annual Statistical Yearbook of the Russian Federation – 1996*. Moscow: Goskomstat.

Inglehart, R. (1997). *Modernization and Postmodernization: Cultural, Economic, and Political Change in 43 Societies*. Princeton, NJ: Princeton University Press.

Inkeles, A. and Smith, D.H. (1974). *Becoming Modern: Individual Change in Six Developing Countries*. Cambridge, MA: Harvard University Press.

Karakovsky, V.A., Novikova, L.I. and Selivanova, N.L. (1996). *Vospitanie? Vospitanie... Vospitanie! Teorija i Praktika Vospitattel'nykh Sistem* [Values Education? Values Education... Values Education! Theory and Practice of School Values Educating Systems]. Moscow: Novaja Shkola.

Marcuse, H. (1964). *One-Dimensional Man*. Boston, MA: Beacon Press.

Nelson, R.R. and Winter, S.G. (1982). *An Evolutionary Theory of Economic Change*. Cambridge, MA, London: Belknap Press.

Nikandrov, N.D. (1997a). *Rossija: Tsennosti obschestva na rubezhe XXI veka* [Russia: Societal values on the threshold of the 21st century]. Moscow: Moscow Institute of Educational Systems Development.

Nikandrov, N.D. (1997b). "Vospitanie tsennostei: Rossijskij variant" [Values Education: The Russian Scenario]. In G. Gleiser and M. Vilotievic (Eds.), *Obrazovanie: Traditsii i innovatsii v uslovijakh sotsial'nykh peremen* [Education: Tradition and Innovation Under the Conditions of Social Changes]. Moscow: Russian Academy of Education.

Przeworski, A. (1995). *Democracy and the Market: Political and Economic Reforms in Eastern Europe and Latin America*. Cambridge, U.K. and New York: Cambridge University Press.

Przeworski, A. (1997). *Sustainable Democracy*. Cambridge, U.K. and New York: Cambridge University Press.

Ravkin, Z.I. (Ed.) (1995). *Obrazovanie: Idealy i Tsennosti* [Education: Ideals and Values]. Moscow: Institute of Educational Theory and Pedagogy of the Russian Academy of Education.

Shils, E. (1975). *Center and Periphery: Essays in Macrosociology*. Chicago, IL: The University of Chicago Press.

Soloveichik, S.L. (1994). "Chelovek svobodnyj". Manifest gazety *Pervoje Sentjabrja* [A Free Person. Manifesto of the newspaper *September 1*], *Pervoje Sentjabrja* 83.

Stark, D. and Bruszt, L. (1998). *Postsocialist Pathways: Transforming Politic and Property in East Central Europe*. Cambridge, U.K. and New York: Cambridge University Press.

Tubelsky, A.N. (Ed.) (1994). *Shkola Samoopredelenija: Shag Vtoroi* [School of Self-determination: Second Step]. Moscow: Politext.

Valitskaya, A.P. (1997). "Sovremennyje strategii obrazovanija: varianty vybora" [Contemporary Educational Strategies: What are the Choices], *Pedagogika* 2: 3-8.

Vygotsky, L.S. (1996). *Pedagogicheskaya Psikhologia* [Pedagogical Psychology]. Moscow: Pedagogika-Press. (First edition, 1926).

Woolcock, M. (1998). "Social Capital and Economic Development: Towards a Theoretical Synthesis and Policy Framework". *Theory and Society* 27: 151-208.

North America
and
the "Far" West

CHAPTER 3

MEXICO: THE CONSTRUCTION OF A NATIONAL IDENTITY UNDER CENTRALIZED LEADERSHIP[1]

Maria Teresa Tatto
Lilian Alvarez Arellano
Medardo Tapia Uribe
Armando Loera Varela
Michael Rodriguez

Introduction

Over the last decade, Mexico has intensified its active search for democracy and invigorated its march towards modernization. Both of these trends have proven to have important influences on the values the Mexican state and educational authorities see as necessary to be transmitted via education. Concern with values and values education in Mexico is evident through the number of studies that have been carried out recently to both uncover those values held as important by Mexicans and to discuss the incorporation of new values congruent with a modern Mexico (Alducin-Abitia, 1989; Alducin-Abitia, 1991; Muñoz-García, 1996). Moreover, Mexico's National Development Plan from 1995 to the year 2000[2] underlines the need for a concentrated effort to develop values that will support the five objectives proposed in the plan:

> (a) Strengthen national sovereignty as a supreme value of our nationality and as the first and foremost responsibility of the Mexican State; (b) consolidate a social regime ruled by the law that will apply to all equally and where justice will be the path to solve conflict; (c) construct a democracy based on trust, political peace and intense participation by citizens as the foundation for the Mexican identity; (d) stimulate social development for all individuals and communities under principles of equity and justice; (e) promote vigorous and sustainable economic growth for all Mexicans (Plan Nacional de Desarrollo, 1995, p. x, our translation).

---

[1] The authors acknowledge the support of all those individuals who collected and processed the data for this study. Special thanks go to Jose Bonifacio Barba of the Universidad Autonoma de Aguascalientes; Maria Elena Madrid, Maria Teresa Yurén and Aurora Elizondo from the Universidad Pedagogica Nacional (UPN) in Mexico City; and to Francisca Quezada, Olivia Verdín, Miguel Angel Izquierdo, Hilda Constantino C., Guadalupe Poujol, María Rosa Quiñones, Erick Castillo, Mauricio Robert, Raúl Burgos Fajardo, Víctor Aguilar, Antonio Corrales Burgueño, Carmen Audelo, and Ismael Alvarado. We also want to thank all our respondents for sharing their valuable insights and their disinterested contribution to this research project.

[2] The Plan's introduction makes a point of explaining that to develop the Plan the central government carried out a national, popular and democratic consultation, organizing ninety-seven fora where more than 12,000 position papers were read. In addition the state received more than 300,000 suggestions from the people in postal boxes and reception centers set up for that purpose across the nation (Plan Nacional de Desarrollo, 1995, p. ix).

The National Development Plan communicates the Mexican State's intention to strengthen its role to guarantee national security, law and order, and the role of its institutions throughout the country, while attempting to group Mexicans under a set of cohesive national norms. Modern Mexico is a country that has gone through a number of changes from domination and exploitation to independence and self-determination, and is still struggling to reconcile seemingly paradoxical value systems. While there is a push to move along with modern societies as a growing global economy and pluralistic society, there is also a push to maintain values that are seen as characteristic of Mexican society. This push in different directions creates a tension that challenges the formation of a consonant Mexican identity and introduces important dilemmas for curriculum designers.

The school curriculum, which had typically dealt with values education through specific subject matter such as civics and history, currently integrates "so-called modern values" across all the subjects. Values such as the importance of critical and independent thinking, the value of constructing a technologically advanced society and the importance of individual independence and entrepreneurship are quickly gaining strength over the more traditional values supporting the family and the nation. These new modern tendencies could seem threatening to holders and supporters of mainly traditional values. This was seen in the recent reintroduction of sexual education in primary schools, where public opinion asked for children to be taught both critical thinking skills and autonomy as well as traditional values.[3]

The reform of the school curriculum is akin with reform tendencies in the United States and indeed worldwide. In Mexico, adoption of constructivist principles via the current educational reform has implied the adoption of a theoretically grounded view of learning that attempts to shift traditional conceptions of knowledge as being "out there" to knowledge developed by those who are involved in the teaching and learning process. It has also meant the inclusion of a concept-based curriculum across the subjects, the encouragement of teaching to accommodate students' different learning needs and styles, the arrangement of learning opportunities so that all participants in the teaching-learning process can be contributors in mastering knowledge, and the intention to construct understandings through reflection, dialogue, and critical thinking in context. Thus the reform through its proposed curriculum and larger principles is *de facto* altering the traditional content and pedagogy of values education. The messages of the new reform are that individuals can become agents of change (an idea that challenges indirectly the central role of the state), the importance of learning based on deep understandings of disciplinary knowledge, the need to understand diversity as an essential element in the teaching-learning process, and the heightened relevance of critical thinking in context. All these values are integrated across the curriculum.

The reform, however, comes at a time when the influence and image of the Mexican system of public education has been strongly debated. The character and authority of the Mexican school has changed dramatically in recent years in part as a result of the economic hardship that has affected the country since the early 1980s and in part as a result of the increased influence of American culture and media on the life of Mexi-

---

[3] Sex education has been a controversial proposal dating at least since the early 1930's when Bassols was the Minister of Education.

cans. There are problems related to the low efficiency and quality of the primary school, as well as wider inequity between rural and urban schools. The system has undergone a decentralization process since 1992 that has permitted some innovation at the state level but in general the policy-making power among educational stakeholders has not been evenly distributed. The academic environment at the school level, the teachers' pedagogical proficiency and the involvement of parents and other community actors in schools' activities have not changed significantly in spite of policies and programs designed to train and motivate teachers, allocate teaching materials, and improve social participation. Some of the factors that explain the failure of modernization at the school and classroom level are connected with the shortage of funds and the inadequate institutional capabilities of the states, the authoritarian and top-down perspective of central bureaucracies, and a strong and unique teacher's union driven by a clientelistic logic. However, in spite of the many shortages, decentralization has improved the quality of the educational policy dialogue by motivating new actors to debate on the current and future role of education. Without any doubt, one of the most ardently debated topics has been values education.[4]

Values education had been kept out of the official curriculum of basic education until 1999 when the federal government via the central ministry of education (Secretaria de Educacion Publica or SEP) introduced a new program for teaching ethics at the secondary school level. However, even before or concurrently to these actions, public agencies at the state or municipal level as well as non-governmental organizations (NGOs) had been introducing value programs in the schools. On the other hand, many teachers under their own personal initiative introduced some modality of values programs mostly to deal with disciplinary problems. Two major perspectives have dominated in these efforts. On one side the conservative view, shared by most of the private sector and some local governments, claims the need to develop values education programs that would facilitate the creation of a climate favorable for private business, by extolling the virtues of personal effort and initiative, individual responsibility, trust, and legitimacy of profit. On the other side the more liberal view, sees values education programs as an intervention towards democratizing the school and inducing values and skills needed by a more open, participatory, pluralistic, and critical society and advocate values such as conflict management, democratic leadership, and tolerance.

Current federal and state efforts to develop a value cohesive nation have begun to consider not only the reform of the school curriculum but also the development of context-relevant values education programs.

In this chapter we report on the results of a study designed to understand the approaches to values education in Mexico as viewed by educational authorities and individuals that have important influence and insight in this arena. After describing Mexico's political economy, we present the study's theoretical framework and the findings from a survey regarding approaches to values education. We conclude with a discussion on how this study may help initiate a policy dialogue on values education in Mexico and support future research to include rank and file teachers, parents and stu-

---

[4] For a review of innovations produced by decentralization see Pardo 1999.

dents' views on values education. As our data will show, one of the most surprising findings of our study is the strong homogeneity in the thinking of our respondents. This relative lack of diversity can be explained in great part by a strong national central system of education that has fulfilled its proposed role of uniting a divided nation by transmitting values such as nationalism, the separation between church and state, and in short by constructing a consonant Mexican identity. There is without a doubt an openness to new ideas such as pluralism and multiculturalism but only to a certain degree and in accordance with what is historically familiar (e.g., a pointed preference to teaching socialist values vis-à-vis Asian or Islamic values). Although we expected consensus in some aspects, our initial hypothesis of regional differences in a country as vast as Mexico seemed plausible. However among those in the group we surveyed there was not as much divergence as expected. This could be as much a characteristic of commonly shared values among those individuals in positions of authority and influence in Mexican education as well as a fair representation of more generalized views. Given Mexico's ongoing decentralization reform, a more marked contrast in views could evolve within the new generations, the ones that are being currently educated within regional and even more parochial views. The consequences of these changes to democracy, national unity and the notion of a Mexican identity will remain an open question for some years to come.

Mexico's Political Economy

Mexico's history is punctuated by periods of prosperity, domination, oppression and sovereignty. Mexico had a variety of well developed indigenous cultures with defined values, societal norms and established commerce well before Christopher Columbus arrived in the Americas in 1492 and before the Spaniards invaded and conquered Mexico in 1521. It is not until 1821—after more than 300 years of domination—that Mexico achieved independence from Spain. The next challenge of the new independent and weak nation came when in the years between 1846-1848 Mexico lost half of its territory to the United States in one of the most unequal wars in American history. Less than twenty years later Mexico once more defended its territory—this time successfully—against the colonization efforts of the French. In 1893 Mexico gave Belize to the United Kingdom in return for the United Kingdom's commitment to stop its support (materialized in guns and liquor) for the Mayan Indian insurrection, known as the Guerra de Castas, in Yucatan, southeast Mexico.

An important and defining moment for the Mexican nation was the revolutionary period in 1910-1917, which overthrew the dictatorial Diaz regime, an initially liberal government that remained in power for thirty years, and established a new constitutional state based on nationalistic, federalist and populist principles. This was a social revolution that has continued to these days. The guiding principles of the revolution were the improvement of the life conditions of the working class, the incorporation of the working class to the political and social life of the nation, the cessation of exploitation of the Mexican people and of Mexico's natural resources by foreign capitalism. The principles of the revolution crystallized in the political Constitution of 1917, which has been amended a number of times since. Shortly after, in 1929, an official government party named PNR, or Partido Nacional Revolucionario, established a strong, authoritarian central state apparatus that has persisted to these days. Although the name of the party has changed from PRM, or Partido de la Revolución Mexicana, in 1934 to PRI, or Partido Revolucionario Institucional in 1946, the style of government changed little until the end of the 1980s when tendencies towards political pluralism began to emerge, having as an outcome more representation of other political parties at the state and municipal levels as well as in the Federal Congress.

Throughout Mexican history, the Catholic Church has played an important and—especially after the Reform Movement (1848)—often unwanted role in internal political affairs and in the shaping of Mexican identity. The major challenge for the church vis-à-vis the new state came when at the end of the nineteenth century the Mexican Liberal Party demanded the strict enforcement of the Reform Laws which among other mandates banned the church's access to the economic, political, and otherwise social life of the country limiting its role within the confines of religious activity strictly defined. These laws had the effect of formally separating the church and the state. This separation had important implications for education as reflected in the 3rd Article of the Constitution of 1917: "Education will be free; and it will be secular—not only that given in official educational institutions but also that given in private institutions at the primary, elementary, and superior levels. No religious corporation or ministry of any cult may establish or direct schools of primary education. All private primary schools will be subject to official supervision..." (Constitucion Politica de los Estados Unidos Mexicanos, 1994, p. 11, our translation). This act had enormous implications for the educational system, and in particular for values education. From this moment on, civic values were promoted and put in the center of the public education's curricula. At the same time, moral and religious values were considered to be a private matter, the responsibility of each individual's family and church with the result that the approach to religious and moral values became predominantly Catholic and patriarchal.

An important influence in Mexican values education was represented by José Vasconcelos, a philosopher and politician who proposed the redemption of mankind—in particular of the Mexican people—through culture and education. As Minister of Education at the end of the revolutionary process he spread throughout the nation what he considered to be the classical works of the East and the West. He called teachers "cultural missionaries" and expected them to have a missionary zeal. His nation-wide literacy campaign included not only the "three R's" but also, cultural and political literacy. Therefore, his was a values education agenda along with Alfonso Reyes and other thinkers that influenced the new teachers of the revolution who were trained to illuminate the conscience of the Mexican people. Later, nationalistic policies under President Calles (1924-1927) and subsequent presidents made civic instruction the core of values education. During the Lazaro Cardenas period (1934-1940) Mexican education acquired strong socialist tendencies. The socialist school was used as an instrument to transmit socialist ideals through the study plans, textbooks and school ceremonies where the children learned to sing the National Anthem along with the Communist International. This was to change gradually as the federal government headed towards the modernization of the country, in the aftermath of World War II.

In the late 1970s and early 1980s and after thirty years of unequal but sustained economic growth the economy, heavily dependent on oil exports staggered, the peso faltered and austerity measures were imposed, all of which negatively affected the performance of all sectors of the country, including education. President Miguel de la Madrid (1982-1988) launched an economic program downsizing the government and restructuring its role in a liberal fashion, departing from the until then dominant welfare state notion. Mexico entered the GATT (General Agreement on Tariffs and Trade), giving serious impulse to education decentralization policies but, paradoxically, only as way to strengthen the central state (see Tatto, 1999). President Salinas' agenda (1988-1994) was dominated by a commitment to prepare the country for participation in a growing global economy; this intention became a salient feature of the political environment, and the explicit goal of many policies of the Mexican State, including education. This transition was marked by the North American Free Trade Agreement (or NAFTA) signed between Mexico, the U.S., and Canada in 1993 with the purpose of liberalizing the economy, promoting exports and attracting foreign investment. In the mid-1990s as the country's agenda became dominated once more by globalization concerns, the federal government added to a nationalistic focus an emphasis on hard work, competitiveness, productivity, and "international literacy". The achievement of this value shift was seen as a task for the educational system. Global awareness and economic competition were the main concerns of the government when at the beginning of 1995, while President Salinas was celebrating the formal beginning of NAFTA, an Indian uprising emerged in the southern state of Chiapas, calling into question the assumptions of the modernization project. The national impact of the "Zapatista Movement", as it is known, was to put into question the whole idea of modernization by recasting traditional indigenous values and moving forward the cause of the indigenous population's rights. From the educational point of view this meant for society an opportunity to rethink very seriously the aims of education, the values it was to promote, and the legitimacy of alternative implementation venues.

The dominant political discourse during the Salinas period, known as social liberalism, urged the Mexican people to abandon the Revolution's ideology and rally around a government program initially designed to reduce poverty called "solidarity". At the end of 1994, with the change of administration Mexico had a severe economic crisis. A number of factors have been suggested to help explain the crisis such as the global economic crisis created by speculation in the international financial market, mistakes in the planning and internal management of the economy, the lack of efficiency and solvency of some members of the public and private sectors, and the insufficiency of social programs. It was not until 1998 that the country was able to recover its stability and growth.

The current discourse that permeates Mexico's educational, economic, and political reform stresses the development of more democratic structures of governance in the country as a whole. Two national values rooted in Mexico's painful history of domination—sovereignty and nationalism—are highlighted in the National Development Plan, and defy the strong currents of change. They are defined as follows:

[S]overeignty is the most important value in our nationality; its defense and

---

[5] Since the National Development Plan was written after consulting with a large number of Mexico's population, these values can be taken to reflect the national consensus.

strength are the first objective of the Mexican State. Sovereignty consists in assuring the capacity of the Mexican people to make free policy decisions in the interior and with independence from the exterior. For this reason Mexican sovereignty does not recognize in the country or in the exterior a higher power than that of the State. In the exercise of our sovereignty we build and recognize our own interests, propose collective goals, protect what is ours, and promote Mexico worldwide (Plan Nacional de Desarrollo, p. 3, our translation).

[N]ationalism is the set of values, feelings, and aspirations that characterize and define a group of people in the large landscape of nations. The Mexican nationalism is inclusive, aware of the richness of the values of which it is formed, and because of that, respectful of the diversity of other cultures. Our nationalism, forged in the course of our history, has as a fundamental quest the defense of our own values, the strengthening of peace and understanding with other countries. Nationalism is the basis of sovereignty; it feeds from the diversity and vitality of our popular culture and is an essential factor of our unity and popular cohesion. Our nationalism is the trust and faith we have in ourselves, the love for what is ours. Our nationalism is the source of strength against adversity. In our nationalism there is no room for antagonism or for disintegration of our territory; it does encourage neither intolerance nor rejection of alien values. Our nationalism guides our behavior abroad and sustains our future (Plan Nacional de Desarrollo, p. 3, our translation.)

Thus the reaffirmation of Mexico's sovereignty and the strong call for national values shape the contours of a Mexican identity. The current debates on the goals of education vis-à-vis the traditional and the modern, and the national and the global define the context of our study.

Theoretical Framework

Research on social and cultural capital framed our study. Research on social and cultural capital has pointed out that the values a culture holds as important are strong forces that help shape societies and influences such aspects as form of government, schooling, productivity and social well being (Putnam, 1993; Coleman, 1994; Bourdieu, 1977; Bourdieu and Passeron, 1977; Inglehart, 1997). These studies also observe that important societal changes are often preceded—and accompanied—by dramatic changes in values and cultural beliefs (Diamond and Plattner, 1996; Inglehart, 1997). Societies that have moved from authoritarian to more democratic forms of government see this change reflected not only in the organization of their government and in the school curriculum but also in the media and in the relationships individuals have with one another.

In this study our aim was to understand the approaches to values education in Mexico as an important force in shaping and re-shaping Mexican identity and the broader society, and as an avenue to social capital formation. As Mexico moves from a traditional to a modern and even late-modern society and from a centralized-one-party system to a more democratic form of government, we expect to see these changes reflected in the thinking of those that decide on or influence educational priorities. Moreover as Mexico has been for many years a highly centralized country we expect to see—in spite of the current tendencies towards decentralization—a fairly uniform agreement regarding different aspects of values education such as rationale, design and target population. These similarities are what allow our respondents to call themselves Mexicans, and what enables them to construct a shared future.

Nevertheless, in spite of this agreement we also expect to find differences regarding implementation and more particular aspects of the values education curriculum. Consequently an initial premise of our work was that even in a centralized country such as Mexico we could not talk about "Mexican values" as a unity taking only one regional sample. Thus our research attempted to include a sample of distinctive regions and perspectives. In this chapter we expand on both themes—differences and similarities—in approaches to values education and ask the following questions: (a) What are those values that are seen as important to include in schooling? How should they be taught and when? (b) Is there an underlying vision among the respondents regarding the why, what and how of values education? (c) What might be the most important challenges to values education development and implementation in Mexico? Our study is informed by previous work on values education in Mexico (Alducin-Abitia, 1989 and 1991; Gonzalez, 1996; Muñoz-García, 1996), in Asia and the West (Cummings, Gopinathan and Tomoda, 1988), in the U.S. (Butts, 1988; Lickona, 1993a, 1993b, 1996a, 1996b; Tomoda et al., 1997), in Europe (Touraine, 1997), and across different cultures (Inglehart, 1997).

Methods and Data Source

The central methodology of this study was survey research (Cook and Campbell, 1979; Warwick and Lininger, 1975). We asked respondents to answer a questionnaire designed to collect their views on fifteen Likert-type questions. The questionnaire was developed by an international steering committee that considered detailed feedback from cross-country teams including the Mexican team. The instrument originally de-

---

[6] This consensus may break down at the implementation level (e.g., the pedagogy and curriculum of values education).

[7] We used a common purposeful sampling frame across the country covering several educational authorities and individuals likely to influence policy decisions. The sample included individuals who had an interest/connection with values and values education and some influence regarding curricular decisions in this area. The respondents had the following characteristics: they formed part of the central educational authorities, or were leading educational intellectuals, religious leaders who had educational positions, leaders of related NGOs, politicians, people in educational institutes, academic leaders (e.g. deans of education schools and prominent professors), curriculum designers in moral education, and/or values/moral education specialists. The sample refers to those who were contacted and agreed to participate. No more than 30 percent of the sample were individuals directly involved in curriculum design and/or teaching of values education as it was expected that such individuals would be more likely to complete and return the instrument, and we did not want their voice to dominate the response pattern.

veloped in English was translated into Spanish and then back translated into English to insure faithfulness in the content of the instrument. The data was collected in mid-November of 1997 from a purposeful sample drawn from six different states in Mexico. The regions included Mexico City (the capital and traditionally the decision making center of the country), two states in the North (Chihuahua and Sinaloa), one state in the Northwest (Aguascalientes), one state in the Center-South (Morelos) and one state in the Southeast (Yucatan) of the country. The total number of respondents was 309 spread across the six states (see Table 3.1 showing the distribution and characteristics of respondents).

Three major questions framed the survey: (1) Why should there be values education? (e.g., what should be the relative stress in values education programs between "old" values as contrasted to the "new" values that will be needed for living in a future characterized by globalization of economic activity, the unbounded availability of information, and increased life-spans? What should be the balance in values education programs between universal and unique values? What should be the balance between character, civic, political, religious, and personal values; and what should be the links between these sub-groups? What should be the balance between a uniform national set of values and the encouragement of multiculturalism, that is, distinctive values for the various cultural groupings in Mexico?); (2) What should be taught in schools? (e.g., should the same program of values education be provided to all young people, or should different groups receive different programs? What should be the role of schools in conveying controversial values relating to such issues as civic responsibility, religious commitment, and sexual behavior? To what extent should future generations be encouraged to appreciate/tolerate the values of others?); (3) How should values education be conducted? (e.g., are values best conveyed through classroom instruction, through community and family-based instruction, and/or through experiential interaction in community service and internships? At what age should values education begin, and what should be the difference in content and methodologies for different age groups? Assuming the desire for broad-based representation in the development of values curricula, what are the options for realizing this representation?).

The next sections describe the results of the study. The survey data was analyzed using simple descriptive statistics, and analysis of variance. Using factor analysis we attempted to define the big ideas or visions underlying the why, what and how of values education that—according to educational policy makers and intellectuals—may guide the development of a Mexican identity for several years. Uncovering these mayor constructs allowed us to understand the common ideas around which people's views coalesced when thinking about a policy agenda for values education in Mexico.

Approach to Values Education's Design and Implementation

What Are the Most Pressing Reasons for Values Education?

The first question in our survey was directed at understanding the most urgent reasons for values education as seen by our respondents and read: "Many arguments have been advanced for stressing values education. In your view, which are the most persuasive reasons for improving values education in your society today?" Table 3.2 shows the ranks the respondents assigned to the diverse reasons for values education. We

Table 3.1 Respondents' Characteristics

Characteristics	State Percent						Total Count
	Aguascalientes	Chihuahua	Mexico City	Morelos	Sinaloa	Yucatan	
Gender							
Male	42	71	47	67	88	70	199
Female	58	29	53	33	12	30	108
Age							
20-29	7	5		2			9
30-39	38	9	9	16	17	5	48
40-49	26	45	41	39	42	46	119
50-59	25	31	25	29	35	26	26
60-69	2	4	16	10	4	9	20
70-79	2	3	9	4	2	14	15
80-89		3					2
Position							
Central educational elite	24	10	3	6	8	11	34
Leading education intellectual	8	15	6	15	17	9	37
Religious leader with ed. position	5	8	6	12	4	9	23
Leader of NGO	10	18	22	6	10	11	39
Politician	3	13	6	12	6	5	24
People in educational institutions	29	17	16	12	23	12	56
Academic leader	2	8	13	27	17	9	36
Curriculum designer/Moral ed.		7	22	6	15	18	30
Values/ Moral ed. specialist	19	4	6	4		16	25
Political Orientation							
Radical		11		6		9	14
Reformist	32	36	34	31	49	44	106
Moderate	32	24	41	37	36	28	91
Conservative	30	24	25	26	15	19	66
Ultra-Conservative	6	5					6
Workplace							
Capital city			100				30
Other major city	100	97		88	77	98	255
Local city		3		8	23	2	18
Peripheral area				4			2
Total Count	59	76	33	49	48	44	309

found that the highest ranked reasons for stressing values education in Mexico were: "To strengthen families", "to encourage greater civic consciousness and thus strengthen democracy", "to increase the sense of individual responsibility", and "to help young persons be reflective and autonomous". Given this evidence most of the

Mexican respondents seemed to believe that to build a strong society it is necessary to support the development of reflective, autonomous, and responsible individuals but within the context of a strong family and social structure.

A second layer of priorities indicated the need to provide individuals with a moral basis for behavior in daily life with a strong foundation on one's heritage and values of justice and equity. Accordingly, our respondents called for values education "to develop an appreciation for our heritage and to strengthen national identity", "to provide a guide for behavior in daily life", "to promote values of justice and equity", "to combat juvenile delinquency including bullying, gang violence, and drug abuse", and "to provide a foundation for spiritual development".

Table 3.2 Why Should There be Values Education?

Why should there be values education?	Mean*	S.D.
First layer		
Strengthen families	8.38	5.9
Encourage civic consciousness	9.45	5.9
Increase sense of individual responsibility	9.72	6.5
Help young persons be reflective / autonomous	9.75	6.9
Second layer		
Develop appreciation for heritage	10.10	5.4
Provide a guide for behavior in daily life	10.40	6.4
Promote values of justice and equity	10.66	6.5
Combat juvenile delinquency	10.93	5.3
Provide foundation for spiritual development	11.79	6.3
Third layer		
Combat ecological abuse	11.91	5.2
Foster economic development	12.40	5.5
Combat social prejudice / promote tolerance	12.50	5.5
Promote world peace	12.71	5.4
Promote orderly, caring school communities	12.83	5.2
Improve the respect and opportunities for women	12.93	5.2
Help youth interpret values transmitted by media	13.91	5.0
Promote pride in local communities	14.13	4.5

* Ranked from most to least important (1=most important, 17=least important); N= 309.
Note. Responses left blank were given a ranking of 17.

A third layer of concern had to do with social and world security and justifies values education as a vehicle "to combat the recent trends of ecological abuse", "to foster economic development by strengthening values such as hard work, creativity, and individual competitiveness", "to combat the tendency for social prejudice and to promote greater tolerance for ethnic, language, and racial groups", "to promote more orderly and caring school communities and thus facilitate learning", "to improve the respect and opportunities extended to girls and women", and "to promote world peace". Arguments that were ranked as less prevalent in justifying values education had to do with tendencies associated with "the globalization of information" and with local concerns including the idea that values education should serve "to help youth interpret the values transmitted by the mass media, the Internet, and other information technologies", and the idea that values education should help "promote pride in local communities".

In sum, the most important reasons for values education in Mexico were the pre-servation of the family and the development of reflective, autonomous, and responsible individuals to function in a democracy. Next in importance was providing individuals with a strong moral and civic basis for individual behavior, and a just and equal inter-action of individuals with their social context. A third priority for values education was the concern for teaching values dealing with social and world security. According to these responses Mexico's conception of values education requires preparing indivi-duals to act reflectively, autonomously, and responsibly as they move across a series of nested and permeable circles from the most immediate personal context to the family, the community and the world.

Table 3.3 Factor Analysis: Why Should There be Values Education?

Underlying Concepts:	Mean*	Loadings	Cumulative %
Social Responsibility			37.8
Combat social prejudice	.5016	.7682	
Respect & opportunities for women	.4563	.6867	
Pride in local communities	.4077	.5969	
Values of justice and equity	.5598	.5880	
Youth development of reflective/autonomous self	.5695	.5185	
World peace	.5145	.5015	
Civil consciousness	.6860	.4860	
Ecological abuse	.6407	.3943	
Modernity			45.4
Foster economic development	.5598	.5732	
Help youth interpret values	.3883	.4977	
Combat juvenile delinquency	.7055	.4888	
Orderly caring schools	.4983	.4556	
Foundation for spiritual development	.5113	.4292	
Sense of individual responsibility	.6213	.4060	
Cultural Continuity			51.6
Strengthen families	.7734	.6111	
Develop appreciation of heritage	.7443	.4010	
Guide for daily behavior	.6084	.3823	

* Based on the proportion of respondents who ranked values as prevalent. N=309.

So far we have presented only rankings regarding a number of reasons for values education. While these rankings are interesting as indicators of those areas policy makers and educational intellectuals perceive as priorities in Mexico, they tell us little about the larger vision shared—if any—by our respondents. The results of our factor analysis show three important dimensions concerning the most pressing reasons for values education (see Table 3.3).

According to our analysis the most important reason for values education in Mexico is anchored in three interrelated concepts: "social responsibility", "modernity", and "cultural continuity". Values concerning "social responsibility" include ideas about the need to combat social prejudice and promote greater tolerance for ethnic, language, and racial groups, respect and opportunity for girls and women, promoting pride in local communities and community life, social justice and equity, the need for youth to develop a reflective and autonomous personality, promote world peace, encouraging civic consciousness and thus strengthen democracy, and the need to combat ecological abuse. The concept of "modernity" was associated with fostering economic development through values such as hard work, creativity, and individual competitiveness, helping youth interpret values transmitted by the mass media and technology, combating juvenile delinquency, promoting orderly and caring schools to facilitate learning, providing a foundation for spiritual development and increasing a sense of individual responsibility. The concept of "cultural continuity" was associated with the need to strengthen families, developing an appreciation for heritage, strengthening national identity, and providing a daily guide for behavior.

This overarching rationale for values education—"social responsibility", "modernity", and "cultural continuity" seems to grow from an ongoing re-interpretation of the Mexican identity. The new Mexican identity is not introspective and individualistic as it might have been after the revolution when the need for self-definition had of necessity to occur within national parameters. The new Mexican identity evolving as part of a global economy is more open and globally interactive, reflexive and bound by two equally powerful and often contradictory forces: modernity and tradition. It is this tension that may facilitate a productive policy dialogue on values education. A dialogue that may open for questioning deep-rooted beliefs about what Mexican values education should be about. Whether this policy dialogue will be regional or national or both remains an empirical question.

In the next section we delve deeper into understanding the diverse rationale for values education by exploring questions dealing with ideas regarding the content of values education.

What Values Should be Included in the School Curriculum?

Questions about what should be included in values education are primarily concerned with content. We were interested on the themes that should form the locus of values education in the schools. We asked the following question: "values education tends to cluster around a number of themes; in your view, which of these themes requires the greatest emphasis in the schools, and which is best left for other institutions?" The responses are shown in Table 3.4. In average, Mexican policy makers and educators, reflecting the current influx of democratic tendencies sweeping the country, gave a very strong emphasis to values of personal autonomy and reflection, values related to democracy, and to civics. Strong emphasis was also given to themes dealing with gender equity, ecological awareness, moral values, and peace and conflict resolution. Some emphasis was given to diversity and multiculturalism, national identity and patriotism, family and work values, and global awareness. Faithful to the traditional separation between church and state, Mexican respondents indicated that religious values should be left out of the schools.

Table 3.4 What Should be Emphasized in the Values Education Curriculum?

What should be the emphasis in values education?	Mean*	S.D.	N
Values of personal autonomy and reflection	1.71	1.17	298
Democracy	1.75	1.26	299
Civic values	1.90	1.13	299
Gender equality	2.04	1.40	293
Ecological awareness	2.07	1.30	297
Moral values	2.13	1.58	294
Peace and conflict resolution	2.14	1.46	294
Values of diversity and multiculturalism	2.34	1.50	293
Work values	2.36	1.67	295
National identity and patriotism	2.38	1.44	296
Family values	2.50	1.76	288
Global awareness	2.54	1.55	290
Religious values	5.34	2.09	277

* 1=very strong emphasis; 7= should be left out

While we now understand what values seem important to emphasize in schooling and which should be left out, we know little about the larger vision underlying our respondents' choices. The results of our factor analysis show three important dimensions concerning the suggested content for values education in Mexico (see Table 3.5).

Table 3.5 Factor Analysis: What Should be Emphasized in the Values Education Curriculum?

Underlying concepts:	Mean*	Loadings	Cumulative %
Social Change			31.4
Value of diversity	2.36	.7027	
Gender equity	2.05	.6975	
Conflict resolution	2.11	.6922	
Global consciousness	2.50	.6633	
Ecological consciousness	2.01	.6195	
Democracy	1.77	.5995	
Autonomy	1.72	.3259	
National Progress			47.7
Civic values	1.90	.8159	
National identity	2.33	.7101	
Work values	2.35	.3687	
Character Development			57.9
Family values	2.49	.7468	
Moral values	2.07	.7048	
Religious values	5.26	.4260	

* 1=very strong emphasis; 7= should be left out. N=229.

Table 3.6 Views with Respect to the Following Controversial Issues as Content Areas in the Values Education School Curriculum

Relative emphasis that should be placed by schools on:	Mean*	S.D.	N
Autonomy			
teaching critical thinking in schools	1.43	1	305
help children understand they have individual rights	1.65	1.1	301
help children develop own values	1.77	1.3	302
help children understand they have the right to be happy	2.15	1.5	293
recognize importance of personal pride and identity	2.54	1.6	296
Civic values			
all are equal before the law	1.67	1.23	303
help young people understand all political/social viewpoints	2.0	1.36	299
respect hierarchy and support the government	4.71	2.0	285
Nationalism			
First promote an understanding and love of nation	2.59	1.66	299
Venerate heroes and promote national pride	3.50	1.86	292
Religion			
help children understand their own religion	5.57	1.89	285
schools should foster an understanding of all religions	3.77	2	294
Work			
stress habits of loyalty, obedience, hard work and punctuality	3.03	1.93	296
competitiveness /creativity for social / economic success	4	2	293
Tolerance			
empathy for people of different backgrounds	1.79	1.29	299
common values to all children	1.83	1.5	301
understanding of unique origins and heritage	2.54	1.68	296
the fortunate to help those who encounter difficulties	3.53	2.2	294
Gender			
equal opportunities and encouragement for girls and boys	1.35	1	305
encourage mutual respect between boys and girls	1.38	1	304
take up issues relating to human sexuality and health	2.27	1.6	287
destiny of girls is to have home-building responsibilities	5.56	2	285
Community			
promote values of solidarity within communities	1.55	1.1	305
foster values supporting the family	1.96	1.2	300
promote a truly global view of the world	2.26	1.5	295
appreciate role of unions in work conditions and fair wages	3.82	1.7	290

* Ratings: 1=very strong emphasis; 7=should be left out

The answers regarding the content for values education in schools were anchored in three interrelated themes: values for "social change", "national progress", and "character development". Within the concept of "social change" our respondents believed it important to include values of diversity and multiculturalism, gender equality, peace and conflict resolution, global and ecological awareness, democracy, and values of personal autonomy and reflection. The concept of "national progress" included the need for civic values, national identity and patriotism, and work values. "Character development" included the need for family values, and moral and religious values.

In contrast to the more philosophical vision regarding the why of values education discussed above, this set of values appear more operational. Thus while values education at a more philosophical level is important in the formation of aware and socially responsible individuals able to negotiate the contradictory forces of modernity and tradition, these traits become a necessity in a climate of continuous and vigorous social change. Especially important for responsible social change is the preservation of national identity and patriotism, two values included in the definition of the larger concept of national progress. Equally important to social change and national progress is character development a concept founded in the deep rooted family and religious values that seem to—and will continue to—remain fixed in the evolving redefinition of a Mexican identity.

While we discussed in this section the larger themes for values education, in the following section we asked more specific questions about content including some issues that may be considered controversial in values education.

What are the Major Issues to be Considered in the Values Education Curriculum?

In addition to understanding the priorities and common agenda for the kind of values that should be included in the curriculum we also wanted to understand what values are seen as major issues for schools to deal with—even if these are controversial. We asked our respondents to more explicitly indicate what content areas should have more emphasis in the school curriculum. Their response range from "very strong emphasis" or "1" to "should be left out" or "7". These content areas included issues dealing with autonomy, civic values, nationalism, religion, work, managing diversity, gender, and community. Table 3.6 shows the responses.

Autonomy

The value of teaching critical thinking in schools was seen as a strong aim of values education, as was the need for schools to help children understand that they have individual rights, and for schools to assist each child in developing their own individual values as a foundation for their acceptance of broader social values. Less importance but still considered relevant as a content area was the importance of helping each child understand they have the right to be happy and the need for schools to recognize the importance of personal pride and identity.

Civic Values

Two content areas were considered important for fostering civic values "the need to stress that all are equal before the law", and the idea that schools should help young people gain an understanding of all political and social viewpoints from the most conservative to the most liberal. The idea that people should be taught to respect hierarchies and support the government did not receive positive support.

Nationalism

Ideas dealing with nationalistic values received mixed endorsement. For instance, the idea that schooling should first promote an understanding and love of nation was deemed somewhat important for inclusion in the curriculum, but the idea that people should venerate heroes and promote national pride was seen as less important. This shared opinion indicates a period of intense questioning and introspection in Mexican society as the heroes and ideals of the revolution have been somewhat associated with the traditionally dominant but now weakened PRI (Institutional Revolutionary Party). Thus the lack of enthusiasm with some of these questions may be due to the association of the concept of nation with the Federal Government and this in turn with the PRI.

Religion

Mexico's constitution mandates the separation of church and state making the teaching of religion in public schools strictly forbidden by law. This situation may help explain our respondents' rejection of ideas such as "schools should help every child gain a deeper understanding of their own religion" in contrast with the less negative reaction to the idea that "schools should foster an understanding of all religions" which is not totally rejected as study of world cultures does include understanding, albeit at a superficial level, of different religions.

Work

Similarly, a number of ideas related to "hard work" were mildly endorsed as having a place in the curriculum by our respondents. The idea that "as sound preparation for the world of work, habits of loyalty, obedience, hard work and punctuality need to be stressed in school" was seen as acceptable as a content area. Less popular was the idea that "values education should highlight the role of individual competitiveness and creativity in realizing both social and economic success". These answers indicate that at least for our respondents, education should be seen first, more in terms of its contribution to intellectual and spiritual growth and second, as a way to increase productivity or economic gain. It seems that at least in this area reinforcing ideas about social responsibility (one of the three core reasons for values education discussed earlier) may help strengthen ideas dealing with work ethics in Mexican society

Managing Diversity

There was a more positive disposition to including in the curriculum ideas dealing with social integration and equality among our respondents than ideas that would tend to separate groups on the basis of origin or wealth. For instance ideas such as "schools should encourage empathy for people of different ethnic, language, and social backgrounds and create opportunities for growth through shared experiences" and "it is best for schools to teach common values to all children without differentiation on the basis of class, ethnicity, or religion", had more acceptance than ideas such as "schools should help the members of each group gain a clear understanding of their unique origins and heritage", or even than "schools should note social differences and stress the duty of the fortunate to help those who encounter difficulties". This reflects the influence of national campaigns seeking a better understanding and support for the plight of Mexico's more than fifty-six different indigenous groups comprising about 9 percent of the Mexican population.

Gender

Our respondents support an egalitarian and liberal position regarding issues of gender and sexuality. For instance the idea that "girls have essentially the same talents as boys and should be given equal opportunities and encouragement in schools" was strongly supported as a content area in the school curriculum as was the idea that "values education should encourage mutual respect between boys and girls". Similarly the idea that "values education should take up issues relating to human sexuality and health, such as chastity, preserving the integrity of the body against drugs and prostitution, and understanding the risks of promiscuity" also received positive support whereas the idea that "the destiny of girls is to have home-building responsibilities" was rejected.

Community

Values having to do with collective matters ranging from family values to worldwide communities' concerns received mixed support. Strong support was given to the idea that "schools should promote values of solidarity within communities", "foster values supporting the family, such as respect for parents, fidelity, and taking care of children and elders", and "promote a truly global view of the world". Less favorable—and surprising given the strong socialist past of the country—was the view that "schools should help young people appreciate the essential role of unions in guaranteeing safe work conditions and fair wages". The response to this question may reflect the extreme role of the teachers' union in Mexico, which in many occasions has paralyzed government's efforts for educational reform.

In sum, teaching critical thinking in schools, helping children understand that they have individual rights, and helping them develop their own individual values were seen as important content areas for values education. Civic values specially as they relate to understanding the law and to educating citizens vis-à-vis pluralistic ideas were seen as important for inclusion in the school curriculum. We observed a generalized lack of enthusiasm for nationalistic values, and a strong rejection of religious teachings in the school curriculum. There was support to the idea that education should be seen more in terms of its contribution to intellectual and spiritual growth than merely as a way to increase productivity or economic gain for individuals or for society. We found an important disposition to including ideas dealing with social integration and equality rather than ideas that would tend to separate groups on the basis of origin or wealth. Equality of opportunity for boys and girls and solidarity across communities were considered important for the curriculum.

Table 3.7 Factor Analysis: Views with Respect to the Following Controversial Issues as Content Areas in the Values Education School Curriculum

Underlying concepts:	Mean*	Loadings	Cumulative %
Pluralistic and Multicultural Values			24.8
Community solidarity	1.56	.8713	
Equal opportunity for girls	1.36	.7963	
Mutual respect for girls and boys	1.42	.7906	
Critical thinking	1.44	.6218	
Empathy for people of different background	1.88	.6185	
Global view of the world	2.32	.5992	
All are equal before the law	1.68	.5891	
Individual rights for children	1.70	.5758	
Children have the right to be happy	2.23	.4418	
Understanding of all political and social viewpoints	2.09	.4091	
Common values to all	1.87	.3251	
Nationalistic Values			40.4
Understanding and love of nation	2.59	.7286	
Venerate heroes	3.41	.6974	
Values of loyalty, obedience, hard work	2.95	.5558	
Respect hierarchy	4.61	.5253	
Family values	1.91	.5237	
Human sexuality	2.28	.4581	
Social Change and Search for Justice			46.7
Note social differences and help less fortunate	3.47	.6202	
Individual competitiveness	3.90	.5697	
Girls destiny is at home	5.44	.4922	
Belonging to Civic/Religious Organizations			52.0
Understanding all religions	3.77	.5729	
Understanding own religion	5.50	.5394	
Role of unions	3.85	.4168	
Individual Identity within the larger social context			56.3
Children to develop own values	1.74	.5717	
Personal pride and identity	2.56	.3293	

* Ratings: 1=very strong emphasis; 7=should be left out. N=249.

While we have discussed our respondents' views on values education's content based on their perception of their degree of contention in Mexican society, it is more useful—especially in areas of controversy—to understand the larger ideas behind our respondents' choices. We found five distinctive but interrelated concepts in our factor analysis: the need to infuse the curriculum with "pluralistic and multicultural values", an emphasis on "nationalistic values", an emphasis on "social change and search for justice values", an emphasis on the value of "belonging to civic or religious associations", and the need to develop a "sense of individual identity within the larger social context" (see Table 3.7).

The concept of "pluralistic and multicultural values" included ideas such as promoting values of solidarity, equal rights and responsibilities and empathy for people of different ethnic, language, and social backgrounds, the value of critical thinking and global views, the need to teach common values to all children without differentiation on the basis of class, ethnicity, or religion and helping young people gain an understanding of all political and social viewpoints from the most conservative to the most liberal. The concept of "nationalistic values" moved away from the traditional emphasis on the notion that it is important to promote national pride, an understanding and love of nation, and teaching young people to venerate their heroes, to a more modern emphasis on work values such as cultivation of habits of loyalty, obedience, hard work and punctuality. Finally family values and sexual education were seen as essential in forming a strong nation. The concept of "social justice" included the need to stress the duty of the fortunate to help those who encounter difficulties, the need to highlight the role of individual competitiveness and creativity in realizing social and economic success, and gender equality. The concept highlighting the importance of "belonging to civic or religious associations" was seen as less urgent and included the possibility of helping the young understand all religions, and to appreciate the essential role of unions in guaranteeing safe work conditions and fair wages, but to clearly stay away from helping children gain a deeper understanding of their own religion. Underlying the concept of "developing an individual identity within the larger social context" were ideas indicating that schooling should assist each child in developing their own individual values as a foundation for their acceptance of broader social values, and that recognizing the importance of a personal pride and identity, schools should help the members of each group gain a clear understanding of their unique origins and heritage.

Operationally then, the values education curriculum according to our respondents should be guided by the intent to develop "social responsibility", "modernity", and "cultural continuity" in order to achieve "social change", "national progress", and "character development". To accomplish this aim the curriculum should specifically include a number of content areas closely related to five main concepts: promoting "pluralistic and multicultural values", "nationalistic values", "social justice values", the value of "belonging to civic or religious associations", and the need to develop a "sense of individual identity within the larger social context". Whether this vision is likely to be implemented in Mexico remains an empirical question. What is possible however, as a result of understanding this preliminary scheme for a philosophy and content of a values education program, is the beginning of a dialogue at least among the policy makers and intellectuals who participated in our study. Indeed, as our findings indicate, there already exists a strong agreement regarding the need, direction and content of values education in Mexico among our respondents. What is not clear however is whether our respondents are aware of this relatively strong agreement across purposes and content. It is possible that this knowledge may help advance a regional

---

[8] This agreement becomes more evident if we compare Mexico with other countries included in our larger study where we found large discrepancies within countries across the why, the what and the how of values education.

and even a national dialogue that until now has faltered in great part due to the un-founded assumption that there are large gaps in agreement regarding values education across regions. Engaging in a policy dialogue using as basis these shared understand-ings places Mexican policy makers and intellectuals in a promising position. Initial consensus in views may ease work towards the development and implementation of a fresh and responsive approach to values education and may facilitate the incorporation of teachers, parents and students into the dialogue.

Understanding and Teaching World Values

We also asked our respondents what values they were familiar with (e.g., Latin American values, Asian, Islamic or Socialist values) and which should be included in the school curriculum. Their answers, in Figure 3.1, show that the values education curriculum is indeed a contested arena and that familiarity with some values may be a necessary but not a sufficient condition for inclusion. A large proportion of our re-spondents supported inclusion of Latin American and socialist values but rejected for the most part Asian and Islamic values. This position seems to contradict somewhat the values considered necessary for social change discussed earlier where "global awareness" figured as part of the first factor explaining priorities in curricular content. Mexican policy makers are however quite consistent with a regionalist attitude and the country's historical past which has been importantly influenced by socialist thinking.

Figure 3.1. Understanding and Teaching World Values

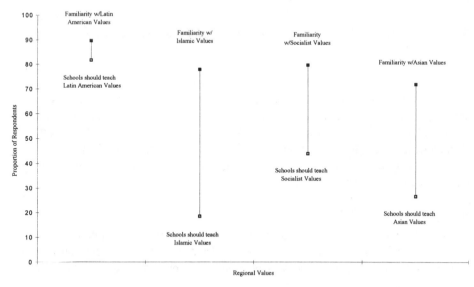

In the previous two sections of this chapter we have discussed the philosophical basis for values education and have presented the views our respondents have regard-ing the content of values education in Mexico. These however may only stay in ideas and great visions if issues of implementation are not explored and its challenges under-stood. Indeed while we find agreement in purpose and content we may find disagreement in implementation. In the next section we discuss implementation issues and ask to whom and where values education should be provided.

How Should Values Education be Implemented?

So far we have a good understanding of the aims and general content for approaching values education in Mexico. In this section we move beyond statements of intent or content to more practical matters related to implementation. Questions about implementation comprise at least three important aspects. One concerns the time or amount of effort that should be given to values education as a whole—indicating the level of importance attributed to this area in the curriculum. The second aspect has to do with target populations, and the third has to do with settings.

How Much Time Should be Given to Values Education in the School Curriculum?

We asked our respondents to indicate what percent of a school budget (money, time and effort) should be devoted to values education. Most respondents indicated that close to 25 percent should be contained in specific classes such as moral education or civics, and close to 45 percent should be integrated across the curriculum. This answer indicates that, at least among our respondents, values education has an important place in schools. Specifically they suggest that close to half of the curriculum should deal with some kind of values education, and that at least one-fourth of the curriculum should have subject-specific treatment of values education.

Who Should Receive Values Education?

In our survey we approached the second aspect by asking who should be targeted for values education. Eighty-five percent of our respondents agreed that values education should begin at an early age under the assumption that the foundations of values are established in early childhood. Conversely, 71 percent of our respondents were in strong disagreement with the notion that values education should only begin in secondary school after young people have a clear idea of what they believe to be important. We also asked how should the values education curriculum be constructed. Sixty-seven percent of our respondents agreed that values education should be integrated throughout the curriculum rather than taught in separate subjects; and 55 percent supported teaching a *common* curriculum for values education (e.g., as opposed to designing different programs according to ability).

Where Should Values Education be Taught?

We also asked more specific questions regarding the relationship between target groups and settings for conducting values education. Answers to these questions varied relative to the different dimensions of religion, moral or civic education (see Table 3.8).

Table 3.8 Who Should Receive Values Education and Where?

	Religious Education %	Moral Education %	Civic Education %
Groups ranked as needing most exposure:			
Inservice teachers	4	13	17
Teacher learners	3	19	31
Young children	14	9	2
Pre-school children	4	5	2
Primary level	35	34	33
Secondary level	7	12	7
High school level	9	4	7
University level	3	2	1
Not ranked	21	2	
Settings ranked as most effective:			
During school as a class	1	6	25
During school through rules of behavior	2	9	28
Outside school activities (clubs, sports, art)	1	1	1
Internship and community service	5	5	13
Camps			
Religious groups and institutions	29	3	
Military training and national service	1	1	
Home and family	59	74	28
Media	1	1	5
Not ranked	1		

N=309

Religious Education

Congruent with the idea that values education should begin at an early age, 35 percent of our respondents agreed that primary level children should receive the most exposure to religious education followed by young children (e.g. preschoolers or younger) and by high school level individuals. Religious education is seen however as a private matter. Close to 60 percent of our respondents believed that the most effective settings for religious education are the home and the family followed by religious groups and institutions, and by internships and community service. These responses highlight Mexico's strong religious beliefs (in spite of the clear separation between church and state) and indicate a desire for the foundations of values education to begin early and at home. The responses are different however when we asked about moral education.

Moral Education

Although close to a third of our respondents persisted in their belief that primary level children should receive the most exposure to moral education, another third also emphasized the need for teacher learners and in-service teachers to be among those who should receive the most exposure. These were followed by students at the middle school level. A complex dilemma however emerges when we ask about the most effective settings for moral education as 75 percent of the respondents still believe that the home and the family should be at the center of this instruction. Only a small percentage believed that the school might have a role in moral education through teaching rules of behavior. Thus one wonders how teachers learners and teachers are expected to receive a "professionally-appropriate" orientation to moral education if this kind of instruction is left outside of the policy realm (that is, the schools and by implication teacher education institutions).

Civic Education

Similarly, we wanted to know who our respondents believed should receive the most exposure to civics/national values education. About a third of our respondents believed that primary level children are a priority group followed by teacher learners and by in-service teachers. Respondents indicated that both the school and the family (in equal terms) are the most effective settings for civic/national education, followed by classroom instruction and in minor degree by the media. Few respondents (e.g., less than 10 percent) mentioned military training and national service.

Answers to implementation questions in values education point to a number of dilemmas that need to be recognized as challenging policy issues. Previously we established that our respondents saw imparting values to young children as an important approach to the formation of reflective, autonomous, and responsible individuals. Moreover teachers were targeted as the second priority group for receiving values education and specifically moral and civic education. But as we approach implementation questions our respondents seem to indicate that values education should be considered as a mostly private matter with the schools—and by implication teachers— playing a relatively minor role. In Mexico, it is common knowledge that a great deal of values education (e.g., religion, morals, ethics) occurs *de facto* in the family and the church. But family dynamics have been typically resistant to policy intervention and the legal separation between church and the state makes it difficult for schools to capitalize on the former's work on values. With the exception of the new program in Ethics at the secondary school level, most of the education on civics occurring in schools seems to be designed to avoid dealing in depth with the moral and ethical life of individuals. If schools are seen as irrelevant in helping develop ethical and moral individuals what avenue may serve as the policy conduit for a values education program? The dilemma posed by advocating a values education curriculum without the creation of transparent structures for discussion, construction and implementation (such as professional development in schools and even in pre-service and in-service teacher education programs) indicates that it may be quite difficult to create values education programs accountable to democratic/popular control. This situation may have important—and undesirable—social consequences as values education has proven to be an important tool used by interest groups to advance their political agenda. If policy dialogue on values education is removed from the public to the private arena the agenda will likely be dictated by a few individuals rather than by the

Mexican people. This dynamic may defeat one of the most desirable outcomes expected of Mexico's current social change movements: the pursuit of a more democratic education and the collective definition of a Mexican identity.

Table 3.9 Cultures/Societies That Should be Given Most Prominence in the School Curriculum

Cultures/societies	Mean*	SD	N
Mexico	1.2	.9	286
Canada	2.7	1.48	258
France	2.8	1.52	261
Japan	2.8	1.57	265
U.S.	2.9	1.73	276
China	3.4	1.73	267
U.K.	3.5	1.61	256
Russia	3.6	1.74	257
Egypt	3.9	1.84	157
Korea	4.1	1.72	238
Thailand	4.4	1.80	247
Singapore	4.6	1.77	232
Malaysia	4.9	1.81	233
Indonesia	4.9	1.65	233

*1=much prominence   7=little prominence

Conclusions and Policy Implications

The results of our analysis lead us to conclude that among the regions and individuals we surveyed, there seems to be a clear tension between traditional and modern values and between nationalistic and pluralistic values. Mexico's fast economic development may accelerate the expansion of modernization values at the expense of the traditional family values that have prevailed in the Mexican society for centuries. Similarly, nationalistic values seem challenged by global and foreign values (see Table 3.9).

This transition in values seems to be fairly uniform across the regions studied, reflecting the strong influence of the global economy and particularly of the central government in values education, in spite of recent efforts to decentralize the governance and content of education in Mexico. As per our findings, the challenge in the Mexican context vis-à-vis policy making is not as much agreement over why there should be values education or over what content should be taught or to whom. Rather the tension is more likely to occur in areas this study has just began to uncover.

We see three important questions that need to be addressed in the development of a values education agenda in Mexico. One of these questions has to do with the development of a coherent regional and national policy regarding values. We have already seen that there is remarkable agreement, at least at the theoretical level, among the policy makers and educational intellectuals we surveyed. Whether this agreement will serve as important leverage to a larger policy including implementation of a values education program is still an empirical question. What is true however is that while current agreement at a theoretical level exists, Mexican reform pushing for decentralization may pose an unintended obstacle to the development of a coherent regional and national policy dialogue as states move away from national norms. Paradoxically however, as the central government's plan to decentralize education by-passes state governments and gives added legitimacy to local power groups, it may be possible for a coherent policy—albeit controlled indirectly by the center—to take hold.

A second question has to do with curriculum design and implementation as a vehicle for values education and social capital formation. We have seen that while there is agreement regarding who should receive values education, there is less clarity regarding the content and vehicle for values education. There are questions as to whether schools would be able to take up this challenge, how should the curriculum be designed and by whom, and how should this emergent reform on values education be implemented. Similarly, there is the question of whether teachers should receive instruction in values education and whether the traditionally inflexible teacher education programs in Mexico would provide an opening for such an instruction to occur. Whether policy may be able to mandate deep-rooted change in teacher education programs and school curriculum will depend not only on community organization and support but also on local and central government's organization of viable initiatives to serve as building blocks of social capital formation using as a foci values education.

A third question has to do with implementation regarding the pedagogical approach that should frame values education. A major anticipated challenge is the relatively recent emergence in Mexico of a constructivist pedagogy that has been used as a guide to develop the curriculum since 1992. This relatively recent approach challenges the more traditional and established autocratic model that has prevailed in Mexican education regarding all subjects and all levels for many years. Although our study did not research specific pedagogical issues vis-à-vis values education, a recent experience in the northern state of Chihuahua illustrates this tension. One of Chihuahua's independent conservative reform groups recently developed and implemented a values education curriculum using a didactic-traditional top-down model of instruction. Educational reformers associated with the state's government and espousing a more liberal approach to values education opposed this model and argued for the need to evaluate its effects before implementing it in more schools. The findings of the evaluation demonstrated that the students exposed to the conservative approach to values education were able to recognize values advocated by the model vis-à-vis students in other schools where the program was not implemented (Personal communication, 1998). Although what this evaluation may indicate is that some instruction in values education is better than no intervention at all, its most important contribution is the opportunity it provides to understand the consequences of and the need for implementing alternative approaches to values education.

In sum, few studies have been carried out in Mexico with the purpose of understanding what changes might lead to "better" values education. Previous to this study, little was known about efforts to link actual practice with a more in depth knowledge of effective values education. The participation of Mexico in this larger study including a number of very important Pacific Rim countries allows Mexican researchers to actively engage as equal partners in a dialogue that will influence education in the region in the years to come. We expect that through this study policy makers and educators from different regions in Mexico, will have the opportunity to have a "voice" in helping others like them understand their views about and approaches to values education thus serving as a conduit for policy dialogue in this area.

References

Alducin-Abitia, E. (1989). *Los Valores de los Mexicanos: Mexico Entre la Tradicion y la Modernidad*. Mexico: Fomento Cultural Banamex.

Alducin-Abitia, E. (1991). *Los Valores de los Mexicanos: Mexico en Tiempos de Cambio*. Mexico: Fomento Cultural Banamex.

Bourdieu, P. (1977). *Outline of a Theory of Practice*. (F. Nice, trans). Cambridge, U.K. and New York: Cambridge University Press.

Bourdieu, P. and Passeron J. (1977). *Reproduction in Education, Society, and Culture*. (F. Nice, trans). London: Sage.

Butts, R.F. (1988). *The Morality of Democratic Citizenship*. Calabasas, CA: Center for Civic Education.

Coleman, J.S. (1994). "Social Capital in the Creation of Human Capital", *American Journal of Sociology*, Supplement: S105-108.

Constitucion Politica de los Estados Unidos Mexicanos (1994). Mexico, D.F.: Procuraduria General de la Republica y Instituto de Investigaciones Juridicas de la U.N.A.M.

Cook, T. and Campbell, D. (1979). *Quasi-Experimentation*. Chicago, IL: Rand McNally.

Cummings, W., Gopinathan, S. and Tomoda, Y. (Eds.) (1988). *The Revival of Values Education in Asia and the West*, Oxford: Pergamon Press.

Diamond, L. and Plattner, M. (1996). *The Global Resurgence of Democracy*. Baltimore, MD: John Hopkins.

Gonzalez, J. (1996). *El Ethos, Destino del Hombre*. Mexico: Fondo de Cultura Economica.

Inglehart, R. (1997). *Modernization and Postmodernization*. Princeton, NJ: Princeton University Press.

Lickona, T. (1993a). "Is Character Education a Responsibility of the Public Schools?" *Momentum* 24(4): 48-54.

Lickona, T. (1993b). "The Return of Character Education", *Educational Leadership* 51(3): 6-11.

Lickona, T. (1996a). "Eleven Principles of Effective Character Education". *Journal of Moral Education* 25(1): 93-100.

Lickona, T. (1996b). "Teaching Respect and Responsibility. Reclaiming Children and Youth", *Journal of Emotional and Behavioral Problems* 5(3): 143-51.

Muñoz-García, H. (1996). *Los Valores Educativos y el Empleo en Mexico*, México: CRIM-Miguel Angel Porrua.

Pardo, M. (Ed.) (1999). *Federalización e Innovación Educativa en México*. México, D.F.: El Colegio de México.

Plan Nacional de Desarrollo (1995). *Plan Nacional de Desarrollo*. Secretaria de Governacion Publica. México, Distrito Federal.

Putnam, R.D. (1993). *Making Democracy Work: The Civic Traditions in Modern Italy*. Princeton, NJ: Princeton University Press.

Tatto, M.T. (1999). "Education Reform and State Power in Mexico: The Paradoxes of Decentralization", *Comparative Education Review* 43 (3): 251-282.

Tomoda, Y. (Ed.) (1997). *Patterns of Value Socialization in U.S. Primary Schools: A Comparative Study*. Osaka: Osaka University Faculty of Human Sciences.

Touraine, A. (1997). *Podremos Vivir Juntos*? Buenos Aires: Fondo de Cultura Economica de Argentina.

Warwick, D. and Lininger, S. (1975). *The Sample Survey: Theory and Practice*. New York: McGraw-Hill.

CHAPTER 4

UNITED STATES: REASON OVER FAITH

William K. Cummings
Maria Teresa Tatto
John Hawkins
Gita Steiner-Khamsi

Introduction

Values educators, particularly those from Asian nations, often ask why American schools take such weak stands on values education and religious and moral issues. They cannot understand why the American curriculum fails to include courses on moral or religious education, whereas such courses are fundamental in most Asian curricula (Bereday and Matsui, 1973). They wonder about the laxity of behavioral rules in American schools that allow pupils to wear diverse clothing, have unusual hairstyles, chew gum, and even smoke; and they are puzzled by about the relative silence schools keep with regard to right and wrong responses to drug use, the value and respect due to human life and other crucial moral issues. Of course, not all American schools are so lax. Still, the general tendency in the U.S. is quite different from that elsewhere. Why?

Implicit in this question is the assumption that values development is an essential component of human development that can/should not be divorced from formal education. American educators are as concerned about the full development of their pupils as their non-American counterparts. Why then have the Americans devised a distinctive educational approach that focuses primarily on the cognitive side of human development, and tends towards a neutral position on religious and moral issues? This study seeks, through comparative and historical analysis, to provide insight on the American approach. The first section explores historical trends in Moral and Values Education in the U.S., and the second part presents the results of our survey of elite perceptions of the current and prospective state of values education in the states of New York, Michigan, California, and Hawai'i.

The American Approach in Comparative Perspective

Plymouth Rock: Faith and Reason

Historians trace many of the peculiarities of American culture to the profound hold of Puritanism on the American conscience. Just as Plymouth Rock still stands on the shores of the Atlantic, so does Puritanism still reside in the American soul.

Puritanism certainly has had a profound impact. It declares that Man can establish a direct relation to God with no church intermediary. Faith is the key to salvation, and Piety a manifestation of faith. Faith is a matter of the heart and soul, which presumably is expressed through morality or virtue and Piety. Puritans developed clear right and wrong answers to most moral dilemmas, and took stands on these dilemmas that seemed as firm as Plymouth Rock. Thus the inhabitants of the New England colonies early on developed a reputation as a moral people.

But what is Faith? To gain the fullest understanding, man needs knowledge and Reason, and proper education can thus assist in furthering this understanding. Because the Puritans valued reason, they felt a strong commitment to public education. From the earliest days that the Pilgrims arrived in America they took the trouble to establish schools in every community. And as a continuation of local education, they supported outstanding colleges: Harvard from 1636, Yale in 1701, and other private and non-private institutions. Consistent with these beliefs, the region where the Puritans first settled has always been pioneer in American education: fostering such new initiatives as the common school, the land grant college, and the research university.

So Puritanism had a profound impact on the birth of American education. Yet curiously the schools set up in Puritan communities had a remarkably non-sectarian curriculum. The goal was to teach Reason, not faith (Cremin, 1970, p. 278 ff) as faith was a disposition cultivated before young people came to school in the homes and churches. So in a curious way it may be that roots of a neutral position on religious and moral issues in American education were imbedded in the Puritan approach to education, with Piety taught in the home and church, and Reason in the school.[1]

Local Government

Of course, Puritanism was not the only faith in early America. Even in New England there were other religious persuasions, some that splintered off of Puritanism and some that were quite different. In the early years of the Puritans the church leaders were determined to set up a local theocracy. But this was defeated, as the other groups refused to be subjugated. After all, why had they come to America? And as time passed such groups were ever more frequent. Indeed within ten years of their arrival, the Puritan monopoly in Massachusetts Colony was broken.

Reinforcing opposition to the Puritan theocracy were the philosophical arguments being propounded on the Continent. John Locke in *Of the Conduct of the Understanding* argued for a separation of church and state as did various of the French Enlightenment scholars. These arguments were particularly persuasive in the colonies, where typically several religions were prevalent making it impossible to identify a set of principles that all could accept.

The rejection by other groups of the theocratic idea led the Puritans to place reliance on local town governments for the preservation of their ideals. Over time, this preference for the sanctity of local government came to be widespread, allowing each distinctive group to protect its own beliefs within the confines of its distinctive township.

---

[1] It is important to point out however that Puritan codes of behavior prevailed as the community was mono-cultural and controlled the school.

Communities, so long as they achieved consensus, were allowed to set their distinctive agendas. Some extremes are the Mennonites in Pennsylvania or the Shakers throughout the Northeast. Some local communities, especially those in New England and elsewhere where the Puritans had strong influence, placed a strong emphasis on schools to be locally controlled and financed. Thus out of this heritage also came the commitment to local control. Communities were encouraged to do as they wished, or to not do, so long as broader principles were not violated.

Over the early years of the American republic, local communities proliferated as the nation expanded its territory. Circa 1900, there were over 100,000 local communities that had established school systems. Some of these communities were of course quite large such as New York City, Chicago, and Boston, while most were small. Over the twentieth century, there was some consolidation of these communities, or at least to their school systems, so that today there are about 15,000 distinctive school systems. Each sets its own curricular rules (Fuller, 1982).

The Contradictory Constitution

While in early America local communities enjoyed much autonomy, the core political unit was the colony and it was at this level that major issues were thrashed out. Thirteen such colonies had been granted charters by the English crown. Miller (1965, p. 36) reminds us that by the time of the Revolution the principle of separation of church and state had been firmly established in all but two of the colonies.

It was the colonial assemblies that one by one decided to rebel against England and it was these same assemblies that financed the soldiers who joined the colonial army. At the conclusion of the war, the colonies drafted the Articles of Confederation, and when these proved inadequate they assembled anew to draft the Constitution forming the federal republic of the United States of America. What stands out in this Constitution is the limited powers that are specifically assigned to the federal government, principally in foreign policy, defense, and international trade. The Constitution specifically notes that those powers not assigned to the federal government reside in the states. Education is one such power of the states.

However, in that the Constitution was the supreme law of the land, certain principles promulgated in it have had a long-term impact on education; of particular relevance for religious/moral education is the first amendment:

> Congress shall make no law respecting an establishment of religion, or prohibiting the free exercise thereof; or abridging the freedom of speech, or of the press; or the right of the people peaceably to assemble, and to petition the Government for redress of grievances.

This amendment clearly articulated the separation the separation of church and state at the federal level. In the early years of the American republic, schools were not a matter of federal concern as their finances were derived exclusively from local revenues. But as the federal government came to be involved in schools through subsidies for particular items such as buildings, textbooks, school lunches and training the federal laws came to have implications for local schools. A series of court cases led to the progressive reduction of religiously specific material in local curricula. The current symbolic issue in this series of legal actions is the appropriateness of requiring children to pray while in school. The current view is that a moment of silence is appropriate so long as that moment is not framed in terms of the precepts of a particular religion. In contrast with some other systems, the American solution currently does not allow for separate religious classes on the premises of public schools for children of different faiths. On the other hand, if a child attends a private school the child may be required to participate in the religious activities characteristic of that school.

The Fourteenth Amendment is another constitutional provision that has had a profound impact on public education:

> All persons born or naturalized in the United States, and subject to the jurisdiction thereof, are citizens of the United States and of the State wherein they reside. No state shall make or enforce any law which shall abridge the privileges or immunities of citizens of the United States; nor shall any State deprive any person of life, liberty, or property without due process of law; nor deny to any person within its jurisdiction the equal protection of the laws.

This amendment has proved particularly instrumental in promoting equal access to public education and to other public opportunities of people from various backgrounds.

The Rise of Common Schools

While separation of church and state is noted in the constitution, it was not rigorously interpreted for several decades. For example, as late as 1833 Massachusetts continued to have established state religion while at the same time non-established religions were allowed to practice as they wished.

The federal constitution made no specific recommendations on education, leaving this up to the individual states and local communities. In some areas such as the Northeast, the local interest in education was comparatively strong and public education was provided free of charge, but it was not until half way through the century that certain states began to discuss the thought of making education compulsory for all young people.

Several factors were behind these discussions. Distinct from the religious need of improving reasoning so as to develop faith, there was the practical need of developing basic literacy and numeracy in order to work in the industrializing economy. With the influx of immigrants from non-English speaking nations, there was also the concern to Americanize these new groups so they could serve more effectively in their various social and economic rules.

A response that, in hindsight, stands out was the move to establish common schools. Up to that time, diverse private groups had led in the establishment of schools. But from the early nineteenth century in some of the states a movement emerged to establish free public education. Massachusetts was a leader in this movement going so far as to establish a statewide Superintendent of Schools. While this state office had little formal authority, its occupant could orchestrate consensus through the holding of state meetings and other means. Perhaps the most noted among Massachusetts' Superintendents was Horace Mann, appointed in 1840 after a successful career as a politician. On the issue of access, Mann proposed

> A Free school system. It knows no distinction of rich and poor, of bond and free, or between those who, in the imperfect light of this world, are seeking through different avenues, to reach the gate of heaven. Without money and without price, it throws open its doors, and spreads the table of its bounty, for all the children of the State (quoted in Bowles and Gintis, 1976, p. 167)

Mann also sought to accommodate religious differences in the schools. In the early years a curriculum had been proposed that met with the approval of the most prevalent religious groups, but this was severely criticized by the Calvinists. Edward Newton, for example, argued as follows:

> The idea of a religion to be permitted to be taught in our schools, in which all are at present agreed, is a mockery. There is really no such thing unless it be what is called natural religion. There is not a point in the Christian scheme, deemed important, and of a doctrinal character, that is not disputed or dis-allowed by some. As to the "precepts" [of Jesus], perhaps, there may be pretty general agreement, and that this one great branch of the Christian scheme we allow. But is this all: all that the sons of the Puritans are willing to have taught in their public schools? (quoted in Glenn, 1988, p. 141).

In the face of continuing criticism of this kind, religious education was gradually re-moved from the schools and with it many of the more restrictive dictums of New England morality. What remained was an exhortation to discipline, good work habits, and clean living, and political participation or what might be called a civil morality.

The common school ideal gradually spread across the United States. It gained impetus in the Western regions with the passage of the Morrill Act (1862), which required each new community established in the new territories to set up a public school. By the turn of the twentieth century, the common school was the prevailing model for the public sector. As Tyack (1974) observes, America developed "one best system".

Private schools, however, could do as they pleased. So during this period Catholic Schools began to be established; starting in the late forties with only a handful of Catholic schools, by 1900 they provided places for over 10 percent of all enrollees in private edu-cation. Some Protestant groups also continued to maintain their own independent schools, though in view of the growing strength of public schools for basic education, these relig-ious groups increasingly focused their resources on higher education. Thus the last half of the nineteenth century brought a big boom in private tertiary education, and a gradual de-cline in the private sector's share of primary and secondary education.

Once established, the common school ideal demonstrated considerable tenacity. Through World War II, in some areas of the United States there was a practice of setting up distinct common schools for blacks and whites, defying the original principal of diver-sity, but that has since been forbidden. Other groups have proposed single-sex schools, also to have that rejected. Similarly, the pressure of particular religious groups to restore some form of religious education into public schools has also been resisted.

While the common school purged the curriculum of religious bias, thereby weakening moral education, it did nevertheless seek to highlight one moral theme, that of patriotism and civil duty. The American flag and commitment to America's democratic institutions was promoted as a unifying moral theme, and specific areas of the common school's curriculum were allocated for the fostering of a sense of civic duty. In particular, a course in civics was proposed for the secondary level, and social studies and history courses at the primary and secondary levels were also expected to stress this moral theme.

The Excesses of Nativism

America has always been known as a nation of immigrants, and especially from the mid-nineteenth century as the economic fortunes of several European nations faltered the numbers heading to the United States began to swell. The first wave of immigrants was from Northern Europe and resembled both in speech and appearance those groups already settled in America. They assimilated relatively easily into the American way of life, and caused little controversy.

However, over time increasing proportions of the immigrants came from the more Southern and Eastern parts of Europe, and from the points of view of some groups already residing in America the new immigrants were perceived as too foreign. While, from an economic point of view, these new immigrants were welcomed to assume low wage jobs in the rapidly expanding industrial sector, they were not welcomed as prospective neighbors and citizens. A political movement known as the "Know-Nothings" emerged to raise the barriers to the immigration of these new groups. A bill was proposed before Congress in the 1850s to extend the number of years of residence required for citizenship from five to twenty-one years; another urged a formal declaration of English as the national language.

These same concerns extended to the schools, where increasing stress was placed on patriotism and nationalistic symbols and customs. It was during this period that school holidays were established to celebrate the fourth of July, Washington's birthday and so on, and the American flag came to appear at the front of classrooms. At the same time, tolerance of ethnic idiosyncrasies was restrained. The common school movement became increasingly popular as a means to make the new immigrants become more American.

The Know-Nothing movement subsided as America moved into civil war and immigration declined. But a similar pattern emerged towards the end of the century as immigration once again boomed, this time with an influx from Asia and even Latin America. After World War II there was yet another revival in reaction to the large inflow of political refugees from Western Europe. And it can be said that the pattern seems to be repeating itself once again in the late eighties as a new wave of immigrants headed to America to escape the repression and poverty found in various third world regimes, including China, Vietnam, Nigeria, Cuba and Mexico. As in the past, politicians have urged a tightening of immigration laws, a declaration of English as the national language, and a stricter enforcement of employment regulations to insure that the new immigrants are not allowed to work for sub-standard wages. Similarly, opposition has risen to provisions for affirmative action that had been designed to give minorities greater access to schools and employment.

Enhancing Minority Rights

The recent re-birth of nativistic politics comes on the heels of nearly four decades of political action to achieve a more equitable balance between the diverse ethnic and racial groups who live in the United States. As noted earlier, the U.S. constitution considers all Americans equal before the law, and the Civil War affirmed this principle through declaring black Americans, many of whom had been enslaved, to have the same rights as white Americans. Despite the accomplishments of that war, for nearly a century thereafter black and white Americans tended to live and work separately. As Gunnar Myrdal (1944) observed, America was divided into two nations, each with their separate places of residence, their separate schools, their separate restaurants, and often their separate workplaces. This was possible through the legal rationale of the "separate but equal" provision of public facilities.

Following World War II, activists began to challenge the separate but equal approach, pointing out that it was not viable. A long struggle for civil rights finally led in the sixties to a series of new laws and regulations aimed at improving the status of minorities. The new provisions included affirmative action in employment to give minorities the prospect of improved opportunities. Concerning education wherever it was found that large numbers of black Americans endured inferior schooling, steps were taken for these blacks to gain access on an equal basis with whites to the same schools. Obligatory busing was introduced in many local areas to achieve this result. Thus the rights gained by blacks were gradually extended to other minority groups.

Initially the reformists stressed equal access to facilities. As time passed, they came to recognize the importance of other factors such as language and culture if the members of the minority groups were to achieve the same accomplishments as members of the majority group. Accordingly, the reformers began to press for greater recognition in schools of the linguistic and cultural needs of minorities. One outcome was legislation to guarantee all children the right to receive education in the language of their upbringing, at least in the initial years of their schooling. Similarly, schools were directed to achieve a greater balance in the cultural lessons they conveyed. The respective policy initiatives are known as bilingualism and multiculturalism.

The American commitment to multiculturalism has had to be worked out within the framework of equality before the law. One implication is that embracing multiculturalism places pressures on educational systems to avoid favoritism to any particular cultural strand. But this very effort to treat all cultures as equal leaves education open to the charge that it has no direction, that all is relative (Bloom, 1990). Where all is equal, it becomes difficult to assert that a particular approach or value should prevail over another, yet in moral education it is often essential to search for such valuation.

As with other educational changes in the United States, the implementation of these reforms has been the responsibility of the various local school systems, leading to extensive variation in outcome. Particularly in the northeastern and western parts of the U.S., there have been comparatively bold approaches.

But these reforms have not always been popular. To the extent that school systems have a relatively homogeneous student body, they tend to be less open to multicultural reforms. On the other hand, the homogeneous communities may sponsor new cultural initiatives focusing on differences between world cultures, by for example building bridges with schools and communities in other parts of the world.

The Rise of Cognitive Psychology

The reformation and the deep religious convictions of that era led many of the earliest immigrant groups to come to America. While these groups sought freedom to practice their faith, most relied heavily on reason to pursue this practice. Thus from the earliest times Americans were firmly committed to logical as contrasted to emotional approaches to problem solving. This commitment to reason was expressed in their preference for a rule of law and in their attachment to constitution to bind the various stages together.

As the young republic evolved, this attachment to reason led to extraordinary innovations in the practice of education. One example is the conviction that all Americans should receive education. One side of this conviction was the belief that reason was required to realize religious progress. At the same time, America's leaders saw value in education as a means to help in solving the problems of everyday life such as bookkeeping and farming. Thus educational institutions prospered in America.

The commitment to reason also had a profound impact on the practice of education. Whereas on the continent, teachers were content to teach traditional subjects in a time-proven manner, Americans began to question those ways. On the one hand, Americans began to introduce major changes in what was taught so as to make American education more relevant to the American condition. On the other hand, these same educators came to ask if there might not be a better way to teach and to evaluate the quality of learning.

Initially in Germany and later in America, interest in learning led to various experiments with mental processes and eventually to the birth of the field of psychology. This field, well established by the end of the nineteenth century, came to play a progressively larger role in the field of education. One of the dictums of psychology was that every child was different, so psychologists proposed various tests to identify differences. Presumably individual differences required different educational approaches, which psychologists sought to devise.

In a cultural setting where schools were not expected to involve themselves with moral education, American educational psychology gradually came to focus on other areas of the psyche, notably the processes of motivation and cognition. Elaborate tests were devised by psychologists to track these processes, and these tests became incorporated in educational decision making ranging from student class assignment to college placement (Boorstin, 1974, pp. 220 ff).

Analyses of the values of young people or their moral behavior was a relatively neglected topic in American psychology until comparatively recently. The first major American theory of moral development, that of Kohlberg (1963), focused primarily on the ability of young people to reason about moral issues, without making any commitment to their convictions. Loevinger's (1976) theory of ego development was equally agnostic. When American schools came to develop an interest in moral education, the initial guidance they received was on moral reasoning rather than moral education. While this approach was consistent with the non-sectarian educational culture of the United States, it did not address the more fundamental concerns of those who sought to strengthen moral education.

The American Frontier

While it is convenient to speak of America as an entity, the original colonies were founded with different purposes. And as America has expanded, it has incorporated new groups and faced many challenges. Thus there is much diversity in the American people. William Ogburn (1966) has helped document the special features of courtly and expressive southern culture as contrasted with the moral inner-directedness of the northeast. Others have suggested that America, as it moved westward and encountered the challenges of the frontier placed increasing stress on public solutions to common problems combined with a new permissiveness with respect to many moral and political issues (Turner, 1920; Walsh, 1981). Finally, as America joined the Orient in Hawai'i, yet other value streams came to shape the American character. Few studies have reached firm conclusions on the dimensions of regional cultures, but one set of working hypotheses worth exploring is that the further west one goes, the more permissive is the moral culture, the more tolerant are the attitudes to people of varying races and cultures (with some exceptions, e.g., right wing attitudes in California), and the more likely are citizens to think of government as a resource for solving problems rather than as an authoritative organ to which they owe allegiance and service.

Current and Future Perspectives on Values Education

Americans are proud of many of their accomplishments over the twentieth century, as their nation has developed to become the most productive and powerful in the world. But with American ascendancy have also evolved various social tendencies that are troubling, including rising crime, violence, and family instability. Reflecting on these signs of social decay, national leaders have proposed various solutions ranging from the strengthening of local community organizations to the strengthening of values. Particularly concerning this latter theme, eyes have turned once again to the schools and the need to promote a stronger and even a more prescriptive values curriculum.

In contrast with the cognitive theories of moral reasoning that have come from American psychology, over the past decade a number of educators with a background in religion and philosophy have offered approaches that are more prescriptive. Table 4.1 lists the values featured in several of the current works. In virtually all cases, these leaders seek to identify an agnostic morality agreeable to the great majority of Americans, and based on the American tradition.[2]

Table 4.1 Moral Values Emphasized in Recent Writings

Butts (1988)	Bennett (1993)	Eyres & Eyres (1993)	Lickona (1991)	Phi Delta Kappa (1993)
Justice	Self-discipline	Values of Being	Respect	Honesty
Freedom	Compassion	Honesty	Responsibility	Democracy
Equality	Responsibility	Courage	Honesty	Ethnic Tolerance
Diversity	Democracy	Peaceability	Fairness	Patriotism
Authority	Responsibility	Self- Reliance &	Tolerance	Caring
Privacy	Friendship	Potential	Prudence	Moral Courage
Participation	Work	Fidelity/Chastity	Self-Discipline	Golden Rule
Due Process	Courage	Prudence	Compassion	Religious
Truth	Perseverance	Values of Giving	Cooperation	Tolerance
Property	Honesty	Loyalty/	Courage	
Patriotism	Loyalty	Dependability	Democratic	
Human rights	Faith	Helpfulness	Values	
		Respect		
		Unselfishness/		
		Sensitivity		
		Kindness/		
		Friendliness		
		Justice/Mercy		

As we see in these lists, there are several common themes:

- Toward individual responsibility and away from individualism;
- Toward ethnic and religious tolerance;
- Toward democratic institutions and civic cultures as mechanisms for promoting and defending common values; and
- Toward respect for religious faith while avoiding a public preference for any particular religion.

But these highly visible spokespeople may not represent the full spectrum of contemporary American thinking on values education. To gauge the generality of their views, we decided to carry out a survey of U.S. educational elites that varied both in terms of where they live (from the four states of New York, Michigan, California, and Hawai'i) and what they do (a combination of top officials and politicians on the one hand and front-line educators on the other hand.[3] So the primary concern in the following analysis is to deter-

---

[2] By this statement, we mean that these educators do not advocate the teaching of the moral and religious positions of particular religions in their proposed curriculums. All of the individuals cited are themselves deeply religious and believe that religious faith is important for individuals. They do not oppose schools teaching some principles of world religions, but they believe the responsibility for conveying an understanding of personal faith lies with families and churches.

[3] The total number of respondents was eighty-eight spread across the four states. As with the other studies in this book, the sample in each area included state education authorities, leading educational intellectuals, religious leaders who have educational positions, leaders of related NGOs, politicians, people in educational institutes, academic leaders, curriculum designers in values edu-

mine whether the proposals of the current values-education opinion leaders are consistent with the views of our elite sample. A secondary concern is to see if there is significant variation in the views of our elite sample that might be related either to their place of residence (e.g., the frontier hypothesis) or their social position (are front-liners more school oriented and practical relative to the idealism of top elites?).

Why Values Education?

The Sigma Values Instrument, discussed in the first chapter of this book, includes several major sections. We first will review the reasons U.S. elites believe values education needs to be strengthened. The options elites were asked to rank are listed in Table 4.2 below.

Table 4.2 Why Should There be Values Education?

Reasons for Values Education*	State				Total
	New York	Michigan	California	Hawai'i	
Increase a sense of individual responsibility	1	.92	.73	.74	.84
Promote orderly, caring school communities	1	.88	.73	.68	.81
Provide a guide for behavior in daily life	.94	.92	.53	.65	.76
Combat social prejudice / promote tolerance	.76	.76	.73	.74	.75
Promote values of justice and equity	.76	.80	.67	.71	.74
Combat juvenile delinquency	.71	.76	.67	.61	.68
Encourage civic consciousness	.82	.80	.73	.45	.67
Help young people develop reflective /autonomous personality	.65	.72	.53	.61	.64
Help youth interpret values	.76	.60	.67	.58	.64
Strengthen families	.59	.68	.53	.58	.60
Develop appreciation for Heritage	.41	.72	.47	.52	.55
Foster economic development	.41	.64	.47	.58	.55
Improve respect and opportunties for women	.53	.48	.47	.58	.52
Promote pride in local communities	.41	.60	.40	.52	.50
Combat ecological abuse	.53	.52	.47	.45	.49
Promote world peace	.29	.52	.27	.55	.44
Provide foundation for spiritual development	.18	.40	.27	.48	.36

* Proportion who believe each argument is prevalent in society

cation, and values/moral education specialists. No more than 30 percent were individuals directly in curriculum design and/or teaching of values education.

American elites were most likely to cite the following as their reasons for strengthening values education in the schools: increasing the sense of individual responsibility was most frequently cited followed by promoting orderly and caring school communities, providing a guide for behavior in daily life, combating social prejudice and promoting tolerance, promoting the values of justice and equity, combat juvenile delinquency, encouraging civic consciousness, and helping young persons develop reflective autonomous personalities.

These reasons reflect a concern, on the one hand, for enhancing the level of social control and responsibility, with, on the other hand, a fostering of the more libertarian concerns for justice and equity, tolerance, and autonomy.

Looking into regional differences, it turns out the East Coasters followed by the Mid-Westerners are the most concerned with enhancing social control through values education: that is the easterners place the greatest stress on the "puritanical" reasons of enhancing individual responsibility and providing a guide for behavior in daily life. In contrast, and in addition to the puritanical values permeating American life even in the West Coast, the Californians place the greatest stress on tolerance and civic consciousness and the Hawai'ians place the greatest stress on promoting values of justice and equity and in promoting orderly, caring school communities, although less so than respondents in New York and Michigan. Similarly, the East Coasters place the greatest stress on developing civic consciousness, whereas to the extent one looks West there is a greater emphasis on promoting pride in local communities, promoting world peace and combating ecological abuse. Michigan respondents place the greatest stress on fostering economic development and on developing an appreciation for the national heritage. In sum, as predicted by the frontier hypothesis, there are significant regional variations.

What Should be Stressed in Values Education?

As indicated in Table 4.3, the preferences of our elite respondents concerning which values should be stressed in the school curriculum are very similar to those advocated by the prominent spokespeople for values education reviewed in Table 4.1. Our respondents urged placing the greatest stress on civic values followed by democracy, diversity, peace, work and moral values, and gender equality.

Again there are striking regional differences. To the extent an elite is located towards the eastern side of the United States, he/she is likely to place a greater stress on civic values and democracy. To the extent the elite lives resides in Hawai'i or the West Coast, he/she places a greater stress on diversity, peace, personal autonomy and national identity. For certain values, particular regions stand out. New Yorkers rank moral values at the top, which was not characteristic of the other states (Hawai'i is closest with a ranking of third). And Hawai'i is exceptional for its stress on family values and on religion. Californian elites give a relatively high ranking to gender equality and to global awareness.

Table 4.3 What Should be Stressed in Values Education?

Curriculum for Values Education*	State				Total
	New York	Michigan	California	Hawai'i	
Civic values	1.53	1.96	2.13	2.00	1.92
Democracy	1.82	1.68	1.80	2.41	1.98
Diversity and multiculturalism	2.29	2.64	1.57	1.57	2.02
Peace and conflict resolution	2.06	2.72	1.67	1.74	2.07
Work values	2.00	2.44	2.07	1.93	2.11
Moral values	1.38	2.64	2.40	1.97	2.13
Gender equality	2.47	2.44	1.64	2.24	2.25
Personal autonomy	2.47	3.08	2.27	2.11	2.49
Global awareness	3.00	2.80	1.87	2.48	2.57
Ecological awareness	2.94	3.24	2.13	2.41	2.71
Family values	3.25	3.48	3.79	2.07	3.00
National identity and patriotism	3.88	3.16	3.33	2.97	3.27
Religious values	5.47	5.63	6.67	4.38	5.35

* 1=very strong emphasis; 7=should be left out

What Are the Major Issues That Should be Considered in Values Education?

In addition to understanding the priorities and common agenda for the kind of values that should be included in the curriculum, we wanted to understand what values are seen as major issues for schools to deal with—even if these are controversial. We asked our respondents to more explicitly indicate what content areas should have more emphasis in the school curriculum. Their responses ranged from "very strong emphasis" or "1" to "should be left out" or "7". These content areas include issues dealing with autonomy, civic values, nationalism, religion, work, managing diversity, gender, and community. Table 4.4 shows these responses.

Table 4.4 What are the Major Issues in Values Education?

Major issues in Values Education*	State				Total
	New York	Michigan	California	Hawai'i	
Autonomy					
teaching critical thinking in schools	1.71	1.58	1.27	1.29	1.45
help children understand they have individual rights	2.35	2.58	2.07	2.36	2.37
help children develop own values	2.53	3.72	2.07	1.96	2.61
help children understand they have the right to be happy	4.06	3.71	2.43	2.54	3.16
Civic values					
all are equal before the law	2.29	1.64	2.13	1.93	1.95
help young people understand all political/social viewpoints	3.06	2.72	2.07	2.36	2.55
respect hierarchy and support the	4.24	5.08	5.60	4.00	4.65

government					
Nationalism					
promote an understanding and love of nation	3.82	4.20	4.73	3.54	4.00
venerate heroes and promote national pride	3.75	4.28	3.73	3.32	3.76
Religion					
help children understand their own religion	5.59	6.60	6.60	4.96	5.86
schools should foster an understanding of all religions	3.12	3.52	3.47	3.21	3.33
Work					
stress habits of loyalty, obedience, hard work and punctuality	2.31	2.84	2.93	1.82	2.42
competitiveness /creativity for social / economic success	3.82	3.50	4.00	3.39	3.61
Tolerance					
empathy for people of different backgrounds	1.41	2.04	1.73	1.54	1.69
common values to all without differences of class, ethnicity and religion	1.53	1.88	2.07	1.68	1.77
recognize importance of personal pride and identity while understanding unique origins and heritage	3.59	4.08	3.27	2.32	3.26
the fortunate to help those who encounter difficulties	2.65	3.36	2.60	2.64	2.85
Gender					
equal opportunities and encouragement for girls and boys	1.59	1.12	1.13	1.64	1.39
encourage mutual respect between boys and girls	1.47	1.20	1.47	1.50	1.40
take up issues relating to human sexuality and health	2.44	3.12	4.00	2.54	2.95
destiny of girls is to have home-building responsibilities	5.24	5.88	6.73	4.93	5.59
Community					
promote values of solidarity within communities	3.80	3.72	3.21	2.50	3.23
foster values supporting the family	2.82	3.04	3.87	1.89	2.76
promote a truly global view of the world	2.59	2.40	1.53	2.00	2.15
appreciate role of unions in work conditions and fair wages	4.88	4.48	4.47	4.21	4.47

* 1=very strong emphasis; 7=should be left out

Gender

Among the issues receiving strong emphasis are those concerning gender. Our respondents support an egalitarian and liberal position regarding issues of gender and sexuality. For instance the idea that "girls have essentially the same talents as boys and should be given equal opportunities and encouragement in schools" is strongly supported as a content area in the school curriculum, as is the idea that "values education should encourage mutual respect between boys and girls". The idea that "values education should take up issues relating to human sexuality and health, such as chastity, preserving the integrity of the body against drugs and prostitution, and understanding the risks of promiscuity" also receives positive support whereas the idea that "the destiny of girls is to have home-building responsibilities" is firmly rejected.

Autonomy

Issues related to individuals' autonomy and empowerment are also strongly emphasized. Notably, the value of teaching critical thinking in schools is seen as a strong aim for values education. Our respondents support the need for schools to help children understand that they have individual rights, and for schools to assist all children in developing their own individual values as a foundation for their acceptance of broader social values. Not all respondents agree on this last value, however. Respondents from Hawai'i are highly supportive of this idea, whereas Michigan respondents tend to be indifferent or reject the idea. Values relating to the importance of helping each child understand they have the right to be happy were not accorded strong emphasis.

Tolerance

There is a more positive disposition to including in the curriculum ideas dealing with social integration and equality among our respondents than ideas that would tend to separate groups on the basis of origin or wealth. Accordingly, respondents support ideas such as "schools should encourage empathy for people of different ethnic, language, and social backgrounds and create opportunities for growth through shared experiences" and "it is best for schools to teach common values to all children without differentiation on the basis of class, ethnicity, or religion". They are less sympathetic to ideas such as "schools should note social differences and stress the duty of the fortunate to help those who encounter difficulties". The need for schools to recognize the importance of personal pride and identity on average, are not accorded strong emphasis, Hawai'i respondents are most favorable to this idea whereas New York and Michigan respondents tend to be indifferent or even reject the idea. These general trends reflects a tendency towards understanding diversity and racial tolerance across the nation.

Civic Values

Two content areas are considered important for fostering civic values: "the need to stress that all are equal before the law", and the idea that schools should help young people gain an understanding of all political and social viewpoints from the most conservative to the most liberal. Respondents differ significantly across the regions regarding the idea that people should be taught to respect hierarchies and support the government. Respondents from Hawai'i and New York are ambivalent, and respondents from Michigan and in a major degree California, reject the idea.

Community

Values having to do with collective matters ranging from family values to worldwide communities' concerns receive mixed support. Strong support is given to the idea that schools should "promote a truly global view of the world" and some emphasis is placed on "fostering values supporting the family, such as respect for parents, fidelity, and taking care of children and elders". Respondents in Hawai'i are most supportive of the idea of family values while respondents from California are largely indifferent. The idea that "schools should promote values of solidarity within communities" is acceptable to our respondents while the view that "schools should help young people appreciate the essential role of unions in guaranteeing safe work conditions and fair wages" provokes indifference or negative views. The response to this question reflects the generalized anti-union stance of a large section of American society.

Work

A number of ideas related to "hard work" are endorsed as having an important place in the curriculum by our respondents. The idea that "as sound preparation for the world of work, habits of loyalty, obedience, hard work and punctuality need to be stressed in school" receives positive support. Less popular though still supported is the idea that "values education should highlight the role of individual competitiveness and creativity in realizing both social and economic success". These answers indicate that, at least for our respondents, education is seen as a means both to increase one's personal autonomy and individual power, and to contribute to increased productivity or economic gain.

Religion

Unlike some Asian countries in our study and like others in the West, the U.S. maintains that the teaching of religion has no place in public schools. This situation may help explain our respondents' negative responses to ideas such as "schools should help every child gain a deeper understanding of their own religion" in contrast with the more positive reaction to the idea that "schools should foster an understanding of all religions". The study of world cultures with some emphasis on the different religions is acceptable, whereas a stress on particular religions is not.

Nationalism

Ideas dealing with nationalistic values are not strongly endorsed. For instance, the idea that schooling should "first promote an understanding and love of nation" is viewed with indifference. Similarly, the respondents were not enthusiastic about the idea that "people should venerate heroes and promote national pride". This shared opinion indicates a period of doubt about the power of traditional institutions that have served to unify American society. This disillusionment may be associated with the recent scandals at the higher levels of government.

In sum, equality of opportunity for boys and girls and solidarity across communities are considered important themes for the curriculum, as is teaching critical thinking in schools. We find a definite disposition to including ideas dealing with social integration and equality as contrasted to ideas that tend to separate groups on the basis of their social origins or wealth. Civic values specially as they relate to understanding the law and to educating citizens vis-à-vis pluralistic ideas are strongly supported for inclusion in the school curriculum. Ideas related to promoting a global view of the world are also supported. There is also support for the idea that education should be seen more in terms of its contribution to individual development than as a means to increase productivity or economic gain for individuals and society. We observe a generalized lack of enthusiasm for nationalistic values, and a rejection of religious teachings in the school curriculum.

What Cultures Should We Include in the Curriculum?

Our study not only set out to explore the why, what and how of values education. We also wanted to know how open our respondents were to including the values of other cultures in the school curriculum. We asked our respondents to indicate what cultures they thought should be given more prominence in the schools. Their answers show, not surprisingly, that the U.S. should receive the most prominence. Japan, China, Russia, the U.K., Mexico, and Canada are ranked next in importance. These are followed by France and Egypt. Our respondents ranked Korea, Indonesia, Singapore, Thailand, and Malaysia in the tenth through fourteenth places (see Table 4.5). While there were few notable differences across regions, it is interesting that the respondents from Michigan and California rated Mexico as a second and fourth priority respectively. California rated Russia as a second priority, and New York gave high priority to Canada. We also asked our respondents to indicate the degree of familiarity with a number of different societies' values (such as Latin American, socialist, Asian, and Islamic values) and which should be included in the school curriculum. Although respondents expressed a relatively high degree of familiarity with values from these different cultures they seemed reluctant to include them in the curriculum, especially Islamic values. The above discussion highlights areas where further policy dialogue may be needed to build shared understanding regarding the introduction of different cultures to values education.

**Table 4.5 Cultures/Societies That Should be Given Most Prominence
in the School Curriculum**

Cultures/societies*	State				Total
	New York	Michigan	California	Hawai'i	
USA	1.19	1.39	1.08	1.28	1.26
Japan	2.25	2.32	1.92	2.17	2.19
China	2.44	2.26	1.85	2.44	2.29
Russia	2.56	2.48	2.33	2.65	2.53
UK	2.81	2.52	2.08	2.77	2.59
Mexico	3.13	2.09	2.00	3.23	2.63
Canada	2.88	2.52	3.08	3.50	2.99
France	3.50	3.41	3.31	3.50	3.44
Egypt	3.81	3.45	3.08	4.05	3.64
Korea	3.93	3.91	3.67	3.59	3.77
Indonesia	4.63	4.23	4.55	4.10	4.33
Singapore	4.94	4.50	4.33	4.30	4.51
Thailand	4.88	4.19	4.85	4.38	4.52
Malaysia	5.13	4.27	4.77	4.33	4.57

*1=much prominence   7=little prominence

How Should Values Education be Carried Out?

In the previous section we have begun to understand the aims and general content of values education in the U.S. In this section we turn to three issues concerning the implementation of values education. One concerns the time or amount of effort that should be given to values education as a whole—indicating the level of importance attributed to this area in the curriculum. The second aspect has to do with the target population, and the third has to do with settings.

How Much Time Should be Given to Values Education in the School Curriculum?

We asked our respondents to indicate what percent of a school budget (money, time and effort) should be devoted to values education. Most respondents indicated that, in average, close to 10 percent of the curriculum should be contained in specific classes such as moral education or civics, and close to 20 percent should be integrated across the curriculum. This answer indicates that, at least among our respondents, subject-specific values education does not seem to have a very prominent place in the school curriculum. These views however, vary significantly across the regions. California and New York respondents would like to see more of the curriculum reserved for subject-specific values education classes while respondents from Michigan and Hawai'i would like to see less. New York respondents also are most likely to propose an integration of values education across the curriculum, whereas Michigan and California respondents are intermediate and Hawai'i respondents are the least supportive of this approach.

Who Should Receive Values Education?

In our survey we approached the second implementation aspect by asking who should be targeted for values education. Overall our respondents agreed that values education should begin at an early age under the assumption that the foundations of values are established in early childhood. Conversely our respondents are in strong disagreement with the notion that values education should only begin in secondary school after young people have a clear idea of what they believe to be important. We also asked how the values education curriculum should be constructed. Congruent with responses examined in the section above, our respondents agree that values education should be integrated throughout the curriculum rather than taught in separate subjects; and they support teaching a common curriculum (e.g., as opposed to designing different programs according to ability). We did not find significant differences across the regions in this aspect (see Table 4.6).

Table 4.6 Who Should Receive Values Education?

Target group for Values Education*	State				
	New York	Michigan	California	Hawai'i	Total
Begin in secondary school	6.65	6.80	6.87	5.71	6.40
Begin at an early age	1.35	1.24	1.47	1.58	1.42
Different values programs by academic ability	6.65	5.92	6.27	5.45	5.95
Integrated throughout the curriculum	2.18	1.68	1.80	1.87	1.86

* 1=strongly agree; 7=strongly disagree

Where Should Values Education be Taught and to Whom?

We also asked more specific questions regarding the relationship between specific target groups and settings for conducting values education. Answers to these questions vary relative to the particular orientation of the curriculum such as religion, moral or civic education (see Table 4.7). Simply put, religious education is seen primarily as a private matter to be carried out in the home and church. Moral education is seen as a shared responsibility of the home, the school, and the community. Concerning civic education, the elite respondents placed the greatest emphasis on the role of the school relative to other educational venues.

Our respondents' answers to the implementation questions in values education point to a number of dilemmas. Whereas their answers to the why and what questions indicate their concern for schools to play an important role in the formation of responsible, autonomous and productive individuals, in their discussion of implementation they downplay the role of schools relative to other venues. One possible explanation for their indifference to schools may be the perception of our respondents that teachers are not adequately prepared to play an effective role in values education. To the extent they are right, this naturally leads to a consideration of greater emphasis on values education in the curriculum of teacher preparation programs.

Table 4.7 Where Should Values Education be Taught and to Whom?

	Religious Education (count)	Moral Education (count)	Civic Education (count)
Groups ranked "first" as needing most exposure:			
Inservice teachers	2	9	10
Teacher learners	3	7	5
Young children	11	7	3
Pre-school children	8	8	0
Primary level	23	32	26
Secondary level	14	7	19
High school level	5	7	13
University level	4	1	3
Not ranked	18	10	9
Settings ranked "first" as most effective:			
During school as a class	4	9	24
During school through rules of behavior	1	8	17
Outside school activities (clubs, sports, art)	3	1	3
Internship and community service	0	0	5
Camps	1	2	0
Religious groups and institutions	25	1	0
Military training and national service	0	0	1
Home and family	47	56	27
Media	0	1	0
Not ranked	7	11	11

N=88

Discussion

Over the past two decades, values education has been given considerable attention in the United States, in both policy and research circles. An academic society has been established to co-ordinate thinking on moral education, and there are several action groups. Thus there is considerable information to draw on for clarifying the principal characteristics of the American approach:

1. Morality is closely associated with religion. In the West and the Middle East where Christianity and Islam prevail, this association is common. Moreover, it is common in Western societies for more than one religion to be practiced by the citizenry. This condition of religious pluralism leads to moral pluralism; among Western nations, perhaps none has such a diversity of religions as the U.S., the world's melting pot. The condition of moral pluralism creates pressure for a creative solution that minimizes conflict between the various religious groups. In contrasts to the Western condition of religious and moral pluralism, in many Asian societies (Japan, China, Taiwan) morality is not associated with religion but rather with the state philosophy. In that there is one state, it is relatively easy to agree on a common morality. In other Asian societies, there may be a number of religions practiced, some of which take di-

vergent positions on certain moral issues. In these cases, as for example in Malaysia and Indonesia, the state may allow for parallel moral coda, with each group expected to practice the coda it affirms.

2. Values education should take place in the family. In all societies, values education begins in the family. What seems exceptional about the United States is the conviction, even in the colonial period, that family education was sufficient to establish sound values and moral convictions—though this may have been justified given the homogeneity of the population at the time—in modern days this assumption is questionable. Schools from the earliest days were considered vehicles for the development of reason, as a complement to piety. In contrast, in most other societies schools were also looked to as vehicles for character education whether through the curriculum or, as in the case of England, primarily through the co-curriculum of school chapels, athletics, and dormitory living.

3. Values reasoning can be taught. Commitment is personal. In view of the complexity of modern American society, much stress is placed on values reasoning as contrasted with particular standards or dogma. America was the first society founded with a mission to promote change, to realize progress. This activist American conviction extended to the frontier and even beyond: on the international scene, Americans often express a mission to involve themselves in foreign settings so that other peoples can enjoy the benefits of the American experiment. Because of the open-ended quality of the American dream, American moralists have been reluctant to set firm standards for individual behavior. Even in the American home, a young person is often told to figure out things for themselves. Parents stress self-reliance over fixed prescriptions. The same principle of figuring things out has influenced American thinking on values education which is characterized by such concepts as values clarification and moral reasoning, as contrasted with the more directive approaches common in other settings.

4. American morality is in crisis. In recent years there has been considerable debate and reexamination of the American approach. Robert Dreeben (1968) in a classic study of youth socialization referred to the American school's approach to moral education as the hidden curriculum. Gerald Grant (1988) in a recent study of a New York high school notes that this curriculum was once neglected but over the past decade has moved to a more prominent position in school planning as a result of the combined efforts of parents, administrators, teachers and students. As evident by this study, politicians and educators have come to raise frequent and major questions about the American way. It is often argued that youth's susceptibility to drugs or the high incidence of crime in American society is a sign of moral decay, of relaxation in the moral upbringing and standards of the American people. However, in terms of the new debate the concerns in the U.S. seem to parallel those in most other modern nations.

5. Consensus on many issues, deep divisions on others. While on most issues, there is still much flexibility and common ground, around a few issues such as the right to life

there is deep polarization. The polarizing issues tend to be grounded in religious differences commonly characterized as fundamentalism versus liberalism. On the particular issue of the right to life for pre-natal fetuses as contrasted with the right of a mother to choose an abortion for an unwanted child, various protestant denominations as well as the Catholic Church have taken official positions. This tendency of religious-based polarization is characteristic of many Western societies, and in some instances has been behind the movement to divide these societies: witness the schisms in the former Soviet Union, the former Czechoslovakia, Yugoslavia, and Canada. In the U.S., separatist movements as such have not emerged. Nevertheless, the religious-based sentiments stand in the way of reform.

6.   In a new America, schools may have a greater role in values education. Similarly there has been a reexamination of the role of schools. Many of America's current critics believe that at least a part of America's moral decay can be traced to the neutrality regarding values characteristic of the American school. Former Secretary of Education William Bennett (1993) has proposed a new role for moral education in the schools. At the other end of the political spectrum, President William Clinton has come to advocate the restoration of "prayer in the schools", a code-phrase for strengthening religious and moral education.

7.   There are several common themes among the contemporary proponents of values education:

   • Toward individual responsibility and away from excessive individualism;
   • Toward ethnic and religious tolerance;
   • Toward democratic institutions and civic cultures as mechanisms for promoting and defending common values; and
   • Toward a respect for religious faith while avoiding a public preference for any particular religion.

There is no inherent reason why American schools need to eschew values education so long as the principles taught are disembodied from the associated religions. Our survey indicates that most respondents concur with these themes, differing only in the relative emphasis on particular dimensions. These differences in emphasis relate to personal conviction as well as local culture. Over the past decade, a growing number of school systems have found ways to define and teach religion-neutral values education (e.g., Michigan has instituted the Michigan Model, which directly deals with values education). While there is no comprehensive survey yet available of the incidence of such programs, they are extensive. Thus it can be said that the American approach to values education, as with the American approach to so many other things, is more complex than might be suggested by the title of this chapter. The American public is continually searching for the best way to realize values education, and in recent years that search is leading to a new focus on the role of schools in this important challenge.

References

Bennett, W. (1993). *The Book of Virtues*. New York: Simon and Schuster.

Bereday, G.Z.F and Matsui, S. (1973). *American Education through Japanese Eyes*. Honolulu: The University of Hawaii Press.

Bloom, A. (1990). *The Closing of the American Mind*. New York: Simon and Schuster.

Boorstin, D. (1969). *The Americans: The National Experience*. New York: Penguin. (Text refers to 1974 edition.)

Bowles, S. and Gintis, H. (1976). *Schooling in Capitalist America*. New York: Basic Books.

Butts, R.F. (1988). *The Morality of Democratic Citizenship*, Calabasas, CA: Center for Civic Education.

Cook, T. and Campbell, D. (1979). *Quasi-Experimentation*. Chicago, IL: Rand McNally.

Cornbleth, C. and Waugh, D. (1995). *The Great Speckled Bird*. New York: St. Martins Press.

Cremin, L. (1970). *American Education: The Colonial Experience 1607-1783*. New York: Harper and Row.

Cremin, L. (1988). *The Metropolitan Experience 1876-1980*. New York: Harper and Row.

Cummings, W.K., Gopinathan, S. and Tomoda, Y. (Eds.) (1988*). The Revival of Values Education in Asia and the West,* Oxford: Pergamon Press.

Degler, C.N. (1959). "Out of Our Past". In *The Forces That Shaped Modern America*. New York: Harper and Row.

Diamond, L. and Plattner, M. (1996). *The Global Resurgence of Democracy*. Baltimore, MD: John Hopkins.

Dreeben, R. (1968). *On What Is Learned in School*. Reading, MA: Addision-Wesley.

Eyres, L. and Eyres, R. (1993). *Teaching Your Children Values*. New York: Simon and Schuster.

Fuller, W.E. (1982). *The Old Country School*. Chicago, IL: The University of Chicago Press.

Glenn, C.L. (1988). *The Myth of the Common School*. Amherst, MA: University of Massachusetts Press.

Grant, G. (1988). *The World We Created at Hamilton High*. Cambridge, MA: Harvard University Press.

Inglehart, R. (1997). *Modernization and Postmodernization*. Princeton, NJ: Princeton University Press.

Kohlberg, L. (1963). "Moral Development and Identification", in H.W. Stevenson (Ed.), *Child Psychology*. 62nd Yearbook of the National Society for the Study of Education. Chicago, IL: University of Chicago Press.

Lickona, T. (1991). *Educating for Character*. New York: Bantam.

Lickona, T. (1993a). "Is Character Education a Responsibility of the Public Schools?" *Momentum* 24 (4): 48-54.

Lickona, T. (1993b). "The Return of Character Education", *Educational Leadership* 51(3): 6-11.

Lickona, T. (1996a). "Eleven Principles of Effective Character Education", *Journal of Moral Education* 25(1): 93-100.

Lickona, T. (1996b). "Teaching Respect and Responsibility. Reclaiming Children and Youth", *Journal of Emotional and Behavioral Problems* 5(3): 143-51.

Locke, J. *Of the Conduct of the Understanding.* New York: Teachers College Press.

Loevinger, J. (1976). *Ego Development.* San Francisco, CA: Jossey-Bass.

Miller, P. (1965). *The Life of the Mind in America.* New York: Harcourt, Brace and World.

Myrdal, G. (1944). *An American Dilemma: The Negro Problem.* New York: Harper and Row.

Ogburn, W. (1966). *Social Change with Respect to Cultural and Original Nature.* New York: Dell.

Phi Delta Kappa/Gallup Poll (1993). *Phi Delta Kappa*, October.

Tatto, M.T. (1998). "The Influence of Teacher Education on Teachers' Beliefs about Purposes of Education, Roles and Practice", *Journal of Teacher Education* 49 (1): 66-77.

Tomoda, Y. (Ed.) (1997). *Patterns of Value Socialization in U.S. Primary Schools: A Comparative Study.* Osaka: Osaka University Faculty of Human Sciences.

Turner, F.J. (1920). *The Frontier in American History.* New York: Henry Holt and Co.

Tyack, D. (1974). *The One Best System.* Cambridge, MA: Harvard University Press.

Walsh, M. (1981). *The American Frontier Revisited.* Atlantic Highlands, NJ: Humanities Press.

Warwick, D. and Lininger, S. (1975). *The Sample Survey: Theory and Practice.* New York: McGraw-Hill.

CHAPTER 5

VALUES EDUCATION OF HAWAI'I: THE INTERSECTION OF HAWAI'IAN, AMERICAN, AND ASIAN VALUES

Gita Steiner-Khamsi
Ying Ying Joanne Lim
Walter P. Dawson

Introduction

Which values should be taught in Hawai'ian schools according to Hawai'ian elites? In this chapter we are able to scratch at the surface of convergence, divergence, and indigenization in the Pacific region by taking a closer look at what is occurring in Hawai'i, the geographical center of the Pacific Basin region. Hawai'i is, in more than one sense, at the crossroads of American and Asian spheres of influence. The United States and Japan, in particular, have had a visible impact on the economy and demography of Hawai'i. To what extent, and how, did these two countries also have a cultural impact on Hawai'ian values education? Have Hawai'ian educational elites also adopted the value systems from these two countries? What we will examine here in more depth for Hawai'ian elites might reflect trends within values education in other countries of the Pacific Basin region that are similarly exposed to American and Asian value systems. The study helps to address a topical question that is genuinely comparative (Steiner-Khamsi, 2000): Are there signs of transnational convergence or divergence in Pacific Basin countries?

Social and Political Context

The first introduction of a foreign value system in Hawai'i came in 1819 when Hiram Bingham was sent by the American Board of Commissioners for Foreign Missions to establish the Sandwich Islands Mission as the first Christian mission in Hawai'i. His arrival along with the 1778 arrival of Captain James Hook are commonly pointed to as the beginning of Hawai'i's modern history (Tabrah, 1984: xiii). The subsequent promotion of immigration was prompted by the decrease in the Hawai'ian population from around one million to 82,000 resulting from the introduction of Western diseases. The following waves of immigrants consisted of predominantly Asian immigrants who provided labor for the sugar plantations in the late nineteenth and early twentieth centuries.

The sheer number of immigrant populations in Hawai'i has given the immigrants a prominent role in the formation of Hawai'ian culture in the twentieth century. The following examples of waves of immigration illustrate the magnitude of immigration in Hawai'i. A tax on agricultural land in Japan, introduced in 1873, impoverished many farmers leading to the immigration of 180,000 Japanese to Hawai'i between 1885 and 1924. In addition to the Japanese population, over 46,000 Chinese had settled in Hawai'i by the time of annexation in 1898. The Hawai'ian government made several attempts to curtail Japanese immigration in particular. For example, the "Gentlemen's Agreement" between Japan and the United States was signed in 1908 to prevent further immigration from Japan. However, as soon as controls for Japanese immigrants were imposed, restrictions for immigrants from other Asian countries were lifted. By 1932, for example, 126,000 Filipinos had immigrated to Hawai'i. In addition, during the first two decades of the twentieth century, 5,600 Puerto Ricans, 7,000 Koreans, and 8,000 Spaniards immigrated to Hawai'i to offset the predominance of Japanese immigrants in the territory (Tamura, 1994). Although the American government of Hawai'i sought to curb the alien influence of the Asian immigrants, the new immigrants proved themselves resilient in their efforts to take the reins of economic and political as well as educational leadership from the Americans.

Nevertheless, throughout these power struggles, the exclusion of the native Hawai'ian in the governance of education remained the one constant in the administration of the Hawai'ian system of education. The systematic subjugation of the native Hawai'ians by subsequent groups of power-holding elites, such as the *nisei* or Hawai'ians of Japanese descent, is elucidated by the following citation (Benham and Heck, 1994, p. 445):

> "The American missionaries saw a heathen society in need of Christian values and thus employed education as a means of devaluing native culture while creating their heaven on earth. The American business elite saw paradise in a governing structure in which their economic desires were met, thereby creating a school system that gave Caucasians privileges over Hawai'ians and Asians. The Democratic nisei saw education as a means to attain the benefits of such American ideals as private land ownership and economic prosperity."

The conscious creation of inequality was manifest in the dilemma faced in the early 1920s by Governor Farrington and Superintendent Givens. They were confronted with the bureaucratic conundrum of how to "maintain an elite organization on one hand, and the need to uphold the ideals, or at least the rhetoric, of democratic parity on the other" (Benham and Heck, 1994, p. 151). Both men supported opening secondary schools to instruct non-*haole* (non-whites) as long as the curriculum of those schools was heavily focused on manual labor and agricultural industry[1]. The result was the creation of the "English Standard School" by the administration of Superintendent Givens in 1924 and the institutionalization of segregation in the Hawai'ian education system. The "English Standard School", as its name suggests, was an institution conceived of as a bastion of linguistic and cultural purity (American language and culture) where whites were placed in much better supplied schools with better teachers in comparison to the schools for non-whites. The curriculum consisted of English-only academic instruction for whites and vocational education for local youths. Stueber (1981, p. 6) refers to the ideology of the colonial administration at this time as "corporate liberalism" describing the marriage of co-opting democratic rhetoric and collusion with the corporate industrial interests leading to "severe erosion" of Hawai'ian culture and community.

The education system in Hawai'i was viewed as a means to incorporate the Ha-

---

[1] In other dependent territories and countries of that time this focus on manual labor and agricultural education was known as "Adapted Education" (see, for example, Barrington, 1983, Bude, 1983).

wai'ian people into the industrial superstructure by devaluing their native culture and using compulsory education to provide for better accountability and acculturation of the youth, ensuring the socialization of American values. To this end, the expansion of secondary schooling, originally carried out for establishing vocational training, had an important additional effect on acculturation processes. They became the most prevalent sites for peer pressure which, in turn, undermined the values and native languages of native Hawai'ian parents and, subsequently immigrated parents. In thus trying to give the public schools primacy in the acculturation of Hawai'ian youth, the colonial administration sought to create "common identity across ethnic lines" (Stueber, 1981, p. 6).

The colonial school culture itself also alienated Hawai'ian children from their communal values in more direct ways. Benham and Heck point out that Hawai'ian culture favors cooperation, with learning taking place in a variety of informal and formal settings. In contrast they state that American classroom structures served to "foster individual competition [...] which forces some to lead, others to follow, while still others become marginalized" (Benham and Heck, 1998, p. 192). This erosion of Hawai'ian culture was by no means incidental, as ethnic communal life was viewed by reformers of the time as reactionary and as a barrier to social progress and modernization. Therefore, in line with the ideology of the "white man's burden" the objectives of colonial education were often clothed in the language of "social progress" which was endemic of the educational climate of the mainland U.S. during the early twentieth century.

The Interpretive Framework of the Hawai'i Case Study

It is instrumental for our case study to explore the impact of Hawai'ian, American, and Asian values on educational policies in Hawai'i. Our literature review of Hawai'ian, American, and Asian values will therefore serve us, later on, as an interpretive framework for analyzing the empirical findings of the case study.

Hawai'ian Values

It is interesting to note that when the state of Hawai'i decided to commemorate Captain Hook's 1778 expedition to Hawai'i, Governor appointee Kenneth Brown chose to commemorate the arrival by creating a Bicentennial Conference on Hawai'ian Values to rediscover the values of the Hawai'ian peoples whom Captain Cook encountered. Although this project was cut short for lack of funds, its inception is indicative of the degree to which Hawai'ians wish to revive indigenous Hawai'ian values.

George Kanahele in his book, *Ku Kanaka, Stand Tall: A Search for Hawai'ian Values* (Kanahele, 1986), tries to approach this effort through his own study of texts pertaining to Hawai'ian culture. In examining the Hawai'ian cultural tradition, Kanahele describes the value system of the indigenous Hawai'ians as being characterized by "spiritual attunement with the gods, harmony with the cosmos and nature, loyalty to leaders, unity with companions, physical and mental health, personal achievement, hospitality and generosity, and aloha" (Kanahele, 1986, p. 13). However, Kanahele does not restrict his search for Hawai'ian values to ancient Hawai'ian texts. It is in surveying present day Hawai'ians that Kanahele seeks to define a set of Hawai'ian values relevant to the lives of people whose value system has been shaped by interaction with many different groups of immigrants.

George Kanahele (1986) asked one hundred native Hawai'ians to rank values that are important to them today. The three highest-ranking values were: aloha, humility, and spirituality (Kanahele, 1986, pp. 19-20). Despite the shortcomings of Kanahele's research methods—the respondents participated at one of his "Ho'okanaka Training Workshops" and, therefore, were prompted to reflect on native Hawai'ian values—it is interesting to note that several of these values are similar to the values that Kanahele (1986) discusses for the pre-colonial period in Hawai'i. Moreover, he should be credited for abstaining from romanticizing all pre-colonial Hawai'ian values only because they are "ancient" and "traditional". In fact, he is not remiss in pointing out the rigidity of the pre-colonial value system (Kanehele, 1986, p. 16): "Some people maintain, for example, that the political system under the sacred *ali'i nui* of ancient Hawai'i was so repressive that commoners exercised almost no freedom in choosing their values, but that, rather, those were dictated to them by the chiefs and priests in power." This is attested to by the extremely rigid moral code of the indigenous Hawai'ians called *kapu*.

The *kapu* system dictated the relations between the Royal line of *ali'i* or chiefs who were regarded as living deities and the commoners. The *ali'i* could be contaminated by the slightest contact with commoners. As a result the *kapu* system consisted of a moral code which "prescribed the proper conduct for everything from land ownership to sexual relations" (Tabrah, 1984, p. x). The penalty for violating *kapu* was death and taboo actions included actions such as letting ones shadow pass over the possessions of a chief. Tabrah (1984, p. x) describes this system as follows:

> "As representatives of the gods, the *ali'i* presided over the elaborately detailed *kapu* system that regulated the everyday life and buttressed the ancient Hawai'ian religion. Because these laws were believed to be divinely given, violation was an offense to the gods and thus required punishment by death lest an offended god take his revenge out on everyone."

It is interesting to note that the *kapu* system was abolished in the same year that the American missionaries arrived in Hawai'i. In 1819 King Kamehameha purposefully committed many taboos thus overturning the *kapu* code as a result of the Hawai'ians' contact with the Western settlers. Depending on different interpretations, it is not clear whether the King lost faith in the power of the gods, was corrupted by the power of Westerners who increasingly joined his group of advisors, or sought to consolidate his worldly power in the face of worldly threats. Whichever the case, the rejection of the *kapu* and the gods could only have been triggered by a sense of profound disillusionment which the King felt in the face of American hegemony. It would be wrong to assume, however, that the rejection of the *kapu* system signaled an abolishment of all Hawai'ian values. However, the end of the *kapu* system can be seen as the end of a purely indigenous set of Hawai'ian values.

American Values

In pre -1776 America, the experience of the American colonists' economic subjugation under British rule forms the background for the formation of Anglo-American values, and those origins have had residual effects on the interplay of economic and social values in the United States to the present day. While the colonization of North America was motivated by Puritans escaping religious persecution, the American preoccupation with the concept of liberty arose, primarily, from the desire to escape the exploitative taxes placed on the American colonies by the British Crown culminating in the Stamp Act of 1765. Several scholars therefore suggest that libertarian economic forces have had primacy over liberal social forces in the establishment of American values (see Greene, 1992).

Tracing American values to the history of European settlement in the Eastern regions of the United States, however, only partially illuminates the foundation of American values. A nation of immigrants with an extensive history of slavery, racism and exclusion of African Americans, native Americans, and non-European immigration groups, the formation of American values need to be discussed against the backdrop of race relations in the United States (see Kaplan and Pease, 1993). As James D. Anderson points out with regard to the United States history of education, there are two traditions that have existed side by side. He identifies "schooling for democratic citizenship and schooling for second-class citizenship" as the two basic traditions in American education and this pattern holds true for Hawai'i (Anderson 1988, p. 1).

With respect to the mainland's colonization of Hawai'i, the forces of assimilation in Hawai'i clearly leaned more towards the goal of "Americanization" to the detriment of self-determination and democratic citizenship, and, thus pursued "schooling for second-class citizenship". The creation of a "common identity" in Hawai'i relied on the standard menu of nationalist symbols and curriculum. Throughout Hawai'i, in schools using American textbooks, the standard nationalist rituals (flying the American flag, saying the Pledge of Allegiance, and singing the national anthem) were followed.

The beginning of the institutionalized form of cultural dominance can be dated to the U.S. Marines' invasion of Hawai'i in 1893, for as soon as the Republican colonists came to power education in the Hawai'ian language was outlawed in 1896 (Benham and Heck, 1994, p. 436). However, the devaluation of Hawai'ian culture extended beyond linguistic discrimination to the realm of socio-economic relationships and communal structures. Teachers were charged with the task of conveying to Native Hawai'ian students the values of individual labor, private ownership, and individual responsibility for economic and spiritual well-being. The long-held Native belief in community (*ohana*) "gave way to valuing personal accumulation of wealth" (Benham and Heck, 1998, p. 171).

The bearers of the canon were teachers educated on the mainland and sent to Hawai'i to serve as models of American culture and language. Influenced by the Progressive Education Movement on the mainland, this influx of Progressive educators in the 1930s brought with them "progressive ideas" about equal opportunity, political participation, and school governance and earnestly introduced these ideas into the secondary school curriculum. Nevertheless, within these efforts was a hidden curriculum geared towards forced acculturation that was manifest in the degree to which Progressive educators, until the late fifties, sought to undermine the cultural heritages of native Hawai'ians and Asian immigrants.

The promotion of values education by the Progressive educators is outlined in a 1930 publication of the Hawai'i Department of Public Instruction titled, "Character Education". It is interesting that this book compares values education in the present (the 1930s) to the past, in analyzing the writings of R. Armstrong, Minister of Education in 1848, who stated "indolence" as "one of the great master evils which hinders the progress of the Hawai'ian race" (Hawai'i Department of Public Instruction, 1930, p. 18). This statement seems to indicate some effort to instill the Puritan work ethic or the value of "industry" in the native Hawai'ians.

For example, the character education project implemented at McKinley High Schools during the 1929-1930 school year was based on the "character traits" outlined in the school's "code of honor" (Hawai'i Department of Public Instruction, 1930, p. 82):

"As a student of McKinley, I stand for HONESTY in all I do and say;
for INDUSTRY in study, work and play;
for PURITY in spirit, thought and deed;
for COURAGE to meet life's every need;
for BROTHERHOOD of races all combined,
and LOVE for GOD and all mankind"

The students participated in this project by writing essays on the six "character traits" and staging a play in which the traits were personified by George Washington, Thomas Edison, Sir Galahad, Charles Lindbergh, Abraham Lincoln, and Florence Nightingale respectively (Hawai'i Department of Public Instruction, 1930, p. 84). The institution of this list of "character traits" or values is interesting, in that it parallels the development of lists of values in the character education curricula of Georgia, Virginia, and Hawai'i a half-century later. Therein lies a continuity in the evident mainland dominance of Hawai'ian values education, which suggests hints of convergence with mainland models of character education.

Asian Values

Underlying the Asian value systems is the Confucian philosophy of what constitutes a "cultivated" or "superior" person *(shi, chun-zhi)*, which combines the ideal of being both knowledgeable as well as human *(jen)*. Several scholars have examined how Confucius' philosophy has been translated into educational practice (see Hu and Robinson, 1999). Ren (1987), for example, analyzes in detail Confucian educational philosophy and finds that there is a strong emphasis on moral education. Confucius stressed the importance of teaching literature *(wen)*, behavior *(xing)*, loyalty *(zhong)* and reliability *(xin)*. Except for literature *(wen)*, these subjects are mainly focused on students' moral improvement. In his analysis of Confucian values, Ren (1987, p. 45) lists the following five characteristics that are targeted in moral education. Students should become honest and gentle, comfortable with poverty, responsible, diligent, and persevering.

In the case of Hawai'i, however, Asian values translate more concretely into Japanese values. The large immigrant populations in Hawai'i were subject to the same

Americanization efforts as the native Hawai'ians. However, from the very beginning of their presence in Hawai'i, the Japanese, in particular, made great efforts to preserve their language and culture while adapting to their new situation as residents of Hawai'i and citizens of the United States. It was this Japanese refusal to reject their native culture which led to the intense conflict over the Japanese language schools in Hawai'i. The movement against the Japanese language schools started with the xenophobic movements arising from the entry of the U.S. into World War I. Soon after, in a report issued in 1920, the Japanese language schools were accused of being "un-American". In addition, Americanizers of the time blamed them for "retarding" the *Nisei* "in accepting American customs, manners, ideals, principles, and standards" (Tamura, 1994, p. 152). However, in response the Japanese argued that Japanese sought to "incorporate the best of Japanese culture with the best of American culture" (Tamura, 1994, p. 152).

> "While Americanizers believed that language schools retarded Nisei 'in accepting American customs, manners, ideals, principles, and standards,' Japanese believed the schools advanced acculturation by teaching moral education, or *shushin*, one of the most important subjects of study in Meiji Japan. Moral values taught at language schools, Japanese correctly believed, were compatible with American values and helped Nisei become better citizens. To that end, all revised textbooks continued to advocate filial piety, duty, honesty, perseverance, industry, courtesy, cooperation, and courage. The only value that may have conflicted with American thinking was filial piety, since it subordinated the individual to the family and thereby discouraged individualism. On the other hand, respect for parents and siblings and honoring family obligations, all part of filial piety, were certainly compatible with American values" (Tamura, 1994, pp. 154-155).

What this citation illustrates is not the compatibility of Japanese and American values that Tamura (1994) seems to embrace, but rather conflicting notions of cultural adaptation (see, for example, Dawson, 1999). Where the "Americanizers" saw Japanese culture as an impediment to acculturation, the Japanese community recognized the need to revise the Japanese language textbooks being used to teach Japanese language and culture to *Nisei* in Hawai'i. Tamura (1994) reports that the teachers of Japanese language in Hawai'i complained that textbooks from Japan were "inappropriate for Hawai'i-born children", and these teachers were "uncomfortable with books encouraging emperor worship and Japanese nationalism" (p. 153). As a result in February of 1915, the Hawai'i Japanese Education Society was formed and with the help of Professor Yaichi Haga from Japan, textbooks were adapted for use in Hawai'i and were subsequently revised in 1924, 1927, and 1937. This continued until the closing of all Japanese language schools after the beginning of World War II. Thus, in contrast with other educators in Hawai'i, the efforts of the Japanese were unique in that they attempted to adapt the values education curriculum to the local situation in Hawai'i and thus enacted their own indigenization of a curriculum originating in Japan.

Values Education Policies in Hawai'i

We need to acknowledge that several values associated with Asian societies are different from American values. At the same time, we would like to point out that there is a tendency in the research literature to unnecessarily define Asian values as being diametrically opposed to American values (see, for example, Kim, et al., 1994). As other researchers have pointed out, more often than not, differences between Asian and American values are overemphasized and stereotyped (Cummings, 1989; Finkelstein, et al., 1991). This results in a binary construction of value systems in which American values of individualism, diversity, and personal freedom are placed at one end and Asian values of collectivism, homogeneity, and social responsibility are located at the opposing end. Worse, yet, are the stereotypes associated with the two value systems such as the American stereotype that Asian values epitomize blind obedience towards authority, and the Asian stereotype that American values promote immorality. It is important to emphasize that the articulation of Asian values has been conducted almost exclusively at the national and international levels; therefore, an examination of this discourse is important to frame our single case study of Hawai'i within the wider context of this regional discourse.

At the heart of the Asian values debate is the question whether there is a specific Asian conception with regard to the role of the state that is fundamentally different from non-Asian conceptions. Some have argued that in Asian countries the state embodies and, in fact, acts as the guardian of public goods and interests. Scholars emphasizing this specific model of state sovereignty, point at several Asian states that have pursued a model of the state that can be best described as one that is based on a single, state-defined ideology. For them, it is therefore not surprising that schools in many Asian societies promote values such as "orderly society" and "respect for authorities" (see Hitchcock, 1994). Critics of this supposedly Asian model of the state have not held back in pointing out the dangers of co-optation of other ideologies driven by elites' political self-interest. However, the problem lies in the dichotomy between the Asian and non-Asian conceptions of the state that the Asian values debate is assuming. There are numerous studies that critically reflect on this assumption of dichotomy and, instead, call for a more differentiated perspective that draws attention to the intersection of different value systems.

Richard Robison, for example, argues that the "'Asian Values' thesis represents one ideological pole in an ongoing political struggle between conservatism, liberalism and social democracy which straddles East and West" (Robison, 1996b, p. 307). In divorcing the debate from its ideologically anchored component, Robison and other researchers (Robison 1996a; Rodan, 1996; Freeman, 1996) have pointed out many similarities between Western and Asian values. Freeman, for example, finds that "Asian elites would not differ fundamentally from many conservative Western elites who have woven more or less genuine elements of traditional culture into the 'political formula' that legitimates their rule" (Freeman, 1996, p. 363). Further doubt is shed on the culturally relativistic argument in that some Westerners have embraced Asian values, while some prominent Asians such as Kim Dae Jung and Aung San Suu Kyi have rejected them (Robison, 1996b, p. 321). To further confuse matters, the key proponent of Asian values, Malaysian Prime Minister Mohammad Mahathir, has stated that "Asian values" were once "Western values" before the West went morally bankrupt because of rampant liberalism (Robison, 1996b). This divergence in credence in the

Asian Values thesis, irrespective of nationality and regionalism, lends support to Gary Rodan's (1996, p. 346) conclusion that "the sharp East-West cultural dichotomy is an invalid one".

Furthermore, Asian countries are not the only places where ethics is being taught. The resurgence of character education in the United States lends support for further discrediting the dichotomy which suggests that Asian countries are strongholds of moral education, whereas schools in the United States abstain from moral education, promote diversity of values, and merely focus on preparing critically thinking citizens by means of civic education. The resurgence of character education in several states and in Hawai'i is a case in point to illustrate the intersection of Asian and American value systems. While some comparativists would argue that character education is "typical" of Asian value systems, and thus view the current character education movement as a Westernized form of Asian moral education, other more domestically-oriented researchers contend that character education has been, since the 1930s, a re-curring theme in American public debates on values education (Bebeau, Rest and Nar-vaez, 1999).

The Georgia Board of Education, for example, formulated and eventually imple-mented a character education policy based on the teaching of thirty-seven "core val-ues". These values are classified in three categories: citizenship, respect for others, and respect for self. The values listed under the category titled "respect for others" are the following: altruism, civility, compassion, courtesy, integrity, honesty, truth, and trust-worthiness (Heslep, 1995, p. 122).

The moral education program developed by the Virginia Department of Education has very similar categories for the designated value set including civic virtues, per-sonal well being, and moral virtues. However, the moral education program has one key difference in comparison to the program in Georgia. Virginia's program was pro-posed within the framework of outcomes-based education with an emphasis on mea-surable outcomes and comparatively inflexible control of curriculum content (Heslep, 1995, p. 122). As the issue of moral education has traditionally been a contentious one involving the intersection of private and public life as well as religious and secular education the degree to which local communities are given the right to shape and de-termine these curricula seem to determine the success or failure of character education programs. Thus the character education curriculum in Georgia has enjoyed much wider acceptance than the curriculum in Virginia.

By 1997, character education had also made its way into Hawai'ian education policy. The movement towards promoting values education in terms of character edu-cation is evident in the Hawai'i Board of Education's adoption of a Character Educa-tion Policy (Policy 2101.1) in September, 1997 (Hawai'i Board of Education, 1997). Within that document the definition and creation of character education is prescribed in the following terms:

"Character education is the process through which students are provided opportunities to learn and demonstrate democratic principles and core ethi-cal values such as civic responsibility, compassion, honesty, integrity, and self-discipline. The Department shall identify a common core of ethical standards for student behavior and character development" (Hawai'i Department of Education, 1997).

It is interesting to note that four of the five values listed in this policy document (civic responsibility, compassion, honesty, and integrity) are identical to values listed in the Georgia character education curriculum. The Character Education Policy states that the Hawai'i Board of Education's vision of character education is characterized by a cross-curricular approach informed by the participation of school staff, students, parents, and other members of the community. However, the apparent borrowing from the Georgia curriculum calls into question the degree to which this values education curriculum was defined by local community members.

In March of 1998, the Hawai'ian Character Education Policy was linked to the Improving America's Schools Act in order to fund "Partnerships in Character Education Pilot Projects" (Hawai'i Board of Education, 1998). The Hawai'i project called "Infusing Character Education in the School Curriculum" funded seven pilot schools from around the state, which designed programs for their schools. These pilot programs were implemented in the fall of 1999 and there will be ongoing evaluation of the programs throughout the years 2000 and 2001. Schools will develop draft versions of their curriculum framework and a resource handbook, which will be ready for dissemination around the state to other schools by the end of 2001.

In addition to this project aimed towards the public school system, Punahou School, one of the most prestigious private schools in Hawai'i, developed a two-year program and disseminated it in the form of a handbook called "Character Education Handbook", written by Chaplain John Heidel and Marion Lyman-Mersereau (1994). Their work is particularly interesting because it highlights twenty-four virtues (one for each month, for two years), translates them into Hawai'ian, provides definitions, lists sources for readings and videos for each level from kindergarten to eighth grade, provides discussion questions and proverbs, then provides suggestions as to how to put the virtues into action. The Punahou curriculum is one important resource that the pilot schools are expected to tap into in formulating their own curricula (Heidel & Lyman-Mersereau, 1994).

Character education programs have been criticized for emphasizing content over teaching practices that promote social skills and the personal growth of students. The danger of creating a value set for values education for any population always lies in the un-democratic process by which the values are defined. Character education programs that focus on content have therefore come under serious attacks for compiling lists of values that purport to be American virtues, whereas in reality they are often conservative, middle-class Anglo-American values (see also Nash, 1997). Nevertheless the movement to introduce character education and moral education in U.S. schools has been quite successful. Despite vocal opposition, the National Council for the Social Studies issued a position statement in 1997 urging social studies teachers "to refocus their classrooms on the teaching of character and civic virtue" (National Council for the Social Studies 1997).

Methods and Data Source

The survey was sent to thirty-five educational elites, and thirty-one persons (values education and social studies experts in higher education and high schools) responded.[2] One third of the respondents chose not to disclose background information on their gender, ethnicity, or profession so that we do not have sufficient information with regard to the sample bias. The non-response rate was extremely high for the question regarding age; only thirteen respondents stated their age. Despite these incomplete responses, we assume that there is a sample bias towards an over-representation of female elites (thirteen females, eight males). The two other sample characteristics, ethnicity and age, seem to correspond to the features of Hawai'ian elites, who tend to be Asian American, Pacific Islanders, and over forty years old. Six elites did not indicate their ethnicity, and an overwhelming majority (n=20) of the remaining twenty-five respondents identified themselves as Asian American and Pacific Islanders. Unfortunately, the survey did not distinguish between Asian Americans and Pacific Islanders, a distinction that would have been helpful for the Hawai'ian case study. The majority of respondents are between forty and sixty years old.

This paper focuses on the analysis and interpretation of one set of survey questions (Question 4) which used a Likert scale as the method of response (range 1 – 7). Question 4 of the survey was formulated as follows: "Concerning each of the themes listed above, there are differences of opinion on content. What are your views with respect to the following controversial issues?" Following this question is a list of twenty-five items from Question 4 (e.g., "Schooling should first promote an understanding and love of nation and then teach about the rest of the world", "Schools should foster an understanding of all religions", etc.). All twenty-five items deal with themes of values education. Thus, the items measure elites' opinions with regard to which of these themes should be included or excluded in values education.

Findings

A Principle Components Factor Analysis with Varimax rotation was performed on the items from Question 4. Table 5.1 summarizes the results: five significant factors were extracted from this analysis. From Table 5.1, we see that they comprise 64.15 percent of the variance with the first 3 components encompassing the majority of these variances (22.82 percent, 14.24 percent, and 11.98 percent, respectively). In addition, we performed a scree plot to decide how many factors should be considered in the interpretation of our finding. An additional scree plot confirmed our decision to only consider five factors in our interpretation. The remaining factors would have consisted of 1 or 2 items and added very little to explaining the variance.

Included in the tables for each factor are the mean values on the seven-point Likert scale for each item in the factor. These Likert scale mean values (in the tables referred to as "means") represent the relative emphasis which respondents thought should be placed on each of the themes in values education. A numerical value of "1" indicates "very strong emphasis", a numerical value of "4" indicates a "neutral" stance, and a numerical value of "7" indicates that this item "should be left out" of the school curriculum.

[2] We would like to thank Professor Gay Garland Reed, University of Hawaii, for helping us with contacting educational elites and for her detailed and helpful comments on the first draft of this chapter. Dr. Shyril Matias was an invaluable help for distributing the surveys.

Table 5.1 Principle Components Analysis of the Sigma survey data from Hawai'i

Factor	Eigenvalue	% of Variance	Cumulative %
1	5.71	22.82	22.82
2	3.56	14.24	37.06
3	2.99	11.98	49.04
4	2.16	8.65	57.69
5	1.62	6.46	64.15

After reviewing the thematic foci for each group of items that are associated with the five different factors, we discussed the interpretation of the extracted factors. Based on these discussions and the review of literature, we chose to label the five factors as follows:

Factor 1:   Family and Community Values
Factor 2:   Gender Equality and Human Rights Values
Factor 3:   Social Cohesion and Social Harmony Values
Factor 4:   Personal Growth Values
Factor 5:   Legalistic Values

Factor 1

From Table 5.2, we can see that items 4g, 4a, 4s, 4w, 4o, 4q, and 4e load together on the first factor. This factor seems to incorporate family and community values. The Likert scale means show more preference for emphasizing familial and community values (4s, 4w, 4q, 4e) as opposed to national values (4g, 4a, 4o) although these means all range from a "neutral" value of four to a maximum value of 1.82 for "strong emphasis".

Table 5.2 Items that Load on Factor 1: Family and Community Values

Items	Loadings	Means
4g: Schools should teach young people to venerate their heroes and promote national pride	.92	3.32
4a: Schooling should first promote an understanding and love of nation then teach about the rest of the world	.83	3.54
4s: Schools should foster values supporting the family, such as respect for parents, fidelity, and taking care of children and elders	.83	1.89
4w: Schools should promote values of solidarity within communities	.77	2.50
4o: Schools should teach children to respect hierarchy and to support the government	.73	4.00
4q: Recognizing the importance of a personal pride and identity, schools should help the members of each group gain a clear understanding of their unique origins and heritage	.64	2.32
4e: As sound preparation for the world of work, habits of loyalty, obedience, hard work and punctuality need to be stressed in schools	.55	1.82

Factor 2

Table 53 illustrates that items 4u, 4r, 4x, 4m, and 4v load together on factor 2 under the direction of gender equality and human rights. These Likert scale means are all high indicating that the Hawai'ian elites in our sample wish to see the curriculum place a strong emphasis on these themes.

Table 5.3 Items that Load on Factor 2:
Gender Equality and Human Rights Values

Items	Loadings	Means
4u: Values education should encourage mutual respect between boys and girls	.87	1.50
4r: Girls have essentially the same talents as boys and should be given equal opportunities and encouragement in schools	.72	1.64
4x: Schools should help children understand they have individual rights, and that they sometimes must fight for these rights	.71	2.36
4m: Schools should teach each child the value of critical thinking	.71	1.29
4v: Schools should promote a truly global view of the world	.60	2.00

Factor 3

Table 5.4 documents that items 4h, 4l, 4c, 4b, 4i, and 4f load on factor 3. We have classified these items as measures for social cohesion and social harmony. It is important to note that items 4h and 4l have means that are greater than the numerical value 4.00 (4=neutral, 7="should be left out") indicating that respondents prefer to place less emphasis on these two themes (4h="Schools should help every child gain a deeper understanding of their own religion", 4l="Schools should help young people appreciate the essential role of unions in guaranteeing safe work conditions and fair wages") in comparison to the other themes loading on this factor. This means, they do *not* wish to emphasize students' individual religious beliefs (item 4h) nor would they like to see students being taught the "essential role of unions in guaranteeing safe work conditions and fair wages" (item 4l). This factor clearly suggests that attention should be given to social cohesion and social harmony rather than emphasizing values that the Hawai'ian elites in our sample see as socially disruptive such as religious beliefs (item 4h), unions (4l), and students' individual values (note that item 4c carries a negative loading).

Table 5.4 Items that Load on Factor 3:
Social Cohesion and Social Harmony Values

Items	Loadings	Means
4h: Schools should help each child gain a deeper understanding of their own religion	.80	4.96
4l: Schools should help young people appreciate the essential role of unions in guaranteeing safe work conditions and fair wages	.64	4.21
4c: Schools should help each child in developing their own individual values as a foundation for acceptance of broader social values	-.64	1.96
4b: Schools should foster an understanding of all nations	.56	3.21
4i: Schools should note social differences and stress the duty of the fortunate to help those who encounter difficulties	.50	2.64
4f: Schools should help children gain an understanding of all political and social viewpoints from the most conservative to the most liberal	.44	2.36

Factor 4

In Table 5.5, we can see that items 4t, 4p, and 4k load on the fourth factor. This factor includes themes of values education that address issues related to personal growth such as health education, promotion of empathy and prevention of gender stereotyping. It is important to note that the Likert scale mean for item 4k ("Girls are destined to have significant home-building responsibilities and the schools should prepare them for this future") is almost "5" (4= "neutral", 7= "should be left out"). This means that the Hawai'ian elites in our samples wish to place little emphasis on preparing girls for "home-building responsibilities". We have therefore interpreted that the Hawai'ian elites oppose gender stereotyping in school.

Table 5.5 Items that Load on Factor 4: Personal Growth Values

Items	Loadings	Means
4t: Values education should take up issues relating to human sexuality and health, such as chastity, preserving the integrity of the body against drugs and prostitution, and understanding the risks of promiscuity	.80	2.54
4p: Schools should encourage empathy for people of different ethnic, language, and social backgrounds and create opportunities for growth through shared experiences	.61	1.54
4k: Girls are destined to have significant home-building responsibilities and the schools should prepare them for this future	.55	4.93

Factor 5

Table 5.6 documents the loadings and means for items 4d and 4h. Both themes measure constitutional or legalistic values: equality before law as well as no discrimination based on class, ethnicity or religion. Both items in the factor have very high means indicating a desire for strong emphasis of these values in the curriculum.

Table 5.6 Items that Load on Factor 5: Legalistic Values

Items	Loadings	Means
4d: Schools should stress that all are equal before the law	.91	1.93
4n: It is best for schools to teach common values to all children without differentiation on the basis of class, ethnicity or religion	.56	1.68

Conclusions and Policy Implications

The results from the factor analysis lead us to confirm that Hawai'i is at a crossroads of different value systems. This applies especially for the first three factors: "Family and Community Values" (factor 1), "Gender Equality and Human Rights Values" (factor 2), and "Social Cohesion and Social Harmony Values" (factor 3).

The second factor "Gender Equality and Human Rights Values" corresponds clearly to American values, whereas the third factor "Social Cohesion and Social Harmony Values" is associated with Asian values. As discussed in the literature review section of this chapter, American values tend to emphasize, among other things: gender equality, individual rights, and critical thinking. All items measuring these values loaded high on factor 2: "Gender Equality and Human Rights Values".

We have traced an equally consistent pattern corresponding to a specific value system for the third factor, labeled "Social Cohesion and Social Harmony Values". The values loading on factor 3 are commonly referred to as Asian values. A clear example of an Asian value is item 4i, which is characterized by the downplaying of social differences and stressing obligations to "help those who encounter difficulties". The same line of argumentation can be found in two other items: Schools should understate social differences based on religion (item 4h) or social class (item 4l) in order to promote social cohesion and social harmony. The common theme of "Social Cohesion and Social Harmony Values" is the emphasis on commonalities rather than on issues that are potentially disruptive to social cohesion and social harmony. Thus, differences should be downplayed in values education, and commonalities or "broader social issues" (item 4c) should be stressed. Closely related to the emphasis on social cohesion and social harmony is the teaching of empathy and tolerance which schools should promote by helping students "gain an understanding of all political and social viewpoints from the most conservative to the most liberal" (item 4f).

There is an abundance of solid research literature discussing Asian and American values (see, for example, Ban and Cummings, 1999; Cummings and Altbach, 1997; Cummings, Gopinathan and Tomoda, 1988). However, we have restricted our review of the literature on studies that, in particular, discuss American, Asian, and Hawai'ian values in Hawai'i. Based on this review of literature, we were able to identify those values that are listed under "Gender Equality and Human Rights Values" as American values, and values loading on "Social Cohesion and Social Harmony Values" as Asian values. Nevertheless, there is a need for caution given that all societies, Asian and American alike, are multicultural, and thus, are comprised of residents of different cultural backgrounds holding different value systems. Hence, "American values" or "Asian values" do not refer to actual cultural practices in these countries but rather reflect on the cultural norms that residents, especially immigrants and minorities, are expected to assimilate to and internalize.

Whereas "Gender Equality and Human Rights Values" (factor 2) and "Social Cohesion and Social Harmony Values" (factor 2) correspond to clearly defined cultural norms in American society and in Asian societies respectively, we are not able to identify one consistent set of values within "Family and Community Values" (factor 1) that corresponds to one specific value system. Instead, we are left with a series of dazzling questions: Are "Family and Community Values" Hawai'ian values or a mixture of Hawai'ian, American and Asian values? As we will illustrate in the following, we can make a compelling case for each of these two interpretations.

First, there is empirical evidence for interpreting "Family and Community Values" as the Hawai'ian dimension of values education. Two of the seven items (items 4s, 4l) explicitly address themes that are associated with Hawai'ian values (supporting the family, solidarity within communities) because they emphasize the need to care for the community *(ohana)*. As mentioned earlier, the most recent Hawai'ian policy stresses the importance of teaching these *ohana* values. This factor can therefore be interpreted as a revival of Hawai'ian values. The highest loading items 4g ("Schools should teach young people to venerate their heroes and promote national pride") and 4a ("Schooling should first promote an understanding and love of nation then teach about the rest of the world") lend further support to the interpretation that this factor reflects a nationalistic, Hawai'ian values education revival in schools. Eric Yamamoto (1979) has characterized the resurgence of emphasis on "local culture" in Hawai'i as being focused on multiculturalism, a shared value orientation, and the creation of a new culture. Thus it can be stated that "Family and Community Values" (factor 1) reflect an emphasis on Hawai'ian "local culture". In addition, the inclusion of nationalism (items 4g and 4a) can be explained by the fact that as Wooden (1995: 128) states, "there is increasingly a strong nationalistic feeling within local culture, and an increasing polarization away from the mainland".

Second, there are also compelling arguments for interpreting the first factor as characteristic of "Pacific values" because we can see a set of indigenous and nationalistic values (items 4g, 4s, 4w) that are supplemented with Asian values (items 4o and 4e) and American values (item 4q). Two items are closely associated with Asian values because they reflect a strong work ethic including the need for loyalty, obedience, punctuality at the work place (item 4e) and demand that "schools should teach children to respect hierarchy and to support the government" (item 4o). In contrast, item 4q comprises a set of values that are associated with the American norms of individualism ("recognizing the importance of personal pride and identity") and diversity (understanding students "unique origins and heritage").

In sum, based on the interpretation of the individual items, "Family and Community Values" (factor 1) can be either interpreted as a factor that represents Hawai'ian values or as a factor that integrates Hawai'ian, American and Asian values. A closer examination of Hawai'ian educational elites, presented in the following, has led us to opt for the latter interpretation. Consequently, we feel that "Family and Community Values" should be regarded as an integration of Hawai'ian, American and Asian values, and therefore be interpreted as "Pacific values".

Eighty percent of our Hawai'ian elite sample is comprised of Asian Americans and Pacific Islanders. All but two of the thirty-one respondents agreed that there is a distinctive set of Asian values (survey question 16a), but only half of the respondents would want to see schools "make an effort to teach Asian values" (survey question 16b). What does this discrepancy between familiarity with the Asian value system and distancing oneself from this very value system suggest? Are we dealing here with Asian Hawai'ian elites who are assimilated, that is, have internalized three different value systems: Hawai'ian, Asian and American? There is much to support this interpretation.

Our investigation of the opinions of Hawai'ian educational elites has revealed interesting findings that advance our understanding of globalization processes. Globalization theories in comparative education that deal with convergence and divergence processes, tend to overemphasize the role of external forces in shaping local realities. Furthermore, these theories tend to neglect agency on the part of the local communities that resist, adapt, or modify global forces in ways that suit their local contexts. The process by which values education models have been imported and borrowed and the degree to which those models have been accepted or rejected in the Hawai'ian context is not haphazard. Bearing these shortcomings of convergence theories in mind, we would like to add that not enough has been said about the impact of migration on international convergence processes in education. Transcultural realities within a nation—in this case within Hawai'i—are as much a consequence of globalization as are the transnational flow of capital, technology, finance, media, and other spheres that are most commonly associated with globalization processes. Our Hawai'ian elite sample epitomizes transculturalism; they are transnationals. Being mostly second or third generation Hawai'ians of Japanese background, they have managed to integrate values from three different value systems. Lately, scholars in Postcolonial Studies have coined the term "hybridity" to denote this integration of different value systems. We purposefully avoid using this term in this context because it might lead to the inference that cultural spheres can be divorced and selectively adopted.

The Hawai'ian elites' integration of different value systems explains only part of our findings. It does not explain why this complex value system promoted by Asian Hawai'ian elites has found entry into the Hawai'ian policy on values education. It would be naive to assume that educational elites can simply impose their own ideas of values education on the education community. Given the contested nature of new reforms, especially in values education, it is pertinent to examine which reforms are most likely to be accepted by the local community. "Power" alone is not sufficient for understanding cultural reproduction in schools. Such an explanation falls short of explaining why the Asian Hawai'ian elites have found political support for the new policy on values education.

A closer look at "indigenization" or local recontextualization processes allows us to understand why Asian Hawai'ians were able to exert influence on values education in Hawai'i. We suggest here that certain Asian values such as emphasis on community and family values are closely related to what are perceived in Hawai'i as typical indigenous values. These Asian values have therefore found fertile ground in Hawai'i and now pass as Hawai'ian values. An analysis of which Asian values found great resonance (family and community values), and subsequently were indigenized, and which values have remained contested (e.g., respect for hierarchy) helps us to understand local resistance and adaptation processes in Hawai'i.

Coming full circle back to policy issues related to values education in Hawai'i, we now can understand why from all existing U.S. educational policy options, Hawai'ian educational elites have chosen to adopt character education that had been previously implemented in several states of the United States. The values promoted in character education—civic responsibility, compassion, honesty, and integrity—strongly resonate with Pacific values held by Hawai'ian educational elites. Although character education was adopted from other states in the United States, the values promoted in character education are closely associated with Asian values, or better, with Americanized Asian values or Pacific values. We find it noteworthy that from all educational policy options regarding values education, Hawai'ian educational elites have chosen the least American version, or, the version that is most closely associated with Asian values: character education.

We started out by searching for a factor that would manifest unique Pacific values that are quite distinct from the well known Asian and American values. What we found in our Hawai'i case study, instead, are transnational realities integrating three distinct value systems: Hawai'ian, Asian, and American. Upon reflection, we proceeded with labeling this intersection of native (Hawai'ian), Asian and American values as "Pacific values". Admittedly, this is a tentative connotation that needs to be substantiated by additional case studies in other Pacific countries.

A more "detached", de-contextualized cross-national analysis in which we compare the data from the ten participating Pacific countries is needed to further explore whether this intersection of native, Asian and American values also applies to other countries in the Pacific Rim. Pacific values might be, after all, an integration of various value systems rather than exhibiting divergence from Asian and American value systems.

Our case study highlights a particular bias in Pacific studies. Could it be, for example, that we lack research on value systems in Pacific states, and therefore unfairly compare Pacific states with regard to their similarity and difference to Asian and American value systems? Postcolonial Studies in Education certainly would suggest that we should stop seeing the Pacific states as being placed "in the middle" between Asian countries and the United States assuming that they are automatically exposed to these two "big value systems". Instead, we should place our object of study—values education in Hawai'i and other Pacific states—at center stage and analyze what is occurring around these countries. From this postcolonial perspective in which we locate the Pacific Ocean at the center, the United States needs to be referred to as an Eastern country and the Asian countries at the Pacific Rim as Western countries. Taking on the perspectives of those whom we study needs to be an imperative for comparative education researchers who attempt to be culture and context-sensitive.

References

Anderson, J.D. (1988). *The Education of Blacks in the South, 1860-1935.* Chapel Hill, NC: The University of North Carolina Press.

Ban, T. & Cummings, W.K. (1999). "Moral Orientations of Schoolchildren in the United States and Japan*", Comparative Education Review* 43(1): 64-85.

Barrington, J.M. (1983). "The Transfer of Educational Ideas: Notions of Adaptation", *Compare* 13(1): 61-68.

Bebeau, M.J., Rest, J.R. & Narvaez, D (1999). "Beyond the Promise: A Perspective on Research in Moral Education", *Educational Researcher* 28 (4): 18-26.

Benham, M.K.P. and Heck, R.H. (1998). *Culture and Educational Policy in Hawai'i: The Silencing of Native Voices.* Mahwah, NJ: Lawrence Erlbaum.

Benham, M.K.P. and Heck, R.H. (1994). "Political Culture and Policy in a State-Controlled Educational System: The Case of Educational Policies in Hawai'i", *Educational Administration Quarterly* 30(4): 419-450.

Bude, U. (1983). "The Adaptation Concept in British Colonial Education", *Comparative Education* 19(3): 341-355.

Cummings, W.K. (1989). "The American Perception of Japanese Education", *Comparative Education* 25(3): 293-307.

Cummings, W.K. & Altbach, P.G. (Eds.) (1997). *The Challenge of Eastern Asian Education: Implications for America.* Albany, NY: State University New York

Press.

Cummings, W.K., Gopinathan, S. & Tomoda Y. (Eds.) (1988*). The Revival of Values Education in Asia and the West.* New York: Pergamon.

Dawson, W.P. (1999). *The Cultural Synthesis of Liberal Democratic Ideology and Confucian Values: An Analysis of Japanese Civic Textbooks and the History of Ideological Struggle in Japan.* Unpublished Master's thesis. New York: Teachers College, Columbia University.

Finkelstein, B., Imamura, A.E. & Tobin, J.J. (Eds.) (1991). *Transcending Stereotypes, Discovering Japanese Culture and Education.* Yarmouth, ME: Intercultural Press.

Freeman, M. (1996). "Human Rights, Democracy and 'Asian Values,'" *The Pacific Review* 9 (3): 352-366.

Greene, J.P. (1992). "The Origins of American Constitutionalism", in Howard, A.E.D. (Ed.), *The United States Constitution: Roots, Rights, and Responsibilities.* Washington, DC: Smithsonian Institution Press.

Hawai'i Board of Education (1998). *Character Education, Reg. 2101.1.* Honolulu: Hawai'i Board of Education.

Hawai'i Department of Education (1997). *Character Education, Policy No. 2101.* Honolulu: Hawai'i Department of Education.

Hawai'i Department of Public Instruction (1930). *Character Education.* Honolulu: Hawai'i Department of Public Instruction.

Heidel, J. & Lyman-Mersereau, M. (1994). *Character Education Handbook.* Honolulu: Punahou School.

Heslep, R.D. (1995). *Moral Education for Americans.* Westport, CT: Praeger.

Hitchcock, D.I. (1994). *Asian Values and the United States: How Much Conflict?* Washington, DC: Center for Strategic and International Studies.

Hui-Chen, H. & Robinson, A.E. (1999). "Eastern and Western Educational Philosophies: A Comparative Study of Confucius and Dewey". Unpublished course paper.

Kanahele, G.S. (1986). *Ku kanaka, Stand Tall: A Search for Hawaiian Values.* Honolulu: University of Hawai'i Press.

Kaplan, A. & Pease, D.E. (Eds.) (1993). *Cultures of United States Imperialism.* Durham, NC: Duke University Press.

Kim, U., Triandis, H.C., Kagitcibasi, C., Choi, S. & Yoon, G. (Eds.) (1994). *Individualism and Collectivism: Theory, Method, and Applications.* Thousand Oaks, CA: Sage.

Nash, R.J. (1997). *Answering the Virtuecrats. A Moral Conversation of Character Education.* New York: Teachers College Press.

National Council for the Social Studies (1997). "Fostering Civic Virtue: Character Education in the Social Studies". *Social Studies* 61: 225-227.

Ren, S.S. (1987). *Chung Kuo jiau yu shi shian shi* [History of Chinese Educational Philosophy]. Taipei: Taiwan Shan-Wu.

Robison, R. (1996a). "Introduction to Special Issue on Politics and Economics in the Twenty-First Century: Is There an Asian Model?" *The Pacific Review* 9(3): 305-308.

Robison, R. (1996b). "The Politics of 'Asian Values'", *The Pacific Review* 9(3): 309-327.

Rodan, G. (1996). "The Internationalization of Ideological Conflict: Asia's New Significance", *The Pacific Review* 9(3): 328-51.

Steiner-Khamsi, G. (2000). "Transferred Education, Displaced Reforms". In J. Schriewer (Ed.), *Discourse Formations in Comparative Education.* Frankfurt/New York: Peter Lang.

Stueber, R.K. (1981). "Twentieth-Century Educational Reform in Hawai'i: History and Reflections", *Educational Perspectives* 20(4): 4-19.

Tabrah, R. (1984). *Hawaii: A History.* New York: W.W. Norton.

Tamura, E.H. (1994). *Americanization, Acculturation, and Ethnic Identity: the Nisei Generation in Hawaii.* Urbana and Chicago, IL: University of Illinois Press.

Wooden, W.S. (1995). *Return to Paradise: Continuity and Change in Hawaii.* Lanham, MD: University Press of America.

Yamamoto, E. (1979). "The Significance of the Local", *Social Process in Hawaii* 27: 101-115.

CHAPTER 6

JAPAN: EDUCATING FOR SOUND MINDS

Tsunenobu Ban
Mayumi Nishino

Introduction

The teaching of values is a long-standing concern in Japanese education. Japan carried on its Confucian tradition of education under Government patronage of the Tokugawa shogunate from the seventeenth century. The schools established by feudal lords put extreme stress on training for the mind using a curriculum focused on the teaching of Confucius, mainly consisting of virtues such as humanity, justice, loyalty, and filial piety.

Even after the formation of the modern educational system in the Meiji era, the Confucian values were emphasized as the basis for nationalistic moral education. The 1880 Education Order gave precedence to morals (Shushin), over other subjects and the 1890 issuance of the Imperial Rescript on Education including Confucian tenets was the most significant development in the formation of guiding principles of moral education in Japan. The Rescript stressing absolute loyalty to the emperor on every aspect of life as well as school life continued to be effective until the end of World War II.

After Japan's World War II defeat in 1945, the General Headquarters (GHQ) undertook government functions and issued a directive to remove the subject of morals (Shushin) from the educational curricula with the purpose of abolishing militaristic and ultranationalistic thinking. In place of morals, social studies was acclaimed as the core of the new curricula, and it had the formal objective of educating children for democracy. As the deletion of morals as a subject of study caused much criticism, the Ministry of Education published a handbook of moral education in 1951, and then instituted moral education as a formal subject in 1958. In spite of the formalization of moral education as a subject in the school curriculum, teachers were reluctant to implement it due to popular feelings of rejection regarding values that could be identified with the prewar military regime.

Recurrence of Moral Values

Recently there has been a resurgence of interest in moral and values education under the slogan "Educating for Sound Minds" triggered by a shocking case of murder at a junior high school in Kobe where a student killed a boy and put the cut head in front of the school gate. At the same time, the above case triggered a rush of bloodshed at the hands of junior high school students. In January 1998, a junior high school female teacher in Tochigi prefecture was killed at school with a knife by a seventh-grade student who suddenly flew into a blind rage when he was admonished for coming late to class. In March 1998 in Saitama prefecture another seventh-grade student killed a classmate out of revenge for being bullied for a long time. The opposite case of a suicide of a eighth-grader to stop money blackmail by senior students came to light in March 1998 in Chiba prefecture. These incidental cases astounded Japanese people who had always considered schools to be safe places.

Parallel to these cases, a phenomenon named *Gakkyu Hokai* (collapsed classes) at the elementary level has become known to the public through inside reports of mass media. Even the experienced teachers find it difficult to control children in class as they display behaviors such as: strolling during class, tearing up test papers, picking up quarrels with classmates over trifles, and talking loud while disregarding teachers. The causes of this phenomenon are, people think, to be considered in the context of lack of proper discipline in both home and school and of excessive emphasis on freedom of children in kindergartens.

Moral deterioration among Japanese elite has also been exposed. After the breaking of the "bubble economy" of the 1986 to 1991 period, many bribery cases of top officials at the central government such as Ministry of Welfare, Finance, and Defense have been exposed to the public eye. This phenomena posed the question about the deficiency of Japanese moral education which fails to convey basic values to the population.

In light of this situation, the Interim Report of the 16th Central Council for Education issued in March 1998, placed a strong emphasis on moral and values education with the strategic goal: "To Cultivate Children's Sound Minds to Develop a New Era—A Crisis of Losing Confidence in Bringing up a Next Generation." Although the governmental report in general steers clear of definitive references to values, it rather positively sets out the values that Japanese education should foster. It mentions that in addition to the Japanese traditional values like sincerity and diligence, the spirit of harmony, the respect for natural environment, and religious sentiments, children are expected to acquire the core of the "zest for living", which consists of the following elements:

1. Tender sensibilities to beauty and natural environment.
2. A sense of justice and a respect for fairness.
3. Basic moral sense including a respect for life and human rights.
4. Consideration for others and a spirit of social contribution.
5. Self-reliance, self-control and sense of responsibility.
6. Coexistence with others and acceptance of individual differences.

Methods and the Data Source

The sigma survey in Japan was conducted in January 1997. The questionnaire was distributed to a total of 140 elites selected from among various positions, such as central educational elites, leading educational intellectuals, politicians, people in educational institutes, academic leaders and moral educational specialists. The number of responses was forty with a rate of response of 28.6 percent. Tables 6.1 and 6.2 show the characteristics of the respondents. Among the respondents, overwhelmingly 87.5 percent of them are male. This shows that, although the number of the women working in society has dramatically increased recently, Japan is still a male-dominated society at least at the policy making level. As for age, 42.5 percent of the respondents are in their sixties, 42.5 percent are in their fifties and 15.0 percent of them are in their forties.

It should be noted that, among our respondents there are many "moral education specialists", reflecting the actual situation in Japan, thus special attention was paid to increase the number of the elites who were not particularly interested in moral education increase the number of the elites who were not particularly interested in moral education in our study. As for the work place of the respondents, 82.5 percent of the respondents live in the capital city, Tokyo.

Table 6.1 Percent of Elites with the Following Characteristics

Male	Capital City	Age in 40's	Age in 50's	Age in 60's
87.5%	82.5%	15.0%	42.5%	42.5%

Table 6.2 Percent of Elites with the Following Social Positions

Central Elite	Intellectuals Academics	Religious Leaders	NGO	Politics	Education & Curriculum	Moral Education Specialists
5.0%	27.5%	5.0%	12.5%	12.5%	20.0%	17.5%

What Are the Most Pressing Reasons for Values Education?

Table 6.3 presents the results of the respondents to thirteen items, each of which represent arguments for values education.

The highest ranked concerns were "to help young persons develop reflective/autonomous personalities", "to provide a foundation for spiritual development", and "to increase the sense of individual responsibility and community consciousness".

After the recurrent misconduct of young people in late 1990s, there has been an increasing public demand to curve juvenile delinquency. Considering the fact that Japanese educational policy today intends to reinforce moral education to solve this serious situation, it is surprising that moral education to guide "behavior in daily life" and to combat "juvenile delinquency" were ranked as second in importance among Japanese elites. These results may suggest that the expectation for values education is seen as more intrinsic than extrinsic to individuals.

The ongoing educational reform places more emphasis on reviving curriculum to cope with a more closely interconnected global information-oriented society. However, global issues in values education such as "environmental ethics", "world peace", and "information technology" received only moderate attention among elites.

Despite the fact that some values which were once highly praised in Japanese society and schooling are becoming obsolete such as "work ethics" and "national identity" among elites, other traditional values such as "family values" still received a high priority.

Table 6.3 Why Should There be Values Education?

Arguments	1st	2nd to 5th	6th to 9th	10th to13th	Total
A. information technology	0 0.0%	3 8.3%	15 41.7%	18 50.0%	36 100.0%
B. spiritual development	9 24.3%	20 54.1%	2 5.4%	6 16.2%	37 100.0%
C. orderly school	0 0.0%	6 16.7%	12 33.3%	18 50.0%	36 100.0%
D. autonomous personality	14 38.9%	17 47.2%	4 11.1%	1 2.8%	36 100.0%
E. national identity	2 5.6%	3 8.3%	19 52.8%	12 33.3%	36 100.0%
F. behavior in daily life	1 2.8%	17 47.2%	6 16.7%	12 33.3%	36 100.0%
G. juvenile delinquency	3 8.3%	8 22.2%	16 44.4%	9 25.0%	36 100.0%
H. work ethics	0 0.0%	2 5.6%	11 30.6%	23 63.9%	36 100.0%
I. environmental ethics	1 2.7%	8 21.6%	14 37.8%	14 37.8%	37 100.0%
J. world peace	1 2.8%	9 25.0%	13 36.1%	13 36.1%	36 100.0%
K. tolerance	1 2.8%	11 30.6%	10 27.8%	14 38.9%	36 100.0%
L. community life	7 18.9%	23 62.2%	6 16.2%	1 2.7%	37 100.0%
M. family life	1 2.8%	16 44.4%	16 44.4%	3 8.3%	36 100.0%

What Values Are Important to Include in Schooling?

Table 6.4 shows the answers to the question "What should be taught in school?" "Autonomy" and "ecological awareness" received the highest points, followed by "moral values " and "global awareness".

Japanese elite gave the least emphasis to the teaching of religious values in school, a response congruent with Japanese law prohibiting religious education in public schools. Most of the Japanese elite de-emphasize "national identity", issues while the attitude towards cultural diversity among Japanese elite seems to be more subtle. Overall, Japanese elites do not assign as much priority to "multiculturalism" as they do to "global awareness".

Since the educational reform in 1980s, "international understanding" has long been emphasized as an important content area in moral education. Still, the way Japanese education approaches this theme is, first, by cultivating a national identity and, then, by helping develop attitudes of tolerance towards different cultures. Therefore, Japanese elites see "global awareness" as a theme to be taught in school. On the other hand, "multiculturalism" is not seen as relevant to the Japanese curriculum, as traditional values related to a closed society still shape national culture.

Table 6.4 What Should be Taught in School?

Themes	1	2	3	4	Total
Religious values	1 2.5%	15 37.5%	20 50.0%	4 10.0%	40 100.0%
Autonomy	18 46.2%	21 53.8%	0 0.0%	0 0.0%	39 100.0%
Moral values	15 37.5%	17 42.5%	8 20.0%	0 0.0%	40 100.0%
Civic values	13 32.5%	24 60.0%	3 7.5%	0 0.0%	40 100.0%
National Identity	2 5.0%	20 50.0%	16 40.0%	2 5.0%	40 100.0%
Family Values	3 7.7%	30 76.9%	6 15.4%	0 0.0%	39 100.0%
Multiculturalism	11 28.2%	20 51.3%	8 20.5%	0 0.0%	39 100.0%
Work Values	2 5.0%	32 80.0%	6 15.0%	0 0.0%	40 100.0%
Peace	11 27.5%	25 62.5%	4 10.0%	0 0.0%	40 100.0%
Ecological Awareness	16 41.0%	23 59.0%	1 2.6%	0 0.0%	39 100.0%
Global Awareness	14 35.0%	21 52.5%	3 7.5%	0 0.0%	40 100.0%

1 Very strong emphasis (1)
2 Moderate emphasis (2-3)
3 Lower emphasis (4-6)
4 Should be left out (7)

What Are the Major Issues That Should be Considered In Values Education?

Autonomy

Table 6.5 presents the answers to the question of issues in values education. As we have already seen, "autonomy" gets highest priority regarding the "why" and "what" of values education. However, when we take a closer look at the issue of autonomy, we see subtle differences of meaning among Japanese elite. What is most striking is elite's evaluation of critical thinking, a value assumed to have a close link to autonomy. As we've already seen, there is an overwhelming agreement on the need to help children and young people develop an "autonomous personality" as a main objective of values education among Japanese elite. In contrast, there is relatively low agreement with the idea that "schools should teach each child the value of critical thinking". Although 56.4 percent of the respondents place emphasis on the importance of critical thinking, this is not as high when compared to other items, such as "solidarity within community" (62.5 percent) or teaching "common values" (72.5 percent). These results indicate that autonomy does not necessarily include goals related to "critical thinking" among Japanese elites.

Table 6.5 Which Theme Should be Emphasized in Values Education?

	1	2	3	4	Total
Religious Values					
Schools should help every child gain a deeper understanding of their own religion.	2 5.1%	14 35.9%	16 41.0%	7 17.9%	39 100.0%
Schools should foster an understanding of all religions.	16 40.0%	19 47.5%	5 12.5%	0 0.0%	40 100.0%
Autonomous personality					
Schools should teach each child the value of critical thinking.	22 56.4%	13 33.3%	4 10.3%	0 0.0%	39 100.0%
Schools should assist each child in developing their own individual values	23 59.0%	13 33.3%	2 5.1%	1 2.6%	39 100.0%
Civic Values					
School should help young people gain an understanding of all political and social viewpoints.	17 42.5%	20 50.0%	3 7.5%	0 0.0%	40 100.0%
Schools should promote values of solidarity within communities.	25 62.5%	11 27.5%	4 10.0%	0 0.0%	40 100.0%
Schools should stress that all are equal before the law.	29 72.5%	11 27.5%	0 0.0%	0 0.0%	40 100.0%
Schools should note social differences and stress the duty of the fortunate to help others.	29 72.5%	9 22.5%	2 5.0%	0 0.0%	40 100.0%
Work Values					
Habit of loyalty, obedience, hard work and punctuality need to be stressed in school.	7 17.5%	23 57.5%	9 22.5%	1 2.55	40 100.0%
It is important to highlight the role of individual competitiveness and creativity.	28 70.0%	9 22.5%	3 7.5%	0 0.0%	40 100.0%
School should help young people appreciate the essential role of unions.	9 22.5%	26 65.0%	5 12.5%	0 0.0%	40 100.0%
National Identity					
School should teach young people to salute the national flag and sing the national anthem.	12 30.0%	16 40.0%	7 17.5%	5 12.5%	40 100.0%
Multiculturalism					
Schools should help the member of each group gain a understanding of their unique origin and heritage.	25 62.5%	14 35.0%	1 2.5%	0 0.0%	40 100.0%
It is best for schools to teach common values to all children.	29 72.5%	9 22.5%	1 2.5%	1 2.5%	40 100.0%
School should encourage empathy for people of different ethnic, language and social background	34 85.0%	6 15.0%	0 0.0%	0 0.0%	40 100.0%

Table 6.5, continued

Gender and sex					
Girls should be given equal opportunities and encouragement in schools.	30 75.0%	10 25.0%	0 0.0%	0 0.0%	40 100.0%
Girls are destined to have a home-building responsibilities and schools should prepare them.	6 15.0%	17 42.5%	11 27.5%	6 15.0%	40 100.0%
Values education should encourage mutual respect between boys and girls.	29 72.5%	11 27.5%	0 0.0%	0 0.0%	40 100.0%
Values education should take up issues relating to human sexuality and health.	28 70.0%	12 30.0%	0 0.0%	0 0.0%	40 100.0%
Global Education					
Values education should stress the differences in the values of various societies and regions.	21 53.8%	17 43.6%	1 2.6%	0 0.0%	39 100.0%
Values education should stress the differences between Asian values and western values.	7 17.9%	22 56.4%	8 20.5%	2 5.1%	39 100.0%

1 Higher emphasis (1-2)
2 Moderate emphasis (3-4)
3 Lower emphasis (4-6)
4 Should be left out (7)

Civic Values

Japanese elite tend to emphasize civic values, such as equity, solidarity, and social justice in values education. Elites, however, are not as definite regarding political education. Only 42.5 percent of Japanese elite had very strong or strong supportive views on the issue "Schools should help young people gain an understanding of all political and social viewpoints."

Nationalism

In Japan the issue of nationalism has a great deal to do with symbols such as the national anthem and the flag. In this sense nationalism may have a more specific meaning in Japan than in other regions. Answers to this question may be influenced by the long-standing debate on the national flag and anthem. For instance, although the national flag is hoisted at ceremonies in most public schools, answers to our questionnaire show the ongoing struggle between preserving or doing away with long held traditions.

Religion

Congruent with the law prohibiting the teaching of religion in public schools, the item: "schools should help every child gain a deeper understanding of their own religion" received the lowest approval rating of all the issues in the list (just 5.1 percent).

Work

Elites' responses show a tendency to replace work ethics and traditional work values, such as habits of loyalty, obedience, and hard work, with "modern" values such as, "individual competitiveness and creativity". This indicates that once typical Japanese work ethics may be seen as obsolete in current Japanese society, as elites want Japanese children to be more creative and competitive in order to further Japan's economic success.

Managing Diversity

Most of the Japanese elite we surveyed, (72.5 percent) strongly approved of teaching "common values" to all children. On the other hand, 53.8 percent of the elite placed strong emphasis on teaching children the "differences in the values of various societies and regions". Close to forty-three percent (43.6 percent) were less certain.

Japanese elites seek "common" and universal values in education, and place less stress on teaching so-called "Asian values". It is often said that Japanese people are more interested in U.S. and European than in Asian values. Such tendency may help explain why Japanese elites show only moderate interest in Asian values. Another explanation of course is that Asian values are assumed to already form an important part of Japanese people life's experience, thus more interest is placed into bringing understanding from other cultures.

Gender

The data on gender values should be interpreted with caution as 87.5 percent of our respondents were male. Their responses to these items, however, indicate dispositions towards values of equality and mutual respect between genders. It should be noted that there were no female respondents who agreed with the idea "girls are destined to have home-building responsibilities and school should prepare them".

Community

There are two issues related to community values in our survey. Both of them received higher emphasis among Japanese elites. Close to 62 percent of our respondents agreed that "schools should promote values of solidarity within communities", and 72.5 percent of the respondents agreed with the issue "it is best for schools to teach common values to all children".

In the previous question related to the reasons for values education, only 18.3 percent of the respondents ranked "community life" first. This indicates that there may be important discrepancies between the theory of the values education (the objectives of values education) and what the elites see as actually being implemented.

Which Societies Should be Given Most Prominence in the Curriculum?

Table 6.6 shows the answers given to the question "Which societies should be given most prominence in the curriculum?" Naturally, Japan comes first, followed by Korea, China, the U.S., and the U.K. According to these responses, Japanese elite gives more priority to the learning of Asian values. This is an answer that potentially contradicts our previous conclusion regarding the low interest of Japanese elites in Asian values.

Table 6.6 Which Societies Should be Given Most Prominence in the Curriculum?

Societies	1&2	3&4	5&6	7	Total
Japan	36	3	0	0	39
Korea	30	9	1	0	40
China	29	10	1	0	40
USA	28	10	2	0	40
UK	22	17	1	0	40
France	18	20	2	0	40
Thailand	17	14	8	1	40
Russia	16	19	5	0	40
Singapore	14	20	6	0	40
Malaysia	11	23	3	0	37
Egypt	9	20	10	1	40
Mexico	6	23	9	0	38

1 Much prominence
7 Should be left out

How Should Values Education be Implemented?

The question on the method of values education reveals that almost 60 percent of respondents felt that it was appropriate for values education to begin at an early age.

A significant number of respondents (63.5 percent) agreed that pupils of different abilities should undergo different values education program conforming Japanese elites beliefs in tracking. The general curriculum in Japan has been centralized, consequently, the curriculum in values/moral education has been uniform over all the Japanese public schools. Our survey suggests that Japanese elite feel the need for differentiation in the values education curriculum.

Table 6.7 Views on Curricular Emphasis

	Strongly agree		Strongly disagree	
	1&2	3,4 & 5	6 & 7	Total
Values Education should begin in secondary school.	5 12.5%	20 50.0%	15 37.5%	40 100.0%
Values Education should begin at an early age.	24 60.0%	15 37.5%	1 2.5%	40 100.0%
Pupils of different abilities should undergo different values education programs.	26 65.0%	15 37.5%	9 2.5%	40 100.0%

Who Should Receive Values Education?

To the question "What group should receive values education?" a significant number of respondents see in-service teachers as prominent recipient of all kinds of values education including religious education. Children at the primary and secondary levels were given high priority regarding education in civic and moral values (see Table 6.10).

Table 6.8 What Groups Should Receive Values Education?

	Religious	Civic	Moral
Inservice teachers	46	31	30
Teacher learners	30	25	21
Young children	9	1	15
Preschool Children	23	10	30
Primary	32	47	59
Secondary level	26	60	50
High school level	30	47	20
University level	23	19	10

Weight
1st   +3
2nd   +2
3rd   +1

Where Should Values Education be Taught?

"During school as a class" scored second to "home and family". Although there is a long-standing debate concerning the incorporation of "moral education" into the curriculum, and the expectation is for teachers and schools to function as vehicles for values education, the family is seen as the moral center of society. Elites seems to think that teacher's awareness of the importance of values education should be the key to implementing effective values education. Other important settings were internships and community service.

Religious Education

Religious education is prohibited in Japanese public school. Therefore, most of the respondents named "home and family" and "outside of school activities" as a vehicle of religious education. This does not mean that religion is seen as unimportant, indeed, there was high agreement regarding the importance of religious education for "inservice teachers" and "teacher learners".

Moral Education

Respondents named "home and family", "during school as a class" and "during school through the rules" as the three most important settings for moral education. This result reflects the long-standing dispute on moral education whether it should be conducted in public school as a class or left to the home.

The answers to the question "What group should receive moral education?" show that elites think children in primary and secondary school level should learn moral values.

Civic Education

Most elites think that civic education should be included in the school curriculum. Unlike moral education, many respondents named "high school level" students as one of the important receivers of civic education. This result reflects the current curriculum in Japan, which puts more emphasis on moral education in primary and secondary school, while, on the other hand, civic education is implemented at the secondary and high school levels.

Table 6.9 Most Effective Settings for Values Education

	Religious	Civic	Moral
During school as a class	33	75	57
During school through the rules	25	49	50
Outside of school activities	21	16	7
Internships and community service	34	35	21
Camps	12	3	3
Military training and national service	2	0	0
Home and family	107	61	102

Weight
1st   +3
2nd   +2
3rd   +1

Policy Implications

Our survey is limited both by the size of the sample and by the characteristics of the respondents. Still it draws attention to some longstanding problems in values education in Japan. One interesting finding relates to "Religious Values". As previously mentioned, it is prohibited in the constitution to teach religious values in public school in Japan. Because of the restriction, most of the respondents expressed the hesitation to answer the questions related to religious values. Still, some respondents (not only the elite in the religious sector) agreed that it is important for children to learn religious values.

In fact, the Course of Study on Moral Education includes, though controversial, some religious values that are rooted in the Japanese traditional sacred feeling such as "reverence for life". In accordance with the surge of violence and bullying in school resulting in tragedies, more people expect values education to teach the importance of life. It is seen as a big challenge for values education in Japan to conduct values education without any religious bases. This is paradoxical in a society, which is traditionally deeply religious.

Another important feature is the meaning of autonomy in Japan. Autonomy has been regarded as one of the principal educational aims in Japan after the World War II. Therefore, the course of study on moral education in Japan stipulates autonomy as one of the main contents of moral education. Our survey also shows that most of the elites find autonomy an essential factor of values education. However, as mentioned before, values related to critical thinking were not strongly supported by Japanese elite. This indicates that the meaning of autonomy in Japanese society is different from that in western countries. Autonomy in Japan, does not mean to freely choose personal viewpoints, instead it means being reflective and willing to obey rules in the society (e.g. without coercion).

Moreover as it is still important for Japanese people to act in conformity with the society they belong to, autonomy in Japan also means to let citizens pursue values amongst those sanctioned by the community. This may explain why Japanese elites do not place strong emphasis on critical thinking under the values related to autonomy.

The great challenge for values education in Japan in the new century is how to encourage critical thinking in children while also preserving traditional values.

Japan has traditionally been a country with a strong work ethic. Prompted by the demands of a global economy, Japan is now struggling to transform its expectations for its work force to include not only values of hard work but also creativity an individual achievement. This shift is reflected in the final report of the Curriculum Council issued in July 1998.

Our survey shows that Japanese educational policy regarding values education is now in the middle of a transition between a curriculum including values related to globalization or traditional values. One obstacle may be a widening generation divide. Although the Japanese elite surveyed seems to approve of the new educational policy, most of them, as we have seen before, hesitate introducing critical thinking in Japanese society where "being critical" means being offensive.

The new "Course of Study", to be first implemented in the year 2002, will place more emphasis on "learning to learn", shifting its traditional focus on knowledge-centered to one emphasizing intellectual curiosity, creativity and originality, where moral and cognitive competence may be integrated under the rubric of an "autonomous personality".

Conclusions

Japan's educational reform calls for the educational system to revise its traditionally uniform curriculum to prepare the transition to a pluralistic society. This is not an easy proposition as, in spite of the introduction of a number of reforms, Japan so far has not yet achieved the development of a curriculum conducive to these purposes.

What's at stake in Japan's values education policy is the balance between individual creativity and traditional values. It seems that the goal of a pluralistic Japanese society for the twenty-first century will depend on whether Japan as a policy community will be able to build enough consensus to determine the direction of values education in this globalized era.

References

Ban, T. and Cummings, W.K. (1999). "Moral Orientations of Schoolchildren in the United States and Japan", *Comparative Education Review* 43(1): 64-85.

Japanese Institute for Child Study (1985). *Report on Lower Secondary Students Survey in the US and Japan.* Tokyo: Japanese Institute for Child Study.

Monbusho (1972). *Gakusei Hyakunenshi (Japan's Modern Educational System – A History of the First Hundred Years)* Tokyo: Ministry of Education, Science and Culture.

Monbusho (1998). *Atarashii Jidai o Hiraku Kokoro o Sodaterutameni (To Cultivate Children's Sound Minds That Develop a New Era)* Tokyo: Ministry of Education, Science and Culture.

CHAPTER 7

TAIWAN: TOWARDS A MORE RESPONSIVE SOCIETY

Hsin-Ming Samuel Huang

Introduction

Unlike values education in the U.S. or Japan, where teaching values in schools is still a controversial issue, neither the government nor the people of Taiwan have ever questioned the importance of values education. The government mandates the values that are to be taught, and it relates the successful instilling of those prescribed values to the nation's survival. Until recently, three mechanisms have been used to ensure that those values were unerringly conveyed to, and earnestly studied by, the students: a highly centralized educational system, unified school curriculum standards, and a competitive joint entrance examination system. The people have always placed the teaching of virtues above the teaching of knowledge. Academically successful students are often criticized and disdained if they are perceived as morally deficient. It is also a common belief that the values conveyed through schools are more appropriate and moderate than what may be popular outside the campuses.[1]

Nevertheless, the consensus on the importance of values education is not necessarily equal to the approval of the content. Though resistance to government-prescribed values was always suppressed in the past, such resistance remains common. In recent years, Taiwan has experienced radical changes in almost every aspect, including a dramatic shift toward political democratization since 1987 (Ger, 1998), an uninterrupted economic prosperity for a half century (Yu, 1998), and a revolutionary educational reform beginning in 1994 (Huang, 1999). Not only are the government-endorsed values facing serious challenges, but also the three above-mentioned educational mechanisms, which the government has used to maintain its values system, are dissolving.

This chapter[2] intends to establish a foundation on which to predict the focus of Taiwan's values education in the future. To do this, a study was made of the nation's social context, major features of thought, and its recent development. Our project researchers share the view that elites, especially educational elites, in most societies may either represent the mainstream or have greater influence than other parties in values education. Accordingly, the author conducted interviews and administered the Sigma Elite Survey to ask the elites in Taiwan why there should be values education, what values should receive the greatest emphasis, and how the values should be transmitted.

---

[1] For example: In the early 1990s a slogan "as long as I like, why not?", first used in a TV commercial, became the most popular phrase among adolescent throughout Taiwan. Many teachers and parents strongly expressed their concern and worry.

[2] Field studies were conducted in Taiwan during late July and August 1997, and January and June 1998.

Social and Political Context

Taiwan, also known as Formosa,[3] is considered a stateless nation[4] (Minahan, 1996). This sweet potato-shaped island, located about 160 kilometers (100 miles) off the southeast Hokkien coast of the People's Republic of China (PRC), is the world's second most densely populated nation.[5] Twenty-three million people live within 36,000 square kilometers[6] (13,900 square miles), of which three-quarters of the land area is mountainous. It lacks natural resources, relying on imports for 99.3 percent of its oil supply (Lee, 1992). Since 1945, it has been under the jurisdiction of the Republic of China[7] (ROC). To cope with the PRC's constant military threat to take over Taiwan, the ROC government has, until recently, set aside more than 40 percent of its national budget for defense (Lee, 1992). Internationally, the ROC has official diplomatic relations with fewer than thirty countries and has been rejected from participation by the United Nations, World Bank, International Monetary Fund, and most other international organizations.

Four Factors Which Shape Taiwan's Values Education

Taiwan's colonial history, political and economic development, and outside cultural influences have shaped its approach to values education. According to Ong (1979), Taiwan enjoyed independence for only twelve days before Japanese occupation in 1895. The colonial history brought diverse populations and cultures. In addition to causing tension between ethnic groups, it also fostered a unique national identity problem. In order to maintain political stability and to enhance national integration, the government strictly regulated its school system so that values disapproved by the government would not be taught. As a result, the ROC national government became the sole authoritative source for the "correct" values in school education.

Dynamic political and economic development together transformed the social structure, rearranged social order, and altered people's living style and personal relationships. The recent political democratization has released once-suppressed ideologies and allowed people to criticize the government as well as the values it advocates. Economic prosperity has caused people's attention to drift to educational issues and has increased people's interest in participating in educational policy-making. Democracy and prosperity have also opened Taiwan's society and exposed it to outside cultural influences. Newly introduced values flow vigorously into Taiwan's society

---

[3] The Portuguese named Taiwan, Ilha Formosa, which means the beautiful island, in late 16th century voyages.

[4] The British custom conventionally stamped "stateless" on Taiwanese passengers' passports.

[5] Next only to Bangladesh.

[6] That is about 660 people per square kilometer, compare to the USA, where the population density is about 22 people per square kilometer.

[7] Most people outside Taiwan confuse Taiwan with the ROC. The ROC is not the national name of Taiwan; rather Taiwan is only a very small part of the ROC's official territories. Taiwan became the ROC's 35th province in 1945. The ruling authorities of the ROC lost the Chinese Civil War and the Chinese Mainland to the Communists in 1949. Since then the ROC controls only Taiwan and a few islets.

through flourishing mass communication media.[8] While the colonial history has formed the basis of Taiwan's values education, the development of the other three aspects, political democratization, economic prosperity, and outside cultural influences, provided impetus for change.

A History of Colonialism

Taiwan's colonial history can been seen as a history of Chinese immigration to Taiwan. In the early seventeenth century, Taiwan was covered with primitive forests and mainly inhabited by aboriginal tribes, believed to have descended from Indo-China or Malay-Polynesia thousands of years ago. The earliest two colonial powers, the Dutch (1624-1661), who occupied the south-west part, and the Spanish (1626-1642), in the north, first encouraged coastal Chinese to immigrate to the island to become plantation workers.

Later, Zheng Cheng-Kong, also known as Koxinga, a warlord loyal to the Chinese Ming Empire who was defeated by Manchurians, forced out the Dutch and established a Chinese kingdom in Taiwan (1661-1683). The Manchurian Empire finally dissolved Zheng's kingdom and annexed Taiwan into its territories (1683-1895). In 1895, Taiwan was ceded to Japan (1895-1945) as the result of the 1894 Sino-Japanese War. In 1912, the Chinese Nationalist Party or the Kuomintang (KMT) overthrew the Manchurian Empire and established the ROC on the basis of the Empire's territories. In 1945, the ROC acquired Taiwan from Japan on behalf of the Allies.[9] The KMT later lost the Chinese civil war to the Chinese Communist Party (CCP) and fled to Taiwan with its entire government and two million non-Taiwanese speakers during the year of 1949. Before that time, Mandarin, the ROC's sole official language, was foreign to the approximately six million Taiwanese residents.

Uninterrupted Economic Prosperity for a Half Century

Despite its defeat in China and its international isolation, the ROC on Taiwan has achieved remarkable prosperity and democracy. International media and academia praised Taiwan's economic success as "Taiwan Miracle" (World Bank, 1993). The average economic growth rate overall from 1952 through 1995 was 8.63 percent. Such an astonishing rate of growth has seldom been seen in other countries (Yu, 1998). Taiwanese annual per capita income rose from less than US$100 in 1949, US$186 in 1952, to US$1,193 in 1977 and to over US$12,000 by 1998 (Ger, 1998). Its trade amounts to US$220 billion a year and it has almost no foreign debt. While the "Asian Financial Crisis", beginning in mid 1997, swept down most other east or south-east

---

[8] Cable television stations were legalized only after the passage of the Cable Television Law in 1993. In 1999, Taiwan had more than 70 television stations, with more than 100 satellite channels, and all compete for the news audience. At one time, as many as eight of these stations were devoted wholly to news 24 hours a day (Teng, 1999). The U.S. has a population 12 times more than Taiwan, yet the Cable News Network (CNN) is the only 24 hours news channel.

[9] After the War, the U.S. on behalf of the Allies put Japan into its trustee. Because the ROC occupied Taiwan through the same means as the U.S. did on Japan, the people who promote Taiwan independence argue that the ROC does not have legitimacy to permanently put Taiwan under its jurisdiction.

Asian nations, the International Monetary Fund (1998) rated Taiwan the third least
"painful" economy in the world. Its misery index lies behind only those of Singapore
and Switzerland. At the end of January 1999, the island's foreign exchange holding
rebounded to US$91.92 billion, third highest among world's economies (Shen, 1999).

Moreover, Taiwan's rapid economic growth is combined with equitable distribution of wealth and low unemployment. The ratio between the household income of the
top fifth and the bottom fifth is the most popular instrument to measure a society's
wealth distribution. In 1995, the ratio was 5.34 in Taiwan, only 0.01 higher than that
of in 1964 (Directorate General of Budget, Accounting and Statistics, 1995). During
the latter half of the 1980s, the unemployment rate dropped below two percent and a
labor shortage emerged, forcing Taiwan to begin employing foreign laborers (Yu,
1998). Although the Asian Financial Crisis did have an impact on Taiwan's economy,
for all of 1998, the unemployment rate was kept at 2.69 percent (Cheng, 1999), a
lower unemployment rate than is seen in most of the world.[10]

Dramatic Shift toward Political Democratization Since 1987

Taiwan's political democratization is no less impressive than its economic performance. The transition from authoritarianism to democracy without major social
upheaval is unparalleled (Alexander, 1998). When the ROC government moved to
Taiwan in 1949, it enacted the "Measures to Eradicate Espionage during the Period of
Communist Rebellion". Until the repeal of Martial Law in 1987, Taiwanese suffered
from nearly 40 years of "white terror" (Hsieh, 1999). Many people were sentenced to
tens of years in jail for offenses as minor as making a political joke or being friends
with a political dissident (Hsieh, 1999).

The lifting of Martial Law revitalized Taiwan's society (Ger 1998). The struggles
of political dissidents and democracy advocates finally dissolved the authoritarian political system of the KMT government and drove the ruling authorities to initiate a
series of political and legal reforms (Tien and Chu, 1994). In today's Taiwan, the people are guaranteed civil liberties, freedoms of assembly, association, speech, and publication, and the right to hold demonstrations and strikes. A recent constitutional interpretation by the Council of Grand Justices even extends freedom of speech to advocating the overthrow of the government.

Popular elections are held regularly at all levels. The voting rate in most elections
averages around 70 percent. It is the governments' obligation to register all eligible
citizens to vote and to provide each candidate a minimal exposure to the voters.[11]
Through the flourishing mass media (Teng, 1999; Wang, 1999) and political campaigns that cut no corners, political and societal issues inundate Taiwanese daily life.

---

[10] During the 1990s, for most West European nations, the unemployment rates have been
around 20 percent. For its best record during 1990s, the unemployment rate was about 5 percent in the U.S.

[11] After each candidate's slot number is picked, the authority concern is accountable to mail
each voter a list, which includes a verified background information and platform provided by
each candidate. The local government in each district is mandated to organize equal amount
of public speeches for each candidate. In 1998 Congress election, the Taipei city extended
this service to television. The purpose is to make it as fair as possible for less wealthy candidates.

Under Taiwan's unique "multiple seats, single vote" district[12] system in its representative elections, empirical statistics[13] show the bigger the district is, the higher percentage of citizens went to vote, the better the voters can have the candidates they support elected.[14] Comparably speaking, Taiwan's Congress is more reflective of the demographic and ideological structures than are elected bodies in North America.

Vulnerable to Outside Cultural Influence

Probably due to its colonial history, trade-oriented economy, and geographic location, Taiwan's most important outside influences have been from classical China, Japan, and the United States. The Taiwanese share substantial cultural heritage with Hokkien and Canton Chinese. Since 1949, when the PRC engaged in the "Cultural Revolution", which aimed to destroy traditional Chinese culture, the ROC has made every effort to preserve classical Chinese culture on the island. Nevertheless, modern China has much less cultural influence on Taiwan's society than Taiwan has on its. The Taiwanese seem more interested in China's past than its present.

Fifty years of Japanese colonialism not only left Japanese food, clothing, music, and living style, but also the Japanese language and cultural values. The samurai spirit[15] and frugality are examples. A great number of senior Taiwanese were educated in Japanese or in Japan and tend to praise Japan rather than China. As it recovered from the destruction of World War II, Japan impressed the world with its economic success and technological prowess. Unlike the Koreans, and despite the unwillingness of the KMT government, the Taiwanese enthusiastically embraced Japanese innovations and spirit.

Taiwan's newest and the most prominent influential power must be the United States. To the younger generation, the U.S. virtually represents the Western World and symbolizes modernism and fashion. The U.S. was the KMT's major political and military supporter from 1949 to 1978. It provided shelter for Taiwanese political dissidents until recent democratization, and satisfied Taiwanese demand for higher education (Huang, 1999). These factors facilitated the spread of U.S. culture to Taiwan and secure its dominant position among western influences on Taiwan.

---

[12] Western political scientists name it "Single-Non-Transferable-Vote" system. In Taiwan, the election district was drawn according to the administrative boundary. For district with larger population, it may have more than one seat for people's representatives. Regardless of the number of seats open, a voter can only vote for one individual candidate. By that it assures each vote has the same value.

[13] Related electoral information and statistics can be obtained from the ROC's Central Election Commission. http://www.cec.gov.tw/

[14] In the second electoral district of Taipei City during the December 1998 Congress election, for example, thirty candidates competed for ten seats. Totally 617,189 out of the 722,224 valid votes cast went to the ten elected. Since each voter can only vote for one candidate, it implied about 85.5 percent of the voters had their supported candidates elected.

[15] Taiwanese conceive the major features of samurai spirit to be loyalty, sacrifice, frugality, courtesy, and bravery.

National Identity Conflict Problem

Interrelated with the above-mentioned factors, the single most important problem is a unique national identity conflict among the people of Taiwan. Since the Chinese immigrated to Taiwan in late Ming and early Qing dynasties, the people of Taiwan have faced three major political identity crises. The first was the split of loyalty between the Chinese Ming and Manchurian Qing dynasties, the second, after 1895, between the Japanese rulers and the Sino-nized Manchurian Empire. Finally after the "February 28 incident"[16] and the 1949 defeat of the KMT on the Chinese mainland and fled to Taiwan, the Taiwanese people were once again torn between Taiwan independence (TI) and reunification with China (Huang, 1995; Chiou, 1994). The identity issue was further complicated by the dispute over the interpretation of "one China" between the Nationalists and the Communists, and the divisions between the ethnic Taiwanese and ethnic Chinese identities.

Taiwan independence advocates have long challenged the legitimacy of the ROC government's rule over Taiwan. They charge that the ROC has neither sufficient legal bases (Shen, 1995)[17] nor Taiwanese consent to rule. In their view, China and Taiwan are two separate nations,[18] so they demand the right of self-determination from China (whether it is the ROC or the PRC). On the other hand, the pro-reunification people condemn the TI supporters as "offspring with no filial piety" of Chinese ancestry. They denounce the idea of Taiwanese as not Chinese or the pursuit of TI as simply an unforgivable sin.

Emergence of the "New Taiwanese"

This problem missed its opportunity for resolution during the years of authoritarian rule. After democratization, the once-suppressed opposing voice was released and has caused escalated tension between different identity groups in almost every single political event.

Ironically, since the contact across the Taiwan Strait was reestablished in 1987, the number of people in Taiwan who rediscovered their Taiwanese consciousness and felt alien to China has significantly increased. The term of "New Taiwanese" emerged in the political arena (Legislation Yuan, 1996; Gau, 1998). Both past Taiwan Province Governor Soong and current Taipei City Mayor Ma were Mainland Chinese-born.[19] The governor employed this term in his 1994 campaign while the mayor raised it right

---

[16] On February 28, 1947, an island-wide rebellion arose to demanding more autonomy. On March 8, 1947, Chinese reinforcement troops arrived at Taiwan on U.S. transport ships and started a brutal suppression. This event is called the 2-2-8 incident or massacre and was believed to be the initiative of the modern Taiwan independence movement.

[17] The San Francisco Treaty does not regulate the ownership of Taiwan. The Cairo Declaration is the only legal base for the Chinese authorities to declare sovereignty over Taiwan. Nevertheless, it was discovered to be an unofficial document because no national delegates signed (Shen, 1995).

[18] The ROC government refuted this argument until July 9th, 1999, in an interview with a German radio station Deutsche Welle, ROC President Lee Teng-hui defined cross-strait relations with the PRC as a "a special state to state relationship." See Sinorama, v.24, n.10 pp. 73-76 for detail (Chen, 1999).

[19] Soong was born in Mainland China. Mar was born in Hong Kong.

before the eve of the Election Day in early December 1998. They both defeated their ethnic Taiwanese opponents despite the fact that Chinese mainlanders and their off-spring consist of only about 14 percent of Taiwan's population.

Although the "New Taiwanese" phenomenon can be seen as a political strategy used by ethnic Chinese candidates to attract votes from ethnic Taiwanese, it also sym-bolizes the rise of Taiwanese national identity or consciousness, which seriously con-tradicts Chinese nationalism, the most emphasized value in Taiwan's education for a half century.

Major Values Taught in Schools

The three doctrines of the ROC's prescribed values system in education are: tra-ditional Confucian morality and teachings, Chinese nationalism, and a living style of democracy and modernism. This can be verified by the PRC Constitution[20] (1947), its national purpose of education[21] (Gou-min-zhen-fu, 1929), the repeatedly revised school curriculum standards, and other values related educational mandates. Among the three doctrines, Chinese nationalism is the top principle. Since Confucianism is an inalienable part of Chinese tradition, it contributes to Chinese nationalism because it can promote a sense of Chinese identification. Democracy and modernization are the founding goals of the ROC; they contribute to the modern aspect of Chinese national-ism.

Traditional Confucian Morality and Teaching

Confucianism is the essence of traditional Chinese culture. Since the KMT takes the stance as the protector of the Chinese cultural heritage, it heavily emphasizes Con-fucianism in schools. The major content of the Confucian morality and teachings in-clude, but are not limited to, the four *Wei* (ethical principles) and eight *De* (cardinal virtues), the three *Gan* (bonds) and five *Chang* (constant virtues), and, though always implicitly, a rooted "literate official"[22] (*sh-dai-fu*, in Mandarin) value. Those teachings are all extracted from the traditional Confucian schooling and have been systemati-cally summarized, phrased together, and interpreted in a way easy to remember so as to increase acceptance.

---

[20] In the ROC Constitution (1947) article 158 states: "Education and culture shall aim at the development among the citizens of the national spirit, the spirit of self-government, national morality, good physique, scientific knowledge and ability to earn a living. "Generally, the na-tional spirit here refers to nationalism. The spirit of self-government and national morality are included in Confucius schooling, while the others can be seen as part of modernization.

[21] The official national educational purpose (Gou-min-zhen-fu, 1929) affirms, "the purpose of the education of the Republic of China is according to the 'three principles of the people', to materialize people's livelihood, sustain the society's vitality, and develop populace's eco-nomic living and continue our nation's life. We determine to achieve national independence, prevailed civil rights, developed commonwealth, and then to promote world harmony." The "three principles of the people" are the teachings bequeathed by Dr. Sun Yat-sen, the found-ing father of the ROC. It advocates building a democratic republic of the people, to be gov-erned by the people and for the people (ROC Constitution, Article 1, 1947). Its content is na-tionalism, democracy, and livelihood.

[22] Literally, sh-dai-fu means a learned government official. It refers to getting government post, considered the most prestige position in imperial time, through education.

Each *Wei, De, Gan,* or *Chang* symbolizes a virtue and some may overlap with each other. Notice the following translation is only the closest meanings in English. The three *Gan* refer to the bonds or relationship between ruler and subject, father and son, husband and wife. The five *Chang* are *Ren* (humanity/benevolence), *Yi* (righteousness/justice), *Li* (propriety), *Zhi* (Wisdom), and *Xin* (sincerity). The four *Wei* are *Li* (propriety), *Yi* (righteousness or justice), *Lien* (honesty), and *Chih* (sense of shame), considered as the norms for personal behaviors. The eight *De* are *Zhung* (loyalty), *Xiao* (filial piety), *Ren* (humanity), *Ai* (philanthropy), *Xin* (credibility), *Yi* (righteousness/justice), *He* (harmony), and *Ping* (peace).

The "literate official" value originated from feudalism, referred to either scholarly civilians or educated warriors, loyal to their landlord. It demands the qualities of an educated people "to investigate things, then to achieve true knowledge; thereafter to set right your heart and make your will sincere; thereafter to cultivate personal life and regulate your family; thereafter to rule the nation in order, then to subjugate the world" (Da Xue) [23] During Chinese imperial period, it advocated the ideal of earning a civilian post through learning Confucian classics as the most prestigious channel to esteem oneself. The meaning of the term evolved into a concept of getting academic credentials in order to secure prestigious social status. The teaching reads, "every other career is at low rank, only scholarship is the highest". For most of the time, it functions to tempt students to study with the promise of earthly rewards (Miyazaki, 1976).[24]

Chinese Nationalism

In general, Chinese nationalism can be characterized as both a political and cultural ideology that advocates a strong Chinese identity, inclusive Chinese membership, and the aspiration to have an invincible China. Modern Chinese nationalism was stimulated by the invasion of Western imperialism in the late nineteenth century. It was further strengthened by the loss of the 1894 Sino-Japanese War and the Japanese invasion of 1937 because the Chinese had long seen Japan as a small and inferior nation.

The early teaching of Chinese nationalism applied to ethnic Han peoples only. Sun Yat-sen, the founding father of the ROC, and his followers prescribed the aim of the founding mission of the KMT: "to drive the alien Manchurian enemies away from China" and "to restore Chinese sovereignty". Nevertheless, after the ROC inherited the territories of the Manchurian Empire, Sun broadened the definition of Chinese nationals and claimed that the Republic of China be a "five peoples' republic".[25] Since then,

---

[23] Extracted from Da-Xue or "the Great Learning", one of the four Confucian classic readings. The translation may have different interpretations. This teaching was written two thousand years ago when China was in a feudal system. "Family" may refer to a big household including a large number of relatives and subjects. "Nation" may refer to the feudal landlord or a kingdom.

[24] The most classic and vivid description of this function could be a poetic prose written by a Chinese emperor in Sung Dynasty. The prose, titled "the pleasure of studying," says: "In books are found houses of gold...In books there are girls with faces of jade. A boy who wants to become a somebody, devotes himself to the classics, faces the window, and reads."

[25] The five peoples refer to the five major ethnic groups residing in the territories of Manchurian Empire: Han, Man (Manchurian), Mon (Mongolian), Hui (Moslem), Zhan (Tibetan).

the line between cultural ethnic identity and political national identity has blurred. Chinese membership includes not only the Han people but also all the other ethnic groups residing in Chinese-controlled territories and those who have Chinese origins or were once ruled by past Chinese empires.

Deeply implanted with this ideology, the ROC government was embarrassed when they encountered remnants of Japanese influence remaining in Taiwan. In order to force Taiwanese to become Chinese, the KMT adopted an assimilation policy similar to the one the Japanese adopted for the Taiwanese (Yang, 1994). In schools, the only language allowed was Mandarin. The native tongue was considered savage. The school curriculum overwhelmingly emphasized traditional Chinese literature, Chinese history and Chinese geography. Taiwanese students were exposed daily to teachings that showed China as having the most beautiful literature and classical culture, a glorious imperial history, the most intelligent people, the richest national resources, and as being the best place in the world to live. Until the introduction of the "native soil" program, which teaches native culture and languages, and the "discover Taiwan" curriculum, which focuses on Taiwan's history, geography, and society, around 1996-97, Taiwan had hardly any importance in the school curriculum (Lee, 1998; Legislation Yuan, 1994; 1996; Lee, 1993).

Democracy and Modernization

The third most important doctrine is the new living style, which embraces the values of democracy and modernization. This sounds contradictory since for decades the KMT had ruled Taiwan with an iron fist. Nevertheless, as described earlier, democracy is one of the founding principles of the ROC. Dr. Sun Yat-sen persistently advocated the four political rights of the people: election, recall, initiative, and referendum. Since the ROC's founding, there has been an explicit design of a three-stage-plan toward democracy. They are, in order: military, tutelage, and constitutional administration. Chiang Kai-shek, who regarded himself as Sun's official heir, tried to accelerate the procedure. Under his efforts, the ROC Constitution was drafted in 1936, and ratified in 1947. In his mind, democracy meant ruling by laws.

Democratic Practice from Elementary Schools

In the educational domain, the teaching of democracy begins in the early elementary level. In Taiwan, a class of students is not just a teaching unit but also a stable student organization that consists of a group of students who own the classroom and eat, rest, and take most of the classes there. At the very beginning of each semester, under the assistance of the class advisory teacher assigned exclusively for their class, the students elect their own officers, set up a student government, collect and manage their own class dues. A general class meeting once per week is part of the formal curriculum. The student officers are accountable to give reports about their duties and answer questions raised by their classmates. By this, students experience some of the basic democratic processes such as to raise issues, to place motions, and to discuss matters related to their class.

At the secondary level, the students are required to write journals and submit them to the class advisory teacher each Monday. Following the pre-designed format of the journals, students record the major national news of the past week, examine their own academic progress, and give comments on any matters they want to address. The class advisory teacher is required to read the journals and give feedback to the students. This establishes a regular communication channel between the students and the advisory teacher. In senior high schools, the school authorities are obliged to help students set up a "united class committee" to serve as the school-wide student representative body. The chair or the president of the committee, in theory, enjoys parallel status with the school principal.

Another distinct feature of Taiwan's schools is the establishment of a "cooperation society" within almost every public school. This society manages the business of retail stores in the school. Every student, staff person, and faculty member of that school is a shareholder of that "society". The board of the cooperation society is accountable to hold shareholder meetings on a regular basis, give reports, and distribute a certain portion of profits to its shareholders.

The New Life Movement

The "New Life Movement" was initiated by Chiang Kai-shek in 1934. He intended to use this movement to correct the four Chinese problems: poverty, ignorance, selfishness, and weakness, by modernization and discipline in daily life (Common Wealth, 1991). He borrowed the traditional four *Wei*, gave them new interpretations, used them as the principal disciplines, and mandated that all levels of schools adopt them as the common school mottoes. In his interpretation, *Li* (propriety) implies a well-behaved (gentleman-like) attitude; *Yi* (righteousness/justice) implies proper conduct, *Lian* (honesty) implies strict distinction of right from wrong, *Chih* (sense of shame) implies thorough awareness. "Neat, clean, simple, plain, prompt, and valid" are the criteria. All of these teachings have been seamlessly integrated into the KMT-prescribed curriculum standards and textbooks at all levels.

Recent Developments

Although the KMT's values education is thorough, strongly supported with political power, and has achieved considerable success, resistance and criticism have always existed. The teachings of Confucian morality and paragons, once the mainstream of moral education, have been brought into question. Ou Yung-sheng, president of the National Taipei Teacher College and chairperson of the "morality committee" of the National Institute for Compilation and Translation, also one of our interviewees, charged that many historical or legendary paragons used in textbooks are actually promoting problematic values that may become divorced from current realities (Li, 1998). [26]

---

[26] Ou questioned many role models from literature and history seen in school textbooks, for instance, Hua Mulan was guilty of misrepresentation, Kuang Heng's "knocking a hole in the wall to steal light" for study involved "the destruction of public [should be private] property" (Li, 1998, pp. 120-121). Even more serious is the story of Guo Ju, who planned to bury his beloved son alive in order to concentrate on looking after his aged mother. Hua Mulan was a legendary girl who joined the army in her father's place. Kuang Heng was a high-ranking civilian and scholar in Han Dynasty. In his early age, too poor to afford a light at night, he

In the political arena, Chinese nationalism is a major target of criticism. Under Chinese nationalism, native tongues were banned in schools. Taiwanese literature, history, geography, and culture had almost no place in school curricula (Lee, 1998; Legislation Yuan, 1994; 1996). The suggestion to extend the teaching of English to elementary school was turned down because of the fear of possible negative influence on students' Chinese identity.

Simultaneously, the Taiwanese demanded that the government enhance educational quality and expand higher education. On April 10, 1994, a decisive demonstration for these purposes was organized by Huang Rong-tsun, at that time a professor in the National Taiwan University, and currently head of the Division of Humanities of the National Sciences Foundation, also one of our respondents. This demonstration lit the fuse of a revolutionary educational reform.

Revolutionary Education Reform Since 1994

In the same year, the government had the Seventh National Educational Conference and launched a major education reform. Based on a recommendation from the conference, the government formed a cabinet-level mission-oriented Evaluation Committee for Education Reform (ECER). In December 1996, the Committee (1996) submitted its final report to both the Executive Yuan and Legislation Yuan and recommended an "unfasten policy" (removing restrains) for almost every aspect of education.

The "unfasten policy" is a response to the criticism of the KMT controlled educational system, officially mandated textbooks (Chen, 1997; Chen, 1995; Zhou, 1994), and the Joint Entrance Examinations. It aims to liberalize Taiwan's educational administration by decentralizing the educational system, allowing free competition for school textbooks, granting schools or local authorities the right to set up their own curriculum, and most importantly, abolishing the joint entrance examinations. These recommendations pleased both people within and outside the government. Nongovernment organizations saw it as a chance to fulfill their educational proposals. On the government's part, after democratization, as education is no longer an effective means to control ideologies, it was willing to decentralize the educational system to unload its responsibility. From 1994 to early 1999, the KMT has twice replaced the minister of education to bring more reform. Some reformists now have complaints that some changes are too radical.

Extensive Curriculum Standard Revisions

Along with educational liberalization, new values generated from inside the island, or introduced from outside, have received greater attention than before. Accord-

---

drilled a hole to his neighbor and got the light to study. Guo Ju's story is one of the "24 paragons of filial piety," a compilation of legend and true stories used to teach filial piety. Encountered famine, Guo Ju and his wife decided to sacrifice their son to save the food for his mother. No sooner than he was digging to bury his son alive, he found gold under the ground, interpreted as an award by the heaven for his "virtue." With the gold, he then could well support both his son and mother.

ingly, the government revised its curriculum standards[27] to add new values and/or modify many old values. Filial piety, of which the spirit is obedience to the parents, for example, has been replaced with "filial respect" (MOE, 1993). What attracts most attention is the implementation of the "native soil" curriculum and "understand Taiwan" program. They reflect the rediscovery of Taiwanese consciousness and the KMT's indigenization.

The Sigma Elite Survey

The above review of the social context including recent developments and the major feature of Taiwan's values education suggests that many old values are destined to be modified, and that newly introduced values will be strengthened. Despite all the changes, the government still mandates the curriculum standards and the three most important KMT values. Will this situation continue, or is change just a matter of time? So far, there are many other important values we did not cover, for example, the attitude to religions. The Sigma Elite Survey has a broader focus and would be a useful reference for possible answers.

The Taiwan team conducted the Sigma Elite Survey based on the assumption that a survey of a carefully selected elite group's attitude and opinion of values would be useful to predict the future development of values education, since they are always influential people in terms of policy making. To better interpret the results of the survey, the author first acquired an understanding of Taiwan's values education and social context through multiple sources. In addition to the literature related to Taiwan's politics and economics, the research began with the collection of official documents from the Ministry of Education and Congress in Taiwan. Comments and reports from official or prestigious magazines and newspapers helped in grasping the big picture of current educational practice and reform. Thanks to Taiwan's highly centralized educational system and open society, the information we obtained has high validity.

Before conducting the survey, the field study started in August 1997. The author interviewed two prominent educational scholars, two members of congress who were on the education committee, two division heads of central government's cultural or education department, and one executive director from a non-government organization for educational reform. In January 1998, the questionnaires were delivered to eighty-six carefully selected people by mail or in person. In June 1998, the author sent out an international comparison and a brief report written in Chinese to the thirty-one respondents and conducted seven follow-up interviews in Taiwan. Follow-up interviews were conducted to collect more information and to clarify the ideas of the respondents with special opinions.

Content of the Questionnaire

The questionnaire was developed collectively by the international team. The purpose was to ascertain why elites in these countries felt the need for values education,

---

[27] The Ministry of Education published its revised elementary school curriculum standard in September 1993 and implemented it in August 1996; junior high published in October 1994, implemented in 1997; senior high published in October 1995, implemented in 1998.

what content they deemed appropriate for values education, and how and when they felt it could best be taught. The author translated it from English to standard Chinese and pre-tested it with several native Chinese speakers to ensure its accuracy in translation.

Methodologies

In developing the sample list, based on the project agreement, respondents were sought from nine groups: central educational elites, leading educational intellectuals, religious leaders who have educational positions, leaders of related non-government organizations, politicians, people in educational institutes, academic leaders, curriculum designers in values education, and values education specialists.

The Taiwan team used these definitions: the "central educational elites" referred to the people who had some role in educational policy making at the central level. "Leading educational intellectuals" referred to the people in the field of education who might not have held offices but were influential. Among the "politicians", the ones chosen were only those who were at the central level and influential in educational policy-making. The "people in educational institutes" were those who might not have held positions of educational leadership at that time, but could represent a certain influential elite group or had potential to be influential in the near future. Some younger professors or researchers, below forty, fit into this category. In the category of "academic leaders", selections were made solely from the deans, presidents, or prominent professors in the schools of education or teacher colleges.

For the major purpose of this study, to predict the future focus and development of Taiwan's values education, the author applied additional criteria to select the sample. With the exception of the "people in educational institutes", "curriculum designers in values education", and "values education specialists", the respondents must have been of great influence on Taiwan's education. Although these three groups of people represent the largest population and can be influential in some ways, based on the definition, they did not hold decisive power in policy making at that time. To prevent them from over-represented, and yet being careful to include their ideas, they were selected not to exceed 15 percent of the whole sample. Keeping strictly to these definitions and standards, eighty-six respondents were finally chosen.

A special feature of Taiwan's elite sample is that a large number of them have multiple positions, especially those in the field of education. For this reason, their categories were assigned according to their main positions. The decision was made using two criteria. The first was the position in which the elite was most active. The other was according to the elite's self-preference or self-identification. As a result of the respondents' descriptions, no one was assigned to the categories of "curriculum designers" or "values education specialists". However, some respondents' names are listed as committee members for the official curriculum standards and some have publications on values education.

It was difficult to expect a high level of cooperation from a group such as this. The list includes the highest political authorities, the most distinguished scholarship, and the most influential spiritual figures in Taiwan. It also includes nine congress people from three major parities, presidents of normal universities or teacher colleges, deans of schools of education, and prominent professors. Younger professors were more willing to help, but they were limited in number. The researcher also suffered from time constrains. This survey was conducted during the Taiwan's lunar New Year, traditionally the longest holiday for families. To increase participation, before or during the time the questionnaire was sent out, the author made some 300 phone calls and tried to build connections through secretaries, or colleagues. When a connection was built, the surveys were delivered in person. About one third of those on the list were reached directly by phone or in person.

Description of Respondents

A total of thirty-one of the eighty-six prospective respondents returned a completed survey for a response rate of 36 percent. It would be a risk to assert that this small sample could represent the elite group intended. However, after examining the respondents' background, it is encouraging to find that the distribution is similar to that of the Taiwan's active influential elite structure as conceptualized by gender, age, position, politics, and workplace, just as they were in my original sample list (Table 7.1). In addition, the majority of the respondents (twenty-six out of the thirty-one) were already influential people in their domains and education. Their responses were by all means important.

Findings

Why Should There be Values Education?

In this section we provided seventeen arguments for values education from which the elites could choose. We first asked them to select the ones that prevail in their society and then rank them in terms of their persuasiveness with "1" being the most important. This confused a few respondents. One ranked all the seventeen items; another only ranked according to his own preferences. One even gave two sets of rankings. The first set is in the order on what he perceived that the society in general advocates; the other is according to his own opinion (this was learned from a follow-up interview).

Since the respondents ranked variedly on items and on the number of them, the mean is not a reliable measure on which to decide its importance. Instead, "ranking frequency" was used along with an indicator to reveal the emphasis. The formula for this indicator on each argument is: the number of the first rank x 17 + the number of the second rank x 16, and the rest can be done in the same manner until the number of the 17th rank x one. Therefore, the larger indicator points to the greater emphasis.

The indicators show the elite respondents were worried about the perceived "adolescent problem", which accompanied rapid industrialization and economic prosperity. While the old social structure was dissolving and the new order had yet to establish itself, younger generations appeared to lose their direction. With this understanding, it is not surprising that the top five reasons for values education, as shown in Table 7.2, are "to help young people develop autonomous personality", "to combat juvenile delinquency", "to guide daily behavior", "to provide a foundation for spiritual development", and "to increase the sense of individual responsibility". What needs to be noticed is that spiritual development for Taiwanese implies hardly any relationship with religion, at least not a direct one. Rather, it is a kind of self-reflection or self-inspiration, such as the courage to overcome difficulty, determination to be successful, or self-sacrifice in order to benefit others or the society. .

Table 7.1 Description of Respondents

Respondents (issued 86 copies, received 31 copies; return rate=36.04 percent)		Number of respondents	Percentage
Gender	Male	24	77.42
	Female	7	22.58
	Total	31	100.00
Age (By estimate)	30-40	6	19.35
	40-50	15	48.39
	50-60	9	29.03
	60-70	1	3.23
	Total	31	100.00
Position	Central educational elite	3	9.68
	Leading educational intellectuals	5	16.13
	Religious leaders who have educational positions	2	6.45
	Leaders of related NGOs	4	12.90
	Politicians	4	12.90
	People in Educational institutes	5	16.13
	Academic leaders	8	25.81
	Total	31	100.00
Politics*	Radical	3	9.68
	Reformist	5	16.13
	Moderate	12	38.71
	Conservative	9	29.03
	Ultra-conservative	2	6.45
	Total	31	100.00
Workplace	Capital City	19	61.29
	Other Major Cities**	12	38.71
	Total	31	100.00

*The estimation is according to the mass media's comment and the norm of Taiwan's society
** Taiwan is a highly urbanized and densely populated society. There is almost no rural area.

As perceived by the respondents, the least important reasons are, in order, "to promote world peace", "to foster economic development", and "to promote community pride" (Table 7.2). In a small island, lacking natural resources, with the second highest population density, it would be difficult to persuade Taiwanese that they are accountable to promote world peace. The elites are seemingly aware of Taiwan's limitations and the extent of Taiwan's strength. Nevertheless, in reality, world peace has been emphasized in school curriculum through the teaching of Confucianism and "the Three Principles of the People". It will be interesting to see if this teaching will be left out in later revisions of curriculum standards.

Table 7.2 Reasons for Values Education (Question 1)

Rank	Most pressing reasons	1st	2nd	3rd	4th	5th	Indicator*
1	To help each young person develop a reflective and autonomous personality	6	5	3	1	4	373
2	To combat juvenile delinquency including bullying, gang violence, and drug abuse	3	4	2	4	6	361
3	To provide a guide for behavior in daily life	3	7	1	2	1	314
4	To provide a foundation for spiritual development	7	1	2	4	1	313
5	To increase the sense of individual responsibility	0	4	5	2	1	295
	Least important reasons						
17	To promote world peace	0	0	0	0	1	34
16	To foster economic development by strengthening values such as hard work, creativity, and individual competitiveness	0	1	2	1	0	127
15	To promote pride in local communities and community life	0	0	1	3	0	146

*Indicator =(1st frequency x 17+2nd frequency x 16 + 3rd frequency x 15 +.... + 17th frequency x 1)

As described earlier, Taiwan has experienced uninterrupted economic growth for half a century. The society is more concerned with the negative impact of "materialized society" than the use of education as a means to foster economic development. In an interview, a politician expressed that although education can help the economy, the purpose should not be achieved at the expense of students' "good spiritual development".

Lately "community consciousness" has become a trend in Taiwan's society. Thus it is surprising to see that elites seem to neglect using schools to promote local community. A possible explanation is that elites may not see how education is related to this issue, as community consciousness should be something that belongs to the community. However, a more possible answer could be that the elite groups tend to be people who focus more on "central level" than local business.

What Should be Taught in the Schools?

In this section the first question is about the arrangement of school time for values education. In Taiwan, values are taught both through specific and integrated subject matters. In the interviews, two people expressed the idea that all subject matters deliver values. Knowledge itself, they both argued, is not value free. Mathematics, for example, demands logical thinking, which is important for a person to be rational. To study the history of one's own nation helps foster patriotism. One respondent argued that values should not be taught as knowledge. When morality is taught as a subject matter, it becomes knowledge. She said students are concerned only with how much the knowledge is useful to get high scores in the examinations and not for their daily lives. Another proposed that values should be amalgamated into daily life. They can only be taught from modeling and self-awareness. However, one scholar took the opposite stance. He said some values are problematic. If values are not to be taught as knowledge, we can hardly anticipate that our children will be able to distinguish right from wrong on their own.

Table 7.3 School Time and Arrangement for Values Education (Question 2)

		Mean	SD
a.	Percent in specific classes (e.g. moral education, civics, religion)	25.8	23.39
b.	Percent of time/effort in values education integrated across the curriculum	32.5	24.66

Table 7.3 shows a mean of 25.8 percent of school time should be focused on specific classes for values and 32.5 percent for integrated across the curriculum. Both standard deviations[28] (SD) are around 24 percent, which indicates the respondents' have a large gap between them. Because the respondents did not receive clear instructions on whether the two approaches (teach values through specific classes or through integrated curriculum) are exclusive, we cannot say the elites think the overall school time for values education should be 58.3 percent (25.8 percent plus 32.5 percent) or 29.2 percent (the 58.3 percent divided by 2). The only conclusion which can be drawn is that the elites disagree largely with each other on the approaches.

The top three most strongly emphasized values were, in order, "Values of Personal Autonomy and Reflection", "Civic Values", and "Democracy". The first emphasis is consistent with the findings found in the first section. The other two reveal elites' concern on political development. The memory of nearly forty years of Martial Law ruling is not easy to erase, especially for the elites, who are generally a more political sensitive group than others are. To Taiwanese, civic values and democracy are inseparable concepts. Democracy has to be built upon the foundation that the citizens are of solid civic values.

These three values have the three smallest SDs among all the choices. Their means are tightly close as well. The elites were found to be in agreement on the importance of these three values. In the seven-scale ranking, "1" means the most important, all the choices, except one, are located from the first rank to the third rank. In contrast, the three least important values in schooling, "Religious Values", "National Identity and Patriotism", and "Global Awareness", happen to have the largest SDs among all others (Table 7.4). This indicates that the elite respondents disagree more with the least important than with the most important.

---

[28] Standard Deviation is the most stable measure indicates that 68.26 percent of the responses distribution locate in between "the mean ± SD." Therefore, the bigger the SD is, the more difference among the variables distribution.

Table 7.4 The Most Important Values in Schooling (Question 3)

Rank	Strong emphasis	1st	2nd	3rd	4th	5th	6th	7th	Mean	SD
1	Values of Personal Autonomy and Reflection	21	7	2	1	0	0	0	1.45	.77
2	Civic Values	19	8	4	0	0	0	0	1.52	.72
3	Democracy	18	9	3	0	0	0	0	1.50	.68
	Weak emphasis									
13	Religious Values	1	2	6	4	3	4	11	5.00	1.91
12	National Identity and Patriotism	6	7	10	2	3	1	1	2.87	1.55
11	Global Awareness	9	10	6	1	3	0	1	2.43	1.50

The item "Religious Values" receives a mean of 5.00, denoting a strong disapproval of teaching religious values in schools. School education, heavily subsidized by the government, is seen as within the public domain. Religions are popular in Taiwan's society; however, religious belief is regarded as part of a person's private life, and has nothing to do with public affairs.

The low emphasis on "National Identity and Patriotism" and "Global Awareness" should not be interpreted to represent a neglect of those values. For the former, as described earlier, Taiwan has a serious national identity conflict between its people. The premise for patriotism is that there is a nation to love, but which nation is it? Some elites may have been troubled with this when they made the selection. When analyzing the data, one has to keep in mind that most of the less emphasized values still receive mean scores smaller than 4, which means the elites are still positive on those values. In reality, global awareness has been promoted in Taiwan for some time. One example is the change in language policy. Before 1998, schools offered English classes no earlier than grade seven, now it has extended down to elementary schools. Second or third foreign language instruction has been widely introduced.

What Content Should be Emphasized?

Regarding the emphasized content, as the SDs indicate, similar to previous questions, the elite group tends to have more agreement on the most emphasized items, but opinions differ on the least emphasized items (Table 7.5). Five of the top six emphasized items, with the exception of "critical thinking", all relate to equality and tolerance issues. This reflects a major concern of Taiwanese society. That critical thinking receives high attention is not surprising. One of the major reasons for current educational reform is the widely accepted conception of Taiwanese students' lack of creativity and ability for critical analysis due to the long conservative and stiff political and educational environment. As to "empathy for differences", this probably reflects the fact that Taiwan's major domestic political tension is caused, or at least believed to be caused, by ethnic and identity conflicts. In previous questions, the elites wished school not to over-emphasize the teaching of national identity, so as to not exacerbate the tension. Here, they hope to use education to help ease the conflict.

The four with the least emphasis are close to being seen as disapproval. Although "teaching children to respect hierarchy and to support the government" and "to venerate their heroes and promote national pride" have been long stressed in schools, simultaneously Taiwanese see the government as a "public servant" employed by the people. Dr. Sun Yat-sen said the government is a taxi driver while the people are the customers. The customers pay the driver and rely on the driver's professional skills and knowledge, while the driver has to take the passengers to the destination decided by the customers. Based on this well-known analogy, the people within a country are to pay the taxes and to make demands, while the government is obliged to take orders or to be replaced. The Taiwanese elites, as educated people, are probably familiar with Sun's teaching.

As discussed earlier, it is not surprising that religion receives low priority. Although religious belief is common in Taiwan's society, in the Taiwanese' mind, religion has never been considered included as a part of school curriculum. What is interesting is that "supporting government" and "national pride" got even less emphasis than religion. Yet, it would be a mistake to conclude that this represents a mistrust of the current government. Many respondents are part of the government, and various elections show the current government still earns majority support. Rather, the response is more likely because of the above-mentioned ideology that government is seen as a public servant, which gets paid by the people. It is the servant, the government, who needs to follow the orders from its masters, the people.

Which Society Should be Given Most Prominence in the Curriculum?

Identical to the three most influential outside cultures on Taiwan, our respondents selected China, Japan, and the United States, as the countries that should be given most prominence in the school curriculum (Table 7.6). In the blank spaces we provided, one filled in Mainland China, and seven filled in Germany. Again, a very special issue here is the definition of China. Surveys from studies in other countries suggested that their respondents overwhelmingly selected their own countries respectively as the most prominent society for school curriculum. In this case, does "China" actually mean Taiwan (or ROC) to the respondents? Or does it mean the "greater China", which includes both the PRC and ROC? The author regrets that he neither listed Taiwan or its official name, the ROC, nor changed China to PRC. Stated as it was, this question may have given the respondents an impression that they were to choose nations other than Taiwan. It is unknown why Germany received such a high attention.

How Should Values Education be Conducted?

When asked how values education should be implemented, the respondents were concurrent supporting the idea that values education should start in early childhood. This thinking can be traced back to "Yan Family Precepts" (Yan, around 550 AD), the forefather of Chinese family precepts which is still popular in Taiwan's society. Yan, the author, points out that if children are raised properly from the time they are infants, this will greatly reduce the occasions for punishment (because of their wrong-doings) when they grow up. It is believed that it would be too late to "correct" people's false beliefs after they have been formed.

Among the thirty-one respondents, five disagree with the idea that values programs should be designed according to different academic abilities but twenty-three
agree with it.

Table 7.5 Values Content School Should Stress (Question 4)

Rank	Most emphasis	1st	2nd	3rd	4th	5th	6th	7th	Mean	SD
1	Stress all are equal before the law	23	8	0	0	0	0	0	1.26	.44
2	Give equal opportunities and encouragement to girls	22	9	0	0	0	0	0	1.29	.46
3	Teach the value of critical thinking	24	5	2	0	0	0	0	1.29	.59
4	Encourage empathy for people of different backgrounds	22	6	3	0	0	0	0	1.39	.67
5	Help the members of each group gain a clear understanding of their unique origins and heritage	18	11	1	1	0	0	0	1.52	.72
6	Encourage mutual respect between boys and girls	20	7	2	0	1	0	0	1.50	.90
	Least emphasis									
25	Teach children to respect hierarchy and to support the government	2	5	4	6	4	4	5	4.23	1.91
24	Teach young people to venerate their heroes and promote national pride	1	1	12	6	4	2	5	4.19	1.64
23	Help every child gain a deeper un-derstanding of their own religion	1	3	9	5	5	4	3	4.13	1.63
22	Foster an understanding of all religions	1	7	10	3	2	2	6	3.90	1.92

**Table 7.6 Which Society Should be Given Most Prominence in the Curriculum?
(Question 5)**

Rank	Country	1st	2nd	3rd	4th	5th	6th	7th	Mean	SD
1	China	17	7	4	2	0	0	0	1.70	.95
2	USA	14	11	2	3	0	1	0	1.94	1.21
3	Japan	12	12	3	2	0	1	0	1.97	1.16

The elites responded positively to the next statement: "values education should
not be taught in separate subjects; rather it should be integrated throughout the curriculum". The author suspects the elites may choose the answer mainly because they
saw the importance of an integrated values curriculum and were not necessary against
teaching values in separate subjects. "Civics and Morality" has been a subject taught
in schools for decades; calls to abolish it have never been heard. The result of these
four questions is integrated in Table 7.7.

Table 7.7 How Should Values Education be Conducted?
(Question 6-9. 1 for Strongly Agree, 7 for Strongly Disagree)

Statements	1st	2nd	3rd	4th	5th	6th	7th	Mean	SD
6. Values education should only begin in secondary school after young people have a clear idea of what they believe to be important.	1	1	0	2	5	7	15	5.90	1.51
7. The foundations of values are established in early childhood so values education should begin at an early age.	20	9	1	0	0	1	0	1.52	1.00
8. Pupils of different academic abilities should undergo different values education programs.	15	6	2	2	0	2	3	2.47	2.08
9. Values education should not be taught in separate subjects; rather it should be integrated throughout the curriculum	17	8	1	2	1	1	0	1.83	1.32

What Settings are Most Effective and What Groups Should Receive Exposure?

In this section, values education is divided into religious education, moral education, and civic education. Nine settings and eight groups of people are provided to choose from for the most effective setting and for the group who should receive the most values education respectively (See Table 7.8 and Table 7.9). Respondents were to choose only three settings or three groups for each question and rank them, with "1" as the most important. For the same reasons previously explained, an indicator with the same formula is used where the greater indicator denotes the greater emphasis.

The author regrets having omitted "religious groups and institutions" by mistake, but it is expected it may have received the most agreement for its effectiveness in religious education. Again, religions are not considered as part of formal school curriculum. This concept prevents the respondents from choosing school as an effective setting. Should school settings be effective for civil education and moral education as our survey suggests (see Table 7.8), they should be effective for religions too. The major purpose of schooling in Europe or America was once to teach religions (Urban and Wagoner, 1996; Ornstein and Levine, 1997), but this has never been the case in Taiwan. In general, most elites responded to this question according to where the religious education should be conducted and not to where they think it should be effective.

Table 7.8 What Settings are Most Effective? (Questions 10, 12, 14)

Settings	10. Religious Ed.				12. Civil Ed.				14. Moral Ed.			
	1st	2nd	3rd	*I**	1st	2nd	3rd	*I**	1st	2nd	3rd	*I**
a. During school as a class	2	1	5	*13*	11	7	3	*50*	5	5	4	*29*
b. During school through rules of behavior and classroom procedures the school establishes	3	1	0	*11*	9	9	2	*47*	7	5	6	*37*
c. Outside of school activities such as clubs, sports, arts.	4	8	3	*31*	2	4	5	*19*	0	5	3	*13*
d. Internships and community service	1	5	10	*23*	2	4	6	*20*	1	9	6	*27*
e. Camps (e.g. during vacation)	2	3	3	*15*	1	1	3	*8*	2	0	0	*6*
f. Religious groups and institutions**												
g. Military training and national service	0	1	0	*2*	1	0	2	*5*	2	0	1	*7*
h. Home and Family	19	3	3	*66*	3	1	7	*18*	13	5	5	*54*
i. Media	0	9	6	*24*	2	5	4	*20*	1	2	6	*13*

* Indicator = (1st x 3 + 2nd x 2 + 3rd x 1). Bigger number indicates more effectiveness.
**Data missing at all cases.

School settings are regarded among the most effective settings for both civil and moral education. However, the elites believe morality can be better cultivated at home, while civil education constitutes a knowledge which needs to be taught in school settings.

On the question of what group should receive the most exposure, the attitude toward religion education is consistent: it is an adult's business. "In-service teachers", "teacher learners", and "university students" are among the top (Table 7.9). It has been commonly taught in teacher education that teachers should devoted themselves in education with religious spirits, and that teachers should have knowledge of various religions and not only the one they may believe in, if any. Most of our respondents involved with teacher education or received teacher education in Taiwan. In-service teachers earn the highest score probably due to the influence of this teaching.

Teachers, and teacher learners, get high scores in the other two focus areas as well. This should not be interpreted as a sign of distrust. Teachers' social status in Taiwan is no lower than medical doctors, or high-ranking civilians. Rather, it should be viewed as an expectation that they possess higher civil knowledge and moral standards. The elites believe civil education and moral education should start earlier. Civil values require higher cognitive skill; therefore, it is felt that it can wait until the children enter elementary schools. None of the respondents places any importance on civil education for children below five years old. As for morality, it is believed to be a behavior and habit. The respondents felt teaching should begin as early as possible.

Table 7.9 What Groups Should Receive the Most Exposure?

Groups	11. Religious Ed.				13. Civil Ed.				15. Moral Ed.			
	1st	2nd	3rd	I*	1st	2nd	3rd	I*	1st	2nd	3rd	I*
a. Inservice teachers	18	4	3	65	10	3	1	37	8	3	2	32
b. Teacher learners	2	16	4	42	2	7	6	26	4	6	3	27
c. Young children (3-4 yr. old)	2	0	0	6	0	0	0	0	3	0	1	10
d. Pre-schoolers (5 yr. old)	0	2	2	6	1	1	1	6	3	7	0	23
e. Primary (6-11 yr. Old)	0	0	7	7	11	4	4	45	9	4	7	42
f. Secondary level (11-14 yr. Old)	1	1	2	7	4	11	4	38	1	7	7	24
g. High school level (15-17 yr. old)	2	2	2	12	2	2	10	20	0	3	6	12
h. University level (18 yr. old or older)	4	4	9	29	0	2	4	8	2	0	4	10

* Indicator = (frequency of 1st rank x 3 + frequency of 2nd rank x 2 + frequency of 3rd rank x 1)

Policy Implications

In general, the result of the Sigma Elite Survey conforms to what is happening in Taiwan's society. Unlike the old practice in which values education mainly served political purposes, it now focuses on individual needs and wishes to nurture a harmonious society rather than specific national goals, such as economic growth or national integration. Individualism is now an important value (Lee, 1996). Although the young generation has been criticized for being ungrateful, selfish, and egotistical (Hu, 1994), some interviewees strongly disapproved of a paternalistic or authoritative approach to correct this problem. The youth need to be guided, they argued, and not to be suppressed. Nevertheless, collectivism or self-sacrifice is still stressed in a gentle way, to prevent over-selfishness and arrogance, which are held as undesirable characters accompanied with individualism.

Great political participation is one of the national characteristics of the Taiwanese. Democracy is regarded as a universal value which contributes to maintaining social order. Theoretically, national identity and patriotism are necessary for national consolidation. However, this theory cannot apply to Taiwan's society. The people of Taiwan, supposed to be of one nation, have two conflicting national identities. A safe policy would be to bring about small changes over time so as not to provoke strong counter reactions.

The survey results also suggest strong support for the newly developed or introduced values, such as gender equality, indigenization, individualism, and respect for diversity. Along with environmental protection, these have been the subjects of major efforts in schooling. The public is more aware of the importance of these "modern" values than ever before. With elites' support, this policy is likely to carry on. Critical thinking has become an important educational objective. Many non-governmental organizations for educational reform have charged that Taiwan's education is limited to training students to be "recital machines". They argued that the centralized educational system is ossified with the least amount of innovation and has discouraged students' creativity and logical thinking.

Many Taiwanese education reformists conclude that a centralized and highly subsidized educational system symbolizes an authoritarian rule. Nevertheless, this argument does not have a solid ground. Germany and France are considered free nations. Germany provides free higher education and France adopts a highly centralized education system. The PRC is a single party-state. Its government bloodily repressed student peaceful demonstration with bullets in 1989, yet it has engaged in dramatic education decentralization and gradually abolished free higher education since late 1980s. In the U.S., national government has no accountability to equalize educational resources or to enhance educational quality. As a result, pupils in certain school districts suffer from below standard education. On the contrary, Taiwan's centralized educational system has made the government accountable to equalize educational access to the masses, to secure and balance educational resources between rural and urban areas, to enhance educational quality, and to maintain school administrative efficiency (Ministry of Education, 1995). On the other hand, many authoritarian nations provide inadequate or no education for their people. It is clear that authoritarian governments and centralized education have no cause-effect relation. A centralized educational system should not be used as an indicator for a nation's democracy. Rather, judgment should be made according to the content of centralization.

In the past, the KMT tightly controlled education to prevent unauthorized values from being taught. As this practice is unfeasible or unnecessary now, decentralization can significantly release the central government's responsibility. The KMT government has taken measures to unload its "burden" to local authorities. In the latest Constitution revision (1997), the KMT secretly and successfully mobilized its party assembly people to abolish the mandate of at least 15 percent of the central government's budget to be assigned for education, science, and culture. Nevertheless, it is still premature to predict that the central government will diminish its role in education in the near future. Taiwanese, on the one hand, seek more autonomy; on the other hand, they demand that the government be responsible for educational opportunity and quality.

Conclusion

In conclusion, the elite respondents' attitudes toward values education are consistent with Taiwan's recent political and societal development. Confucianism and Chinese nationalism are facing serious challenges while democracy remains the most important value. Our respondents stressed the importance of most newly developed or introduced values, such as gender equality, self-realization, cultural diversity, and Taiwanese consciousness. Taiwan's values education is at a transition point wherein no single power can manipulate its contents and directions as in the past, but government still plays an important role in setting up criteria. Individualism needs to be a greater focus than collectivism. The elites believed values education should be used to foster students' spiritual development and to help self-realization rather than to achieve a national political or economic goal. The government may try to unload its responsibility of providing guidelines for values education or maintaining educational equality, but it is still premature to predict the how much role the government will play in the near future.

Four sets of written documents are useful in indicating the directions of contemporary Taiwan's education. They are: *Final Report for Educational Reform* (in Chinese; Evaluation Committee for Educational Reform, 1996), *White Paper of ROC's Education: Outlook Toward the 21st Century* (in Chinese; Ministry of education, February 1995), the latest revised curriculum standard issued by the Ministry of Education (1993, 1994, 1996), and the president Lee Teng-hui's Inaugural Address on education (May 20, 1996). In Lee's address, he said:

> Reform in education aims to put into practice concept of education that imparts happiness, contentment, pluralism and mutual respect. Such education is designed to develop potentialities, respect individualism, promote humanism, and encourage creativity. All unreasonable restrictions will be removed to allow the emergence of a life learning system. Ample room will be reserved for individual originality and personal traits to ensure the continued pursuit of self-growth and self-realization. The new generation will be assisted to know their homeland, love their country and foster a broad international view. Fortified in this manner they can better meet international challenges and map out a bright future for their country in an increasingly competitive global village.

From then to the present, Lee's remarks on education seamlessly match Taiwan's values education development. Nevertheless, the statement "the new generation will be assisted to know their homeland, love their country..." has raised several different and opposing interpretations. For example, why does the new generation require assistance so they can know their homeland? What is the "homeland"? Is it China or Taiwan? According to him, Lee has claimed literally two hundred times that he does not support TI; however, whether the president has been promoting TI secretly has been a heated debate among both identity groups and there is no single answer can be agreed upon.

On March 2 1999, Taiwan's Central Bank announced a total redesign of Taiwan's currency for the next millennium (Reuters, 1999). Sun Yat-sen's and Chiang Kai-shek's images on most banknotes will be replaced with symbols of high technology, sport, and education. The Free China Journal, an official weekly of the ROC government, changed its name to Taipei Journal in its first issue of the year 2000. An act like this before 1987 was a serious offense to the national policy. Do they imply that the government is trying to lead the people to modern themes, or do they only reflect the societal changes in values? Pertinent to this study is the related question: Will the elites' ideas affect the society or do their responses indicate that it is they who are following society change? In Taiwan's case, it appears to be the latter.

References

Alexander, D. (1998). "Sizing up ROC's Success in Light of Current Events". *The Free China Journal*, (Sept. 4): 6.

Central Election Commission. (1999). http://www.cec.gov.tw/

Chen, E. (1995). "Cover Story: Opening a 'Window' on Ideology—A Comparison of School Textbooks in Taiwan, Hong Kong and Mainland China", *Sinorama* 20 (6): 6-27.

Chen, J. (1997). "Cover Story: The Textbook Revolution: Deciding What Children Learn", *Sinorama* 22(10): 6-17.

Chen, J. (1999). "Cross-Strait 'Special State-to-State Relationship' Controversy Continues", *Sinorama* 24(10): 73-76.

Cheng, J. (1999). "Jobless Rate Down Slightly Despite Continuing Layoffs", *The Free China Journal* (Feb. 5): 3.

Chiou, C.L. (1994). "Emerging Taiwanese Identity in the 1990s: Crisis and Transformation". In G. Klintworth (Ed.), *Taiwan in the Asia-Pacific in the 1990s*. St. Leonards, Australia: Allen and Unwin.

Cohen, M.J. and Teng, E. (1990). *Let Taiwan Be Taiwan*. Washington, DC: Center for Taiwan International Relations.

Common Wealth (1991). "New Life Movement—Start from Daily Life". In *Discover Taiwan: 1620-1945*. Taipei: Common Wealth.

Directorate General of Budget, Accounting and Statistics. (1995). *The 1995 Survey Report on Family Income and Expenditures in Taiwan, Republic of China* (in Chinese). Taipei: Directorate General of Budget, Accounting and Statistics, Executive Yuan, Republic of China.

Evaluation Committee for Educational Reform (1996). *Final Report for Educational Reform* (in Chinese). (Dec. 2).

Gou-min-zhen-fu (the ROC government) (1929). *The Purposes and Methods of the ROC's Education* (governmental document, in Chinese.)

Gau, X. (1998). "Direction for the New Taiwanese" (in Chinese), *Sinorama* 23(5): 65-66.

Ger, Y. (1998). *Politics, the Story of Taiwan*. Taipei: Government Information Office.

Hsiao, F. and Sullivan, L. (1979). "The Chinese Communist Party and the Status of Taiwan, 1928-1943", *Pacific Affairs* (Fall): 446-462.

Hsieh, D. (Feb 1999). "Tragedy and Tolerance—The Green Island Human Rights Monument", *Sinorama* 24(2): 44-53.

Hu, J. (1994). "Youngian Psychology—Taipei's New New Youth on Life", *Sinorama* (19)11: 8-17.

Huang, H.S. (1999). "Educational Reform in Taiwan: A Brighter American Moon?" *International Journal of Educational Reform* 8(2): 145-153.

Huang, Z. (1995). "An Insight on the 100 Annual of Shimonoseki Treaty", (in Chinese). *China Times*. (Apr. 17).

International Monetary Fund (1998). *World Economic Outlook, October 1998.* Washington, DC: International Monetary Fund.

Lee, Teng-hui, ROC President. (1992, May 25). "Address to the Asia and Pacific Council Symposium". Taipei: Governmental Information Office.

Lee, Teng-hui (1996, May 20). *Presidential Inaugural Address.* (Governmental Document).

Lee, Tian-Jian (1993). "A Compilation of the Interpellation in Legislate Yuan" (in Chinese), *Ren-Ben Education Notes* 47: 33-37.

Lee, Y. (1998). "Education Reform Should Start from Revising Textbooks" (in Chinese). (Incumbent congressman. Records both from the interview with him and in his personal website.)

Legislation Yuan (1994). *Minutes of the Seventh Meeting of Education Committee* (Oct. 12), Fourth Assembly, Second Legislation Yuan.

Legislation Yuan (1996). *Minutes of the Third Meeting of Education Committee* (Apr. 15), First Assembly, Third Legislation Yuan.

Li, L. (1998). "The Passing of the Paragons—The Changing Role of Moral Role Models", *Sinorama* 23(3): 116-125.

Minahan, J. (1996). *Nations Without States: A Historical Dictionary of Contemporary National Movements.* Westport, CT: Greenwood Press.

Ministry of Education (1993). *Curriculum Standard for Citizens' Elementary Education* (in Chinese). Taipei.

Ministry of Education. (1994). *Curriculum Standard for Junior High School Education* (in Chinese). Taipei.

Ministry of Education (1995) *White Paper of ROC's education: Outlook toward the 21th Century* (in Chinese).

Ministry of Education. (1996). *Curriculum Standard for Senior High School Education* (in Chinese). Taipei.

Miyazaki, I. (1976). *China's Examination Hell* (C. Schirokauer, trans.). New York and Tokyo: Weatherhill.

Ong, I. (1979). *Taiwan: A History of Anguish and Struggle.* Tokyo: Taiwan Youth Society

Ornstein, A. and Levine, D. (1997). *Foundation of Education* (6th ed.). Boston: Houghton Mifflin.

Reuters (1999). A news article on Mar. 2.

ROC Constitution (1947). "Article 158".

ROC Constitution (1997). "Introduction" of the fourth revision.

Shen, D. (1999) "CBC Rebuts US Magazine Report", *The Free China Journal,* (Feb. 5): 3.

Shen, J. (1995). "The Cairo Declaration Fraud", electronic article posted in Taiwan Culture and Scholarship Network. (Dec. 28).

Teng, S. (1999) "TV News—Fighting for Survival", *Sinorama* 24(5): 78-87.

Tien, H.M. and Chu, Y.H. (1994) "Taiwan's Domestic Political Reforms, Institutional Change and Power Realignment". In G. Klintworth (Ed.), *Taiwan in the Asia-Pacific in the 1990s.* St. Leonards, Australia: Allen and Unwin.

Urban, W. and Wagoner, J. (1996). *American Education: A History.* New York: McGraw-Hill.

Wang, A.Y. (1999). "The Road to Press Freedom—Looking at Taiwan's Fourth Estate", *Sinorama* 24(6): 98-103.

Wees, G. (1989). "Taiwan's Sovereignty and International Economic Relations: The European Perspective", *NATPA Bulletin,* 8(2): 22.

World Bank, The (1993). *The East Asian Miracle: Economic Growth and Public Policy.* New York: Oxford University Press.

Yan, Z. (around 550 AD) *Yan Family Precepts.*

Yang, T.R. (1994). "Nationalization and Indigenization—Ethnic Identity Movements and Their Educational Impact in Taiwan" (in Chinese), *Education Journal.* 21(2) and 22(1): 127-137.

Yu, T. (1998). *Economy, the Story of Taiwan.* Taipei: Government Information Office.

Zhou, C. (1994). *Position Paper to Urge Deregulation of School Textbooks* (in Chinese). Unpublished paper presented in Legislative Yuan (the Congress) by Zhou (was a Congresswoman).

The Confucian "Middle Way"

CHAPTER 8

KOREA: CONFUCIAN LEGACY, GLOBAL FUTURE

Gay Garland Reed
Sheena Choi

Introduction

While the social and cultural impacts of modernity have democratized South Koreans, the Confucian legacy is perpetuated in the social rules which guide intergenerational interactions, in linguistic conventions which reflect status differences and in the attitudes which underlie behavior. Although it has been argued that Confucian values and practices are not transmitted through schools, worship services, or the mass media, but only through spontaneous family indoctrination (Koh, 1996), it seems more probable that Confucianism, as a force in shaping perceptions and generating social behavior is, in fact, perpetuated through multiple social institutions, including schools.

Confucianism, with its emphasis on ritual, tradition and focus on the past can only partially explain the passion with which Koreans of past generations have cleaved to tradition. For a better understanding of this characteristic it is useful to examine the historical context. Always vulnerable to the influence of China and Japan, Korea maintained her political and cultural sovereignty until 1910 when she was annexed by Japan. The period from 1910 until 1945 was a period of systematic deculturalization. Korean children were forbidden to speak Korean at school, and educational opportunities for Koreans were limited. Access to tertiary education was largely limited to those few who were willing to become loyal servants of the Japanese. There was strong resistance to colonization both at home and abroad where Korean churches became the sites for political resistance and the maintenance of Korean language and cultural traditions.

The division of Korea into North and South at the end of World War II had important educational repercussions that paralleled the political division. During the period between the end of World War II and the Korean War, North Korea sought educational advice from the Soviet Union (Reed and Chung, 1997) at the same time that South Korea was adopting educational models and practices from the U.S. The Korean War brought the focus on education to a temporary halt and three years of civil war were devastating to the educational infrastructures of both parts of the peninsula. The result of Korea's historical vulnerability, colonization, civil war and division into North and South has nurtured a national characteristic that we might call cultural tenacity. It is this characteristic that preserved Korean language and traditions in the face of cultural imperialism and helped Korea to maintain its uniqueness in the face of forces that pushed it towards cultural homogenization and globalization. More recently cultural tenacity is an impetus for the renaissance in Korean traditional art forms and helps to explain why Confucianism remains such a powerful cultural force.

The educational implications of the political division into North and South must be underscored. Our research and this chapter focus on values education policy in South Korea, but we cannot ignore the significant repercussions of living in a divided country and must take into account the fact that educational policy in the South is partly designed in opposition to the values orientation of the North. In a divided country, a country that measures its own values and constructs its own identity in relation to a national "other", values are often more carefully articulated and adhered to than in countries where there is no immediate "enemy". Children grow up with a clear notion of what they are *not* as a means of differentiating themselves from the political other.

Korea's historical, geographical and political divisions are only part of the values puzzle. Another division, which has significance for this study, is the generation divide between those who recall the War years and those were born after Korea had recovered from the War. One of our informants noted that some people say that there is a new generation in Korea every hour—an expression of the dramatic social changes, which have taken place in Korea over the last several decades. Others underscored the generation differences by saying that Korean young people are another race.

Perhaps there is nothing that separates the present generation(s) more from past generations of Koreans than the access to affluence [1] This issue was discussed by several of our informants who noted that this societal problem is also an educational problem. Ironically, the examination system, the engine which drives education in South Korea is also woven into the pattern of excess because parents spend exorbitant amounts of money for private tutoring and cram schools to give their children the education edge despite the fact that legislation has been enacted to stop this practice. Because education is such an important determinant of social status, the commodification of education seems inevitable.

This research was conducted at a significant moment in Korean political history. During the months that the initial phases of this research were conducted, the country was in the throes of the *Hanbo* scandal[2] and President Kim Yong-sam's popularity was on the wane. When Kim Young-sam became the first president of South Korea he ran on a strong anti-corruption platform. His promise of clean government devolved into the *Hanbo* scandal and made the issue of corruption front-page news. There was a general sense that corruption had never been worse than it was then. This perception led to a wave of nostalgia for the "good old days" and a re-evaluation of the presidency of Park Chung-hee who was recast as a relatively incorrupt leader. In terms of education, the "wave of corruption" in 1996-97 led moral educators to consider the idea of including business ethics as part of the curriculum in moral education classes at the high school level. This was one of several ideas that appeared in an unpublished internal discussion paper from the Presidential Commission on Education Reform (interview with Moon Yong-lin, 1997).

Another factor that influenced the political and economic climate during the months that we were conducting this study was the Asian Economic Crisis, which had particularly dire consequences for Korea and helped to pave the way for the election of President Kim Dae-Jung. The unique economic and political conditions of the months when we were conducting this research impacted our results in that interviewees were particularly sensitive to issues related to political scandal and societal ex-

---

[1] One informant noted that the Seoul Olympics were the turning point for Koreans who suddenly realized their affluence and saw their role as an international player crystallized.

[2] This was a corporate scandal in which the president's son was implicated.

cesses and spoke often about the moral climate of Korea. We must also assume that this charged political atmosphere had some effect on the survey, which was conducted in the midst of the presidential campaign.

Values Education Policy

Like other modern societies in Asia that have a strong Confucian tradition, Korea requires moral education as an essential and regular part of the formal school curriculum at both the elementary and secondary levels. As historical conditions have changed Korean society and education, educational reformers have responded by re-conceptualizing the purposes, content and pedagogy used in moral education classes. In other words, the "why", the "what", and the "how" of moral education have changed over time in response to internal and external historical, economic and societal pressures.

The content and purposes of the South Korean Education system are grounded in a set of social and political values which are reflected in the provisions that are laid out in the Education Act of 1949. This Act, which was amended by laws throughout the succeeding five decades, is an important document to examine, not simply because of its relevance for the present education system in general, but in particular because of its moral tone, the values which it promotes, and its historical relevance for this study.

Article 1 states that "the purpose of our education is to achieve the integration of character and instill the abilities of an independent life and the qualifications of citizenship and thus contribute to the development of a democratic nation and realize the idea of co-prosperity based on the idea of *Hongik Inkan*—the greatest service for the benefit of mankind". In order to achieve this purpose, Article 2 of the Education Act lists seven guidelines:

1. Nourishment of the knowledge and habits necessary for the sound growth and maintenance of the body and cultivation of an indomitable spirit.

2. Nourishment of a patriotic spirit for the country and nation in order to preserve and develop the nation's independence and advance the cause of world peace.

3. Inheritance and enrichment of our national culture and thus contribute to the development of the world.

4. Fostering of a spirit of truth seeking and an ability to think scientifically for creative activities and a rational life.

5. Encouragement of peaceful associations with the community with a spirit of faithfulness, cooperation, respect, love of freedom and high regard for responsibility.

6. Development of an aesthetic sense in order to appreciate and create sublime fine arts, enjoy the beauty of nature, and to utilize leisure time effectively for an enjoyable life.[3]

---

[3] This guideline notes the importance of aesthetics as an integral part of education. The connection in traditional Confucian thought between morality and art and the importance of this

7. Encouragement of thriftiness and faithfulness to one's work in order to become an able producer and a wise consumer for a sound economic life.

These guidelines will be referred to later in this paper because they are useful in interpreting the results of our survey. They are also useful in pointing out the inevitable contradictions between policy and practice which characterize most educational systems.

There are other documents which help to illuminate the purposes of education and its role in the development of Korean values. A document produced by the Korean Ministry of Education (1980) redefines educational ideals and goals to meet the needs of societal change and notes that education should not only develop productive manpower but should also help students cope with the "problems of the new dimension, such as those associated with value conflicts, moral deprivation, and dehumanization inherent in a highly industrialized society" (p. 117). All textbooks used in Korean schools are approved by the Ministry of Education, including texts for Moral Education which have been revised six times. (National Institute for Educational Research, 1991). In a study published by the National Institute for Educational Research (NIER), representatives from Korea analyzed the changes in the texts from 1960-1989. Their analysis indicated that earlier texts stressed conformity and practice of existing moral principles. The tone of those books tended to be admonitory and authoritative (NIER, 1991). By 1989, the tone of the texts was markedly different. Moral dilemmas had been introduced and the emphasis was on moral judgement, Socratic questioning, rational thinking and understanding the principles underlying practice. The content of the books falls into five values domains: individual, family, neighborhood and community, society and nation and international (NIER, 1991).

According to a Ministry of Education official, the 7th National Curriculum, which takes effect in 2003, will see some reduction in the requirement for moral education at the lower and upper secondary levels. This official pointed out that this is not an indication of the reduced importance of moral education but a response to complaints from parents that schools have too many requirements. The reduction in moral education classes is part of a general reduction in requirements for students at the secondary level. According to this official, at the upper secondary level, the 7th National Curriculum reduces the current six credits over three years of moral education to two. Although this official saw the problems with the six-credit requirement as primarily a problem of overburdened students, other informants have pointed out problems with the system (personal communication, 1998).

Seoul National University professor and Chief Member of the Presidential Commission on Educational Reform during the Kim Young-sam presidency, Dr. Moon Yong-lin, argues that moral education has not been very successful over the last fifty years because of problems with an inconsistent curriculum and an over emphasis on pro-government moral messages. But he also suggests that aside from content and cur-

---

aesthetic sense in the development of a moral human being were not taken into account in our study. In retrospect, our survey should have included at least one option related to this important aspect of moral cultivation.

ricular issues, there are pedagogical issues which have hampered the teaching of moral education. Large classes do not permit the kind of discussion and interchange that is conducive to moral development, and teachers are not prepared for this type of discussion. He notes that fewer than 50 percent are licensed to teach moral education. He also argues that the emphasis on paper and pencil tests hampers good moral instruction, and he suggests that the "strong delinquent and violent flavor" of Korean schools sometimes overrides the effects of formal moral education (Moon, 1995; personal communication, May, 1997).

Two of our informants recalled their own experiences as students in moral education classes and explained that these classes were just like other classes where the material had to be studied and was tested. In some cases the time set aside for moral education classes was usurped by subject matter that was more crucial for passing the college entrance exam. According to our interviewees, the content of moral education classes was not fully integrated into lives, it was seen as something separate from living.

A Seoul National graduate and former moral education teacher who is currently working at the Korean Educational Development Institute (KEDI), made the observation that "moral education is taught as a body of knowledge like Korean or math" (personal communication, 5/1997). This teacher noted that this has disadvantages as well as advantages. The disadvantage is that "knowledge for credit does not have implications for actions" (personal communication, 5/1997). In other words, one can learn the content, do well on the examination and gain the credit but there might be little actual effect on behavior, which is, after all, the goal of moral instruction. The advantage of having moral education as a separate subject is that there is time set aside in the regular curriculum to address issues of a moral nature.

While this study focuses on moral education in school settings, it is important to note that formal moral education classes in school settings are only part of values education. Both traditional and contemporary values are communicated explicitly and implicitly in other classes in the formal system as well as through non-formal and informal educational experiences in and out of school.

Description of the Study

This study combines data from multiple sources. Field research was conducted in South Korea in May of 1997 and January of 1998. We consulted with colleagues in Korea and conducted interviews as part of the first phase of our research on values education policy in Korea and later as a means of illuminating the survey data. This chapter includes data from formal in-depth interviews and from numerous conversations and informal discussions with professors and administrators (including a former university president) from academe, government bureaucrats from the Ministry of Education and the Presidential Educational Reform Commission, and researchers and curriculum developers from other government sponsored agencies like KEDI, the Institute for Korean Unification, the Institute of Curriculum and Evaluation and the Academy of Korean Studies.

The interview data was only one component of the study. The Sigma Survey used for the larger study was developed by our team of scholars from Asia, Russia, Mexico and the U.S. Its purpose is to ascertain why elites in these countries feel there is a need for values education, what content they deem appropriate for values education, and how and when they believe it is best taught. The Sigma Survey was translated into Korean, and 107 respondents completed the survey between November 1997 and February 1998. Koreans elites who represented the previously mentioned constituencies as well as the media, politics, law and business participated in the study; in addition, respecting the special role of teachers in formulating values education policy in Korea, thirty-four teachers were included in the sample. The respondents ranged from age thirty to seventy. Twelve percent were female; 75 percent of the sample were from the capital city of Seoul.

Nearly one-third of the survey respondents were teachers of moral education at the elementary and secondary levels; in the Korean context, teachers can be thought of as front-line elites. Teachers, even when given a standard curriculum to teach, are constantly making important decisions that influence educational outcomes. Some of these decisions are of such import that they may even subvert the intention of the curriculum developers and other high level experts who determine policy. This point was reinforced when we interviewed a former moral education teacher who discussed the disparity between the government-mandated curriculum and what was actually taught by teachers. Of course the degree of disparity varies, but this teacher suggested that, at least among a group of the teacher's colleagues, it was significant. The teacher noted that the university entrance exams include only a limited number of questions on moral education. Teachers could easily predict what type of question would be asked so they allotted a limited amount of class time to memorizing that material, expecting at least an 80 percent success rate on the examination. They made substantial adjustments to the text in terms of emphasis and interpretation. For example, instead of emphasizing anti-Communism, which was a central theme in their government sanctioned curriculum, they emphasized unification and non-confrontation. When the textbook discussed Confucianism, stressing the paternalistic role of government by metaphorically casting the government in the role of the "father", these teachers made the point to their students that Confucian ethics were fundamental to Korean family life but had no place in a democratic system of government. Interviews, like this one, that reveal the degree to which teacher intentions can alter and even subvert the curriculum, are instructive for researchers who are trying to make sense of the ways in which values are actually transmitted in school settings while ostensibly teaching a standard, government-sanctioned curriculum. They also help to support our contention that teachers are important as interpreters and conveyors of curriculum content.

Limitations

The results of the survey were analyzed in order to illuminate contemporary Korean attitudes towards values education and to use as a basis for comparison and contrast with other settings in Asia and the West. Throughout the process we were aware of the limitations of survey research and were faced with the inevitable problems that attend research of this nature. Although the group that developed the survey represented multiple cultural perspectives, the process of data collection was clearly situated in the Western tradition. As noted in other chapters, translation of some of the items was a problem. For example, the survey results from our setting indicated that the respondents from Korea, when compared with respondents in other settings in our survey, placed the least value on critical thinking. In fact, this number may have reflected a translation problem rather than actual attitude because two respondents noted, in follow-up interviews, that the word that was used to translate "critical" actually meant "crucial". The concept of "critical thinking" was therefore "lost in translation" and may have skewed the results. We therefore must be cautious in drawing our conclusions from the data.

Besides problems in translation we also note that there are inevitable issues of interpretation. Even words that are "accurately" translated from one language to another, may have different meanings and nuances in those contexts. Later in this chapter, we will discuss an issue that arose for us related to the interpretation of a particular word and provide contextual clues and evidence that will help to clarify its meaning in the Korean context.

The Purposes of Values Education

In response to the first question, regarding why values education is important, respondents from Korea gave special weight to the following points: (a) to help each young person develop a reflective and autonomous personality; (b) to provide a foundation for spiritual development; and (c) to encourage greater civic consciousness and thus strengthen democracy (see Table 8.1). For this question, we had 104 valid questionnaires from respondents who ranked the seventeen responses.[4] The scores for the top three and the bottom three responses are reported below in Tables 8.1 and 8.2. Fifty-eight percent of the respondents chose "Help young persons develop reflective autonomous personalities" as their top choice. Forty-four percent of the respondents chose "Provide foundation for spiritual development" as their second choice. Forty-one percent of the respondents chose "Encourage civic consciousness and thus strengthen democracy" as their third choice.

Table 8.1 Why Should There be Values Education? (Most Important Reasons)

Rank	Reason	Percent
1	Help young persons develop reflective autonomous personalities	58
2	Provide foundation for spiritual development	44
3	Encourage civic consciousness and thus strengthen democracy	41

N=104

The second response, "To provide a foundation for spiritual development", requires contextualization and analysis because it might be misleading. The term "spiritual", from a North American point of view, often connotes religious belief but this is not the case in Korea and in some other Asian countries. Former Minister of Education, Rhee Kyu Ho, helped to illuminate the concept of spiritual education in the Ko-

---

[4] It should be noted that the directions for this question were somewhat misleading. Some respondents rank ordered all 17 of the responses. Most respondents rank ordered 4-5 responses and some only ranked the first one or two.

rean context presented in May, 1981, in a speech entitled "Enhancement and Internalization of National Identity", on the occasion of Education Week:

> As you know, one of the objectives of our educational system reform is the strengthening of spiritual education. What we call spiritual education here is a combination of what is generally called moral education and political education.
>
> (Rhee, 1981, p. 102).

Later, Minister Rhee explained that "Spiritual education's core on the primary level is to implant national pride and love for country into the minds of the children" (Rhee, 1981, p. 107). In a departure from traditional Confucian notions of valuing the work of the head over the work of the hands, Dr. Rhee said, "I think that physical labor education bears a very big significance for the spiritual education at secondary schools. A person who has not ever worked in sweat cannot realize the meaning of life" (Rhee, 1981, p. 109).

Rhee Kyu-ho noted that the objectives of educational reform for that period included a strengthening of spiritual education from kindergarten through university (Rhee, 1981, p. 102). In his speech, he warned against selfish ambitions and encouraged discipline, propriety, hard work, the cultivation of civic spirit and respect for laws and regulations.

What seems to be most essential in the definition of spiritual education that Rhee Kyu Ho offers is its social nature; e.g., the sense that spiritual education can only take place in a social setting, through interaction with others. It is also clear that there are no religious overtones to this concept in the Korean context, rather it is clearly a secular value that has moral, civic and political dimensions.

Just as the top three responses are of interest to us, the responses that received the lowest scores and were not seen as a priority for values education are illuminating. The answers that fell into the category of least important are listed in Table 8.2. Two percent of the respondents ranked "strengthen families" in the top three preferences; 2 percent ranked "improve the respect and opportunities for girls and women" in the top three preferences; and fewer than 1 percent of the respondents ranked "promote pride in local communities" in the top three preferences. They are presented below in order of their rank ordered scores:

Table 8.2 Why Should There be Values Education? (Least Important Reasons)

Rank	Reasons	Percent
15	Strengthen families	2
16	Improve the respect and opportunities for girls and women	2
17	Promote pride in local communities	1

N=104

Although two people in our survey felt that values education should focus on improving the respect and opportunities for girls and women as a first priority, this answer received one of the lowest priorities by a significant margin. We can interpret this answer in two ways. It may reflect a continuing pattern of undervaluing women common in many cultures or it might be that values education is not seen as an appropriate vehicle for promoting respect and opportunities for women, or on the contrary they may consider this issue as already properly addressed. Likewise the low priority given to "promoting pride in local communities" and "strengthen families" might indicate that these were not seen as very important content for a values education program and might be emphasized elsewhere.

An answer that fell into the middle range of apparent Korean priorities (median score = 4.0) but was a high priority when compared with other settings (Singapore was the only country which saw this as a more important reason for values education), was the answer related to the role of values education in "developing an appreciation for heritage and strengthening national identity". Both in our initial interviews and in the literature, the importance of values education as an essential tool for preserving Korean national and cultural identity was stressed. During the interviews we were not surprised at the emphasis which was placed on this value given the historical need for Koreans to create and maintain a unique identity, and were somewhat surprised that it did not receive more emphasis in our survey. Part of the explanation for this might be that heritage and national identity were subsumed into the category of "spiritual education" as indicated by the quote above from Rhee Kyu Ho. This might also indicate that there is a trend to focus away from national and cultural identity in favor of developing the individual.

One of our interviewees made the observation that "the older generation (in Korea) is concerned with national identity and the younger generation with self-identity". (Dr. Lee Kwang-Ho, personal communication, 1998). There are several possible explanations for this generational difference. One is the expendable income[5] which permits young people to express their individuality, their cosmopolitan tastes and trendiness through their pocketbooks. Another is the gradual democratization of South Korea which gives political impetus to self-expression. A third possible explanation might be the historical circumstances which separate the generations. Emile Durkheim once made the observation that when countries live in a state of war they tend to shape their people according to a nationalistic model but when international competition takes a more peaceful form, education serves somewhat different social ends. A more subtle issue, which may have shifted the attention away from national identity as it was conceived in the decades of the 1950s through the 1980s, is a softening of the passionate anti-Communist stance and a movement towards a political agenda which favors unification with the North. If unification is to be successful, the conception of Korean national identity will have to be adjusted to fit a different political reality. It is also possible to attribute the decrease in the emphasis on national identity to the forces of globalization that tend to encourage less emphasis on the nation state.

National guidelines for education in the past spoke about education with a national imprint which combines aspects of traditional cultural identity with patriotism and nation building. Four goals of this type of education were:

1. All education activities should stress the spirit of patriotism and love of nation.

---

[5] Even though the IMF effect severely curtailed spending habits in 1998, the material wealth of young Koreans in this generation is far greater than in previous decades.

2. The cultural heritage and historical continuity of the nation should be stressed.
3. All doctrines and theories regarding education must originate from the peculiar historical environments and conditions of the Korean people.
4. Education should seek to breed a national cadre of capable and force-ful leaders. (Ministry of Education, 1980, p. 23).

While this is an older education document, the concern that Korean education re-flect Korean cultural identity and historical experience is still important, even in this age of globalization. Every nation faces the inevitable tension between traditional no-tions of nationalism or statism and globalization. It is clear that in order to manage this tension, a new breed of nationalism has to be developed. Professor of international relations at Seoul National University, Dr. Yoon Young-kwan, suggested that for Ko-rea, this new nationalism should be one that is magnanimous, forward-looking and open (1995).

The Content of Values Education

In response to the question, "What should be taught in schools?" "personal auton-omy", "moral values", and "civic values" all received the same high mean score as indicated in Table 8.3.

Table 8.3 What Should be Taught in Schools? (Higher Priority)

Rank	Content	Mean
1	Personal Autonomy	1.9
2	Moral Values	1.9
3	Civic values	1.9

The areas represented in Table 8.4 were seen as having a slightly lower priority.

Table 8.4 What Should be Taught in Schools? (Lower Priority)

Rank	Content	Mean
10	Global Awareness	3.0
11	Diversity and Multiculturalism	3.0
12	Peace and Conflict Resolution	3.0
13	Religious Values	4.1

Korea was not unusual among the sites that our research teams studied in its pre-ference for avoiding the teaching of religious values in schools. Most sites did not fa-vor the teaching of religious values in schools. What is of greater interest for this study is the clustering of the other three values "diversity and multiculturalism", "peace and conflict resolution" and "global awareness" still positive but lower on the priority scale. Koreans described their country as homogenous. Although there are many Kore-ans living in diaspora there is a strong sense of cultural rootedness. Korea simply does not have significant numbers of minorities living within its national boundaries. Chi-nese are the largest minority group in Korea and, while their numbers have fluctuated over the years, they have never amounted to even one percent of the total population.

A revolving population of American troops has been stationed in the country for decades, and presently Korea is seeing an influx of guest workers, but there are relatively few long-term foreign residents. This is partly because of the restrictions against foreigners owning land, which was a law until recently. This may be one reason that an understanding of diversity and multiculturalism was not seen as a priority to the respondents in our survey. The same seems to be true of global awareness. If we refer back to the third guideline for promoting the purpose of education, as stipulated in the Education Act, "Inheritance and enrichment of our national culture and thus contribute to the development of the world", there is a clear sense that the focus is on the national culture with residual influence on the global community by becoming a self-sufficient member of that community. This is quite a different notion from global awareness, which includes peace and conflict resolution as part of the process towards achieving global community, and may explain why these three answers were clustered at the bottom.

The third question in our survey had to do with the views on emphasizing controversial content. Respondents were asked to rate twenty-five items on a Likert scale of one to seven as to whether they should receive strong emphasis in the curriculum or be left out. The means scores for Korea ranged from 1.7 (strong emphasis) to 4.2 (weaker emphasis). Those items receiving the strongest emphasis and weakest emphasis are shown below in Tables 8.5 and 8.6.

Table 8.5 What Content Should be Emphasized? (Most Emphasis)

Rank	Content	Mean
1	Assisting each child in developing his/her own values	1.7
2	Encourage mutual respect between boys and girls	2.0
3	Foster values supporting the family	2.1

Table 8.6 What Content Should be Emphasized? (Least Emphasis)

Rank	Content	Mean
22	Appreciate the essential role of unions	3.8
23	Foster an understanding of all religions	3.8
24	Gain deeper understanding of their own religion	4.1
25	Respect hierarchy and support the government	4.2

In analyzing those controversial content issues which Koreans marked as higher priority for values education, it is useful to note the compatibility between the top priority answer in this section, "Assisting each child in developing his/her own values", and the top priority answer to the first question, where respondents chose "Help young people develop autonomous personalities". The preference for fostering autonomy and the ability to develop one's own values was seen in the other settings in this study as well, so Korea fits the international pattern.

The second most popular answer, to "Encourage mutual respect between boys and girls" offers us some insight into what seemed to be an earlier indication that values education should not be concerned with improving the respect and opportunities for girls and women. This answer suggests that Koreans would agree that it is important to place their emphasis on the relationship between boys and girls, concerning their mutual respect for each other, rather than focusing on girls and women as a separate category. The mean scores on these two questions were very close to the total mean score for all of the sites where the survey was conducted.

In response to the question, "Which country examples should be most prominently featured?" Korean respondents predictably answered: Korea (1.7), U.S. (1.9) and Japan (2.0).

The Implementation of Values Education

Respondents from Korea tended to feel that values education should begin in the early years rather than later, but they were less likely than people in other settings to feel that it should be integrated across the curriculum. These responses are consistent with the way that values education is presently conducted in Korea. It begins at an early age and continues through the upper grades and is taught as a stand-alone course.

When asked about appropriate settings for religious education, Korea was in concert with most other sites in the study agreeing that home and family and religious groups and institutions were the best venues for such education. For this set of questions related to religion, the mean scores, for all countries surveyed, ranged between 1.5 and 2.4. Korea was at the mean or within .3 of the mean on all questions except one, where it deviated rather significantly. Among the ten sites in the original study Korea stood out in its response to the question that asked if "military training and national service" were appropriate settings for values education. Korean respondents were far less inclined to see this as an appropriate venue for values education than people in the other sites. This data is included on the following table, which combines data from three questions and shows both the international mean and the Korean mean.

Table 8.7 What Is the Best Setting?

Settings	Religious Ed.		Civic/Nat Ed.		Moral Ed.	
	Korea	I. Mean	Korea	I. Mean	Korea	I. Mean
1.During School as a class	2.4	2.1	1.7	1.6	1.9	1.9
2.During school through rules of behavior	2.1	2.2	1.6	1.8	1.9	2.0
3.Outside school activities (clubs, sports, arts)	2.2	2.4	2.2	2.3	2.6	2.3
4.Internships and community service	2.4	2.4	2.1	2.0	2.3	2.1
5.Camps	2.5	2.3	2.3	2.2	2.3	2.1
6.Religious Groups and Institutions	1.7	1.8	2.4	2.2	2.3	2.2
7.Military training and national service	4.0	2.4	2.0	2.1	3.0	2.1
8.Home and family	1.7	1.5	2.0	1.8	1.6	1.4
9.Media	2.7	2.4	2.3	2.3	2.3	2.3

1=strongly agree; 7=strongly disagree

Table 8.8 looks at the data which was collected in reference to what groups should receive the most exposure to religious education, civic/national education and moral education.

Table 8.8 Who Should Receive the Most Exposure?

People	Religious Ed.		Civic/Nat Ed.		Moral Ed.	
	Korea	I. Mean	Korea	I. Mean	Korea	I. Mean
1. Inservice Teachers	1.6	1.9	1.4	1.7	1.4	1.7
2. Teacher Learners	2.2	2.2	1.8	1.8	2.0	1.9
3. Young children	1.5	1.7	1.0	1.9	1.4	1.7
4. Pre-schoolers	1.8	1.8	1.0	1.9	1.9	1.8
5. Primary Level	2.1	1.8	1.8	1.7	2.0	1.8
6. Secondary Level	2.2	2.0	2.2	2.0	2.5	2.1
7. High School Level	2.2	2.2	2.5	2.3	2.6	2.4
8. University Level	2.0	2.3	2.4	2.3	2.2	2.4

1=strongly agree; 7=strongly disagree

Considering that all of the answers for these questions were clustered at the "strongly agree" end of the scale, we can assume that our respondents were in favor of religious, civic and moral education for all of the constituents represented, with the strongest emphasis on civic and national education for the very youngest children. The scores suggest that Koreans also feel that teachers, in particular, need exposure to these areas of values education and that as students move through the system the need to emphasize values education diminishes slightly.

Interviews

Comments made by informants have been integrated throughout our discussion. While the interviews reflect the diversity of concerns of the elite who talked with us over the period of this study, we can note some recurring themes. The most common thread that runs through the interviews is a sense of values tension. This tension was expressed in a variety of ways. It was generated both from internal as well as external forces and from the tension between the two. While all of the factors are intercon- nected, we can identify specific areas of tension. It appears that the values tension is due to the following multiple factors: (a) the rapid pace of change, (b) generational differences, (c) the need to embrace western as well as traditional values, (d) the ten- sion between national identity and globalization, (e) the inevitable reunification of Korea, and (f) the constraints and contradictions in education (see Figure 8.1).

Sometimes this tension around values was described as confusion, other times it was seen as a kind of balancing act where particular values systems were applied in different situations. For example, one interviewee contributed: "Western values in the day time and Confucian values at night [....] when we are doing business we have to rely on the Western rational values...but when we meet our friends or when we meet our father's brothers we have to use our Confucian values". This interviewee acknow- ledged that many people see this as confusing but preferred to see the possibilities of

Figure 8.1 Factors Influencing Values Tension

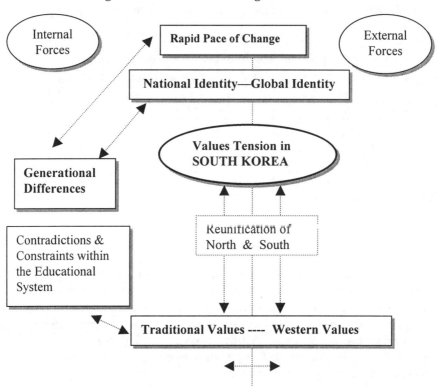

creating a harmonious union of the two systems and underscored the point that traditional values were an essential part of being Korean. This view complemented the point of other informants who spoke about "grafting" Western values to traditional values. This image suggests that the fundamental values are Korean and the new values were grafted to the Korean root.

The kind of discussions around values suggest that the tension has both negative and positive aspects. On the one hand, the tension demands the development of means for reconciling competing views and institutional contradictions and constraints, of holding on to the aspects of tradition which enhance and inform the present, while relinquishing those aspects which undermine reform efforts. At the same time, the values tension generates a sense of potential dynamic change, which was acknowledged by some of our informants.

Policy Implications

In looking at the policy implications of this study, we can ask the following question: Do current policies and planned policy revisions speak to the values concerns that were raised by the results of the survey and in the interviews? As indicated earlier in the paper, an educational reform package scheduled for implementation in 2003 reduces the number of hours spent in formal moral education classes at the secondary level. Our informant explained that the impetus for this decision was concern from parents and educators that students had too many academic requirements. As indicated earlier in the paper, there are other problems with the moral education component of the curriculum which make this an easy target for reduced hours. A related educational reform that may help to alleviate the academic pressure within the education system is the plan for the abolition of the all-powerful entrance examination. It is difficult to gauge how values education will fare, in the midst of all this reform. When the hours are reduced, will teachers of other subjects feel the need to integrate it into their curricula in a more intentional manner? Might the proposal to use other criteria besides the entrance examination for college entrance be the decisive factor in creating a less competitive society? Or will the implementation of new criteria for entrance to college simply create a new hierarchy of status and achievement markers that open up new venues for competition that have repercussions for students, parents and teachers at the lower levels? It is not possible to answer these questions at this moment in time.

One must tread lightly when discussing policy implications of a study like ours. This is partly due to the fact that our study conceived of values education policy and practice as normative and prescriptive. It might be that issues that were given low priority were given this status only within the parameters of values education as it is currently conceptualized. This certainly seems to be the case in questions that referred to teaching religion in the schools.

Some of our informants wondered about the success of the system in preparing people for the acceptance of cultural diversity and were concerned that the educational system was not putting enough emphasis on multiculturalism or transnational competencies. This concern was not strongly reflected in the survey.

The ideological tensions between South Korea and North Korea and the issue of eventual reunification pose a continuing dilemma in values education. In an article describing the six major shifts that have taken place in the moral education curriculum from 1945 to 1992, Dr. Moon Yong-lin suggests that the current version of the moral education curriculum—which was instituted in 1992—emphasizes communitarian ethics as a preparation for eventual unification with the North (Moon, 1995). Issues related to peace and conflict resolution which might have been seen as relatively less important themes in values education might become more central to the values discussion as North and South Korea move closer to reunification.

The guidelines presented in the Korean Education Act are very comprehensive and reflect both breadth and depth of thought about the nature and purposes of education. If there appears to be something missing from this document, it might be because we look at it from the perspective of societies that are more diverse and multicultural rather than relatively homogeneous. However, the concerns that were raised about the insular nature of Korean culture and the need for a more inclusive and multicultural attitude should be taken into account. While there are clear social and historical reasons for Korea's tendency to mono-culturalism, nevertheless, this may indeed be the area of values education which requires more thought and emphasis in the future.

Woo and Lee (1998) have argued that the superb performance of Korea's youth on standardized tests is as much an indication of the failure of Korean education as an indicator of its success. Their point is that the test driven system places an emphasis on rote learning. Large classes and the need to maintain order result in unimaginative pedagogy that favors order and obedience over creativity, critical reasoning and spontaneity. Time spent in and out of school on preparing for the college exam leaves little opportunity to develop skills in creative thinking, critical reasoning and social interaction. This problem will be partly rectified by new guidelines for college entrance which will go into effect in 2002, making the exam a less important criterion for college entrance. If there is concern that students are not developing their creative, thinking and social capacities, values education might the be domain in which these can best be promoted. Despite the problem of class size which may continue to plague Korean education and make Socratic pedagogy difficult, it appears that the moral education curriculum has been designed as a participatory one in which students are required to actively seek for moral principles and use moral dilemmas as a means to develop rational thinking. Furthermore moral education, particularly if it is realized through social action projects, might result in important educational experiences for Korea's youth while promoting general social consciousness. The new education policy, which reduces hours in moral education, as described earlier in this paper, may actually turn out to be a policy that does not serve Korea's larger educational interests, which must go beyond creating a technologically competent work force.

References

Durkheim, E. (1980). "Education and Sociology". In E. Steiner, R. Arnove and E. McClellan (eds.), *Education and American Culture.* New York: Macmillan.

Kim, S. (1997). "Debates Raised Over Partial Ban on Out-of-school English Lessons", *Korea Newsreview 26*(12): 15-16.

Koh, B. (1996). "Confucianism in Contemporary Korea". In W. Yu (ed.), *Confucian Traditions in East-Asian Modernity.* Cambridge, MA: Harvard University Press.

Ministry of Education (1980). *Education in Korea 1979-1980.* Seoul, South Korea: National Institute of Education.

Moon, Y. (1995). "The Status and Perspective of Moral Education in Korea", *The Seoul National Journal of Education Research* 5(12): 1-10.

National Institute for Educational Research (1991). *Education for Humanistic, Ethical/Moral and Cultural Values.* Tokyo: NIER.

Reed, G. and Chung, B. (1997). "North Korea". In G. Postiglione and G. Mak (eds.), *Asian Higher Education: An International Handbook and Reference Guide.* Westport, CT: Greenwood Press.

Rhee, K. (1981). *To the Young Korean Intellectuals.* Elizabeth, NJ: Hollym International Corp.

Woo, C. and Lee, J. (1998). *Education in Korea: Attainments and Challenges.* Paper presented at the meeting of the Korea Development Institute, Seoul, South Korea.

Yoon, Y. (1995). "Globalization: Towards a New Nationalism in Korea", *Korea Focus* 3(1): 13-28.

CHAPTER 9

CHINA: BALANCING THE COLLECTIVE AND
THE INDIVIDUAL

John N. Hawkins
Zhou Nanzhao
Julie Lee

Introduction

Educators in China have for centuries stressed the importance of values education as a critical component of the educational system. In the Asian region, certainly in East Asia, many of the values that find their way into the educational system originated in China (Cummings and Altbach, 1997). Educators in China today and during the past decade have debated which values should be stressed and how they should be taught. In this essay, we will look specifically at China focusing first on the social and political setting, then on the post-1949 period, followed by a discussion of the agencies responsible for teaching values (the formal schools, non-formal institutions, and agencies external to the schools), and conclude with a discussion of the effectiveness of values education in general. This discussion will take place in the context of an elite survey conducted in China to illuminate the questions of: "why" teach values; "what" values should be taught; and "how" should they be taught.

Research on values education has long been a contentious and emotional area of inquiry. The literature is vast but it is useful in the China case to note that at least two opposing views can be identified. What might be termed a conservative view is proposed by Doyle (1997) who makes the distinction between education (character development) and training (narrow and focused) and suggests that from the ancient Greeks right down to the late nineteenth century "education's greater purpose was to shape character" (p. 440). He notes that humans are distinct in this sense and have always needed a supportive social order, culture, values and language to survive. In this view, children have no innate capacity to be good and need to be taught the rules of correct social behavior. They may be hardwired for language but not for values. Rather than disagree with values education, educators should embrace the notion and openly explore ways to teach them. Thus in this view there are two elements to values education: 1) There is no such thing as a value free school; 2) There are good and bad values and like it or not schools shape character. Values are imbedded in all areas of the curriculum (even science where students are taught honesty in collecting data, maintaining a consistent methodology, willingness to change one's views based on new evidence, and so on). This is a point that educators in China would agree with (Yuan and Shen, 1998).

His colleague Kohn (1997) disagrees and attacks the "fix the kid" and Hobbesian views that Doyle espouses. His view of Doyle and others who support this version of values education is that what passes for values education in the schools is "for the most part, a collection of exhortations and extrinsic inducements designed to make children work harder and do what they are told" (p. 430). The "fix the kid" approach represents a dark view of human nature in general and children in particular. It does not engage them in deep and critical reflection about certain ways of acting and be-having. Kohn (1997) stresses the point that "good values cannot be bought" with ex-trinsic rewards or produced through other kinds of punishments. He agrees that values are indeed taught but the real question is, whose values find their way into the cur-riculum: "The character education programs–and the theorists who promote them–seem to regard teaching as a matter of telling and compelling" (p. 432).

As we shall see in this essay, educators in China have struggled with both of these views of values education seeking to come to terms with China's new role as a mod-ernizing, global society in the context of a long and deeply imbedded tradition. As Yuan and Shen (1998) note, issues related to character education, who controls values, and the content of values education are very much alive in both Taiwan and China. Thus the debate on values education is a cross national topic.

Social and Political Context

Core values emerged in the region in the second millennium BC in northern China and over time spread to Korea and Japan. Rozman (1991) makes the point that a typology of societies that includes Confucianism makes more sense than the traditional capitalist and socialist notions that seem to have prevailed on conventional concepts of modernization and development. It is the brand and expression of Confucianism that needs explanation.

Although it is risky to utilize stereotypes based on culture and history, they are nevertheless useful in setting the tone of the discussion. Rozman (1991) and associates found many of the following stereotypes regarding societies influenced by Confucianism to be ". . . relatively true: individuals are characterized by self-denial, frugality, patience, fortitude, self-discipline, dedication, rote learning, and an aptitude for applied sciences and mathematics" (pp. 28-29). Some educational implications for these statements are that individuals from the region excel in efforts that require patience and unstinting effort over long periods of time, with delayed gratification; memorization and repetition are rewarded; individualism is downplayed both at home and in the school. In the school, student diligence, rote learning, memorization, emphasis on test taking at an early age, and moral education highlight motivation and achievement. While all of this may suggest uniformity, in fact the opportunity structure (merit based competition) was quite open both in China and Korea in the early periods (Rozman, 1991).

Other group stereotypes that help frame the discussion have to do with "group orientation, acceptance of authority, deference, dependence, conflict avoidance, interest in harmony, seniority consciousness, and dutifulness" (Rozman, 1991, p. 30). If one would want to locate a unit of analysis that best encompasses these traits then probably the family and its extension, familism, would be a good place to start. Group organizations, whether they are the family proper, or a school, are more strict in the degree of commitment required to join or be admitted and in their exclusivity, than is the case in many other societies.

All of these stereotypes are grounded to some degree in the philosophical mode of thought typically referred to as Confucianism. The modern expression of this system of thought varies between Japan, Korea and China with, however, significant similarities.

In China as far back as the Song dynasty (960 AD), the teaching of Confucianism through formal and "nonformal" educational means became established (Levenson, 1968). At this time the educated class expanded significantly, and schools could be found in most all market towns and certainly at least one at the county level. Ordinary peasants now came into contact with educated people, and even the highest ranking officials were by this time marrying into the local lower class families. Thus, Confucian values were spreading throughout the different classes of Chinese society and were not solely present in the privileged classes. The educational system played a powerful role in this expansion, particularly the memorization associated with the examination system; this became a widespread phenomenon and verses expressing Confucian values were memorized by people at all social levels. Thus, an indirect outcome of the spread of schools was the spread of Confucian ideas and values (Ebrey, 1991). The role of the family in spreading Confucian ideas was also significant, not only in China proper but in other areas populated by Chinese (e.g., Hong Kong, Singapore, Taiwan).

The educational implications of the practice of filial piety are not often discussed. In brief, the hierarchy of family relations (obedience, rites, responsibilities, etc.), polite language towards superiors, and a variety of behaviors associated with superiors and inferiors found their way into the school environment once education became more widespread. In some respects, the family reflected the autocratic nature of traditional Chinese society: superiority of old over young, and males over females. This was modulated, however, by rules based upon mutual responsibility and obligation; a high sense of security and predictability among family members made the system work. Just as the children and mother of a family (the inferiors) had to adhere to the decisions of the father (superior) so did younger siblings to the oldest son. These decisions would range from internal family matters, to property concerns to marriage. Just as there was a high degree of uniformity in the Chinese family, by the end of the Qing dynasty in 1911 there was a parallel high degree of uniformity of belief and behavior regarding learning which if properly approached resulted in uniformly high motivation among students in the Chinese societies (Ebrey, 1991).

Much of this can be summed up in the Chinese term for education, *jiaoyu* the two characters of which are metaphors for training and values. Or, as Meyer (1990) suggests, the effort to reconcile differing patterns of thought can be expressed with the longer phrase in Chinese, *jiaoyu yuren*, or teach knowledge and form character. Education thus came to be seen as a transformative agency capable of bringing about change in the individual not just in the realm of knowledge and facts but behavior as well. Thus, with the impact of the West and Western utilitarian educational values, China's response was to suggest a bifurcated system of Western learning for useful purposes in the context of Eastern values. This milieu was to become even more complicated with the establishment of the People's Republic of China in 1949 and the introduction of the Chinese brand of socialist values.

The People's Republic of China and Education: Some General Comments

From 1949 down to the present China's educational leaders have struggled with the at times contradictory goals of educating students to be both "red and expert".[1] Although the terminology has changed depending on the historical period there has always been a tension between these two goals. The tension culminated in the dramatic and traumatic period known as the Cultural Revolution. China's educational history down to the end of the Cultural Revolution in 1976 has been detailed elsewhere (Hayhoe, 1989; Hawkins, 1983) and will not be focused on here.

The notion that schools should promote socialist values and maintain a balance between "red and expert" remained part of the official rhetoric. And during this period (1977-1980), the idea that schools can and should play a powerful role in transmitting correct values to children was revived. This movement accelerated from 1980-1982 with a concerted effort to rebuild some form of moral base thought to have been destroyed during the Cultural Revolution. Many of the values expressed during this period were focused on individual personal qualities, essentially conservative (following orders and recognizing hierarchy) harking back to Confucian norms. From 1983-1984 the effort moved beyond personal qualities and behaviors to demonstrating a concern over the new freedoms and independence characteristic of the economic liberalization that was taking place. Thus there was a renewal of political education stressing a balance between the economic freedoms that were being promoted ("becoming rich") and the need to "regulate autonomy and obedience; bring wealth back to the collectivity" (Lee, 1996). A renewed emphasis on patriotism among youth was also emphasized during this period.

In the two years following this period China's educational officials faced a paradox of rising economic liberalization coupled with a call for a corresponding intellectual liberalization. Concerned that these two movements might result in some behaviors and values at odds with socialist values and government policy, an interesting mix of values to be promoted in the schools emerged in official publications. Teachers were exhorted to instill in children notions of civilized behavior, courtesy, hygiene, public order, morals, beautification of the mind, moderate language, good conduct, protection of the environment, love of the motherland, love of the people, love of labor, science, and socialism (Lee, 1996). These were essentially values focused on stability and order. Yet they were to be taught through a student-centered, elicitation method designed to stimulate student individual initiatives, independent thinking, self-education, free expression of ideas, and open discussions. There is little research on this period and one wonders how teachers coped with what appear to be contradictory messages.

In the last decade, educational policy documents have revealed a more refined approach to reconciling the values associated with economic liberalization (open discussion, student independence, democratic classrooms, independent thinking, entrepreneurial behavior, etc.), and values associated with socialism (on-going exhortations condemning bourgeois liberalism) (Lee, 1996). Here is the basic conflict between what might be called Western values and Chinese values with a socialist template.

There is clearly some confusion as to how to confront this transition period characterized by a liberal market economy on the one hand and a political desire to

---

[1] "Red and expert" is a standard term used in China where "red" denotes values focused on political awareness, socialism and communism among others, and "expert" the more objective, scientific, value free approach to getting things done.

maintain socialist values on the other. For example, Li (1997) makes the case that there are laws that govern the market and laws that govern education. Both the market and education have differential values and social orientation. He concludes that, "there are often deviations and imbalances between economic development and moral civilization. And that economic development is not necessarily the pre-condition of moral civilization" (p. 1).

It is clear that scholars are grappling with the dilemma of market forces versus native values. Sun Changqing for example argues that "modernization should not be occidentalizing" (1997, p. 2). In his view, China should promote a good "oriental morality"; he quotes both Confucius and Mencius liberally and suggests that China has a special and cultural specific set of morals and values that can be adapted to the modern world. Students need to be taught socialist ethics, all of which are adaptable to the market economy, and the society should mobilize the media, schools and other agencies to educate young people about these values. Guo Zuyi (1997), who adds Confucius to the pantheon of Chinese moral-political leaders such as Mao, Marx, Engels, and Lenin, backs this view.

Part of the reason for the renewal of discussion about values and morals among Chinese educators had to do with a rise in student activism in the 1990s. The State Education Commission reacted quickly by issuing a series of directives stressing the need to reinvigorate moral education (*deyu*) and generally admitting that previous approaches to institute moral education had been ineffective (Guojia, 1990). While these reports decry the over-emphasis on study and examinations they note that students found moral education to be uninspired and propagandistic.

The government seems to be equally adrift and has responded with vaguely worded directives to teachers to "promote socialist morality" or "spirit civilization" (XSJW, 1996, no. 11). Marx, Mao and Deng are all quoted in this report as providing the theoretical guiding principals for "spirit civilization".

Some writers have sought a middle ground by suggesting that the values associated with the market economy and those needed for a socialist society are not necessarily mutually exclusive. Schools and teachers should concentrate on those values that are similar and move away from lecturing and the heavy-handed approach to teaching socialist values that has dominated in the past. Instead, schools should concentrate on discovering, through an experiential approach, those values that are good whether or not they come from a market economy approach or socialist (Yuan, 1997).

What, in fact, did the elite respondents think of this debate? In the sections that follow we will attempt to explore in more detail the expression of these conflicting values as they appear in the various educational agencies in China and illustrate the discussion by reporting on the results of a survey on values in education conducted as part of a broader cross-national study.

Values in Practice: Policy Issues

China's educational system is comprised of an inter-related formal and non-formal system of schools covering precollegiate and collegiate levels. This system is the primary transmitter of values and moral and political education. The State Education Commission has over the years issued general guidelines on what and how to teach morals. A 1986 document reveals that there were both specific and general objectives. The overall objectives were wide-ranging and included the usual goals of loving the motherland and the Communist Party, as well as more general goals of being disciplined, civil, courteous, respectful, frugal, diligent, honest, humble, punctual, responsible, and trustworthy. Interestingly at this time other somewhat conflicting goals were also included, such as fostering independent thinking among students, and encouraging them to ask questions and be creative (Quanrizhi, 1986).

In order to determine more accurately the views of China's educational elite regarding values education the authors conducted a survey in 1998 designed to illuminate the three questions posed earlier in this chapter: "why", "what", and "how".[2]

Regarding the "why teach values" issue our survey of educational decision-makers revealed that this group believed that the dominant reasons for stressing values education had to do with the need to develop greater individual responsibility and social consciousness. This was necessary in order to lay a foundation for "mental development" (the Chinese translation for our category of spiritual development). Also ranked high as to "why" one should study values was the need to foster economic development and national identity while strengthening collective consciousness.

Table 9.1 Why Study Values Education?

Most Important Reasons	Least Important Reasons
1. Highlight individual responsibility	1. Prevent racial discrimination
2. Lay foundation for mental development	2. Strengthen family values
3. Foster economic development	3. Promote world peace

This is an eclectic mix of answers to the "why" question but seems to reflect the confusion over the movement towards a new market economy while trying to preserve traditional, socialist, more collective values. Perhaps unique to China, educators have been struggling with a desire to balance socialist values of stability, collective behavior, and respect for authority and hierarchy with the new demands of marketization and globalization. These latter demands call for more independent thinking, risk-taking, and entrepreneurial values.

The three reasons that ranked the lowest for teaching values had to do with preventing racial discrimination, strengthening family ties and promoting world peace. Respondents seem to believe that these are non-issues in current Chinese society or that they are being effectively addressed. This is especially true in reasons 1 and 3 above. While issues of race and ethnicity are clearly present in Chinese society, there is a general belief that since about 94 percent of the citizens belong to the Han group and most minorities live in border, frontier regions, majority-minority relations are not a critical

---

[2] A multi-nation study of values education was conducted in 1998. The China portion of this study was based on data from 51 respondents using the sigma instrument designed by the research team. We followed a common sample design used by the other members of the project team. Of the 51 China respondents, 25 were affiliated with educational institutes while 13 were values/moral education specialists. The remainder were leading educational intellectuals, academic leaders and leaders of NGOs. One-third were from smaller towns in China while two-thirds were from large cities.

topic for the schools. In addition, there is a stated policy that China is a unitary multiethnic state. And despite China's effort to engage in the global economy, China remains a highly nationalistic state, not overly concerned with conflicts beyond its own borders. More difficult to explain are the responses to reason 2 as other evidence suggests that promoting family solidarity and strength remains a strong Chinese value. One interpretation might be that those surveyed do not view the schools as a proper place for teaching values regarding the family. There was no response on the questions that had to do with gender and educational opportunities for women. Values associated with understanding the media and the internet, both areas the central authorities seek to control, were also ranked low (10th out of 13).

Regarding the issue of "what" the course content should be in values education those surveyed ranked basic moral education, civic values, and autonomous and mature individuality as the top three themes. Religious values, family and gender, and multi-culturalism ranked among the least important.

Table 9.2 What Should be Taught?

Most Important Issues	Least Important Issues
1. Moral education	1. Religion
2. Civic values	2. Family and gender
3. Autonomy	3. Multiculturalism

Again, one can see something of the conflict between wanting children to have basic moral values, especially those associated with socialist Chinese society and be good citizens, yet be independent and autonomous thinkers; the latter values needed for China's move towards a market economy. Regarding the least important issues, religion, in the Western sense of the word, has never been a topic of much interest to Chinese educators, or one might add, to Chinese society as a whole. With a tradition based more on the secular, ethical and moral teachings of Confucianism (and the negative view of religion held by Marxists in general), it is understandable that religion not be ranked very high. Again, multiculturalism, as was the case with racial discrimination, is not a topic at the top of the agenda in the largely Han Chinese society. More interesting was the low ranking given to family and gender. The previous reason for ranking family low as an issue to be taught would probably hold true in this case as well. The reasons for ranking gender low would be worthy of further study. It should be noted, however, that the category "national identity" was also not highly ranked (ranked 7th out of 11). Perhaps it is thought that the schools are simply not the appropriate places for dealing with these issues.

On a set of more specific questions regarding the kind of themes that ought to be included in the curriculum China's educational leaders remained consistent and ranked creativity, individuality, equal treatment between boys and girls, helping children analyze the ideas of others while forming their own independent ideas, and values related to equality before the law among the top four themes. All of these are values that will be important for China's new economic directions.

Table 9.3 Most and Least Important Themes in Values Education

Most Important Themes	Least Important Themes
1. Creativity and individuality	1. Sex Education
2. Boys and girls should be treated equally	2. Involvement in social organizations
3. Analyze the ideas of others	3. Understand unionism defense of work wages and conditions
4. Form own ideas and values	4. Girls are responsible for the foundation of the family
5. Interact with others	5. Emphasize differences between Eastern and Western values

The least important themes had to do with encouraging different views on sex education, involvement in social organizations, and other political issues, and emphasizing the difference between Eastern and Western values. These rankings are also understandable. Sex education has never been considered a topic appropriate for the schools and involvement with trade unionism and social organizations (the most recent example being *falun gong*!) is anathema to China's ruling party. There is also little interest in highlighting Western values in the classroom given that some of them (those associated with representative government and personal freedoms) would surely clash with those promoted by the Communist Party.

Finally, educators were surveyed on the question of "how" the teaching of values education should take place. Educators felt that values education should be a lifelong process, that they should be conducted in formal courses in schools as part of the normal teaching curriculum.

Teaching values outside the school, in summer camps or in religious organizations was not felt to be appropriate. It was noted, however, by one of our Chinese researchers that the religious category was not really appropriate to address in school settings and by the educational system in general in China and would therefore always receive the lowest response. These responses may reflect a lingering dissatisfaction with previous, more politicized efforts at values education associated with such movements as the Great Leap Forward, the Socialist Education Movement and the Cultural Revolution. Part of the goal of sending young people out the countryside in the 1960s and 1970s was to inculcate them with worker and peasant values.

Table 9.4 How Should Values Education be Conducted?

Top Two Responses	Bottom Two Responses
1. In formal courses in school	1. Religious groups
2. As part of the normal teaching curriculum	2. Summer camps

Regarding which groups should receive civic/national education the top ranked answers were preschool children, working teachers, and students in teachers colleges. This is somewhat in contrast to previous, heavy-handed efforts to provide "political education" to college students following the Democracy Movement, and the Tiananmen square military action; efforts that clearly were not evaluated as effective either by the students or the leadership. It is now felt that the appropriate place to begin is with younger children and those who care for them in the schools.

Table 9.5 Who Should Receive Civic Education?

Top Three Groups	Bottom Two Groups
1. Preschool children and toddlers	1. College students
2. Working teachers	2. High school students
3. Students in teachers colleges	

Finally, responses to the question as to who most needs moral education, Chinese educators responded that the top groups were working teachers, then toddlers, and preschool students, while those less in need were high school students and students in teachers colleges. This corresponds with the previous findings on who should receive moral education.

Table 9.6 Greatest and Least Need for Values Education

Top Three Groups	Bottom Three Groups
1. Working teacher	1. High school students
2. Toddlers	2. Students in teachers colleges
3. Preschool children	3. Middle school students

These responses overall reveal that Chinese educators have a strong belief in the value of moral education overall and also believe that young children should develop and acquire a strong sense of individuality and independence while maintaining a sense of civic behavior. Less important were issues that might be ranked higher in a different society and culture such as the role of religion, issues related to sex education, gender, multiculturalism and mass media. The views expressed in our survey are reflected to some degree in the more specific objectives provided to teachers in different parts of China, a topic to which we will now turn.

Goals and Objectives

Course syllabi from the late 1980s offer very specific objectives for both the elementary and secondary school levels. They also provide an interesting counterpoint to the results of the elite survey, generally projecting a more conservative content. With respect to elementary schools, thirteen points were specified. Students should:

1. Know they are Chinese, know the country's name, the national anthem, who the main leaders are, and so on.
2. Learn the name and location of one's home village.
3. Learn correct relationships with other people, such as parents, elders, each other.
4. Learn the concept of collectivism.
5. Learn how to treat others with warmth and courtesy.
6. Develop good personal hygiene.
7. Learn to be punctual.
8. Obey rules of traffic.

9. Learn the value of hard study.
10. Learn to love work and labor, not be arrogant and lazy.
11. Learn frugality in daily life.
12. Learn to be courageous.
13. Learn to confess mistakes and not lie, not to "covet small advantages" such a pocketing money they find on the playground (Quanrizhi, 1986).

At the intermediate and upper grade levels the emphasis shifts to developing social skills and acquiring a basic understanding of the law. Here seven points were specified. Students should:

1. Learn about great figures of history and respect China's national dignity.
2. Understand diversity and that all groups in China should be respectful of each other.
3. Understand that the People's Liberation Army is the defender of the motherland.
4. China should have friendly relations with the world and be courteous to foreigners.
5. Respect parents and teachers.
6. Respect other people.
7. Learn about the collective.
8. Cultivate good learning habits, do not shirk hard work (Quanrizhi, 1986).

These values found their way into state approved texts and were widely applied throughout China. The values expressed in the texts did not differ significantly from those of earlier periods even going back to the early 1960s (Straka and Bos, 1989; Burton, 1986). In the late 1980s and early 1990s two principal classes focused on moral education: *sixiang pinde jiaoyu* (moral thought education) and *zhengzhi* (politics). A content analysis of elementary school texts revealed that patriotism and respect for school rules ranked highest in number of lessons taught; the fewest lessons had to do with "love of science" (Meyer, 1990. p. 11). In literature texts patriotism ranked at the top followed by respecting school rules and authorities and ranked last was modesty and humility (Meyer, 1990, p. 12) In addition to formal classes, students were provided with a booklet (*xiaoxuesheng richang xingwei quifan*—daily rules of behavior for elementary school) and memorized songs that reinforced the moral qualities listed in the texts (Meyer, 1990, p. 12).

This approach was basically teacher-oriented, textbook-focused with little in the way of creative discussion or inquiry. The classes were overseen by a *banzhuren* (home room teacher) who had great authority over content, classroom behavior and so on, and who also would incorporate home visits should any problems with students arise. More recently, some writers are suggesting that this method of teaching morality and values is outmoded and that a more effective method utilizing the "hidden curriculum" should be utilized. It is suggested that students be allowed to participate in the leadership of the school and learn values in an "invisible" manner (Sun, Chen and Lin, 1997, p. 10). However, at this time it appears that the didactic method prevails.

The higher up the educational ladder one climbs, the more the emphasis shifts to a focus on politics and the government. At the secondary level, rulebooks have been prepared for students which deal directly with issues of the state, communism, Marxism, and the Chinese Communist Party (CCP) (Meyer, 1990). At the university level efforts are being made to enhance the CCP's role in higher education through new courses on Marxism-Leninism and Mao and Deng's thought. A new Marxist Studies Foundation has been created to "support and encourage new scholarship on the teaching of Marxism, Leninism, the Philosophy of Mao Tse-tung and Deng Xiao-ping's theories on building socialism with Chinese characteristics" (Hertling, 1996; Wu, 1996). CCP party committees are seeking more power on campuses and there is a general sense of alarm on the part of authorities that students are not being taught "correct" values.

In general, the effort to teach morals and values in a directed manner through the educational system has been a hallmark of China's educational practices since modern times and probably harks back to China's traditional Confucian education. One prevailing problem, however, is that teachers are ill prepared to teach this subject. They tend to rely solely on the texts that have been prepared by the government and the rulebooks that the students receive. Thus, they lack confidence to try more creative methods of teaching values/morals (Meyer, 1990).

While the formal school system is the principal channel through which young people receive values education, the various youth organizations, such as the Young Pioneers (*xiaodiandui*), the Young Communist League (*gongqingtuan*), and various student organizations (the Student Union, monitors etc.) also have an impact on children mostly through their admission policies. Scholars in China have proposed that these organizations are more influential than the family and have been increasing in importance (Li, 1990).[3] Foreign observers have noted that these organizations all have as one of their primary goals: "to train children to have proper attitudes towards their country, their parents, labor, science and socialism" (McClintock, 1987).[4] Others have observed "the eagerness, the enthusiasm, the happiness, the cooperative social interactions displayed by these children. Not once during the whole morning was there . . . a non-compliant behavior, and aggressive interaction" (Sparkes, 1990. p. 21). It appears to these observers and others that the moral/value education that is imparted does indeed have an impact on the children. Often, however, there is little analysis of the process by which this occurs. Other scholars have noted the long-standing use of "role models" (e.g. Lei Feng) as a means to transmit values and that this practice is likely to continue even during the current transition period (Reed, 1995).

Other innovative nonformal education programs designed to transmit values include arts education. Through the arts, observers have noted, young people are taught citizenship education which "will encourage them to participate actively in the political process. . . and in turn enhance their decision-making power" (Lo, 1989, p. 3). However, a recent tendency for teachers and artists to learn more about Western art is seen as problematic by the CCP and has resulted in a conservative reaction (Lo, 1989).

Finally, there are a number of ways in which the local communities are involved in transmitting values through the media, street committees, mass organizations and organized home study programs. For example, the State Education Commission has

---

[3] Other studies, however, show the continued importance of the family among Chinese students in comparison with students in the U.S. (see Nuttal, 1988).

[4] This author, herself an American principal, wrote an objective and mildly praiseworthy article on the order and discipline seen in the Chinese classroom in contrast to her school in Michigan.

recently released a new videotape for students on "being well behaved and polite in school" (GMRB, 3/11/98). The tape includes a textbook and will be used both in and out of school. Another more mainstream film has been released specifically aimed at middle and high school students and is designed to promote "the traditional Chinese virtue of appreciating and returning benefit" (GMRB, 3/13/98). Entitled, "Going to school and carrying father on the back", the film tells the story of a young boy who remembers that his father carried him when he was too little to cross the river and when the father is paralyzed the boy reciprocates.

The theme of respecting one's parents seems to be considered an important one as evidenced by the development of a new three character chant (developed by the Baishulin street community office of Xi'an and emulated elsewhere). The chant reinforces five basic values: 1) Respect parents and take your responsibilities seriously; 2) Provide parents with a nice life when they are alive and a simple funeral when they die; 3) Be polite to seniors; 4) Help and yield to elders when traveling; 5) Be willing to help neighbors (Xi'an RB, 8/28/97). For their part, parents have been receiving special moral education texts (*jiating jiaoyu*) to be used at home and are exhorted to become part of a tripartite alliance to instill proper values among students (parents, school, students) (Meyer, 1990). Obviously, part of the reason for emphasizing values related to respect for elders and authority has to do with a rise in student violence. Conferences have been held on "education and obedience of the law" directed at elementary and secondary students, mass organizations such as the All China Women's Federation and the Working Committee for the Care of the Next Generation, have focused on this issue and government agencies in general are concerned that the move towards a market economy has resulted in a breakdown of morality (XSJW, 1996, no. 8). While our survey showed that strengthening family values ranked among the least important reasons why values should be taught it is likely this had to do with utilizing schools to teach family values, although it would be interesting to follow-up this issue with a more detailed survey.

These concerns are even more pronounced in China's so-called "open cities" or "special economic zones" where traditional methods of deploying moral education are even less respected. Here parents encourage independent thinking and competitiveness and care little about conventional governmental and educational efforts to instill officially sanctioned values (Deng, 1987). A survey conducted in the Guangdong area revealed that secondary students lacked basic knowledge about China's history and culture and cared little about the pronouncements emanating from Beijing. Efforts are being made to confront this problem and special classes have been established to teach young parents how to begin moral education early in a child's life. New techniques are under review to emulate officially sanctioned values but with a more acceptable approach. It remains to be seen how successful this effort will be.

Evaluation

How does China's educational leadership evaluate the effectiveness of their efforts to instill moral and political values among their youth? Within the schools, teachers are encouraged to utilize a variety of measures to assure that students have acquired the proper values and morals. Li (1990) notes that five basic measures are applied:

1. Cognition: general knowledge of Marxism-Leninism, and Mao Tse-tung thought.
2. Emotion: proletarian feelings, patriotism, internationalism, collectivism, ambition, responsibility, obligation, and pride.
3. Will power: overcome any difficulty, obstacles, be good to your word.
4. Belief: needed to leverage knowledge to reality.
5. Action: the final outcome of education; good habits are the best form of action (Li,1990, p. 167).

In sum, it appears that the aim of values education is to strengthen " good" behavior and overcome "bad" behavior, utilize praise, encouragement, criticism and punishment, employ competition in areas of study, discipline, good deeds, health and sports. Finally, to measure all of this, teachers prepare a written evaluation of their students' character and conduct and provide this to the parents each term. Li (1990) points out that the weakness of this system of evaluation is that the values being promoted are essentially those of the leadership rather than more abstract values. Once the students lose confidence in the leadership their value orientation can become confused and lead to chaos. The author concludes: "The Chinese emperors sought to rule by ethics, and consciously or unconsciously, the pattern is being repeated in the country today. In the past, as at present, moral education could and can be described as institution-centered rather than person-centered, and for the advantage of government rather than for individual development" (Li, 1990, p. 170). Our elite survey, however, shows some movement away from this view as independent and autonomous values are ranked somewhat high.

This rather cynical view is not uncommon among social commentators in China today. It reveals a level of pessimism among those who study China's efforts to instill "correct" values. One area where this is most evident is in studies of Chinese juvenile delinquents and other groups that demonstrate a high level of social deviance. Among these groups there is a high level of frustration with the old values of patience and diligence when the opportunity structure is such that only a very few will be able to enter the university or be successful in the world of politics or business. This creates a climate for rebellion against the values that seem to be out of touch with the move towards globalization and modernity (Smith, 1982).

Others have concluded that the real problem the Chinese face in effectively transmitting acceptable values is their use of the "inculcation" method to teach values. The use of exemplary individuals, models of morality (such as Lei Feng) has a long history in China but the top down, heavy handed manner in which these models are utilized every time there is a crisis of leadership, has rendered the public and even school children cynical (Levitt, 1992). The author concludes that as China continues to move towards a market economy, this method will be even less effective; however, he doubts that it will change.

There appears to be no clear answer to the question of the uniqueness of Asian and Western values, or those of China and other parts of Asia and the West. Efforts to apply so-called universal moral reasoning instruments (such as Kohlberg's theory of moral reasoning) have been inconclusive. As Walker has noted: "although in general, the universal applicability of Kohlberg's approach was supported by the data, a subjective analysis of responses revealed some indigenous concepts, fundamental to communist Chinese morality, that are not well tapped by the approach" (Walker and Thomas, 1991, p. 139). Walker's study revealed that Chinese responses demonstrated a stronger indication of support for the maintenance of the social system than North American responses, and a stronger orientation towards utilitarianism than Western samples. More interesting, however, was the extreme reluctance of the Chinese sample to generalize moral decisions beyond specific cases; "thus appropriate moral behavior in concrete situations is not simply deduced from a set of given moral rules or principles" (Walker, 1991, p. 153). This aspect differed strongly from the Western samples.

Conclusion

From the foregoing it appears China's educators are grappling with a variety of forces and factors when it comes to developing a common view on the importance and content of values education. Several trends seem to be distributed across the various studies including the sigma survey this group conducted. Surveys conducted in the 1980's revealed a strong emphasis on both nationalist and collective values. Learning about "being Chinese" and placing value on working cooperatively, respect for authority and others, "learning about the collective", learning how to obey rules, and so on dominated the responses to values studies during this period.

These values certainly have not disappeared in the 1990s but one could see a gradual infusion of individual values as China opened its doors economically to the rest of the world and began to participate in the broad arena of "globalization". Values such as having individual will power, thinking for oneself, and developing good personal habits can be found in the early 1990s. By the time we completed our study the primary reason for including values education in the curriculum was to "highlight individual responsibility". Among the top three topics to be taught was included "individual autonomy". And the most important theme to be taught was "creativity and individuality". Civic values and patriotism as well as fostering economic development and political stability also rank high but it is our view that the degree to which China concentrates on global economic development would reflect the degree to which more individual and personal values will be included in the curriculum. How well this trend will be maintained in the future will bear close scrutiny.

References

Burton, G.M. (1986). "Values Education in Chinese Primary Schools", *Childhood Education* 62: 250-255.

Cummings, W.K. and Altbach P.G. (eds.) (1997). *The Challenge of Eastern Asian Education: Lessons for America*. Albany, NY: State University of New York Press.

Deng, Z. (1987). "Duiwai kaifang qu gongzuo chutan". *Jiaoyu yanjiu yuekan* 3: 32-36.

Doyle, D.P. (1997). "Education and Character", *Phi Delta Kappa* 78: 440-43.

Ebrey, P.B. (1991). *Confucianism and Family Rituals in Imperial China: A Social History of Writing about Rites*. Princeton, NJ: Princeton University Press.

Fifth International Conference on Chinese Education for the 21st Century. (1997). Chinese University of Hong Kong. (Hereafter, FICCE 1997)

Guangming Ribao (hereafter *GMRB*) (1998, March 11), 5.

Guangming Ribao (1998, March 13), 4.

"Guojia jiaoyu weiyuanhui guanyu jinyibu jiaqiang zhongxiaoxue deyu gongzuo de jidian yijian", in *Zhongguo gaige quanshu*. (1990). Beijing: State Education Commission.

Guo, Z. (1997). "The Basic Principles of Citizen's Moral Judgement and the Effective Ways of Developing Moral Self-cultivation". Paper presented at FICCE.

Hawkins, J.N. (1983). *Education and Social Change in the People's Republic of China*. New York: Praeger Publishers.

Hayhoe, R. (1989). *China's Universities and the Open Door*. New York: M.E. Sharpe.

Hertling, J. (1996, May 3). "A Crash Course on Communism". *The Chronicle of Higher Education,* A43.

Kohn, A. (1997). "How Not to Teach Values". *Phi Delta Kappa* 78: 429-439.

Lee, W.O. (1996). Guest editor introduction. *Chinese Education and Society* 29: 5-12.

Levitt, G.A. (1992). "The Legend of Lei Feng: Moral Education in Elementary Schools in China". *The International Journal of Social Education* 7: 37-46.

Li, M. (1990). "Moral Education in the People's Republic of China", *Journal of Moral Education* 19: 159-197.

Li, Y. (1997). "Market Economy, Social Cultural Moral Value and Moral Education". Paper presented at FICCE.

Lo, L.N.K. (1989). "Arts Education in the Mass Culture System of China", *Journal of Aesthetic Education* 23: 101-124.

McClintock, S. (1987). "An American Principal Examines China's Schools", *Principal* 67: 39-43.

Meyer, J.F. (1990). "Moral Education in the PRC", *Moral Education Forum* 15: 3-26.

Nuttal, R.L. (1988). "Views of the Family by Chinese and U.S. Children: A Comparative Study of Kinetic Family Drawings", *Journal of School Psychology* 26: 191-194.

Quanrizhi xiaoxue sixiang pindeke jiaoxue jiaoxue dagang, *Zhongguo jiaoyubao,* (1986, May 31). In: "A Syllabus for a Course of Study in Ideology and Morality for Full Day Primary Schools", *Chinese Education and Society* 29: 38-46.

Reed, G.G. (1995). "Moral/Political Education in the People's Republic of China: Learning Through Role Models", *Journal of Moral Education* 24: 99-111.

Rozman, G. (ed.) (1991). *The East Asian Region: Confucian Heritage and Its Modern Adaptation*. Princeton, NJ: Princeton University Press.

Sheridan, M.K. (1990). "Chinese Symposium: Some Current Directions in China's Preschool Programming", *Early Child Development and Care* 60: 67-72.

Smith, J.P. (1982). "Education in China", *Educational Leadership* 39: 426-428.

Sparkes, K. (1990). "A Visit to a Rural Preschool in China", *International Journal of Early Childhood* 22: 17-22.

Straka, G.A. and Bos, W. (1989). "Socialization Objectives of Chinese Primary Schools: Results of a Comparative Textbook Analysis", *Studies in Educational Evaluation* 15: 257-76.

Sun, C., Chen, J. and Lin, X. (1997). "Some Conceptions on Strengthening Moral

Education for Citizens in the New Era". Paper presented at FICCE.

Walker, L.J. and Thomas, J.M. (1991). "Moral Reasoning in a Communist Chinese Society", *Journal of Moral Education* 20: 139-155.

Wu, Z. (1996). "Control in Colleges Increased". *Hong Kong Standard.* Retrieved April 16, 1996 from the World Wide Web: http://www.hkstandard.com.

Xi'an Ribao, (1997) August 28:1.

Xuexiao sixiang jiaoyu wengao (hereafter, *XSJW*) (1996) no. 8.

XSJW (1996) no. 11.

Yuan, B.J and Shen, J. (1998). "Moral Values Held by Early Adolescents in Taiwan and Mainland China", *Journal of Moral Education* 27: 191-207.

Yuan, G. (1997). "On the Nature of Market Economy and the Actual Effect of Moral Education in Schooling", Paper presented at FICCE.

CHAPTER 10

HONG KONG:
ENHANCING THE QUALITY OF THE SELF IN CITIZENSHIP

Wing On Lee[1]

Introduction

Studies of values and values education have a long tradition in Hong Kong. A common theme is the exploration of the role of traditional oriental/Confucian values in the context of modern society, in terms of orientations towards family, group, and nation versus self and achievement orientations. Past studies also show that these values cannot be dichotomized. For example, finding a higher emphasis on self-oriented values in the Chinese Language textbooks, both Au and Leung argued that this reflected a Chinese traditional emphasis on self as a starting point for social relationships. For example, Au (1995, p. 194) argues:

> Self-cultivation" is the foundation of being a human, and the fundamental requirement of attaining order and harmony of human relationships. "Self-cultivation" stimulates "self-reflection", "self-critique", "seeking one's own self" and "seeking one's truthfulness" from "self-awareness" to "self-love" and "self-control". All this should go further to attain self-determination, [a high degree of] cultivating oneself, self-enrichment, and to attain the four virtues of "benevolence, righteousness, rite and intelligence".

I have summarized value studies on Hong Kong in my other studies. In one study, my observation was that "these studies suggest Hong Kong youngsters are on the one hand achievement-oriented and fond of freedom, but on the other hand uphold significant traditional Confucian values, such as filial piety (to both family and society) and familialism" (Lee, 1997, p. 120). In another recent study, I have analyzed studies on youth values in the nineties, most conducted by The Hong Kong Federation of Youth Groups and Commission on Youths. It is interesting that findings of the various surveys conducted by these two bodies, as well as others, resemble one another to a large extent. Hong Kong youth in the nineties continue to place high priorities towards family, work and education, and have expressed concerns and commitments toward the society (2001).

The past studies on values reveal that we need an on-going reflection upon what we mean by traditional and modern values, and how they can be distinguished and integrated to become meaningful to a population who has inherited certain traditional values but needs to cope with the demands of a modern society. In the Hong Kong context, it is particularly meaningful to make comparisons between the thinking in Honk Kong relative to the thinking of groups from nearby Asian settings. Accordingly in the report below of the Hong Kong findings from the Sigma International Elite Survey of Values Education, most of the analysis will be restricted to Hong Kong-Asia

---

[1] The author acknowledges his gratitude to Sara Wong for her valuable assistance in conducting the study and data analysis. Thanks are also extended to Pong Suet-Ling for her valuable advice in the process of the study.

comparisons. As with the other chapters in this book five questions are addressed: Why should there be values education? What should be emphasized in the values education curriculum? How should values education be carried out? Who should receive values education? What should be the direction of the future values education in Hong Kong?

A Look at Past Studies

Examination of previous various values studies in Hong Kong suggests a diverse picture. A notable study was conducted in 1985 by Lau (1985), who administered the Rokeach Value Survey to 1,463 university students and found that students in Hong Kong had a tendency toward personal and competency-oriented values. In 1991, Kwan and Tse (1991) surveying Hong Kong youth aged eleven to twenty-two, found that "contribution to society" and "having a happy family" were regarded by the respondents as two important criteria of judging a person's success. Moreover, a large majority of the respondents regarded "to build up one's career" and "to repay your parents' love" as the most important objectives of life, whereas "freedom" and "family relationship" were considered the most important tasks in life. In 1992, Wong and Cheng (1992) conducted a survey on "Value Systems of Youth" to secondary students. They found that the students ranked "family relationship", "freedom", "family members", "friends", "filial piety", and "knowledge" at the top among the forty-six value items. In 1994, Au (1994) conducted a content analysis of junior secondary Chinese Language textbooks. She found that self-oriented values were distinctive in the Chinese Language curriculum, in terms of the frequency of themes occurring in the textbooks (60.4 percent for self-oriented values, 24.6 percent for group-oriented values, 11 percent for nation-oriented values). Building upon Au's study, Leung (1996) further analyzed the senior secondary Chinese Language textbooks, and had similar findings (38.4 percent for self-oriented values, 26 percent for group-oriented values, 17.7 percent for society-oriented values, 16 percent for nation-oriented values, 1.8 percent for nature-oriented values), except that the proportion of self-oriented values at the senior secondary level declined.

In 1999, I compared teachers' perception of citizenship in three Chinese cities, namely Hangzhou, Guangzhou and Hong Kong (Lee, 1999a). I found that Teachers of the three cities all gave high regards to traditional values. Placing emphasis on traditions and values notwithstanding, they all see the need to pay attention to current events, and for Guangzhou, even to worldwide needs and responsibilities. Referring to Hong Kong in particular, I have found that Hong Kong is surprisingly Chinese, possessing very common characteristics comparable to the other two Chinese cities developed in social and political contexts very different from that of Hong Kong over the last few decades. Apart from the commonalties, I have also identified that Hong Kong tends to place comparatively higher priorities to the fulfillment of family responsibilities and moral behavior, focusing on the private sphere of citizenship, using Janoski's framework. (Janoski, 1998). In my IEA Civic Education Study for Hong Kong published in the same year, I also found that there were strong concerns for critical and analytical thinking, and a tendency to avoid politics in the teaching of civics (Lee, 1999b).

Research Methodology

Sampling of Respondents

While the above studies sought the views of student and citizen groups, this study focuses on elites who are perceived as having a significant impact in on the future of values education in Hong Kong. The initial identification of respondents was made by the M.Ed. in Values Education class at the University of Hong Kong, at the request of the author. This particular group of twelve students was considered to be appropriate as they had already studied one year in the program, and were familiar with the literature, especially the local literature. The students discussed among themselves the figures in Hong Kong whom they would regard as leaders in various sectors in Hong Kong. When the initial list was drawn up, an invitation letter was sent to each of them. The letter explained the nature of the project and requested further suggestions of names to be included in this study. Eventually, a total of forty persons agreed to participate in this study, with representations in various sectors, as shown in Table 10.1. Among these forty persons, six were identified for a follow-up interview.

Table 10.1 Classification of Respondents in the Study

Category	No. of Respondents
Leading educational intellectuals	5
Religious leaders	7
Politicians	2
Officials in education administration	6
Academic leaders (prominent professors)	2
Curriculum designers in values education	6
Values/Moral education specialists	2
Prominent school principals	10
Total	**40**

Instrumentation

The study comprises a questionnaire survey and follow-up face-to-face interviews with selected respondents. The core questions, developed by the international team of scholars, is presented in the Appendix of this book. Additional questions were also included to fit the national context of Hong Kong. Based on the quantitative findings, we drew up an interview guide. In the main we asked our respondents how they would perceive the differences between the Hong Kong choices and the Asian choices, as well as how and why they made their choices.

Data analysis is mainly focused on a comparison of rank orders between different items within the same section of the questionnaire, and between the Hong Kong score and the average score of the project countries in Asia, including the PRC, Hong Kong, Japan, Republic of Korea, Malaysia, Singapore, Taiwan, and Thailand. Due to unavailability of data during the analysis, Indonesia is not included in the calculation of the Asian average score. For simplicity, this chapter will call those average score as "Asian" scores, preferences or choices. Where a seven-point Likert scale applies (1 for agree and 7 for disagree), we attempt to look at the mean scores in addition to the rank orders.

Why Should There be Values Education?

The questionnaire identifies seventeen reasons for the need to stress values education. As shown in Table 10.2, the choices of the Hong Kong respondents are very similar to the general choices among the Asian project countries. The rank order of the three most important choices are almost identical, all suggesting that values education is important for spiritual development, for the development of reflective and autonomous personality, and for enhancing individual responsibility. Looking at the bottom of the ranks, both the Hong Kong respondents and the Asian respondents give world peace very low ranking, and gender issue is seen as the least important among the choices. The only difference is that juvenile delinquency is among the least important items for Hong Kong but not the rest of Asia, whereas ecological abuse is among the least important for Asia but not for Hong Kong.

Table 10.2 Reasons for Values Education (By Rank)

The Most Important Reasons	
Hong Kong	**Asia**
1. to provide foundation for spiritual development	1. to provide foundation for spiritual development
2. to help young persons develop reflective and autonomous personality	2. to increase sense of individual responsibility
3. to increase sense of individual responsibility	3. to help young persons develop reflective and autonomous personality
The Least Important Reasons	
Hong Kong	**Asia**
15. to promote world peace	15. to combat ecological abuse
16. to combat juvenile delinquency	16. to promote world peace
17. to improve the respect and opportunities for girls and women	17. to improve the respect and opportunities for girls and women

Spiritual Development

From our interviews, the Hong Kong respondents regarded building moral and spiritual values to be intrinsically important for the youngsters in their development because, as many of them said, "Their intrinsic values determine the directions of their development". Values education is regarded by our respondents as a significant foundation for building up these values, and for helping the youngsters develop reflective and autonomous personality as well as critical thinking. These dispositions are essential qualities for making wise judgments. However, the respondents also expressed disappointment about the promotion of critical thinking in Hong Kong schools in practice. They considered that Hong Kong schools are in general conservative. One of them specifically criticized that teaching in Hong Kong is too didactic, and critical thinking is simply ignored.

National Identity

In our survey findings, the most important choices are accorded to those reasons relating to individuals. Collective values such as "to encourage civic consciousness", "to provide a guide for behavior in daily life", and "to develop appreciation for heritage and to strengthen national identity" are generally given secondary importance. Our interviews confirmed such an attitude.

Most of the respondents actually regarded spiritual development, rather than national identity, as the most important reason for values education. Only one of the interviewees considered national identity as the most important reason, and one felt that both spiritual development and national identity are of equal importance.

When asked why they felt spiritual development to be more important than national identity as a reason for values education, in general, they expressed that spiritual development refers to one's personal quality. As compared to values related to nation, it would be more important to emphasize individual quality first, as the nation is comprised of individuals and relies upon good individuals to support the nation. One of them said, "When our intrinsic values are fostered, they can further be extended to other aspects, such as family, society, nation and world". From another perspective, spiritual development has fundamental influence upon one's cultural appreciation and national identity. However, one respondent disagreed. He explained his position quite elaborately. He said,

> Theoretically spiritual development would be the most important reason for values education. However, practically stability of the nation is a crucial environment for one's personal development, and the well-being of the individual and the nation are interrelated. The process of building up our country helps to understand our own selves.... Our Chinese culture represents our national identity.

Community Consciousness

In the survey, "to promote pride in local communities" obtained very low ranking (14) in the Asian score, but a higher rank in Hong Kong (12). This finding suggests that while the Hong Kong respondents, as compared to their counterparts, accord more significance to individual values, they feel that taking pride in the community is also important. Our respondents explained that they are looking beyond their community, as when they were ranking, they were expecting the youngsters to extend their individuality to the community, but this was only the starting point. They also expected the youngsters to develop an international perspective. One of them said, "Promoting pride in community life would definitely help the youngsters to develop an understanding of and concern for issues of their country, nation, and further to the world".

What Should be Emphasized in the Values Education Curriculum?

As seen in Table 5.3, the choice of the Hong Kong respondents is very similar to the Asian choice in putting "values of personal autonomy and reflection", "moral values", "civic values", and "democracy" as important themes for the values education curriculum. The major variation from the Asian choice is that Hong Kong puts values of personal autonomy and reflection before moral and civic values, but it is the reverse in the Asian choice. According to the Hong Kong respondents, values of personal autonomy and reflection is the most important theme, followed by moral values and civic values. If moral values refer to a more personal dimension than civics, the Hong

Kong choice represents a more consistent progression of the continuum starting from the personal dimension, and then extended to the social dimension of values. This is a pattern consistent with what has been found from the previous section on reasons for values education. Moreover, it is very clear that in Hong Kong, the respondents place priority on character and moral education over political and religious education.

In regard to the least important themes in curriculum, the Hong Kong respondents, also in line with the Asian choice, rank "religious values" at the bottom. However, it is interesting to note that in the previous section, "spiritual development" is ranked first, but "religious values" is ranked last in this section. There must be a distinction between "spiritual" and "religious" values in the mind of the respondents. This is an important issue for further study. At this junction, the association of the choices can give us some hints in interpreting the spiritual and religious values. If we look at the top ranks in the previous section, "spiritual development" is closely followed by "autonomy and reflection". In this section, "autonomy and reflection" is ranked first. We can interpret that "spiritual development" actually refers to the kind of quality closely associated with independent thinking and reflectivity, which is related more to the rational dimension than to the religious dimension of values. This interpretation is supported by our interview findings, as the respondents also associated critical thinking with autonomy and reflection.

Table 10.3 The Most and Least Preferred Curriculum Themes in Values Education (By Rank)

The most important curriculum themes		
Hong Kong		**Asia**
1. Values of personal autonomy and reflection	1.	Moral values
2. Moral values	2.	Civic values
3. Civic values	3.	Personal autonomy
4. Democracy	4.	Democracy
The least important curriculum themes		
Hong Kong		**Asia**
11. National identity and patriotism	12.	Global awareness
13. Gender equality	14.	Gender equality
15. Religious values	16.	Religious values

In terms of the relationship between nationalism/patriotism and global awareness, "global awareness" gained a much higher ranking in Hong Kong, as compared to "national identity and patriotism" (rank 7 versus rank 11), whereas the two items are at equal ranking in the Asian choice (both rank 10). This can be explained by the specific background of Hong Kong as a British colony in the past, during which citizenship education and national identity were undermined. This also suggests that while the majority of the project countries place high priority on the national theme in values education, the global theme is relatively under-emphasized. In this regard, the national and global themes in values education appear to be competing concepts, rather than complementary concepts, with one being emphasized at the expense of the other.

Personal Autonomy and Reflection

During this part of the interview, we asked our respondents specifically what they had in mind, when according a high rank for personal autonomy and reflection. In general, their answers confirmed our observation. They associated this theme with a rational dimension of values rather than a religious dimension. Most of them said that they made that choice with an understanding that personal autonomy and reflection are essential elements in making a rational judgment.

Moral Values

In elaborating on the high ranking for moral values, our respondents reiterated that moral and spiritual values are important for the growth of the youngsters because their direction of development will be built on the intrinsic values they have acquired. In regard to the contents for teaching moral values, they suggested such topics as duties towards family and society, treating others with respect, honesty, and tolerance. One respondent said,

> Students are expected to assimilate the moral concepts into their intrinsic values, and apply them in daily life. Most important, with the acquisition of these intrinsic values, students can learn how to analyze and make rational decision against outside influence.

From their response, there is a clear interrelationship between personal and social values. Starting with a concern for personal values, they are expected to link them up with the social aspects, such as duties, family and society, and interpersonal relationships. It is worth noting that, as from the above quoted comment, instead of worrying about uncontrolled autonomy, intrinsic values are emphasized as an important base for rational decision, which further form a base for the youngsters to fight against outside influences. This may be helpful in explaining that the Hong Kong respondents do not regard juvenile delinquents as an important reason, in comparison with the others, for values education. To them, instead of resulting in lack of control, emphasis on personal values, would reinforce self control.

Civics and Democracy

In the interview, the respondents were asked to suggest topics to be covered under civic values. The topics we obtained include national identity, sense of patriotism, government and political institutions, citizen rights and responsibilities, civic consciousness, and social participation. For democracy, they suggested that Hong Kong should teach concepts of freedom, democracy and human rights. In the main, the Hong Kong respondents are aware of the topics normally covered in the areas of civic and democracy values. However, their interests seem to be focused on personal qualities rather than the civic and political dimensions of values.

Religious Values

As mentioned above, "religious values" is seen as the least important theme for the values education curriculum in Hong Kong. Being ranked the lowest, it is not surprising that our respondents were not interested in elaborating on this topic. However, this is also a surprising response if we take into account that half of the schools are run by religious bodies. This can be explained by the gradual movement of Hong Kong religious bodies from an evangelistic approach to a professional approach in running schools in Hong Kong (Lee and Ng, 1993).

Global Awareness and National Identity and Patriotism

This seems to be an interesting topic to our respondents in terms of the time they spent on this topic and the rich answers given to us. We specifically asked our respondents why they ranked global awareness higher than national identity and patriotism. Below were the reasons given to us:

- *Importance of global citizenship*: "In addition to developing personal qualities, students should also learn to be a global citizen to broaden their horizon of concerns."
- *Interrelationships between individual and the world*: "Extending from the level of individual to the level of society, nation and world, these dimensions are interrelated, and should not be seen as mutually exclusive. The well-being of the person, the nation and the world are interdependent."
- *Betterment of humankind*: "We should be concerned with the harmony of the world and the betterment of humankind, as a global citizen."
- *Importance of global view*: "Patriotism should be handled with caution because loving a country is different from loving a government. Holding a global view does not mean that we do not love our country. We can also learn to love and develop our country when holding a global perspective."
- *Patriotism as a narrow perspective*: "Patriotism is a narrow perspective, and is rather subjective. A global awareness can help us understand our nation, and most importantly, to recognize our role in the society and the world."

Table 10.4 Priorities of Values to be Taught in School (By Ranks)

Values education curriculum themes	Hong Kong	Asia
Diversity and multiculturalism	5	8
Ecological awareness	6	7
Global awareness	7	10
Family values	8	6
Peace and conflict resolution	9	9
Work values	10	5

The rich answers we have obtained suggest that the Hong Kong respondents were quite clear about their preferences for the various themes in values education. Again, the historical background helps to explain the emergence of such an attitude, but it should also be noted that they would like the Hong Kong citizens to possess an international perspective even when looking into national affairs.

Priorities on Other Curriculum Themes in Values Education

Apart from looking at those themes in the highest and lowest ranking, it is also worth looking at those items falling at the middle ranks. While the preferences of the Hong Kong respondents closely resemble those of their Asian counterparts, it is interesting to note for some items that there are clearly different rankings between the Hong Kong choice and the Asian choice, namely diversity and multiculturalism, global awareness and work values. In a society with a homogeneous population, one would expect Hong Kong people would pay less attention to social diversity and multiculturalism. Surprisingly, Hong Kong places a higher ranking for diversity and multiculturalism. This will make sense if we associate this choice with the significance of global awareness in the minds of the Hong Kong respondents. If one looks to globalization, it is easier for one to be more aware of diversity and multiculturalism. However, it is not known why work values is not accorded hard rank in Hong Kong, as from our discussion, hard work is very much emphasized by the respondents as well.

Controversial Issues in Value Education

Twenty-five statements on the school's role in teaching a particular value issue are included in the questionnaire. In summary, these twenty-five statements are evolved around such values as autonomy, civics, gender, globalization, morality, nationalism, religion, tolerance and work. In general, the Hong Kong response closely resembles the Asian response, with exception to the issues related to civic values and tolerance.

Table 10.5 Preferences on Values Related to Gender

Controversial content	Hong Kong		Asia	
	Mean	**Rank**	**Mean**	**Rank**
Girls should be given equal opportunity and encouragement	1.4	1	1.7	1
Encourage mutual respect between boys and girls	1.7	4	1.9	4
Destiny of girls to have significant home-building responsibilities	4.7	25	4	24

Gender

Responses to the gender issues are strong and clear: There should be equality and mutual respect between boys and girls, and girls should not be confined to household responsibilities.

Autonomy and Rights

The Hong Kong respondents, as well as their Asian counterparts, place strong emphasis on the value of critical thinking, and therefore children's autonomy. The respondents perceived that critical thinking is an "important tool for learning", "for judging the accuracy and objectivity of information flooding to youngsters through mass media and internet", and "for guarding against indoctrination". However, if we consider the response to rights as well, it is interesting to note that the items on rights obtain relatively low ranking, both in Hong Kong and in the project countries in Asia as a whole. However, the means are still on the positive side. It seems that there is some difficulty for the Hong Kong respondents to extend the notion of critical thinking and personal autonomy to the concepts of rights. This may reflect a general orientation in Eastern societies that responsibilities are emphasized over rights.

Table 10.6 Preferences on Values Related to Autonomy and Rights

Controversial content	Hong Kong		Asia	
	Mean	Rank	Mean	Rank
Value of critical thinking	1.4	2	3	3
Assist each child in developing own values	2.1	8	7	7
Help children understand they have individual rights	2.3	11	14	14
Help children understand they have the right to be happy	3.1	15	16	16

Work Values

It is interesting to note that the work values items are not accorded high significance in Hong Kong and in the Asian project countries in general. The ranking and means for the work values are close to those of rights. This may be a problem of the items, as each of the above items contains more than one descriptor, each of which may mean different things. For example, hard work is generally valued in the Eastern societies, but putting it together with loyalty and obedience may affect the choice of the respondents. The same may be true for individual competitiveness and creativity. This is reflected in our interviews, as hard work is definitely regarded as a very important value for Hong Kong. To quote: "this is an essential quality for the realization of the economic and social success of the society". Nevertheless, we can still look at the relative significance of the two items on work. If we compare the two items, it is clear that in Hong Kong, as well as in Asia in generally, loyalty, obedience and hard work are more important than competitiveness and creativity. This may also be an illustration of the general preference on conformity in Eastern societies. Even though there is a strong concern for personal values in Hong Kong, when one behaves in the work place, one is still expected to be group conscious.

Table 10.7 Preferences on Work Values

	Hong Kong		Asia	
Controversial content	Mean	Rank	Mean	Rank
Habits of loyalty, obedience, hard work, and punctuality	2.3	12	2.5	12
Highlight role of individual competitiveness and creativity	3.1	16	2.9	18

National and Civic Values

The importance accorded to national and civic values is quite low in Hong Kong. The ranks and means for these items in the Asian rating are also quite low, but the means are slightly higher than those of Hong Kong. This is interesting because our previous finding was that there is a clearly higher emphasis on nationalism and patriotism in the Asian project countries as a whole. However, the Hong Kong response is very close to the Asian average, emphasizing equality before law but denouncing hierarchy in government. Coupled with their respect for gender equality, as discussed above, we can well summarize that all the project countries in Asia have strong concern for equality, but nationalism and politics tend to be downplayed in Hong Kong.

During the interviews, our respondents elaborated that they wished the rule of law and the concept of equality be sustained in Hong Kong after becoming a Special Administrative Region of China. They have expressed their pride of the past record in fighting corruption, and a strong wish that such an effort be continued.

Table 10.8 Preferences on National and Civic Values

Controversial content	Hong Kong		Asian	
	Mean	Rank	Mean	Rank
Promote understanding and love of nation	3.2	17	2.7	17
Venerate heroes and promote national pride	3.3	18	3.2 [a]	19
Understanding of all political and social viewpoints	3.9	22	3.2 [b]	20
Respect hierarchy and support the government	4.0	23	4.0	25
Stress that all are equal before law	1.6	3	1.8	2

[a] Before rounding up to one decimal place, mean value for this item is 3.233.
[a] Before rounding up to one decimal place, mean value for this item is 3.238.

Tolerance

In relation to tolerance, Hong Kong places high importance on personal pride and heritage, but low importance on common values. This is in accord with the above findings that Hong Kong scores high on those items related to individuals and personal values. The low importance accorded to common values also suggests the tendency to support pluralistic values in the society. This is an interesting contrast with the Asian choice that on average places medium rankings on these two items.

Table 10.9 Preference on Values Related to Tolerance

Controversial content	Hong Kong		Asia	
	Mean	Rank	Mean	Rank
Importance of personal pride and identity, understand unique heritage and origins	1.8	7	2.4	11
Common values to all without differentiating class, ethnicity, religion	4.5	24	2.6	15

Perhaps, the choice was complicated by the descriptors of class, ethnicity and religion. As many other project countries in Asia have multiple ethnic groups (and accordingly multiple religions), they have a higher tendency to pay more attention to ethnic and religious issues. Whereas in Hong Kong, where the ethnic origin of the population is quite homogenous, there is a higher emphasis on a pluralistic society. Our respondents say:

> By understanding the traditions, culture and customs of their society, students would then know their identity which in turn help to strengthen the personal pride of the students.

> One's values can be developed in different ways in different backgrounds in terms of culture, class, origin and heritage. Teachers are expected to help students understand their unique origins and heritages and treat others' differences with respect.

The Values Education Curriculum

Societies Other Than Hong Kong To be Mentioned

In the survey, China is ranked first, followed by the United States and Britain. Our respondents elaborated that as a part of China, the Hong Kong students should first be familiar with the characteristics and features of the Chinese nation and culture, and find out how we are influenced by the Chinese heritage. However, they also noted that the students should look beyond the mother country, and should compare and contrast our own culture with others' in developing a global perspective. In terms of teaching contents, we see a split of views. Respondents from the school sector and non-governmental organizations mentioned conceptual issues, such as the need to help students recognize their national identity. Those from governmental departments mentioned factual accounts such as the landscape and traditions of China.

Priority of Values Education in the School Curriculum

In the survey, there is great variation in the answers to the question regarding the percentage of moral education, civics, and religion in school subject. One suggests 40 percent and another 80 percent. The average is 14 percent. Similarly, the percentage of time and effort that should be given to values education integrated across the curriculum ranged from 5 percent to 100 percent. The average is 22 percent. These figures show a great diversity of opinions.

In regard to the sufficiency of values education in the overall curriculum, the Hong Kong respondents strongly expressed that the time and effort in such provision is far from sufficient. According to a respondent from the government, civic education and moral education have been included as one of the formal subjects in the school curriculum of Hong Kong, comprising 5 percent of the total teaching time-table in school.

The general comment from our respondents is that values education has not yet been fully developed in Hong Kong. Its content is too "political-oriented", "superficial", and "in lack of focus".

Pedagogy

In regard to pedagogy in values education, two teaching methods were suggested by our respondents: didactic teaching and the activity approach. Those who advocated the didactic approach criticized the activity approach as being impractical and not effective. They felt that students would be serious only when they have to sit for an examination. That is to say, if values education is not a knowledge-based and examination-oriented subject, they do not see that it will be treated seriously by the students.

Those who supported the activity approach argued in an opposite way. A teacher respondent expressed that it is meaningless to use examination as a tool for moral education because morality is not entirely knowledge, and moral concepts have to be internalized in the mind of the students. Another respondent, a curriculum officer, stressed the importance of a comfortable and relaxing atmosphere for students to learn values concepts, and the activity approach would be ideal for this purpose. Moreover, students' interests in learning values can only be enhanced without examination pressure.

What Settings Are Most Effective for Values Education?

This section provides a suggested list of settings for values education. Respondents were asked to rank order the importance of the settings. The list of settings includes "during school as a class", "during school through rules of behavior", "outside school activities", "internships and community service", "camps", "military training and national service", "home and family", and "media".

In this section, the choice of the Hong Kong respondents is very close to the choice of the Asian project countries as a whole. In regard to moral education and religious education, both the Hong Kong and Asian elites rank "home and family" as the most important setting for values education. In Hong Kong, over 50 percent of our respondents have made this choice. However, there is a different opinion for civic education. The Hong Kong respondents regarded "outside school activities" as the most important setting, whereas the Asian ranking place "during school as a class" at most significant. Again, this shows a clear difference in preference for civic education between the Hong Kong respondents and the Asian respondents. Hong Kong people in general still wish to downplay civic education in school, and therefore prefer it to be implemented outside the school curriculum, although there are also disagreements between the Hong Kong respondents.

How Should Values Education be Carried Out?

Should values education be a separate subject or integrated throughout the curriculum? The mean score for the statement "Values education should not be taught as a separate subject..." is 2.6 in Hong Kong, as compared to the Asian mean of 2.3. This suggests that the Hong Kong respondents generally support this statement, but the degree of support is not as high as the Asian project countries' average. In our interviews, we found that the opinions on this issue were quite split. Only one of our respondents supported that values education be taught as a separate subject, while the others supported an integrated curriculum. The respondent who supported a separate subject said, "School teachers have always failed to integrate value issues in their teaching and they would only teach 'hard facts' for the examination.... Integrated curriculum is impractical, as the level of class discussion would become very superficial".

However, for the majority of our respondents, integration is an ideal mode for values education for the following reasons:

- The integrated curriculum can provide flexibility in touching upon any related value issues in any subjects;
- The school curriculum is too tight already, and it is difficult to afford another separate subject; and
- Values are to be internalized rather than taught as subject knowledge, and integration can avoid reducing values education to knowledge-based transmission.

When Should Values Education Begin?

The mean score is 6.2 for secondary school, and 1.2 for early childhood, as compared to the Asian mean scores of 5.3 and 1.6 respectively. This suggests that the Hong Kong and Asian opinions are very alike, all regarding that values education should begin from early childhood. During our interviews, the respondents asserted that children start to develop their values systems from early childhood, therefore we should teach values to our children from the very starting point of their education. Children interact with one another and are influencing one another in school. This gives an additional reason for us to teach values in school.

Should Students of Different Academic Abilities Receive Different Values Education?

There is a clear difference in the level of support to this statement between the Hong Kong respondents and their counterparts in Asia, as reflected by their mean scores: 2.8 in Hong Kong and 3.8 in Asia. In other words, the Hong Kong responses are more positive to the statement. During our interviews, an educational administrator elaborated that students with lower academic ability should be taught more factual content, and the teaching method should be "straight forward", i.e., didactic. For those with higher academic ability, we can afford to raise the abstract level that requires more critical thinking. However, other than this, we were not able to further elaboration from the respondents.

Who Should Receive Most Exposure to Civic Education, Moral Education and Religious Education?

A list of groups is included in the questionnaire for the respondents to indicate priority in values education. These groups are "in-service teachers", "teacher learners", "young children (three to four years old)", "pre-schoolers (five years old)", "primary level (six to eleven years old)", "secondary level (eleven to fourteen years old)", "high school level (fifteen to seventeen years old)" and "university level (eighteen years old or older)". The most important groups to be exposed to the three areas of values education are as follows:

Table 10.10 Groups that Should have Most Exposure to Values Education

Area of values education	Hong Kong	Asia
Civic Education	teacher learners	in-service teacher
Moral Education	in-service teachers	young children
Religious Education	young children	young children

Note: Young children refer to those aged 3 to 4.

It is interesting to note that while the Hong Kong respondents regard teachers as the most significant group who need to be exposed to values education. However, the Asian counterparts see young children as more important. In addition, the Hong Kong respondents also give priority to the older groups of the youngsters, such as students at university level and secondary level. During our interviews, it was suggested that not only teachers need civic education, but also parents, as they are role models for their children. In general, our respondents regarded the teacher as the key-person to convey civic values and knowledge to students, but Hong Kong teachers are not well equipped and their civic teaching is rather superficial. Our respondents clearly opinioned that there should be teacher training in values education. It is also interesting that there is an opinion that young children should be the priority group in receiving religious education. Our respondents suggested that religious values are personal values, and they should start early in life, but the respondents also suggest that those values be taught at home by the family rather than school. Perhaps, this explains why they choose the priority differently for religious values.

Directions of Values Education

Asian and Hong Kong values

The responses to the two questions on Asian values are positive, but the mean score (3.3) for teaching Asian values is close to ambivalence, and is obviously much lower than the Asian countries' average mean score (2.3). It is interesting also to note that the international mean score is 1.8. This suggests that countries other than those in Asia see the presence of Asian values more distinctively than those within Asia. Within Asia, the Asian project countries see the presence of Asian values more distinctively than the Hong Kong respondents do. However, this does not mean that the Hong Kong respondents would regard the teaching of Asian values as insignificant. One of them said, "This section is ignored in the curriculum of Hong Kong. In fact it should begin from Asian values, by viewing the relationship between Hong Kong and the neighborhood countries and then confirm the direction of values, finally viewing the values globally". However, as reflected in the above remark, the concern for Asian values is balanced by a global concern in Hong Kong. This tendency is even clearer in the discussion of Hong Kong values. In terms of mean score, the response is the same as that to the question on strengthening the Confucian tradition, both with a mean score of 3.3. Most Hong Kong respondents pointed to the need to have a balanced values system. Below are some of their opinions:

"There are good things in both new and old values, and they should be complementary to each other."

We need to have an open mind toward other ideologies, select the best, and get rid of the worst. But we still need to take root in our indigenous Chinese values because we need to know who we are."

"Values education should also be balanced by the Western ideology [in addition to the Confucian ideology]."

"We should hold the attitude of critical thinking and decide what to take and what to drop.... One would accept this [Confucian] value after critical thinking. Hence, it is very important for the youth to think critically before any proceedings."

Table 10.11 Opinions on Asian Values (Means of 1-7)

Statement	Hong Kong	Asia
Would you agree that there is a distinctive set of Asian values?	2.6	2.3
Would you agree that schools should make an effort to teach Asian values?	3.3	2.3
Should schools strengthen on the Confucian tradition any more?	3.3	----
School schools strengthen on democratic ideology and life style?	2.0	----

"Critical", "selective", "open-minded", "balanced" and "complementary" are words used by the respondents to justify parallel consideration of Confucian and Western values. It is quite obvious that they were all cautious in presenting the Asian and Hong Kong traditional values in calling for the need to be critical, selective, and receptive to new, Western values.

The Hong Kong respondents were also negative toward the existing "Hong Kong values". Many of them criticized that Hong Kong values are quite "materialistic", "short-sighted", "short of spiritual dimension", "money-oriented", and "superficial". Below are two comments:

In Hong Kong, the economy grows much faster than spirituality.

I find that coming along with the blossoming of economy and democracy [sic] is that 'personal interest' is being superimposed on 'social interest' in today's Hong Kong society. People are just focusing upon their individual needs.

Preferences on Moral Ideologies

As from Table 10.12, the response to the questions on moral ideology in Hong Kong is generally positive, but quite ambivalent. The mean scores are 3.1 for traditional Confucian and 3.3 for Western. The response to the Socialist ideology is negative.

Many of the Hong Kong respondents being interviewed agreed that it is important to teach the moral ideology of Confucius in Hong Kong. Regarding the characteristics of Confucian values, they specifically mentioned such virtues as kindness, modesty,

Table 10.12 Preferences on Moral Ideologies in Hong Kong

Moral Ideology	Mean
Traditional Confucian	3.1
Western	3.3
Socialist	5.2

loyalty and faith, filial piety, familial consolidation and harmonic livelihood. Among these, filial piety and social harmony were most frequently mentioned. It is generally considered that Confucianism, or Eastern ethics, is closely associated with collectivism. However, one respondent interestingly interpreted Confucian ideology as personal rather than public. To quote:

> I think the traditional Confucian moral ideology over-emphasizes the personal aspect, though the concept of helping the others is also advocated. However, the moral ideology of Western countries not only emphasizes personal virtue but also the social interface, e.g. public virtue (*Gongde*). Many countries in Asia are deeply influenced by the Confucius ideology which is more inclined to personal virtue rather than public virtue, where consciousness toward community, countries and nation is rather weak and even ignored.

Whether the respondent's concept is right or not, the interpretation does open up a need for reconsideration of the personal and social dimensions of Confucianism. Certainly, this helps to explain the simultaneous emphasis on both spiritual and personal development of the youngsters discussed at the beginning of the chapter.

Table 10.13 The Role of School in Political Advocacy

Statement	Mean
No preferences, but show all ideas to students	1.1
No preferences, but avoid debating ideas to students	5.2
Cultivate patriotism and nationalism	4.2

The respondents generally regarded that Western ideology is important to Hong Kong. As mentioned above, the Hong Kong respondents were very careful in ensuring that Western values be placed alongside Asian values. While Western values are generally viewed with endorsement in Hong Kong, a couple of the respondents also asked for caution against excessive individualism, marriage breakdown, and over-emphasis on rights.

Role of School in Political Advocacy

As from Table 10.13, it is clear that the Hong Kong respondents suggested that school should not play a role in political advocacy. The responses were very clear cut, in asserting that school should show all the different ideas to students.

Conclusions

The above discussion shows that the Hong Kong respondents have consistently placed high significance on attributes essential for the development of personal quality, with an expectation of extending awareness from a personal level to the social, national and global levels. Our respondents in general view that the person, the nation, and the community are interrelated with one another, and more than that, the extension of concern to the community is viewed as a stepping stone toward the development of an international perspective. Such a continuum resembles the Confucian idioms of "Extending yourself toward the others" and "Cultivate yourself, regulate your family, administer your country, and in the end pacify the world".

Concerning the items that received lower priority in the survey, such as "to promote world peace", "to combat juvenile delinquency", and "to improve respect and opportunities for girls and women", our respondents defended that they should not be viewed as not important. However, among all the listed reasons, they would regard capacity building as more important in values education, and therefore they chose those reasons that have a close relationship to the enhancing of personal quality.

Further examining those personal qualities, the choice of the Hong Kong respondents are quite well rounded and balanced, in choosing "spiritual development", "reflective and autonomous personality", and "sense of individual responsibility" as the top three reasons. There is an emphasis on autonomy and responsibility, as well as spirituality and reflectivity. In view of the continuum we have identified, i.e., extending from a concern for personal qualities to a concern for community, nation and the world, a philosophy of values tends to emerge. The philosophy is characterized by a balanced concern for spirituality and rationality, autonomy and responsibility, as well as self and the collectivity. However, it is interesting to note that the quality of the self has become the center of concern.

If moral values refer to a more personal dimension than civics, the Hong Kong choice represents a more consistent progression of the continuum from the personal dimension to the social dimension of values, which is consistent with what we have found from the section on reasons for values education. Moreover, it is very clear that in Hong Kong, the respondents place priority on character and moral education over political and religious education.

Findings in this study tend to coincide with those of other studies on values in Hong Kong, as mentioned at the beginning of the chapter. The traditional and modern values are far from dichotomized, and may require constant re-interpretation. This is particularly manifested in an interpretation that Confucian values are personal whereas Western values are group-oriented. The findings, as well as the elaboration we were able to obtain from the interviews offer an interesting and coincidental resemblance with Tu Wei-ming's discussion on selfhood in Confucianism. In one of his works, Tu (1985, p. 113) says that self-transformation is a communal act, and this view involves two interrelated assumptions: (1) the self as a center of relationships, and (2) the self as a dynamic process of spiritual development. In another context, I have argued that self-cultivation can be considered a fundamental quality for effective citizenship, and self-realization and collective-realization, rather than being dichotomized, are mutually reinforcement of each other:

> Some societies place stronger emphasis on individualism, while others collectivism. However, the two are not necessarily dichotomized and mutually exclusive. On the contrary, there are subtle relationships between them.

In societies where individualism is more obviously valued, the significance of common interests, common will and common good is also valued. Likewise, in societies where collectivism seems to be dominant, there are various extents of respect for individuality, and self-realization is seen as best achieved through collective realization. In the Chinese tradition, even though collectivism has been a dominant social value, self has been seen as the starting point of civic values.... (Curriculum Development Council, 1996, p. 15).

Whether right or not, this interpretation reflects the changing perception of values by people within a particular society at a particular time. The struggle toward what kind of values to be adopted will certainly continue to characterize the efforts of the Hong Kong leaders and its people. However, a clear trend revealed in this study is the attention toward individual well being.

References

Au, Y.Y. (1994). *Values Orientations in Junior Secondary Chinese Language Ccurriculum of Hong Kong*. M.Ed. dissertation. Faculty of Education, University of Hong Kong.

Curriculum Development Council, Hong Kong (1996). *Guidelines on Civic Education in Schools*. Hong Kong: Curriculum Development Council, Education Department.

Kwan, Y.H. and Tse, W.L. (1991). *A Study of the Attitudes of Secondary Students on Values in Life in Hong Kong*. Hong Kong: YWCA.

Janoski, T. (1998). *Citizenship and Civil Society: A Framework of Rights and Obligations in Liberal, Traditional, and Social Democratic Regimes*. Cambridge, U.K. and New York: Cambridge University Press.

Lau, Sing (1985). "A Value Profile of Chinese University Students in Hong Kong". In A.M.C. Ng and F. Cheung (eds.), *Selected Papers on Youth Studies in Hong Kong*. Hong Kong: Center for Hong Kong Studies, Chinese University of Hong Kong.

Lee, W.O. and Ng, P. (1993). "The Professionalisation of Religious Education", *Hong Kong Journal of Religious Education* 5(5): 1-14.

Lee, W.O. (1997). "Measuring Impact of Social Values and Change". In J.D. Montgomery (ed.), *Values in Education: Social Capital Formation in Asia and the Pacific*. Hollis, NH: Hollis Publishing Co.

Lee, W.O. (1999a). "A Comparative Study of Teachers' Perceptions of Good Citizenship in Three Chinese Cities: Guangzhou, Hangzhou and Hong Kong". In L. Jie (ed.), *Education of Chinese: the Global Prospect of National Cultural Tradition*. Nanjing: Nanjing Normal University Press.

Lee, W.O. (1999b). "Controversies of Civic Education in Political Transition: Hong Kong". In J. Torney-Purta, J. Schwille and J. Amadeo (eds.), *Civic Education Across Countries: Twenty-four National Case Studies from the IEA Civic Education Project*. Amsterdam: The International Association for the Evaluation of Educational Achievement.

Lee, W.O. (2001). "A Story on Hong Kong Youth Values". *Journal of Youth Studies*, Vol. 4, No.2, July.

Leung, S.K. (1996). *Values Orientations in Senior Secondary Chinese Language Curriculum of Hong Kong and Perceptions of Teachers on Values Education.* M.Ed. dissertation. Faculty of Education, University of Hong Kong.

Tu, W. (1985). *Confucian Thought: Selfhood as Creative Transformation.* Albany, NY: State University of New York Press.

Wong, S.W. and Cheng, H.K. (1992). *Value System of Youth: An Exploratory Study of Configuration and Structure.* Hong Kong: City Polytechnic of Hong Kong.

South-East Asia

CHAPTER 11

MALAYSIA: STRENGTHENING RELIGIOUS AND MORAL VALUES[1]

Thomas N. Barone
Ibrahim Ahmad Bajunid

Introduction

Malaysia has historically been concerned with moral values as an essential component of education. This is evident by centuries of Islamic Education and the continued concern with this aspect of education in modern Malaysia. Since the 1980s, Moral Education has been taught as a required subject for Non-Muslims throughout primary and secondary schooling. Part of the reason for Moral Education has been to foster positive moral development and also to unify the nation around core ethical principles. In addition, there has been growing concern with the negative aspects of the "Westernization" of Malaysia and its effect on the moral values and behavior of the young. Since the elites involved with this study are involved in key roles in the educational establishment, it was felt that their perceptions of the role of values education were especially important. Elites also regularly address conferences, report to the media, and issue reports regarding the role values should play in modern Malaysian society and education. Therefore, this study is significant in that it examines the current thinking of Malaysian elites on values education as a potential indicator of future policy directions. It is hoped that this study will also lead to further research in this area especially regarding the role of teachers in the transmission of values. This need has been addressed by Hayhoe who states that "what bears study is the perceptions of teachers about their responsibilities towards students in the arena of fostering values, the pedagogies and relationships they develop in order to carry out their task, and the difficulties they face as they build bridges between the relatively safe and sheltered world of the classroom and that of the wider society" (Hayhoe, 1997, p. 108). In addition, this study examines the "duality" of the Malaysian values education approach, problems associated with the current system of values education, how teachers can foster moral values in the classroom, and the role values play in the quest for racial unity.

A Historical View of Unity and Diversity in Malaysia

The ethnic diversity that exists in Malaysia today is a result of the British colonial policy of bringing Chinese and Indian laborers into the country. Under colonialism, the educational system reflected the larger society and the British policy of divide and rule. The major racial groups were compartmentalized with the indigenous Malays in rural areas and the Chinese primarily in urban areas. This separation led to different

---

[1] For this chapter, "values education" is used as the more general term for moral instruction. In Malaysia, Moral Education and Islamic Education refer to different classes within the National Education System taken separately by Non-Muslims and Muslims.

229

schooling opportunities with urban settlers benefiting most from colonial educational policies. The British encouraged the Malays to stay in rural areas and Malay primary schools provided little chance of any socioeconomic mobility. The Chinese either attended Chinese language schools or attended the English language schools that made them eligible for increased employment opportunities. Finally, Indian students often went to Tamil language primary schools that also provided little chance of advancement (Thomas, 1985). Therefore, British educational policy was passive in that "at no time was universal education a goal...nor did they offer a plan for unifying the society by means of a colony-wide school system" (Thomas, 1985, p. 204). Early in the twentieth century, there were limited educational opportunities for Malays. The major exception to this policy was regarding the education of the traditional Malay elites who were provided English education increasingly in the early twentieth century (Loh, 1974). This access to English education was demanded more by the Malays but was generally blocked by colonial policy. By 1924, only 3,858 Malays were enrolled in English schools while 20,166 Chinese were enrolled (cited in Hashim, 1996). Finally, British policies also had the effect of placing the historical rulers of the Malay Peninsula, the Malays, in an inferior economic and educational position to the immigrant Chinese community at the time of Independence (Thomas, 1985).

In new nations, primordialism is high and loyalties are low with opposing groups competing for scarce resources. Malaysia after emancipation from British rule in 1964 focused on unity and integration by gradually implementing a national language (Malay), a national educational policy and national ideology. This policy was influenced in part by the colonial legacy of segregation, inadequate education, and inequality of opportunity (Hashim, 1983). This focus on unity is seen clearly in the Razak Report (1956) which states that "the ultimate objective of education policy in the country must be to bring together the children of all races under a common education system in which the national language is the main medium of instruction" (quoted in Hashim, 1983, p. 71). This has become a recurring theme in subsequent five-year plans and education in Malaysia can be seen as "an instrument that is indispensable for its sociopolitical cohesion" (Mukherjee, 1988, p. 150). The importance of values education as an overall objective is evident in the National Philosophy of Education stated by the Ministry of Education:

> Education in Malaysia is an on-going effort towards further developing the potential of individuals in a holistic and integrated manner, so as to produce individuals who are intellectually, spiritually, emotionally and physically balanced and harmonious, based on a firm belief in God. Such an effort is designed to produce Malaysian citizens who are knowledgeable and competent, who possess high moral standards, and who are responsible and capable of achieving a high level of personal well-being as well as being able to contribute to the harmony and betterment of the family, the society and the nation at large. (Ministry of Education, 1997)

Attempts at unity were deemed inadequate after race riots in 1969, which led to the development of a political ideology-the Rukunegara. According to Apter (1968), ideology links action with a wider set of meanings that make more explicit the moral basis of action. Political ideology can be defined as "an application of particular prescriptions to collectivities" (Apter, 1968, p. 235). The Rukunegara contains five pillars, which can be viewed as defining the goals of the nation (cited in Syed Zin and Lewin, 1991, p. 248; Hashim, 1983):

1. Belief in God
2. Loyalty to King and Country
3. Upholding the Constitution
4. Rule of Law
5. Good Behavior and Morality

However, some have seen a gradual shift away from the earlier emphasis on unity. The emphasis on unity was stated as a primary objective of the country according to the Second Malaysia Plan (1971-1975) with an emphasis on the principles of the Rukunegara (Jadi and Khamis, 1987). This unity emphasis was also in subsequent Plans including the Fifth Malaysia Plan (1986-1990). However, by the Sixth Malaysia Plan (1990-1995), a shift was evident in educational policy that coincided more closely with the National Education Philosophy of 1987. In particular, an explicitly stated goal of educational policy was now to produce responsible citizens with strong moral and ethical values while national unity is implied in the National Education Philosophy it is not stated directly (Hashim, 1996).

Islamic Education and Moral Education

Islamic Education in Malaysia dates back centuries and the ties between religion and education long predate the colonial era. As a result, when the British arrived in the eighteenth century, Islamic schools were the only ones in existence (Thomas, 1985). The 1980s and 1990s were also a time of increased Islamization of many aspects of Malaysian society and this included an increased emphasis on the importance of Islamic Education (Hassan, 1996). Islamic Education has official status since Islam is the national religion and therefore, all Muslims are required to study the subject throughout primary and secondary schooling. All students are required to increase their knowledge of the Quran. The philosophy of Islamic Education is stated as "a continuous effort to disseminate the knowledge and skills that lead to the internalization of the teachings of Islam based on the Quran [...] This effort is to develop in the Muslim students the attitudes, skills, character, and a view of life that enable him to see himself as a servant of Allah" (Ministry of Education, 1990).

Moral Education was implemented in the 1980s to be taught to non-Muslims while Muslims studied Islamic Education. Moral Education was implemented in primary schools in 1983 and secondary schools in 1989 and is one of the compulsory subjects in the recent Integrated Curriculum of Secondary Schools (ICSS) (Syed Zin and Lewin, 1991). According to the syllabus, Moral Education "stresses the inculcation and internalization of noble values found in Malaysian society and advocated by the various religions, traditions, and cultures of the different communities and which are consonant with universal values". The objectives of Moral Education are as follows:

1. Strengthen and enhance conduct and behavior keeping in line with those moral values and attitudes instilled at primary school level;
2. Be aware of, understand and internalize the norms and values of Malaysian society;

3.   Think rationally based on moral principles;
4.   Make rational, moral and ethical decisions; and
5.   Develop the practices of consistently observing sound moral principles in daily life.

(Ministry of Education, 1989)

The Moral Education Syllabus for secondary schools contains values which are based "on religious considerations, traditions and values of the multiracial society" as well as the Rukunegara (National Institute for Educational Research (NIER), 1990:68). These sixteen core Malaysian values are as follows: compassion, self-reliance, humility, respect, love, justice, freedom, courage, physical, honesty, diligence, cooperation, moderation, gratitude, rationality, and public spiritedness (Abdul Rasid, Haji Maghribi and Mohd Taib, 1994).[2] The core values are implemented in the primary and secondary curricula in different ways with emphasis being given to habit formation at the primary level and problem solving at the secondary level (NIER, 1990). At the secondary level, students are taught to think creatively and rationally in making decisions and teachers are trained in many approaches including values analysis, values clarification, values inculcation, and cognitive development (Abdul Rasid et al., 1994).

There are a number of similarities between Islamic Education and Moral Education in the current system. Philosophically, both classes are in line with the National Education Philosophy in that they attempt to "produce individuals who are intellectually, spiritually, emotionally, and physically balanced and harmonious, based on a firm belief in God" (Ministry of Education, 1997). However, since Moral Education is not based on one specific religious tradition like Islamic Education but based on universal values, Moral Education is taught in a less traditional manner with its focus on moral reasoning (Hashim, 1996).

On the other hand, there are clearly differences in Islamic Education and Moral Education that are related to the practice of these two courses. The Islamic secondary school syllabus emphasizes reading, understanding, and internalizing the teachings of the Quran as a guide to behavior. The learning of the Quran and the following of the required practices of Islam are then often reinforced by the Malay family (Hashim, 1996). The current system of separate values education classes has been criticized by Mukherjee (1988) and Hashim (1996) as establishing a "dual" system of morality that does not help the cause of racial unity. The emphasis on Quran memorization and more traditional learning methods in Islamic education does not necessarily facilitate moral reasoning that is emphasized in Moral Education classes. Hashim (1996) seems to feel that Muslims could also use Moral Education classes:

> This does not help in improving understanding and appreciation of values among the various communities and in overcoming prejudices. Muslim students also need moral education as this subject can expand their horizons and develop the skill of using reason in making moral decisions and choices (p. 147).

However, this is probably not going to happen since this would require Muslim

---

[2] The seventeenth core value of citizenship was added recently to the Moral Education syllabus.

students to take both Islamic Education and Moral Education classes (which now run concurrently) while Non-Muslims would only be required to take Moral Education. Another critique is also possible since Non-Muslims are exposed to a more "secular" system than Muslims; some parents would probably rather their children were in religious education classes like the Muslim students.

In the past several years, in order to enhance morality and national unity, increased emphasis has been given to teaching the Moral Education values across the curriculum to all students in Malaysia (Abdul Rasid et al., 1994). Values across the curriculum emphasizes character building of the individual in line with the Rukunegara and the National Education Philosophy. The inculcation of values in classes is done indirectly and was put in place to make students realize the importance of values in their lives, to improve national unity, and to try to overcome social problems of youth in Malaysia. There is also an awareness that informal ways of inculcating values are also essential including students' own experiences outside of class, students' own observations, students' own self awareness, and students' perceptions of teachers and others as role models (NIER, 1991). However, research by Barone (1998) has shown that some classroom teachers attempt to inculcate values across the curriculum while other teachers claim they do not have time to do this in the current exam driven system. In addition, efforts to inculcate the core Moral Education values across the curriculum are viewed by some Muslim students as less important than the religious values taught in Islamic Education classes.

There has also been concern over several aspects of the teaching of Moral Education and its role in the Malaysian education system. Jadi and Khamis (1987) found that Moral Education teachers understood the subject objectives but were concerned that the subject was boring for students and teachers. Mohd Noordin (1995) described some of the problems of Moral Education as inadequate teacher training, difficulty in assessing values, lack of interest and commitment among teachers and students, and incompatibility between values and social institutions. Elites have also identified the conduct of Moral Education as often problematic. Mohd Noordin (1996) mentions "teaching by moralizing" as one of the most uninteresting ways of getting students to learn. Since critical thinking is a goal of Malaysian education, more teachers need to encourage this in their students. Mohd Noordin (1996) has also stressed (as did several elites in this study) that it is necessary for teachers to be role models of the values they are attempting to foster. This is critical since Moral Education needs to be taught with an emphasis on moral reasoning, this needs to be a major feature of teacher education since a more traditional approach will not facilitate this process (Hashim, 1996).

Our Study

Given the long-standing concern with values education, the purpose of this study was to determine current perceptions of elites regarding values education. The reason for starting with elites in this study was due to their ability to influence values education policy. A long-range goal is to compare the thinking of elites with the thinking of teachers and students and see where gaps are evident in the thinking of these diverse groups. However, the focus of this initial study was to compare the views of values education of elites within each country and between the different countries participating in this research. In Malaysia, elites have frequently spoken of the need to enhance values education

The instrument designed by country participants and administered to elite respondents in the ten countries was organized around the following three key questions:

1. Why should there be values education?
2. What should be taught in schools?
3. How should values education be conducted?

The premise of the study is that only through understanding differences is it possible to generate true mutual understanding and consensus. Respondents were asked to rank their responses according to level of importance to get a clearer understanding of what issues they felt strongly about. Since Malaysia teaches Moral Education and Islamic Education and attempts to infuse values across the curriculum, answers to these questions told us how elites think of these issues that, in turn, has implications for policy.

The sample for the study was comprised of a variety of educational leaders in Malaysia including central educational elites, leading educational intellectuals, leaders of related NGOs, people in educational institutes, academic leaders, curriculum designers, and moral education specialists. Data was collected via a survey questionnaire with a cover letter describing the purpose of the study that also assured the participants of the confidentiality of their responses. A final section of the questionnaire also gave respondents an opportunity to provide written feedback on values education. Thirty-seven usable responses were received back from male and female elites. The majority of elites (54 percent) were from the Kuala Lumpur area while the rest of the elite respondents came from outside the capital area.

Findings

Why Should There be Values Education?

The Malaysian respondents indicated that the two most prevalent reasons for improving values education are:

1. To provide a foundation for spiritual development and
2. To provide a guide for behavior in daily life.

It is clear that these educational elites are in some way reiterating the objectives of Moral Education and Islamic Education classes. Therefore, elites feel that daily behavior is essential, but also recognize the importance of spiritual values as providing the needed base for guiding behavior. This is not surprising given the importance that religious values play in the stated ideology of education and in the conduct of life in Malaysia. The significance of moral values as a guide for behavior again coincides with policy documents that argue that values are to be a basis for moral action. This needs to be stressed since the presence of Moral Education as a separate subject in school which is tested can lead to a student focus on tests and grades and less of an emphasis on values as a "a guide for behavior in daily life".

According to Malaysian elites, the following are the four least important reasons for improving values education:

1. To help youth interpret the values transmitted by the mass media, the Internet, and other information technologies;

2. To promote more orderly and caring school communities and thus facilitate learning;

3. To combat the tendency for social prejudice and to promote greater tolerance for ethnic, language, and racial groups; and

4. To promote pride in local communities and community life.

The response that stands out here is the promotion of a more orderly and caring school community. This goal gets a great deal of attention in American literature as a crucial component in comprehensive character education programs (see Lickona, 1991), but according to these responses it was not viewed as essential by Malaysian elites. Similarly, respondents also de-emphasized the promotion of greater tolerance for ethnic groups. The alternate explanation for these answers is that it is possible that elites believe that Malaysian educators are doing enough to promote an orderly, caring environment and tolerance between different ethnic groups. On the other hand, the results can also be interpreted to mean that these areas are not deemed to be as important as other areas, and clearly this could be problematic given past ethnic tensions in Malaysia.

What Should be Taught in Schools?

The importance of values education in Malaysia is evident in that elites said that quite a bit of school time should be devoted to the learning of values. Respondents stated that 20 percent of school time and effort should be devoted to specific classes in moral education and 10 to 20 percent of school time and effort should be for integrating values across the curriculum. This also reflects current reality since formal religious and moral education classes are offered throughout primary and secondary schools and teachers are expected by the Ministry of Education to integrate values across the curriculum. However, as we shall see later, elites also responded that infusing values throughout content area classes and "teaching" moral values in out of school activities were also an important role of teachers and schools.

The cluster of specific themes that elites felt should be emphasized in values education in schools coincides closely with what is currently taught in schools. Seventy-five percent or more of elites indicated that a very strong emphasis should be given to teaching religious values, moral values, civic values, family values and work values. Not surprisingly, the two most frequent responses by elites—religious values and moral values—are also the values most emphasized in Malaysia education. Civic values were mentioned as important and the prominence here may be due in part to the importance of civics in the 1970s curriculum. Key themes of civics education were then incorporated into the new Moral Education curriculum implemented in the 1980s.

Elites were next asked their opinion of the content of values education, that is, which issues should be given strong emphasis and which should be emphasized less. Of the twenty-five issues provided on the questionnaire, 74 percent or more of elites responded that a very strong emphasis should be placed on the following eight items:

1. Schools should foster values supporting the family, such as respect for parents, fidelity, and taking care of children and elders.

2. As sound preparation for the world of work, habits of loyalty, obedience, hard work, and punctuality need to be stressed in school.

3. Schools should help every child gain a deeper understanding of their

own religion.
4. School should teach each child the value of critical thinking.
5. Values education should encourage mutual respect between boys and girls.
6. Schools should promote values of solidarity within communities.
7. Girls have essentially the same talents as boys and should be given equal opportunities and encouragement in schools.
8. It is best for schools to teach common values to all children without differentiation on the basis of class, ethnicity, or religion.

Several interesting findings are present here including the emphasis on the values of respect, hard work, and solidarity, the teaching of common values, gender equity, critical thinking and religious values. The idea that respect is one of a core of values that should be taught along with the importance of religion is a clear finding from this study. Elites emphasized the need for schools to focus on respect between boys and girls and the need to encourage equal opportunity. The habits of hard work, loyalty, and obedience were also deemed to be more important in Malaysia than in a number of other countries. The Western value of individualism and the importance placed on unique origins and heritage associated with a multicultural perspective are stressed less in Malaysia. A possible reason is due to the primary emphasis placed on using values to forge a common Malaysian identity while downplaying individualism which can be viewed as excessive in the American system (see Bellah et al., 1985). However, a greater focus on individual rights could also be part of a greater democratization movement that although supported by some elites, is feared by others. Recent concerns have also been noted about the inadequacy of the critical thinking abilities of school graduates and this is reflected by responses of the Malaysian elites. According to Yaacob and Seman (1993), schools need to do more to promote reasoning and problem solving skills. For example, the Integrated Secondary School Curriculum encourages this practice, but teachers can do more to act as role models that encourage discussion and debate of issues and foster the critical examination of conflicting points of views. Moral Education could be an especially important area to facilitate critical thinking among students while simultaneously emphasizing higher cognitive levels of thinking.

How Should Values Education be Conducted?

Malaysian elites strongly agreed that values should be taught at an early age. The majority of respondents (60 percent) strongly disagreed that values education should only begin in secondary school and instead all elites stated that values education should commence at an early age. These answers reflect the current practice of starting values education at the primary level in Malaysian schools. However, 47 percent of the elites strongly agreed that values should also be integrated across the curriculum as has been encouraged by the Ministry of Education in recent years. Regarding the different settings for values education, home and family were seen as essential for religious education and moral education. However, for religious education and civic education the next most common answer was "during school as a class". For Moral Education, outside of school influences like clubs and sports were seen as slightly more beneficial than learning morals during school as part of a class. This is interesting since the current emphasis is on learning morals directly through class instruction. A summary of these results is shown in Table 11.1:

Table 11.1 Most Effective Settings for Values Education (percent)*

Setting	Religious Education	Civic Education	Moral Education
Home and Family	82	88	81
During school as a class	60	72	56
Religious groups and institutions	58		56
Outside of school activities such as clubs, sports, etc.		50	65

*Only the top three results are shown for each column

Which Country Examples Should be Featured?

Most elites stressed the fact that their own country should be the primary focus when giving values examples to students. Malaysian elites also emphasized other Asian countries like Japan, Korea, Indonesia and Singapore as being useful for providing positive examples. However, unlike elites in many other countries America was not thought of as an influence. Another country not mentioned in the top three as an example by Malaysian elites was China. This is surprising given that the Chinese are the second largest group in Malaysia.

Are There Regional Values?

A final area in which Malaysian elites indicated a strong level of agreement was regarding the presence of a distinct set of Islamic and Asian values. For Asian values, elites indicated that there was a distinctive set of Asian values (mean=1.2) and that schools should teach these values (mean=1.4). In addition, elites also strongly agreed that there was a distinctive set of Islamic values (mean=1.2) and schools should teach Islamic values (mean=1.2). Again, these results are not surprising in that Malaysian schools teach both moral and Islamic values throughout primary and secondary schooling.

However, it is possible to view the issue of elite support of Islamic values and Asian values as related but also quite separate in its implications. Elite support for Islamic values is not surprising given that Islam is the national religion and as such occupies a special place in Malaysian schools and society. However, elite support for Asian values can be viewed as more problematic given the recent debates over this subject. According to Dupont (1996), the 1990s have witnessed increasing calls for a return to traditional core values common to all Asian societies despite the fact that there is often a great deal of disagreement over the core values underpinning Asian culture. In Malaysia, Prime Minister Dr. Mahathir Mohamed has called for a return to Asian values in his critique of the West although he has acknowledged that certain Asian values are outdated and need to be eliminated (e.g., excessive anti-materialism and deference to authority) (cited in Dupont, 1996). Looking at Malaysian society, Collins (1998) sees the importance of consensus building and respect for authority in both Malay and Confucian value systems. However, the moral authority of the ruler is dependent upon a just and fair treatment of citizens and consultation with local elites.

The critics of Asian values argue that values such as consensus building and respect for authority can be abused by those in power and used to mask authoritarian attempts to stifle the opposition.

Implications for Policy

Malaysian elites are clear in their support for values education as essential for providing a foundation for spiritual development and providing a guide for behavior in daily life. Malaysian elites were less likely than elites in several other countries to assert the primacy of young persons developing a reflective and autonomous personality. However, elites did stress the importance of encouraging critical thinking that clearly is part of developing a reflective and autonomous personality. A clarification of the way these terms are defined by Malaysian elites and how these constructs are reflected by actual practice may be useful questions for future research. However, Malaysian elites did stress the importance of increasing individual responsibility.

Regarding the question of what should be taught, moral values, civic values, and religious values were mentioned as crucial and all of these areas are currently being taught formally and informally in Malaysian schools. Another finding from this study is the fact that elites said that schools should help each child gain a deeper understanding of their own religion while also stated that schools should teach common values to all children. The second part of this is currently being done through attempts to teach the core moral values across the curriculum. However, the schools are not teaching children about their own religion except for Muslim students who are taking Islamic Education classes. This is a potential area to examine in future policy discussions. Gender equity is another clear concern among elites in that they argue that girls should be given the same opportunities as boys and that values education should encourage mutual respect between boys and girls.

There was a slight difference in the way that the different types of values education should be approached in Malaysian schools. It is clear from the results of this study that Malaysian elites believe that values education is the responsibility of all major socializing agents of society with schools and families being the most effective setting for values education. After home and family, the next most effective setting for religious values and civic values was in school as a class. However, for moral values the role of outside of school activities such as clubs and sports were deemed more valuable than moral education classes. This gives a possible implication for policy in that schools, according to elites, should focus more on these out of school activities and less on specific classes to teach moral values. Students have also stressed this issue in stating that it is more important to give students opportunities to practice values (e.g., through co-curricular activities) rather than just talking about them in classes (Barone, 1998).

There are a number of problems which elites have written about and mentioned in this study regarding the current practice of values education. One area of concern is the "dual" system of values education and its implications for national unity. Although there is a certain degree of philosophical concordance between Islamic Education and Moral Education, in practice they are very different. Since students are segregated primarily by race during Islamic Education and Moral education classes, it is also difficult to see how this practice fosters national unity. If teachers were to actively inculcate values across the curriculum, this may help to improve unity. As stated earlier, another problem inherent in teaching moral values as a specific class is that students may be likely to focus more on passing exams than on incorporating the core values into their daily life. Evaluating moral behavior cannot be adequately done through paper and pencil exams since at best this method can only evaluate moral knowledge. Ironically, the reason Moral Education is now tested is that originally the course was not taken seriously since it was not an examinable subject. Also, there have been recurring concerns in Malaysia about the quality of Moral Education teachers and the methodology used by these teachers to keep students interested in the subject. However, the overall educational system is still quite segregated in that a number of students (especially at primary level) attend Chinese, Tamil or Islamic schools and not the national schools. Malaysian policymakers must continue to be concerned that non-Malays do not perceive overt attempts at national unity as threatening to their ethnic identity (Hashim, 1996). Finally, critical thinking and moral reasoning need to be fostered throughout values education in Malaysia. Since Malaysian students are now faced with more difficult decisions regarding moral issues, they need to be prepared in the skills associated with moral reasoning in order to adequately cope with the challenges they face in an increasingly "Westernized" society.

One area that is repeatedly identified as crucial to values education is the teacher-student relationship. In a study by Barone (1998), a number of the concerns regarding values education were expressed by Malaysian secondary school teachers and students which address some of the concerns mentioned by Hayhoe (1997). In one part of this study, Malaysian secondary school teachers and students were interviewed concerning their views of Moral Education class. Both students and teachers recognized the dichotomy that is set up by the current system, namely, while the goal of moral education is to improve behavior, the "system" by testing Moral Education students rewards getting the right answer on tests. Students and teachers both agreed that Moral Education class was useful for teaching core values and for reinforcing concepts of right and wrong, however, much depends on the quality of the Moral Education teacher. One exemplary Moral Education teacher described herself as a role model and consistently tried to "break down the barriers" she perceived in the traditional Malaysian teacher/student relationship. This relationship is especially critical if you are a Moral Education teacher. She described her practice as follows:

> "That's why I always like to walk in the class and be with the students rather than standing in front of them... I like them to treat me as someone older than them trying to share something with them like a sister" (Interview, 8/96).

> "If you have the character only you can teach. The teacher has to set examples of proper behavior... I think the most important thing is the teacher has to show the proper example" (Interview, 8/96).

In addition, she frequently did not use the Moral Education textbook (which she disliked), but used current events from the newspapers as ways to encourage reflection of real-life moral dilemmas. She did this since she found much of the textbook not interesting and tried not to use it too much in her class. She also addressed the issue of exams in Moral Education by stating that her goal was to improve her students' behavior and was less concerned about how well they did on tests.

> "I hope the students will kind of build up their values so that when they do things they do it morally according to our values...Most of all is how they behave in their daily life. That is more important than passing an examination" (Interview, 8/96).

The relationship of the school and the community appears to be an important area to examine in Malaysian education. Since the elites in this study stressed the dual importance of schools fostering values supporting the family and also highlighted the critical nature of the home as the most effective setting for religious, moral and civic education, one would expect a close relationship between parents and the schools. This seems to be an area that needs further strengthening since the centralized educational system in the past has made home/school partnerships difficult. The "barriers" that exist between parents and schools need to be removed so that a caring supportive relationship exists which reinforces respect, discipline and moral values in both home and school. There are home/school partnerships through organizations such as the PTA but these are generally not strongly supported by parents who need to be incorporated more into the life of the school (NIER, 1996). Another area that has been identified as an area of concern is the preparation of teachers to teach moral values. For example, in a study by Jusoh and Ismail (1994/1995), student teachers were found to have an inadequate knowledge of the definitions of the core values and an even greater lack of awareness of how to infuse core values into the subject matter content that they were planning to teach in the future.

In conclusion, the views of the Malaysian elites regarding values education and its role in society are well represented by the written comments they provided at the end of the questionnaire. These comments along with the results presented previously give some direction for future policy. Some of these views are listed below:

1. All education is essentially value-driven; if all the right values are inculcated, the child will be self-propelled and motivated to succeed and be a positive force for good.
2. Values education should be taught as early as possible and the emphasis should be on universal positive values.
3. Values education is the responsibility of the parents, the teachers in schools as well as the general society at large.
4. Values are difficult to teach, as all of us know. It is by example from those with public posts that values are transmitted.
5. For values education to succeed within the school system, the larger environment must in its essence correspond to the values being propagated. It is the contradiction between word and deed that destroys values in society.
6. Values should be integrated in the classes and not taught separately.

In sum, according to one elite, "the foundation of civilization is [in] its religious and moral values—take that away and the destruction of that civilization is imminent. The socialization of the young, the transmission of culture has as their cornerstone, values education".

References

Abdul Rasid, N., Haji Maghribi, N. and Mohd. Taib, A. (1994). "Moral Education Programme: The Malaysian Experience". In *Report: Regional Seminar on Values Education in ASEAN*. Kuala Lumpur: Ministry of Education.

Apter, D. (1968). *Some Conceptual Approaches to the Study of Modernization*. Englewood Cliffs, NJ: Prentice Hall.

Barone, T. (1998). *A Comparative Study of Value Perceptions and Normative Rule Compliance of Malaysian and American Secondary School Students*. (Doctoral dissertation, State University of New York at Buffalo, 1998). Dissertation Abstracts International, 59-09, 3397A.

Bellah, R., Madsen, R., Sullivan, W., Swidler, A. and Tipton, S. (1985). *Habits of the Heart: Individualism and Commitment in American Life*. New York: Harper and Row.

Collins, A. (1998). "The Ethnic Security Dilemma: Evidence from Malaysia". *Contemporary Southeast Asia*, 20(3): 261-278.

Dupont, A. (1996). "Is there an Asian Way?" *Survival*, 38(2): 13-33.

Hashim, R. (1996). *Educational Dualism in Malaysia: Implications for Theory and Practice*. New York: Oxford University Press.

Hashim, W. (1983). *Race Relations in Malaysia*. Kuala Lumpur: Heinemann Educational Books.

Hassan, M.K. (1996). *Towards Actualizing Islamic Ethical and Educational Principles in Malaysian Society*. Petaling Jaya, Malaysia: Muslim Youth Movement of Malaysia.

Hayhoe, R. (1997). "Education as Communication". In J. Montgomery (Ed.), *Values in Education: Social Capital Formation in Asia and the Pacific*. Hollis, NH: Hollis Publishing Co.

Jadi, H. and Khamis, A. (1987). *Values Education in Malaysia*. Malaysia: South East Asian Research Review and Advisory Group.

Jusoh, I. And Ismail, Z. (1994/1995). "The Understanding and Implementation of Values Education: Perceptions of Student Teachers", *Jurnal Pendidik dan Pendidikan* 13: 87-98.

Lickona, T. (1991). *Educating for Character*. New York: Bantam Books.

Loh, P. (1974). "British Policies and the Education of Malays, 1909-1939", *Paedagogica Historica*, 14 (2): 355-384.

Ministry of Education (1989). *Moral Education Secondary School Syllabus*. Kuala Lumpur: Curriculum Development Centre.

Ministry of Education (1990). *Islamic Education Syllabus*. Kuala Lumpur: Ministry of Education.

Ministry of Education (1997). *Education in Malaysia*. Kuala Lumpur: Ministry of Education.

Mohd Noordin, W. Z. (1996). *'Demoralising' Moral Education*. Paper presented at APNIEVE Experts Meeting to Design Values Education at Teacher Training Level, Malacca, Malaysia.

Mohd Noordin, W. Z. (1995). *An Overview of Values and Ethics Education*. Paper presented at the Regional Seminar on the Teaching of Values and Ethics in Schools for Asia and the Pacific: Realities, Reflections, and Expectations, Kuala Lumpur, Malaysia.

Mukherjee, H. (1988). "Moral Education in A Developing Society: The Malaysian

Case". In W.K. Cummings, S. Gopinathan and Y. Tomoda (Eds.), *The Revival of Values Education in Asia and the West*. New York: Pergamon Press.

National Institute for Educational Research [NIER] (1996). *Partnerships in Education: Home, School and Community Links in the Asia-Pacific Region*. Tokyo: National Institute for Educational Research. (ERIC Document Reproduction Service ED 420555).

National Institute for Educational Research [NIER] (1991). *Education for Humanistic, Ethical/Moral and Cultural Values*. Tokyo: National Institute for Educational Research.

National Institute for Educational Research [NIER] (1990). *A New Decade of Moral Education*. Tokyo: National Institute for Educational Research.

Syed Zin, S.M. and Lewin, K. (1991). "Curriculum Development in Malaysia". In C. Marsh and P. Morris (Eds.), *Curriculum Development in East Asia*. London: The Falmer Press.

Thomas, R.M. (1985). "Education as Intergroup Relations—An International Perspective: The cases of Malaysia and Singapore". In J. Hawkins and T. LaBelle (Eds.), *Education and Intergroup Relations: An International Perspective*. New York: Praeger.

Yaacob R.A. and Seman, N.A. (1993). *Towards Achieving A Critical Thinking Society in Malaysia: A challenge to School Libraries and Educational Systems*. (ERIC Document Reproduction Service No. ED 399933).

CHAPTER 12

THAILAND: BEYOND MATERIALISM

M. Elizabeth Cranley
Neon Pinpradit
Kingfa Sintoovongse

Introduction

In current debates about Thai values, two distinct yet interlocking themes emerge: materialism and democracy. These concepts suggest an emerging values system which is in contest with the perceived values of the past. Materialism and consumerism are viewed as a consequence of economic expansion and a cause of recent economic crisis, and they are a challenge to emerging democracy and the formation of a responsible civil society. In this milieu, an array of other values, complementary and contrary to materialism and democracy, are being reiterated and/or reinvented to fit the dynamic Thai society.

In 1996, nearly a year before the crash of the Thai economy, Professor Dr. Kriengsak Chareonwongsak of Thailand's Institute of Future Studies for Development said of contemporary Thai society, "People will do anything possible...for material gain, as society overemphasizes the value of material wealth—which always bring [sic] much prestige and power" (Chareonwongsak, 1996). He is not alone in his indictment. A leading economist in one of the country's top universities remarked that for Thai people "consumerism has become the most vicious enemy" (Interview, 8/6/97). From a more moderate perspective, a senior scholar in psychology felt that the dominant value in Thai society today is the "personal materialistic value". "I think", she remarked in an interview, "it's the same everywhere. People don't care much for the spiritual value or the things that are non-materialistic, but [rather] the things that have more materialistic values. Money, for example. Money, career promotion. The material reward" (Interview, 8/5/97).

Such critiques of current societal values may seem appropriate for many of the world's communities, but for leading Thai academics, policy makers, and social activists and critics, materialism or consumerism is not just a sign of the rapid development that the Thai economy has enjoyed over the past decade. It is also a reflection of a dynamic society, a society characterized by an expanding middle class and the rapid growth of urban areas (Bunbongkarn, 1996, p. 9), a society that is increasingly demanding more participation in public affairs and more accountability from public servants. Thus, closely linked with the consumer culture in which material wealth "always brings much prestige and power", is the political or civic culture.

During this study, which followed the 1997 ratification of a new constitution and the fall of the economy in the same year, Thailand had been undergoing significant reforms economically, politically, and socially. Education reform, with the recent passage of the National Education Act of 1999, is a cornerstone of this reform. This Act will affect the nation in many ways as it expands educational opportunities, reforms teacher education, and decentralizes many aspects of financial and administrative responsibilities and curriculum development. Philosophically, the Act stresses the dual importance of knowledge and morality, once again reiterating that education, especially formal schooling, is a key site for the articulation of ideal values to address societal issues. This paper draws upon the Sigma Elite Values Survey and related interviews in an attempt to understand the Thai "elite" thinking about values and values education in this era.

Social and Political Context

The decade of the 1990s may well prove to be a significant turning point in Thailand's history. For over thirty years, the country's economy experienced steady growth through abundant natural resources, a vital and semi-diversified agricultural sector, high savings rates and high domestic and foreign investment rates, cheap labor, adequate infrastructure, and liberal, export and business-oriented public policies. From 1985 to 1995, Thailand had the fastest growing economy in the world (World Bank, 1997). Consequently, by the early 1990s, with double digit annual economic growth rates and an expanding middle-class, the Kingdom of Thailand, a nation of 60 million people, was considered "Asia's Fifth Tiger" by the world economic press (Hussey, 1993). Thus propelled into the ranks of the newly industrialized countries by the early 1990s, Thailand was prepared for neither the political turmoil of 1991-1992, nor for the economic crash of 1997. These two major events of the 1990s are helping to shape the debates about the direction the nation is moving economically, politically, socially, and psychologically.

Perhaps the most significant change in recent Thai society has been the growth and rise of the new middle-class. On average, the income for Thai households increased by over 10 percent annually between 1988 and 1996 (National Statistical Office, 1999), and in municipal areas, the sites of the middle-class, incomes rose much more rapidly than the national average during the late 1980s and early 1990s (13.4 percent during 1988-90, and 15.2 percent during 1990-92) (*Bangkok Post,* December, 1996). At the same time, the average size of households declined (see Table 12.1).

Table 12.1 Average Monthly Income and Expenditure of Household (Baht)

Year	Average Household Size	Average Monthly Income of Household	Percent of Change per Year	Average Monthly Expenditure of Household	Percent of Change per Year
1975-76	5.5	1,928	---	2,004	---
1981	4.5	3,378	11.87	3,374	10.98
1986	4.3	3,631	1.45	3,783	2.31
1990	4.1	5,625	17.04	5,437	14.31
1994	3.8	8,262	8.16	7,567	7.66
1996	3.7	10,779	14.22	9,190	10.20
1998*	3.8	12,835	9.12	10,982	9.32

Source: National Statistic Office, Table 1 (1999). *1998 data is preliminary.

Data collected by the National Statistical Office of Thailand reveals a sizable increase in the average monthly household income and a subsequent shift in Thai spending patterns. Over a fifteen-year period, the percentage of monthly expenditures for food declined from 44.1 percent in 1981 to 32.2 percent in 1996. Conversely, non-food expenditures have risen from 55.9 percent to 67.8 percent during the same period. Even more striking is the percentage of monthly income spent on non-consumption goods. It has more than doubled since 1981 (National Statistical Office, 1999) (see Table 12.2). Such figures illustrate the rise of the purchasing power of Thai citizens. It also supports the claim of some Thais that excessive materialism has taken root in society. In their critique of recent development in Thailand, Bello, Cunningham and Poh (1998) describe a "culture of consumption" where, for example, Thailand became the primary market of Mercedes Benz outside of Germany (p. 5) and rural Thailand became, after the U.S., the world's biggest market for pickup trucks (p. 8).

Table 12.2 Percentage of Average Monthly Expenditure of Household by Expenditure Group

Expenditure Group	1975-6	1981	1986	1990	1994	1996	1998*
Total Expenditures	100.0	100.0	100.0	100.0	100.0	100.0	100.0
Food and Beverages	46.1	44.1	38.9	36.2	33.7	32.2	33.4
Alcoholic Beverages	1.0	1.2	1.2	1.5	1.6	2.5	1.6
Tobacco Products	2.8	2.4	1.8	1.5	1.2	1.5	1.1
Apparel and Footwear	10.1	7.3	6.2	5.8	5.4	4.8	3.6
Housing	16.9	20.6	23.4	22.4	21.9	20.3	20.9
Medical Care	4.0	3.3	3.5	3.4	3.5	3.7	2.6
Personal Care	2.4	2.2	2.6	2.5	2.5	2.4	2.2
Transportation and Communications	7.5	7.3	9.1	12.8	14.8	15.4	15
Recreation and Reading	2.3	2.3	2.4	2.3	2.2	2.2	1.9
Education	1.6	1.3	1.5	1.4	1.8	1.8	1.9
Miscellaneous	1.3	1.4	1.5	1.1	1.1	1.0	1.2
Non-Consumption Expenditures	4.0	6.6	7.9	9.1	10.3	12.2	14.6

Source: National Statistic Office, Table 1 (1999). *1998 data is preliminary.

Ironically, the growth of the middle class and the burgeoning of the consumer culture coincided with an increasing intolerance of greed and corruption among the nation's political leaders. Phongpaichit and Piriyarangsan (1994) credit the rise of corruption as *an issue* [their emphasis] in the late 1980s to the rise of democratic institutions, including the parliament and the press, and to increasing competition for political power (p. 187). After decades of governments headed primarily by military dictators, Thai civilians, led by the business community, began to call for increased democratization and a civilian government elected by the people. The first civilian government in over a decade was elected in 1988. In February 1991, a military coup overthrew this government, citing corruption in the government as the reason. In May the following year, the middle class took to the streets of Bangkok in massive protests and riots that forced the military regime to step out of politics and brought about a rebirth of democracy (Bunbongkarn, 1996) and the public recognition of the need to control corruption and limit the influence of money in politics.

By the mid-1990s, the political power of the military was fading as civilian governments strengthened. Conversely, the economy began weakening. Investment capital was being diverted from the productive sectors of the economy and channeled into the highly profitable real estate, stock market, and credit creation sectors (Bello, et al., 1998; Phongpaichit and Baker, 1998; Unger, 1998). By 1997, manufacturing lagged while the financial sector overheated, coalescing in the collapse of dozens of finance companies, a massive over supply of real estate, the fall of the stock exchange, the flotation of the baht, zero growth in exports, and the flight of foreign capital (Bello, et al., 1998, pp. 7-8). A year later, Thailand's total external debt amounted to US$86.4 billion, roughly two-thirds of which was private sector debt (Punyaratabandu, 1999, p. 80).

In the face of the seemingly get-rich-quick schemes and rampant conspicuous consumption of the early 1990s, it is not surprising that many Thais are blaming a lack of moral virtues and an absence of a responsible civil society for the troubles. Currently faced with rising prices and dwindling savings, the middle class is questioning its recently acquired materialistic values, its tolerance of greed and corruption, and its view of "development" that is focused narrowly on economic gains (e.g. Bello, et al., 1998; Chareonwongsak, 1996; Mulder, 1997; Phongpaichit and Piriyarangsan, 1994; Phongpaichit and Baker, 1998; Personal Correspondence, 1997-1999).

In recognition of the volatility of current Thai society, The Office of the National Education Commission (ONEC), the government agency responsible for education policy and evaluation, has identified a "New Era of National Education" from 1997 onwards. This is an Era that is responding to drastic social changes and growing demands for radical reform in education.

> Thailand is now confronting the most drastic social changes from within and from its interconnectedness with the complex and rapidly changing world. Such changes are too overwhelming for both individuals and society to cope with, thus causing imbalances in various aspects of development. The present social institutions—be they political, bureaucratic, educational, religious, and judicial or media systems—have failed to adapt themselves to cope with the formidable changes. The result is organizational weaknesses, confusion, conflicts and suffering which might erupt into violence. Social reform is thus indispensable in order to strengthen all sectors of the society. Reform of the education system is one of the most important areas of social reform since it is believed that education is a very important process to enhance individual development, which will contribute to social and economic development of the country. It will enable Thailand to move through the current crisis (ONEC, 1998, p. 12).

An examination of education in such a context of confusion and upheaval suggests that values education may be reevaluated and reemerge as a central component of education reform and as a forum to address a wide array of social, political and economic issues.

Values Education Policy

Thai public schools have always been a vehicle for propagating values. Early in the twentieth century one of the primary justifications for establishing formal education for the masses was to teach what it meant to be Thai, to hold the values and practice the morality that would create social solidarity. Built upon a centuries-old tradition of monastic education, schools were the expected and entirely appropriate site for values education. This is no less the case in current educational policy, which clearly emphases this, both through its overarching principles and goals for the sector as a whole and in the curriculum for every level (ONEC, 1997).

For more than 600 years, from the thirteenth to the middle of the nineteenth century, education in Thailand remained virtually unchanged (Watson, 1973). By the end of the thirteenth century, Buddhism was the dominant force in the intellectual life of Sukhothai, Thailand's first major kingdom, and Buddhist monasteries became the centers of learning and culture. By the fourteenth century, the basic patterns of Thai education were set: education was situated firmly in the Buddhist monasteries with literacy, basic numeracy, and the principles of Buddhism the goals of the loosely structured, individualistic curriculum (Wyatt, 1969).

The second major period in the history of Thai education (1870–1932) marks the beginning of the modern educational system, including the establishment of a formal curriculum, textbooks, and schooling for both boys and girls. Although the earliest schools of this modern era served primarily the nobility in preparation for government service, a 1898 reorganization of education established an aggressive plan to spread education to the provinces by using the monasteries as the sites for modern schools. King Chulalongkorn himself explained,

> No education can be established which is not connected with the monastery, because to the teaching of reading and writing must be added instruction in religion. This is a goal of the first order.... I have investigated in the provinces, and we have seen the decay of Thai people without religion, which has caused them to lose their "morals". I would like to have the educational system connected with religion (Quoted in Wyatt, 1969, p. 225).

Drawing from traditional monastic education, religion was declared one of the cornerstones of the new "secular" modern education, which included separate subjects, formal classroom instruction, lay teachers, graded levels, and examinations, for the purpose of developing a literate and moral citizenry. In the years that followed, various national education schemes advocated the teaching of moral principles and values in the schools.

From 1932 onwards, education policy has stressed modernization and education for national development (ONEC, 1998, p. 10). During this period Thailand has achieved universal primary education and greatly expanded secondary and tertiary education. With these achievements, the focus of education policy has shifted and evolved. The *1992 National Scheme of Education* and the *Eighth National Education Development Plan: 1997-2001* articulates the principles and current goals of education. The four fundamental principles of education are:

- The flourishment of individual wisdom, thinking, mind and morality is a necessary and essential goal.
- Human beings must realize the importance of judicious utilization and conservation of natural resources.
- An understanding of language and culture of Thai society must be as-

certained.

- The proper balance between dependency and self-reliance is an essential basis for cooperation at individual, community and national levels (ONEC, 1998, p. 16).

The goals of education "emphasize balanced and harmonious development of the individual in four aspects: wisdom, spiritual development, physical and social development" (ONEC, 1998, p. 16). Three out of four of these goals—wisdom, spiritual development, and social development—are essentially an articulation of values, including moral, civic, and social values. Wisdom, for example, includes the ability to "differentiate between virtues and vices, right and wrong" and to "be creative and possess an inquiring mind". An educated person who has developed spiritually should be able to "uphold religious principles and train one's mind to become morally developed; be conscious of wrong-doings; self-controlled and self-disciplined; [and] possess concentration and perseverance". Similarly, social development means, among other things, to "possess proper social behavior; extend help unselfishly; preserve the Thai national identity and culture; recognize and observe one's own rights and others' rights and freedom...; [and] be able to utilize and conserve natural resources". (ONEC, 1998, pp. 17-18).

Schools' Role in Values Education

At the school level, via formal curricula and texts, values education, which emphasizes responsibilities toward country, society, family and oneself, continues to be a major component of education. This is especially true in the primary grades (one through six). The current primary school curriculum is divided into four areas of instruction[1]: Basic Skills, Life Experiences, Character Development, and Work-Oriented Experiences. According to the curriculum, Character Development accounts for 20 to 25 percent of instruction time for grades one through six, and is defined as "dealing with activities necessary for developing desirable habits, values, attitudes and behavior, which will lead to desirable character" (ONEC, 1998, p. 47). In separate subject classes in moral education, students study units such as: "Good School, Good Discipline", "Good and Happy Family", and "Conforming to Thai Culture and Traditions"; virtues such as "Honesty", "Responsibility", and "Diligence"; as well as "Buddhist Principles". (MOE, 1995, pp. 49-50, 57, 58, 62). Values education also forms a large component of the other areas of instruction and within school rules, rituals and extra-curricular activities.

When students reach secondary school, the overt attention given to values and moral education in the formal curriculum decreases dramatically. It is confined to social studies classes, which include history, economics, government and Buddhism, and through scouting and club activities. However, teachers are formally encouraged to integrate values education in every subject and activity.

Objective and curricular guidelines for values education, especially civic and

---

[1] Students in grades 5 and 6 have a fifth area, Special Experiences. Although the activities may be drawn from the other four groups or any other area of interest, with very few exceptions, students study English.

moral values, are quite clearly articulated for all levels. Despite this emphasis, values education is perceived to be failing. The director of primary education for a large northeastern province remarked that "values education is currently ignored in schools. Schools emphasize academic subject matter" (Interview, 7/30/97). He explained further that parents are demanding this shift in emphasis as competition for places in the best high schools and colleges increases. An educational researcher elaborated, "Parents are more educated in general, so they understand the significance of education.... They would like their children to get an education to improve the quality of themselves, to have a good mind, to have more choices" (Interview, 8/5/97). For most parents, this means an emphasis on the subject matter that appears on examinations. Consequently, moral education as an evaluated *subject* often receives the same type of intellectual objectification as mathematics or ancient history. It is seemingly divorced from any application to real life. In his critique of primary school textbooks, Mulder (1997) claims that primary school children are given a moralistic, primarily religious view of Thailand, which emphasizes an imagined and idealistic view of history and society, one which is divided into "good" and "not good". He suggests that

> The moralizing image of society offered in school is rather simplistic: you either belong to it, or not at all. The task of the school is to reproduce morally good people who are determined by a rather simple-minded set of values (p. 52).

> The cognitive way ethics is taught and repeated makes it appear that morality equates with a certain knowledge that enables people to classify almost all actions as either "good" or "not good", but since this labeling is done outside of real-life contexts, it remains a purely academic exercise that has little to do with everyday experience" (p. 54).

Secondary school texts offer little enhancement to the primary level lessons. Mulder describes a junior high school text:

> From heroic attempts to analyze the economy as basic to all social dynamics, the narrative slips back to moral observations... What remains in place are a few slogans: without king, no Thailand; the king constitutes the center of Thais' hearts and minds; the Thais love democracy; foreign investment is good; ... Thailand is independent and respected; the past is untroubled, the present problematic (p. 111).

Teachers also come under fire for their inability or unwillingness to teach values. Reflecting the view of many Survey respondents, a professor involved in university affairs, including curriculum development and teacher education, explained the current situation: "The teaching method is lecture. They tell [the students], 'You must do this. You must not do that.' Teachers don't 'give closeness' to students. They don't have the time to devote to students for values and personal development" (Interview, 7/30/97). Similarly, a Chulalongkorn University education professor said of teachers' methodology,

> It seems to me that nowadays we define and practice education or teaching as the *transmitting* of knowledge or skills or values. I think the term 'transmitting' is not a good term to define teaching. ...I think education

sometimes has something artificial. [Teachers] try to [bring an] artificial world into the classroom, just learn in the classroom, just learn from the book only... I think its not enough (Interview, 8/8/97).

The professor, who believes that "very good teachers" are the essential key to successful values education, laments that the quality of teachers has drastically declined.

I think about 50 years ago Thailand had a good policy to bring the tops from each province to train to be the teachers, so we [had] very good teachers. We [had] good people to be teachers by choice, not by chance. They choose to be teachers. Also, the teaching profession [was] very respectable. But 50 years later, we need some people in engineering, medicine...Also the people in [those] areas get very good money... [Now] we are worried because people come to be the teachers by chance. (Interview, 8/8/97).

The professor, whose research has focused on the teaching profession in Thailand, contends that education is often a student's last choice among fields of study and of careers. The best students go to other, more lucrative fields. "So it just by chance [bad luck or poor exam performance] that they get into the teacher education institutions, and then by chance get the degree in education. And if they can't get another job, they will be a teacher" (Interview, 8/8/97).

The quality of teaching is not the only attack teachers face. The quality of their personhood is also being questioned by nearly every Thai involved in this study, from local school principals to high level administrators in the central government. They revealed that next to the family, teachers need to be good models for children. This is more important than what happens in the formal teaching of values and morals; it leaves a more lasting impression on students. One oft-cited example is that teachers frequently get into debt to buy automobiles and other consumer goods. This is a persistent problem among many, especially rural teachers, as the salaries are low and the urge for material gain is high. A few teachers also are known to gamble and drink and have even been known to sell illegal drugs to their students (Interviews, 7/29/97, 7/30/99 (2), and 8/6/97). Many of these teachers live in small villages and or on school grounds, making them highly visible to their impressionable students. When faced with such living examples, the dry moralistic tone of classroom pedagogy has little meaning for children.

From a more benign perspective, some of the "best" teachers are criticized for focusing "on the ability of good teaching, but good teaching so the children in the class get good marks and ...can enter into the university. [This] reflects the good ability of that particular teacher even though that teacher might not be a good moral [model]" (Interview, 8/5/97). This type of teacher reinforces the perception that achievement in academic subject matter is superior to good character development.

Parents, as partners in educating their children, are also criticized for neglecting the social and moral development of their children. Parents are too busy working, either trying to make ends meet or to get ahead. The attention they give to children seems to be much less than in the past. Family structure is also shifting as families become more mobile, migratory labor increases, and upheavals such as divorce increase. Consequently, some families are abandoning this crucial role and expecting schools to fulfill it. This is putting more pressure on schools and teachers and exposing them to greater criticisms.

Although the national education policy is imbued with values, and the propagation of these values is central to the educational enterprise, the practice does not always live up to these ideals. Through interviews and the Sigma Elite Survey, Thai "elites" reveal that they agree with assessments of the volatility of current social situations and the oftentimes inadequacy of current education policy and practice. Nonetheless, they do believe that values education has a definite place in trying to address some of these issues.

Description of the Study

This study began in August of 1997 when we interviewed approximately twenty Thai "elites" to gain a greater understanding of the thoughts and issues regarding values in Thai society in general and the role educational institutions play in values education in particular. Following these interviews and the development of the Sigma Elite Survey, we purposefully identified approximately eighty Thai elites to whom we sent the Survey in January of 1989. In the Thai context, we defined "educational elites" as those people who hold high positions in their respective areas and are in a position of influence, preferably nationally, but at least regionally, in the area of education. Our respondents were drawn from government, both elected officials and civil servants, from institutions of higher education and from the business and religious communities. Following a preliminary analysis of the Survey results, we formally interviewed approximately one third of the respondents to define and clarify some of their answers, and we received written comments from many other respondents.

Of the eighty Surveys sent, fifty elites, almost 63 percent, responded. Of these fifty, the overwhelming majority is from the higher education sector: twenty-one are university administrators and thirteen are administrators of Rajabat Institutes (formerly known as teachers colleges). Eleven respondents are policy-makers at the national/central level. These include a high level politician in the current government, both political appointees and career civil servants in the Ministry of Education and related departments, and an executive of a large bank which has educational interests. Another four respondents are local school administrators. The remaining respondent is a nationally recognized monk whose wide-ranging interests include education. Our respondents can be further divided into more specific categories (Table 12.3).

The respondents, thirty-six men and fourteen women, reside in all five major regions of Thailand—North, Northeastern, Central, South, and the Bangkok Metropolitan Area—with the majority, twenty-two, living and working in Bangkok. The other twenty-eight live throughout the country, but primarily in major cities or provincial capitals. Only two represent the small towns or rural areas. Although the majority of our respondents lives and works outside of Bangkok, many of them are originally from the capital city and/or were educated there.[2] Thus, the influence of Bangkok may be

---

[2] Our data regarding the geographic origins of our respondents is anecdotal, rather than gathered through our Survey. However, this could be considered a fairly accurate reflection of the

far greater among our respondents than our survey indicates.

Table 12.3 Sigma Elite Survey Respondents

Position of Respondents	Number of Respondents	Percent of Respondents
Central Educational Elites	7	14
Educational Intellectuals	3	6
Religious Leaders	1	2
Leaders of NGO	1	2
Politicians	2	4
People in Academic Institutes	6	12
Academic Leaders	21	42
Curriculum Designers for Moral Education	2	4
Values/Moral Education Specialist	7	14
Total	50	100

We recognize that fifty respondents cannot represent a population of 60 million, or even the smaller population of "educational elites" in Thailand. Nonetheless, our respondents do represent an array of familial and educational backgrounds, political persuasions, religious affiliations, geographic locations, and professional lives. Yet, they all share a common interest in education, many of whom are directly involved in values and moral education, and their survey and interview responses display a striking degree of consensus around many of the issues.

Thirty people did not respond to the survey: twelve policy makers (including several high level ministers and secretaries-general of education related departments), eleven university administrators, three Rajapat Institute administrators, one well-known monk, and one administrator of a non-governmental organization.

Limitations of the Study

The sample size and composition is the major limitation of this study. This Thai survey is focused on perceptions of "ideal" policy rather than on current practice. With this in mind, we limited our survey to those "elites" known to us who potentially can influence policy at the national or regional levels, particularly in terms of public policy formation, educational research, and teacher education. Thus our Thai respondents do not include what other settings in this Pacific Rim survey consider "front line" elites or practitioners. Our sample did not include any teachers of the kindergarten through grade twelve levels, and only two respondents are secondary school administrators. We might conclude, then, that our respondents reflect points of view that are somewhat removed from the daily practice of values education in the schools. We recognize that "front line" educators often offer more insightful and realistic portraits of what is and can happen in schools and that they can wield tremendous influence in the lives of their students. However, in the current system of educational policy making in Thai-

---

power structure in education where many high level civil servants, administrators, and university and college professors are from Bangkok, or at least graduated from Bangkok universities.

land, individual teachers have little or no policy influence at any level, except perhaps the grade or building level.[3]

All of the Thai respondents are university graduates, many with advanced degrees from Thai or overseas universities. Many are bilingual in English and Thai. Despite this level of educational achievement, the survey instrument presented a few difficulties. Some of the respondents felt that the Thai language used, which was directly translated from the original English, was somewhat alienating because it sounded "foreign" or "too sophisticated". Some of the words and phrases, although correctly translated, are not part of the everyday lexicon of values in Thailand, thus the respondents were faced with terms that seemed awkward. For example, the phrase "competitive values" was translated as a "fondness for competition", and "a reflective and autonomous personality" as a "private personality that includes independence and thoughtfulness". As a consequence, some of the respondents commented that they felt the survey instrument reflected Western values, although paradoxically, one wrote, "The questions basically followed the ideology of Confucius" (#58, written comment).

Although the survey itself was in Thai, many of the interviews were conducted in English. This allowed for the clarification of terms and concepts, but also resulted in some diversions. One interviewee, rather than talking about "values education", spoke very eloquently about the "value of education" and how it is changing in society. The challenges of research in a multilingual context are evident throughout this research.

Findings

The findings presented below represent responses to the Sigma Elite Survey questions pertaining to the "why", "what", and "how" of values education. Interview data is included to explain and clarify some respondents' interpretation of the questions in the Thai context.

Why Should There be Values Education?

"To increase a sense of individual responsibility" is the unambiguous number one reason for promoting values education today. Forty-nine percent of the respondents listed this argument as one of their top three reasons (among seventeen), and more respondents (thirty-nine) chose this argument than any other. Similarly, the second and third most prominent arguments—"to provide a guide for behavior in everyday life" and "to encourage civic consciousness and strengthen democracy"[4]— also emphasize the role of the individual. All three of these responses had similar means and low standard deviations, indicating a great deal of consensus (see Table 12.4).

---

[3] Current education reform efforts are primarily focused on decentralization, including curriculum development and decision-making. This will potentially allow teachers and local administrators more autonomy in determining resource allocations and curriculum content.

[4] The Thai translation of this concept is more closely back translated as "to improve a sense of responsibility towards society to help make the system of democracy stronger."

Table 12.4 Reasons for Values Education

Rank Order	Most Prevalent Reasons for Improving Values Education in Thailand Today	Mean*	SD	n
1	To increase a sense of individual responsibility	4.10	2.58	39
2	To provide a guide for behavior in everyday life	4.39	2.81	38
3	To encourage civic consciousness and strengthen democracy To provide a guide for behavior in everyday life	4.39	2.83	38
4	To provide a foundation for spiritual development	5.68	4.49	31
5	To develop an appreciation for heritage and strengthen national identity	5.82	3.83	38
6	To promote orderly and caring school communities thus facilitating learning	6.48	3.63	33
7	To strengthen families	6.77	4.57	31
8	To promote pride in local communities and community life	7.03	4.03	36
9	To foster economic development through hard work, creativity, and competitive values	7.07	4.19	28
10	To help young persons develop a reflective and autonomous personality	7.29	4.04	28
11	To combat juvenile delinquency	7.56	4.32	27
12	To help youth interpret values transmitted by the media and information technology	8.07	5.20	27
13	To combat ecological abuse	9.23	4.38	30
14	To promote values of justice and equality	9.41	4.23	29
15	To promote world peace	10.30	5.89	23
16	To combat social prejudice	10.46	5.04	24
17	To improve the respect and opportunities extended to girls and women	11.60	3.70	20

*A lower mean indicates greater importance for those who checked an argument as prevalent.

As the rank order of prominence descends from the most persuasive argument for values education to the least persuasive, the issues become larger in scope, from individual behavior to issues which affect the nation and community, and toward the bottom, those which include a wider, more global perspective. According to many of the respondents, an understanding and practice of a sense of responsibility is the cornerstone of the values that follow. Thus, it must be first. If one has a well-developed sense of responsibility, and behaves accordingly in everyday life for the betterment of self and society, there will be no need to "combat ecological awareness" or "social prejudice", for example.

The argument considered least important is "To improve the respect and opportunities extended to girls and women". Neither male nor female respondents considered this to be important relative to the other issues. Despite documented exploitation of women in Thailand (e.g. Bello, Cunningham and Poh, 1998; Bishop and Robinson, 1998; and Sittirak, 1996), this is not considered to be a compelling reason for values education. Women have made remarkable strides and are at near parity with men in terms of education and employment in many fields, including farming, craftsmen/laborers, and sales (Sethaput and Yoddumnern-Attig, 1992, p. 84). While women still lag behind men in "white-collar" occupations, their numbers are increasing. Thus, from the perspective of the respondents of this survey, it is not a priority issue. When responding to "what should be taught" respondents evinced a similar lack of interest in gender as an issue.

What Should be Taught in Schools?

Considering what should be taught in schools, Thai elites responded again with the social values that affect civil society directly: 1). Civic Values; 2). Democracy; and 3). Work Values (Table 12.5). Within these three themes lie a multitude of values that contribute to the well-being of society, socially, economically, and politically. They especially address some of the societal issues that Thailand is facing in terms of developing democracy and struggling with the economy.

Table 12.5 Values Education Themes

What Emphasis Should be Placed on Each of the Following Themes (1=very strong emphasis)	Rank Order	Mean*	SD
Civic Values	1	1.59	1.19
Democracy	2	1.80	1.38
Work Values	3	1.90	1.12
National Identity & Patriotism	4	2.02	1.30
Moral Values	5	2.04	1.31
Personal Autonomy and Reflection	6	2.15	1.43
Ecological Awareness	7	2.18	1.38
Family Values	8	2.43	1.46
Diversity and Multiculturalism	9	2.67	1.72
Peace and Conflict Resolution	10	2.78	1.77
Global Awareness	11	3.12	1.68
Gender Equality	12	3.25	1.64
Religious Values	13	3.40	1.73

*A lower mean indicates greater importance should be placed on the values theme.

National Identity and Patriotism and Moral Values are given some prominence in this survey, but lack the emphasis that their presence in the school curriculum would suggest. These two themes are the core of the values education curriculum. They are emphasized at morning assembly, in ethics and religion classes, in social studies and history classes, and in scouting and other extra-curricular activities. Yet Thai educational elites are espousing a somewhat different view of "nation", one where civic responsibility and democracy will help to define the national identity and moral values. A deputy prime minister, who felt that National Identity and Patriotism should be left out of schools, explained:

> What I'm afraid of is that when you try to teach this concept of loving the nation, you easily slip into a sort of nationalistic indoctrination and sentiment, which often, in the end, does not serve national interests. I'd like first and foremost for people to think about the love of mankind, humanity... So I'd like people to feel strongly about the common challenge facing the whole world, and to think about themselves as part of the world, much

more than belonging to just a society or a country. But that does not in any way mean that they should not take into account public responsibility. I guess this is about the concept of the nation (Interview, 10/14/98).

Despite the world view of the deputy prime minister, Global Awareness is ranked near the bottom of the themes to be emphasized in schools, followed only by Gender Equality and Religious Values. Certainly there is recognition of the increasing globalization in which Thailand plays an active role. However, themes relating to Thai society and personal development should take precedence in schools, according to the elites.

The Buddhist Religion—one component of the Thai ideological triad of Nation-Religion-King—is quite prominent in most schools via the formal curriculum, observance of Buddhist rituals and holidays, and daily prayers. It seems, therefore, surprising that Religious Values falls last in the list of themes. Among the survey respondents, religious values are important, but not necessarily Buddhist rites and rituals, which is the view of religion commonly taught in schools. Many elites who were interviewed feel that religious values are central to moral development, but not, however, that one particular religion is superior over another. "Religious values. I think this is very important because many good things can be drawn as a guideline for socializing the Thai children, even [for] the children who profess other [not Buddhism] religions. I think the central teachings of other religions are the same—honesty, behave well, control yourself, non-aggression..." (Interview 8/5/97). Thus the respondents state that the *principles* of religion, the moral values, should be given much emphasis, but a particular religion, viewed in terms of religious practices need not.[5]

Controversial Issues

Among the values themes that should be emphasized in schools, "Family Values" ranked in the middle, neither most nor least important. However, out of twenty-five potentially controversial issues presented to the survey respondents, the idea that "schools should foster values supporting the family" was considered the least controversial, indicated by a mean of 1.31 with a standard deviation of only .55 (see Table 12.6). To most Thai respondents, actually *teaching* family values cannot be done in isolation from the family. The schools can, however, *support* these values by emphasizing the importance of respect to elders, the characteristics of "happy families", and the virtues of gratitude and familial responsibility.

Gender issues do not hold a prominent place in the values debate in Thailand. Perhaps this is because there is a strong belief that "girls have essentially the same talents as boys and should be given equal opportunities and encouragement in schools" (ranked #2), as well as a recognition that given these equal opportunities, girls are not necessarily "destined to have significant home-building responsibilities" (#25) any more than boys are. High priority is also given to "encouraging mutual respect be-

---

[5] It should be noted that on a scale of one to seven, where one means that strong emphasis should be placed on the given theme and seven indicates that the item should be left out, the Thai elites as a group indicated that all the themes have a place in schools; the lowest mean score is 3.4.

tween boys and girls" (#6). These attitudes are reflected in the school curriculum that includes housekeeping and handicrafts as well as agriculture and job skills for both boys and girls.

Table 12.6 Controversial Issues in Values Education

Rank Order	What Emphasis Should be Placed on Each of the Controversial Issues (1=very strong emphasis)	Mean	SD	n
1	Schools should foster values supporting the family, such as respect for parents, fidelity, and taking care of children and elders	1.31	.55	51
2	Girls have essentially the same talents as boys and should be given equal opportunities and encouragement in schools	1.33	.71	51
3	Schools should promote a truly global view of the world	1.33	.74	51
23	Schools should help young people appreciate the essential role of unions in guaranteeing safe work conditions and fair wages	3.29	1.36	51
24	Schools should teach children to respect hierarchy and to support the government	3.98	1.67	50
25	Girls are destined to have significant home-building responsibilities and the schools should prepare them for this future	4.08	1.65	51

The third least controversial issue is that "schools should promote a truly global view of the world". Like the issue of family values, this global view issue seems contrary to the relatively little popularity of emphasizing Global Awareness in schools. Accounting for this contradiction is more difficult. Thai people have an awareness of the inter-connectivity of the world, awareness heightened during the economic crisis and subsequent intervention by international institutions such as the Asia Development Bank and the International Monetary Fund. Consequently, respondents may feel that, like gender equality, there is a sufficient degree of Global Awareness relative to other values themes, but that it is a non-controversial issue, which should be promoted where possible.

A principle component analysis of this question revealed no particular clustering, but the rank order of issues does suggest a pattern in the Thai responses. Family, community and civic values promoting solidarity and equality are given greater emphasis. In addition to supporting families and encouraging equality and respect between boys and girls, the Thai respondents indicated that schools should "promote solidarity within communities" (ranked #5), "stress that all are equal before the law" (#8), and "teach common values without differentiation" (#10). Issues that might result in division, or at least a greater recognition of diversity within society, such as schools should "help students develop their own individual values" (ranked #17), "note social differences" (#19), "encourage empathy for people of different backgrounds" (#20), and "help children to gain a deeper understanding of their own religion" (#21) tend to garner less support. Nationalistic values, including the view that schools should "promote an understanding and love of nation"(#15), "promote national pride" (#19), and "support the government" (#24) also receive less emphasis. It is worth noting, however, that the respondents considered all but two of the issues worthy of being included in values education

Out of the twenty-five issues presented in the Survey, only two items have a mean score below 3.5, the mid-point between "very strong emphasis" and "should be left out". These two issues suggest that children should be taught to "respect hierarchy and to support the government" and that "girls should be prepared for their destiny as "home-builders". Although "traditional" Thai values include a respect for authority and seniority, contemporary Thai elites view this attitude as contrary to the democracy and meritocracy that they would like to see develop in Thailand. According to many respondents, people should be respected for their abilities and moral qualities, not for their gender or positions of power and wealth.

In a related question regarding what should be taught in school, we asked respondents to consider which countries should receive prominence in the school curriculum. Japan was given top priority, followed by China, and the United Kingdom, with the United States and Singapore close behind. The respondents indicated that Japan, China, and the United States, the countries that wield great influence in the world, cannot be ignored. According to one politician, "Its not a question of whether you like that or not, but it's just a fact of life. Reality. That's why I think it's important to learn about these countries.... The way the world is shaped today, you would be severely handicapped if you did not know about the powers that be" (Interview, 10/14/98). The United Kingdom and Singapore, though arguably not as powerful and influential as the others, often serve as positive examples: the United Kingdom for its constitutional monarchy and Singapore for its disciplined citizenry and economic performance. Overall, greater emphasis was given to countries that are economically and politically stable. Many respondents wrote in additional countries, including Germany, Australia, and Israel, which also reflect this notion of stability and success.

How Should Values Education be Conducted?

The "how" of values education includes questions about the best settings for values education as well as to whom it should be targeted. Although the Thai elites gave answers across the spectrum of possibilities, there was significant agreement regarding the most appropriate settings for religious, civic/national, and moral education. As indicated in Table 12.7, "home and family" are the most appropriate settings for values education. Over 50 percent of the respondents felt that this is the most important setting for religious and moral values and 40 percent thought civic and national values should be taught first and foremost in the home. Approximately 75 percent felt that this must be among the top three settings. For the elites as a whole, religious education should take place in the home, within religious groups and institutions, and, interestingly, in the media. The respondents were unanimous in thinking that the military is no place for religious education.

Civic/national education is more appropriate in the school setting than is religious education. A separate subject class and integrated within the established rules and procedures of school life are, after home, the most appropriate sites for civic and moral education. This is in keeping with the respondents earlier indication of the importance of civic education and the need to develop civic society and democracy by encouraging individual moral behavior. They consistently support these themes in schools.

Table 12.7 Setting for Values Education

Settings for Values Education	Religious	Civic/ National	Moral
	% 1, 2 or 3*	% 1, 2 or 3	% 1, 2 or 3
During school as a class	40.8	44	46
During the established school rules of behavior and classroom procedures	30.6	40	48
Outside of school activities such as clubs, sports, arts	20.4	38	30
Internships and community service	14.3	28	10
Camps (e.g. during vacation)	16.3	16	12
Religious Groups and Institutions	57.1	18	38
Military training and national service	0	16	8
Home and Family	77.6	64	74
Media	46.9	38	34

* Number indicates the percent of respondents who ranked the setting as 1, 2 or 3.

The annual camping trip with the scouts (cub scouts, girl scouts, and junior Red Cross) is a significant part of most Thai school children's life. It is an opportunity for children to develop many of the ideas of responsibility and teamwork that values education promotes. Yet, camps are not a significant site for any type of values education according to this survey. The scout trip occurs during the school term rather than during vacation and is part of the school curriculum. Perhaps for this reason, Thai elites do not consider this to be the type of camp suggested by the survey. However, they did not give co-curricular or community activities prominence either.

When faced with the choice of settings given in this survey, the Thai elites tended to respond in a way that reflects current practice in schools and communities. That is, they recognize family as the most important setting, but that teaching values as a separate school subject and through school rules are also quite significant.

Contrary to the above discussion, when answering a different, yet related question, Thai elites indicated strongly that values education in schools should be integrated throughout the formal and informal curriculum, rather than treated as a separate subject.[6] The interviews substantiated this view. Without exception, each person we interviewed, backed by many of the written comments, suggested that values education should not only be integrated, but also be experiential in nature. Children must see positive role models, they need to have a contextual understanding of the reasoning behind the emphasis on good values, and they require a chance to practice the values that are taught at home and in school. Values cannot be fully taught and understood in an artificial environment, according to the respondents. Children must be given opportunities to "learn by doing". "And you do that", suggested one man, "by getting

---

[6] In response to the statement "Values education should not be taught in separate subjects; rather it should be integrated throughout the curriculum," the mean score was 1.38, with a SD of 0.95.

them to do extra curricular activities together. Then they learn about how to live with other people. They learn about responsibilities. They learn about how to resolve conflict. Then they learn about democracy" (Interview, 10/14/98). "Learning from a textbook can be beneficial, but it is not sufficient" (Interview, 7/29/97).

Thai elites turn their critical eye on teachers as a weak link in the values education process. They speak and write at length about the necessity of positive role models for children. According to the Thais, role models are clearly lacking in public life, where politicians are constantly under suspicion of corruption, and in the media that glorifies violence and elevates triviality to significance (Interview, 10/13/99). As prominent adults in children's lives, it falls to the teachers to help fill the void. Yet many of them are found lacking. Given these sentiments, it is not surprising that the Thai respondents indicated that in-service teachers should be among the targeted groups for values education[7] (see Table 12.8).

Table 12.8 Recipients of Values Education

Groups for Values Education	Religious Education % 1, 2 or 3*	Moral Education % 1, 2 or 3
In-service teachers	50	53.2
Teacher learners	8.7	14.9
Young children (3-4 yr. old)	19.6	14.9
Pre-schoolers (5 yr. old)	23.9	25.5
Primary (6-11 yr. old)	69.6	74.5
Secondary (11-14 yr. old)	54.3	48.9
High school (15-17 yr. old)	45.7	44.7
University	28.3	25.5

*Number indicates the percent of respondents who ranked the recipients as 1, 2, or 3.

The elites felt very strongly that values education should begin in early childhood, a view that is reflected in the current curriculum, which places much emphasis on values in the primary grades. Nonetheless, the survey results show that more respondents considered in-service teachers to be the most important recipients of values education than any other group.[8] Considering the emphasis on in-service teachers as a target group for values education, the total lack of priority given to pre-service teachers is surprising. When queried about this apparent contradiction, a distinguished former university president explained that his view of values education for in-service teachers involved both in-service training and, more importantly, the creation of a teacher culture of positive values at the school level. "Everyday or every week they [teachers] should come sit together to discuss whether they have a problem in school... [They should] share ideas" (Interview, 10/13/98). Teachers are often in isolation and, consequently, unable to share ideas and learn from their peers. The creation of a positive sharing environment, he suggests, will help teachers to be better role models and to be better teachers of values. In this way, the focus of teacher education is on the school

---

[7] Data for civic/national education is missing.

[8] 34.9 percent of the respondents indicated that in-service teachers should be the number one recipients of religious education and 36.2 percent indicated that in-service teachers should be the number one recipients of moral education.

building culture. Pre-service teachers are not yet part of this environment. "Pre-service teachers can be 'taught'. But if you say 'taught,' well, at least 'made aware of,' that's it". The significant learning experience occurs when the teacher joins the school community.

Other respondents indicate that the curriculum for pre-service teachers is overwhelmed by academic subject matter. "Good values" are treated as an inherent quality that the pre-service teachers should already possess, and by this virtue, be able to teach them as necessary. The Thai elites, many of whom are deans and professors of education, did not comment on the relationship between the abilities and behaviors of pre-service teachers and those of in-service teachers.

Regional Values

In an interview given prior to the Sigma Survey, a university professor and specialist in values education articulated several sources of positive contemporary Thai values. Among these sources are the traditional agricultural society, Buddhism, and increasingly, the global community (Interview 8/8/97). The survey results highlight traditional values such as strong families, individual responsibility, and the important role of teachers, as well as values including democracy and civic consciousness, which may be considered "global" values. Many respondents commented that although there are many sources of values, both good and bad, there is something indefinably unique about their manifestation in Thailand.

This realization of the multiple sources of values may help explain Thai attitudes toward regional values. When asked in a set of questions about regional values, Thai elites seemed rather ambivalent. They somewhat agreed that there are different value systems, but with the possible exception of "Asian" values, there is little compelling reason to teach these distinct values. Even "Asian values" are not easily defined. One respondent said of Asian values:

> I think there is, despite the diversity [within Asia], a great deal in common among the Asian societies that still distinguish them from Western societies. For example, certain institutions like the family, extended family, or the closeness between the people in the local communities set a different pattern of behavior and relationship then in Western societies. The respect for seniority the importance of, I guess, discipline, and the ability to accept what's handed down is certainly more prominent in Asian than it is in Western countries (Interview, 10/14/98).

Other elites are less able or willing to define Asian values. One university professor suggested that the individualistic nature of Buddhism served to create a tension between the stereotypic Asian values of strong familial ties and hierarchical social patterns and the Buddhist culture. Similarly, according to many respondents, the economic development process and increasing globalization is further diluting absolute distinctions among and between value systems.

Discussion

Often described as "highly individualistic and resisting regimentation" (National Identity Board, 1995, p. 111), Thais are considered to be "independent" and "fun-loving". In her landmark study of Thai values, Komin (1985/1998) found that Thai people tend to place high value on self-reliance and independence, while placing low value on obedience and meekness (p. 182). This freedom and independence is mitigated by the Thais' realization that "inner freedom is best preserved in an emotionally and physically stable environment. Therefore, they believe that social harmony is best maintained by avoiding any unnecessary friction in their contacts with others" (NIB, 1995, p. 111). A Chulalongkorn University professor summed up this attitude: "Thai people are very proud to be independent. Sometimes quiet, but independent in their minds. [They] keep quiet, listen a lot. Be their own persons" (Interview 8/8/97). Part of maintaining this social harmony *and* independence is to adhere to traditional values, drawn primarily from Theravada Buddhism. These include virtues such as non-aggression, gratitude, generosity, honesty, and modesty, but also more secular values like respect for authority and seniority, and respect for proper etiquette.

In an idealized past, adherence to these values ensured a harmonious society. However, in the face of rapid social, economic and political change, these values have lost much of their strength according to current Thai social debates and among the respondents in this survey. The president of a Rajabat institute in the south of the country wrote,

> At present, values of "materialism" are so popular among Thais. Everyone realizes that good living with luxurious things could come easily to them only if they have money. Thus, people struggle and sacrifice their lives and time just for money. Only, in the end, they absolutely forget to think about the mind (#26 written comment).

Similarly, a nationally renowned and respected monk felt that there are many prominent values that Thais should abandon. These include

> values that harm society as a whole, such as a preference to be richer and richer, admiration of the wealthy or famous persons, materialism, the love of fun and excitement or any challenging games, dislike of difficult tasks and preference for those which are easy, a total lack of thinking wisely, and a lack of consideration (#80, written comments).

He concluded his criticism by claiming that "the Thais in general are not at all serious about thinking wisely or acquiring wisdom".

The findings of this study suggest that rather than an emphasis on the "traditional" Thai virtues, education should include values that address current problems or issues, especially those associated with consumerism and materialism and the development of a civil society. The Thai elites agree that most of the values cited in the Sigma Survey should be included in a comprehensive values education program in the schools, and they agree with the current school curriculum that values education should focus on individual behavior as a way of strengthening civil society.

This attitude is both a recognition of the "highly individualistic" nature of the Thais and a slight repudiation of that same trait. Many respondents indicated that independence can be a source of strength when thinking and action is directed toward the good of society. On the other hand, it can also lead to the selfish values of which the monk writes. For several elites, the concept of the "public sphere" illustrates the general Thai population's undeveloped or distorted sense of self and society. Rather than belonging to all, "public" is often interpreted to mean either "that which does not belong to *me*", or "if I grab it first, it's *mine*". The willful destruction of public telephone booths is an oft-cited example of the former, while illegal encroachment on protected forests is indicative of the latter (Personal Correspondence). Such attitudes put the individual at the center of decision-making that affects the larger society.

The desire for personal wealth and material accumulation can (and does, according to many Thais) lead to corruption, greed, and abuse of power, all of which have had a role in the political and economic turmoil of the 1990s. It is not surprising, therefore, that developing a sense of individual responsibility and behavior is at the heart of the values debate. Similarly, concepts of civic values and democracy are directly related to the role of the individual in society. Thus, the educational elites take the meaning of "civic"—the rights and duties of citizens—seriously because they perceive that the general Thai population does not. "Democracy", very closely tied to "civic values" in the Thai context, and "work values" all begin with the premise of individual responsibility, an understanding of rights and, especially, duties. The elites promote ideas of democracy and economic development (the result of individual responsibility for the good of society), but reject the resulting materialistic culture (selfish individualism). Furthermore, there is an expectation that families and schools, both as institutions and individuals within the institutions, must take primary responsibility for educating young people in these proper values. They should do this by being positive role models, giving children the opportunities to have valuable experiences as well as inculcating values through traditional classroom pedagogy.

Although the participants in this survey are critical of contemporary Thai society and recognize the challenges to values education, they are hopeful for the future.

Future of Values Education

"You have to lose some if you want to gain some" is one Thai elite's pragmatic approach to the future of values in Thailand. Thailand is at a crossroads; the heady boom years of the late 1980s and early 1990s are gone, but the society that they produced is not. The economic crisis led many Thai people, including the King, to call for a return to the pastoral life of the past, a time that was simpler and gentler (Bello, et al., 1998). But a return to this romanticized past seems impossible considering the shifting social, political, and economic patterns of Thai life (Phongpaichit and Baker, 1998, p. 330). Some of the values held dear by previous generations are all but lost, while new values are gaining prominence. Some "new" values, including materialism and competition, are not welcomed by many Thai elites who hope to mitigate their influence by emphasizing traditional values, such as responsibility and family. Other, newer values, such as a more global perspective, less tolerance of corruption, and a greater appreciation of a strong work ethic and democracy, are considered important and worthy of a place in values education.

The Thai elites who participated in this study indicate that values education is an essential part of any education in order to help young people to become good and useful members of society. They admit, however, that proper, effective values education is problematic. The type of education most favored by the elites, positive role models and experiential learning, is a difficult challenge. Positive role models must be cultivated and rewarded by being given the recognition and respect that frequently goes only to the rich and powerful. According to some of the respondents, the media should take a more proactive role in helping Thais, especially young Thais, understand the benefits of good moral citizenship.

Experiential learning is also problematic for our elites. Values education must be experiential, they claim, but when schools are expected to be the primary site of this education, it is stifled by a social and fiscal structure that seeks tangible (economic) outcomes, such as successful academic advancement or employability upon leaving school. The demand for time and resources devoted to academic subject matter out-weighs the desire for a comprehensive, experiential values program. Similarly, the availability of qualified teachers devoted to values education is minimal at best. Re-gardless of these obstacles, values and values education has a significant place in the public debates about contemporary Thai society.

The recently enacted National Education Act is a testament to and a validation of the perceptions and attitudes of the educational "elite" in Thailand regarding values. This Act is intended to reform all aspects of education by fulfilling the promise of the 1997 Constitution, which states that all Thai citizens are entitled to twelve years of free education, by decentralizing much of the administrative, financial and curriculum decision making, and by reforming teacher training and university administration. This reform effort will also combine several national ministries into one new ministry—the Ministry of Education, Religion and Culture—explicitly linking these value-laded concepts. Framing these institutional reforms is an emphasis on a student-centered approach to education to develop critical thinking skills and an emphasis on moral and civic values, especially values of democracy, a strong work ethic, and responsibility. Furthermore, it emphasizes the importance of "personal and social knowledge", "knowledge of religion", and "knowledge and skills related to work and leading to a 'good life' that is not materialistic". Our findings coincide with these values. Thus, this study serves both as an illustrative background to much of the thinking behind the Na-tional Education Act and as a strong indication of the direction in which Thai policy makers would like their nation to move. The task is now to implement the promises of this new reform Act.

References

Bello, W., Cunningham, S. and Poh, L. K. (1998). *A Siamese Tragedy: Development and Disintegration in Modern Thailand.* London and New York: Zed Books Ltd.

Bishop, R. and Robinson, L. S. (1998). *Night Market: Sexual Cultures and the Thai Economic Miracle.* New York and London: Routledge.

Bunbongkarn, S. (1996). *State of the Nation: Thailand.* Singapore: Institute of South-east Asian Studies.

Chareonwongsak, K. (1996). "Society on trial", *The Nation*, August 11, 1996: B1-2.

Economic review: Year end, (1996). (December). *Bangkok Post.*

Economic review: Year end, (1997). (January, 1998). *Bangkok Post.*

Fairclough, G. and Tasker, R. (1994). Thailand: "Separate and Unequal", *Far Eastern Economic Review*, April 14: 22-28.

Hussey, A. (1993). "Rapid Industrialization in Thailand: 1986–1991", *Geographical Review* 83: 14-28.

Komin, S. (1985). "The World View Through Thai Value Systems". In A. Pongsapich, (ed.) (1998), *Traditional and Changing Thai World View*. Bangkok: Chulalongkorn University Press.

Ministry of Education (1993/1995). *The 1990 revised edition of the 1978 primary school curriculum*. Bangkok: Department of Curriculum and Instruction, Ministry of Education.

Mulder, N. (1997). *Thai Images: The Culture of the Public World*. Chiang Mai: Silkworm Books.

National Identity Board, Office of the Prime Minister (1995). *Thailand in the 1990's*. Bangkok: Author.

National Statistical Office, Office of the Prime Minister (Thailand) (1999). Internet: http://www.nso.go.th/eng/stat/socio/socio.htm.

Office of the National Education Commission [ONEC] (1997). *Education in Thailand, 1997*. Bangkok: Seven Printing Group.

Office of the National Education Commission [ONEC] (1998). *Education in Thailand, 1998*. Bangkok: Seven Printing Group.

Phongpaichit, P. and Baker, C. (1998). *Thailand's Boom and Bust*. Chiang Mai: Silkworm Books.

Phongpaichit, P. and Piriyarangsan, S. (1994). *Corruption and Democracy in Thailand*. Chiang Mai: Silkworm Books.

Punyaratabandu, S. (1999). "Thailand in 1998: A False Sense of Recovery", *Asian Survey* 39(1): 80-88.

Sethaput, C. and Yoddumnern-Attig, B. (1992). "Occupational Role Behaviors Over Time". In Yoddumnern-Attig, et al. (eds.) *Changing Roles and Status of Women in Thailand*. Salaya, Nakornprathom: Institute for Population and Social Research.

Sittirak, S. (1996). *Daughters of Development: The Stories of Women and the Changing Environment in Thailand*. Bangkok: Women and Environment Research Network in Thailand (WENIT).

Unger, D. (1998). *Building Social Capital in Thailand: Fibers, Finance, and Infrastructure*. New York: Cambridge University Press.

Watson, K. (1973). "The Monastic Tradition of Education in Thailand", *Paedagogica Historica*, 13(2): 515-529.

Watson, K. (1980). *Educational Development in Thailand*. Hong Kong: Heinemann Asia.

World Bank (1997). *World Development Report*. New York: Oxford University Press.

Wyatt, D. K. (1969). *The Politics of Reform in Thailand: Education in the Reign of King Chulalongkorn*. New Haven, CT: Yale University Press.

CHAPTER 13

SINGAPORE: VALUES EDUCATION FOR A KNOWLEDGE-BASED ECONOMY[1]

Christine Han
Joy Chew
Jason Tan

Introduction

Singapore is the smallest of the eleven Pacific Basin countries represented in the Sigma survey in terms of land area and population. It has a land area of 647 square kilometres. Its multiracial population of slightly over three million comprises three main ethnic groups, namely the Chinese (77.3 percent), Malays (14.1 percent) and Indians (7.3 percent), while a residual 1.3 percent is made up of Eurasians and Singaporeans of other ethnic origins. Unlike its much larger Southeast Asian neighbours such as Malaysia, Thailand and Indonesia, this island city-state does not have any natural resources except for its strategic nodal location and a deep natural harbour.

In the forty years since self-government in 1959, this former British colony has been ruled by the dynamic and highly proactive leadership of the People's Action Party (PAP) government led first by Prime Minister Lee Kuan Yew and subsequently by his successor Goh Chok Tong.[2] A successful industrialisation program was launched in the 1960s. It was supported by a national education system that was oriented towards manpower planning and human capital investment. By the 1990s, Singapore had become a prosperous financial, trading and internationally oriented manufacturing centre of sophisticated products and services. Until the Asian economic crisis, which has also affected Singapore, the country has enjoyed high economic growth rates averaging 9 percent per annum since 1966 and, in 2000 it had an enviable per capita gross domestic product of around US$23,000, the highest in East Asia apart from Japan. The Singapore government is fervent about maintaining economic growth, and competing globally with other economies for high quality manufacturing investments. It seeks to 'stay ahead of the pack'. Hence, bold measures have been taken in the education system to lay the foundation for a knowledge-based economy in the approaching twenty-first century. These measures include the reduction of curriculum content, the fostering of critical and creative thinking, and the use of information technology.

The Educational System and Values Education Policy

In framing the educational and economic policies of Singapore, the PAP government has also been concerned with fostering social cohesion and developing a sense of national identity among the Chinese, Malay, and Indian ethnic communities. English was adopted as one of the four official languages besides Chinese (Mandarin), Malay,

[1] The authors thank Azam Mashhadi, formerly of the National Institute of Education, Nanyang Technological University, for his help on the statistical analysis for this chapter.
[2] Goh Chok Tong took over as Prime Minister in November 1990.

and Tamil. It is today the lingua franca, serving as a language of commerce, technology, administration and education. English is the main medium of instruction from
primary to secondary schools and post-secondary education. In addition, all Singapore
students are required to learn their mother tongue (Chinese, Malay, Tamil, or other
Indian languages) for at least ten years in the school system. Political leaders have held
strongly to the view that teaching the mother tongue in school will ensure the pre-
servation of the Asian cultural heritage and moral values.

In addition, Singapore schools provide for a compulsory civic and moral education program that will be elaborated on below. Thus, even as young Singaporeans are
being socialized in the education system for work and citizenship responsibilities,
there has always been a great emphasis on values transmission. For this reason, effort
has been made to inculcate such 'Asian' values as thrift, industry, loyalty, placing the
group above the individual, etc. Hence, it can be said that the goals of the education
system are to build a Singapore national identity, to preserve core 'Asian' values, and
to increase the country's capacity for greater economic resilience in the international
marketplace.

Senior education policy makers have recently described the period of Singapore
education from 1959 to 1978 as being 'survival driven', and the period from 1979 to
1998 as being 'efficiency driven' (Ministry of Education, 1998, pp. 2-3). The 'survival
driven' stage was characterized by the need to provide mass education to support economic growth and to build social cohesion. In the last two decades the school system
has been restructured 'to hone the efficiency of the education system and to reduce
educational wastage.' In the 1990s especially, the government has responded to key
trends in the world environment by implementing new measures to maintain economic
growth, and to help Singapore remain economically competitive in the global economy. The next stage of reforms, devised to support the development of a knowledge-
based economy in the twenty-first century, is to implement an 'ability-driven' education system. What this term means, however, is unclear as it is still being determined
and defined by Singapore educators and school practitioners.

Schools operate within a centralized and rigid structure. The curriculum is also
differentiated through the practice of academic streaming to cater for students with
different abilities, interests and aptitudes. Assessment and achievement testing are
conducted regularly to monitor students' performance in core and elective subjects at
the secondary school level. Streaming by language and academic ability is practised
beginning in Year 5 (for eleven-year-olds) at the primary school. Students sit for national examinations at three points of their school career, at the ages of twelve, sixteen,
and eighteen.

There is a distinct technological bias in the school and tertiary education curriculum. English, mathematics, science and information technology (IT) are compulsory
subjects, whereas subjects in the humanities such as literature, history and geography
are offered as electives at the upper secondary school level. In other words, the primary emphasis in education is its utility in terms of progression to higher levels of
education and career prospects. In the same vein, values being transmitted through
official programs like Civics and Moral Education can be said to have a bias towards
economic and technological advancement. For example, teamwork and co-operation

are encouraged, not so much as desirable traits in themselves, but for the reason of enabling future workers to be more productive in the workplace.

It could also be said that, notwithstanding official pronouncements about the desirability of the all rounded development of the individual, there is often an emphasis on academic outcomes to the neglect of the non-academic outcomes of schooling, e.g. the development of personal autonomy. This phenomenon has been exacerbated by the annual publication of school 'league tables', which has been the practice since 1992. These league tables rank schools according to their students' performance in national examinations, and are meant to spur schools towards academic excellence. The Ministry of Education also provides monetary incentives to 'value-added' schools. Many principals are therefore under considerable pressure to concentrate their efforts on improving, or maintaining, their schools' ranking positions, as they are well aware of the impact of these ranking positions on future student intakes (Tan, 1998).

With the emphasis given to academic performance, all non-academic aspects of school life have been relegated to a secondary position. Commenting on her ethnographic study of a Singapore school, for instance, Chew notes that the formal curriculum seeks to promote a certain social morality about the role and social responsibility of citizens, emphasising a group orientation where values such as care and concern for others, loyalty to the group and nation, teamwork, social discipline and cooperation are highlighted. However, she continues,

> there is a conflicting moral orientation in parts of the written curriculum that socializes Singaporean pupils to behave in a very individualistic and self-serving way in their relationships with other people. The message is clear: if an individual and a small nation-state are to survive in a highly competitive world, then they must work smartly to try to 'keep ahead of the pack' (Chew, 1997, pp. 90-91).

The school program therefore poses some serious dilemmas to its students. On the one hand, various efforts have been made over the years to inculcate the desired moral values in students, e.g., being caring, selfless, etc. On the other hand, an approach to education that is both utilitarian and competitive emphasizes a totally different set of values. Given the reward structure of the larger society, students are responding in expected ways, and the consequence is that much of the effort put in by schools to give students a balanced education is in danger of being nullified by the entrenched value system.

History of Values Education in Singapore

Few governments have been as actively involved in promoting a formal civic and moral education component in the national school system as that of Singapore. Since 1965, when Singapore attained its status as an island republic, state schools have experimented with no fewer than five locally developed values education programs. Historically, there was an earlier subject called Ethics in 1959. It was replaced by Civics in 1963 at the secondary school level for thirteen- to sixteen-year-olds. In 1973, an interdisciplinary subject for values education called Education for Living was designed for primary school children (six- to twelve-year-olds). However, it was evaluated as being a weak attempt at providing moral education. Two new programs were developed and implemented by the early 1980s: Good Citizen for primary schools, and Being and Becoming for secondary schools. Before long, in 1984, a controversial Religious Knowledge (RK) program was introduced and made compulsory for upper secondary school students. Students of Chinese, Malay and Indian ethnic backgrounds were required to choose their RK subject from a range of six alternatives: Bible Knowledge, Buddhist Studies, Hindu Studies, Islamic Religious Knowledge, Sikh Studies and Confucian Ethics. Unexpectedly in 1989, the Ministry of Education decided to scrap RK as a compulsory subject. The argument was that it was inconsistent for a secular government to advocate religious education in schools. It was also thought that the RK program had the unintended effect of increasing the religious fervour of each ethno-religious community, and thus posed a threat to multiracial harmony and national unity.

With the scrapping of RK, a revised program called Civics and Moral Education was developed between 1992 and 1995, and implemented in primary and secondary schools (Chew, 1998). Today, it is still part of the official instructional program. It is taught for three weekly periods (of thirty minutes each) in primary schools in the student's mother tongue, and two weekly periods at the secondary level, largely in the English medium. The name given to that program reflects its content and themes: to foster cultural and religious appreciation; to promote community spirit, to affirm family life, to nurture interpersonal relationships, and to develop commitment to nation building. In contrast with the prior values education programs, the subject is formally assessed and graded in schools. Civics and Moral Education teachers are required to plan assessment activities for each year level. Students are awarded letter grades based on their effort in carrying out a variety of group projects, as well as their individual performance in class tests. Students are required to take such classroom activities seriously and to pass the subject at the end of each school year.

The experimentation with new values education programs has not ended. In July 1996, Prime Minister Goh Chok Tong announced the launch of a new component, National Education, which is designed specifically to teach students knowledge and values that are perceived to be needed for the country's survival in the twenty-first century. The explicit purpose of the new program is "to develop national cohesion, the instinct for survival and confidence in the future, by a) fostering a sense of identify, pride and self-respect as Singaporeans, b) by knowing the Singapore story – how Singapore succeeded against the odds to become a nation; c) by understanding Singapore's unique challenges, constraints and vulnerabilities… and d) by instilling the core values of our way of life, and the will to prevail, that will ensure our continued success and well-being" (Ministry of Education, 1997).

What then is the likely consequence of the official attempts to promote values education? As has been noted, the education system is heavily biased toward the economic and technological; at the same time, there is a stated concern about core values, centering not only on such traditional notions as 'Asian' values, but also for utilitarian purposes. Added to this is an education system characterized by a high level of selectivity, and a drive to increase the manpower potential of the schooling population. Taken together, all this means that there are conflicting messages for both schools and students. Hence, while the avowed aim is to create a caring ethos and to provide for the all-round development of the student, what results is a high degree of competitiveness and individualism. In other words, given the conflicting messages and demands made on schools and students, this is a pragmatic response on their part. The debate in Singapore echoes in some senses the wider debate in international perspective (see for instance Kennedy, 1997; Lo and Man, 1996).

Discussion of such issues as rights and obligations, public versus private interests and the dilemmas of values education in a multicultural society, finds resonance in the Singapore case.

Profile of the Respondents

For the Sigma survey in Singapore, questionnaires were sent out to forty-two respondents who had been identified from among the 'elite' in Singapore. Thirty-two percent of these were from educational institutions, 24 percent were leaders of related Non-Government Organisations (NGOs), and 16 percent were academic leaders; 4 percent were from the central educational elite, while the remaining 24 percent were evenly divided among religious leaders with education positions, politicians, and values/moral education specialists. Hence, the respondents were dominated by people in educational institutes, while leaders of related NGOs and academic leaders formed two other large groups.

The respondents were overwhelmingly reformist in their outlook (64 percent); this group was followed by the conservatives (20 percent) and moderates (12 percent) respectively. Radicals made up the smallest group (4 percent). It should be noted, however, that in Singapore the range of attitudes from 'reformist' right through to 'radical' probably rests right of centre relative to that in some other countries. Hence, an individual considered moderate in Singapore might be 'conservative' in the US, while one considered 'radical' in Singapore might be 'moderate' in the US.

Twenty-five people responded to the questionnaire, giving a response rate of 60 percent. The ratio of men to women was 2:1. The average age was about forty-five years. However, this might be misleading as the mode was fifty.

Findings

Why Should There be Values Education?

The respondents gave strongest support for improving values education to serve the following purposes: providing a foundation for spiritual development, increasing the sense of individual responsibility, and improving the respect and opportunities extended to girls and women (Table 13.1). Indeed, the most persuasive reason for improving values education in Singapore today was to 'provide a foundation for spiritual development', while the least persuasive was to 'foster economic development'.

Table 13.1 Reasons for Improving Values Education

Reasons for improving values education	Average ranking (in terms of decreasing importance)
To provide a foundation for spiritual development	2.63
To increase the sense of individual responsibility	2.88
To improve the respect and opportunities extended to girls and women	2.96
To encourage greater civic consciousness and thus strengthen democracy	3.0
To provide a guide for behaviour in daily life	3.25
To promote world peace	3.42
To develop an appreciation for our heritage and to strengthen national identity	3.54
To combat the recent trends of ecological abuse	3.67
To promote pride in local communities and community life	3.75
To help each young person develop a reflective and autonomous personality	3.88
To combat the tendency for social prejudice and to promote greater tolerance for ethnic, language and racial groups	3.88
To promote more orderly and caring school communities and thus facilitate learning	3.92
To help youth interpret the values transmitted by the mass media, the Internet, and other information technologies	4.21
To strengthen families	4.50
To promote the values of justice and equity	4.54
To combat juvenile delinquency including bullying, gang violence, and drug abuse	4.71
To foster economic development by strengthening values such as hard work, creativity, and individual competitiveness	4.75

Hence, spiritual development was considered the most important reason, while the use of values education to promote economic success—and, perhaps, the utilitarian attitude to values education underlying this—was not supported. Given the emphasis in Singapore on national economic success, this result was unexpected. Perhaps the high ranking given to providing a foundation for spiritual development reflected a feeling among the elite that there had been too little emphasis on this, and that the situation needed to be redressed. The low level of support given to fostering economic development would also be consistent with this theory. Its being placed as the least important consideration in improving values education could have been a reaction to the wide coverage already accorded it, not only in schools, but also in the media. Indeed, one respondent, commenting on the need consistently to emphasize values, wrote about the way in which societies, such as Singapore, which placed a high premium on material success created 'negative impact' on values development.

Given the emphasis in Singapore on individual responsibility, it comes as no surprise that this was ranked second. However, considering that Singapore is a secular society, and that the emphasis has for the most part been on secular civic and moral education, the high level of support for values education to provide a foundation for spiritual development was unexpected. Also unexpected was the choice of the third most persuasive argument, since gender equality has had little emphasis in civics and moral education in Singapore.

It is also interesting to note that, while the reason 'to combat the tendency for social prejudice and to promote greater tolerance for ethnic, language and racial groups' was given an average ranking (3.88 in a range of 2.63 to 4.75), there was least disagreement on this (s.d. = 2.74). The reason, 'to combat the recent trends of ecological abuse', which was given a similar ranking, showed the widest disagreement (Mean = 3.67; s.d. = 5.88). These may be two important issues for values education policy in the near future.

What Should be Taught in the Schools?

With regard to the percentage of time for values education in *specific classes*, the suggestions ranged from 0 percent to 50 percent. The average percentage suggested was approximately 16 percent (i.e. about a sixth of the total time), although the largest number of people put the figure at 10 percent.

In other words, respondents felt that slightly more time should be dedicated solely to values education than is the current practice (of three half-hour periods a week or 7.5 percent of curriculum time). However, it is pertinent to note that, with the introduction of the National Education Curriculum in 1997, a concerted effort has been made to implement values across the curriculum; time has also been set aside to promote the values associated with the National Education plan in the informal curriculum.

Table 13.2 Themes

Themes	Average Ranking in terms of decreasing importance (1 to 7)
Moral Values	1.56
Civic Values	1.72
Family Values	2.00
Values of Diversity and Multiculturalism	2.24
Values of Personal Autonomy and Reflection	2.48
Work Values	2.48
National Identity and Patriotism	2.80
Peace and Conflict Resolution	2.80
Democracy	3.00
Ecological Awareness	3.00
Global Awareness	3.20
Gender Equality	3.60
Religious Values	4.52

With regard to the themes that respondents felt required the greatest emphasis in schools, the four most highly ranked were moral, civic, family, diversity and multiculturalism values (Table 13.2). This result, particularly the high placing for moral and civic values, comes as no surprise since values education in Singapore has always been couched both in terms of civic and moral education. Indeed, civic values had the smallest standard deviation (s.d. = 0.94), indicating general agreement among the re-spondents. Similarly, family, diversity and multiculturalism values received a high degree of emphasis, both in schools and in the media.

The school and, specifically, the classroom, were considered to be the most effec-tive setting for teaching civic/national values, and second only to the home and family for moral education.

Values of personal autonomy and reflection came next, and were ranked above work, national identity and patriotism related values. This low ranking may be because the latter two have already received wide coverage in schools; while the emphasis on the first two may be an attempt to redress the situation in Singapore where there has been little emphasis on these aspects.

While there was a high degree of support for improving values education for the purpose of proving a foundation for spiritual development, it was felt that religious values should not be handled by schools. Indeed, there was strong consensus that re-ligious groups and institutions and the home and family (52 percent and 40 percent respectively) constituted the two most effective settings for religious instruction; in contrast, none of the respondents cited religious instruction within the classroom or school as the most effective setting.

Table 13.3 Agglomeration Schedule

Stage	Cluster Combined		Coefficients
	Cluster 1	Cluster 2	
1	Moral Values	Family Values	19.00
2	Ecological Awareness	Global Awareness	26.00
3	Civic Values	Values of Diversity and Multiculturalism	35.00
4	Values of Personal Autonomy and Reflection	Peace and Conflict Resolution	46.00
5	National Identity and Patriotism	Work Values	56.00
6	Values of Personal Autonomy and Reflection	Civic Values	61.50
7	Values of Personal Autonomy and Reflection	Democracy	77.25
8	Gender Equality	Ecological Awareness	90.00
9	Values of Personal Autonomy and Reflection	Moral Values	93.90
10	Values of Personal Autonomy and Reflection	National Identity and Patriotism	112.29
11	Values of Personal Autonomy and Reflection	Gender Equality	131.59
12	Religious Values	Values of Personal Autonomy and Reflection	247.75

A reason for the view that religious values should not be handled by schools could be the belief that, in a multicultural country like Singapore, religion might be divisive and, hence, what should be taught should comprise universal values. As a respondent put it:

> While all religions preach and teach us to be good, there are elements in the principles of every religion that are fundamentally sectarian and so, potentially divisive in nature. So while I believe we should promote understanding and respect for different religions, religious values should not be the mainstay of our Values Education.

> We should base Values Education on universal values such as hard work, self-discipline, love of family, respect for neighbour, love of country, love for peace and harmony in the context of our multi-racial, multi-cultural, multi-religious societies.

Whatever the case may be, the general view was that the school's role in values education should be primarily secular in nature.

Table 13.4 Hierarchical Cluster Analysis

(Dendogram using Average Linkage Between Groups Rescaled Distance Cluster Combine)

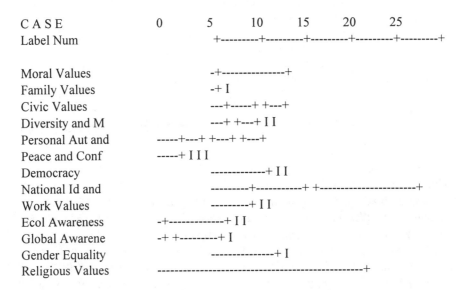

```
C A S E              0     5     10    15    20    25
Label Num                  +---------+---------+---------+---------+---------+

Moral Values               -+---------------+
Family Values              -+ I
Civic Values               ---+-----+ +---+
Diversity and M            ---+ +---+ I I
Personal Aut and     -----+---+ +---+ +---+
Peace and Conf       -----+ I I I
Democracy                  -------------+ I I
National Id and            ---------+-----------+ +----------------------+
Work Values                ---------+ I I
Ecol Awareness       -+-------------+ I I
Global Awarene       -+ +---------+ I
Gender Equality            ---------------+ I
Religious Values           ------------------------------------------------+
```

While the sample size of twenty-five respondents is rather small, *Agglomerative Hierarchical Cluster Analysis* using SPSS was carried out because it was felt that the patterns that emerged could be illuminating.[3] The clusters could reflect archetypes that

---

[3] Cluster Analysis seeks to separate data into constituent groups. The clustering technique used is an Agglomerative Hierarchical, specifically, the Complete Linkage Technique. In this method, the individual statements or variables (not the respondents or cases) are classified into groups, and the process repeated at different levels to form a tree (dendogram graph) through a series of successive fusions of the variables into groups. The groups, which initially consist of single variables, are fused according to the distance between their nearest members.

would be recognisable to those familiar with the distinct value orientations found in Singapore (see Table 13.5). Tables 13.3 and 13.4 show how the individual statements combined to produce the various clusters.

Visual inspection of the dendogram indicated the broad clusters identified in Table 13.5. We found, for instance, that those who supported the teaching of moral values also tended to support the teaching of family values. Both these sets of values are emphasized in schools and by government policies. Hence, it is not surprising that these are related in the mind of this category of respondents. These respondents may align themselves with more 'traditional' positions on values education. An interesting question would be why they might do so, and the extent to which they might have been influenced by the government's views of values education.

Table 13.5 Cluster Analysis

Groupings of Themes
Moral Values
Family Values
Civic Values
Values of Diversity and Multiculturalism
Values of Personal Autonomy and Reflection
Peace and Conflict Resolution
Democracy
National Identity and Patriotism
Work Values
Ecological Awareness
Global Awareness
Gender Equality
Religious Values

Those who supported the teaching of national identity and patriotism also tended to support the teaching of work values. These are two sets of values that are strongly encouraged by the political leaders, and in schools. This group may represent those who endorse a 'nationalistic' position in values education. As with the earlier group, it is not known why they might do so, or the extent to which they might have been influenced by the government's views of values education.

Respondents who supported civic values also supported the values of diversity and multiculturalism, of personal autonomy and reflection, of peace and conflict resolution, and of democracy. Accordingly, the ideal citizen envisioned by this group of respondents is a tolerant, peaceable member of a multicultural society, who supports conflict resolution. The group supporting such values would not be associated with a passive form of 'Asian' democracy (or soft authoritarianism), but rather with a view in which the citizen is seen as an active participant. The inclusion of personal autonomy and reflection in this combination of values, and the form that this should take, should perhaps be seen in this light.

Each fusion decreases by one the number of groups, and proceeds until all the statements are clustered. The Complete Linkage method was used as the values attributed to the statements are ordinal, and it avoids having too many small clusters.

At the same time, it could be said that values of ecological, global and gender awareness have received attention relatively recently, particularly in Western countries, and these are generally associated with 'political correctness'. Not unexpectedly, therefore, those who supported one set of these values tended to support the other two as well, and—in a relatively conservative society like Singapore—these values received relatively little support from the respondents.

With regard to controversial issues in values education, respondents felt that schools should place strong emphasis on teaching children the value of critical thinking; indeed, this theme was given the highest ranking of all (see Table 13.6). It is unclear whether this result was a reflection of support for the Singapore government's current emphasis on critical and creative thinking as a means to maintain the competitiveness of the Singapore economy. Considering that a fairly high degree of importance was given to personal autonomy, as seen earlier, it is possible that the respondents believed that it was important to teach critical thinking to go along with values such as personal autonomy and reflection; such a view might be perceived by some to be 'Western' in nature.

Table 13.6. Controversial Issues

	Controversial issues	Average Ranking in decreasing order (1 – 7)
Most important	Schools should teach each child the value of critical thinking.	1.44
	It is best for schools to teach common values to all children without differentiation on the basis of class, ethnicity, or religion.	1.68
	Schools should encourage empathy for people of different ethnic, language and social backgrounds and create opportunities for growth through shared experiences.	1.68
	Schools should foster values supporting the family, such as respect for parents, fidelity, and taking care of children and elders.	1.68
	Girls have essentially the same talents as boys and should be given equal opportunities and encouragement in schools.	1.84
Least important	Girls are destined to have significant home-building responsibilities and the schools should prepare them for this future.	5.12
	Schools should help young people appreciate the essential role of unions in guaranteeing safe work conditions and fair wages.	5.12

Apart from teaching the value of critical thinking, areas to which respondents felt schools should also give strong emphasis included teaching common values to all children, encouraging empathy for people different from oneself, and fostering such values as supporting the family, fidelity, and taking care of children and elders. Indeed, there was strong agreement among respondents with regard to encouraging empathy for others (mean = 1.69; s.d. = 0.90). In other words, there is the belief that schools should prepare children to live in a multicultural society, as well as to foster the values associated with an 'Asian' society.

Respondents thought that the fostering of gender equality, in terms of girls being given the same opportunities and encouragement as boys, should also be emphasized. At the same time, it was felt that there should not be a strong emphasis on schools preparing girls for home-building. Overall, therefore, there was a sense that greater emphasis should be given to gender equality, and to preparing children for a future where this is practised.

The widest range in views occurred in responses related to the question of whether schools should help children understand they have the right to be happy (mean = 4.20; s.d. = 2.20). According to 'traditional Asian values', rights should not be emphasized over obligations; at the same time, the individual pursuit of happiness as a goal might also be frowned upon. Among our respondents there are some who would be in disagreement with this position.

Values that respondents considered should be given most emphasis comprised elements that were drawn from different sources, (e.g. from what is commonly regarded as traditional or 'Asian' values, from ideas generally considered to be 'Western', and from the values needed specifically for living in a multicultural country). Views with regard to the societies that are important and relevant to include in the Singapore curriculum provide further evidence of this.

The clustered results, in decreasing order of perceived importance place Singapore, China and Malaysia in the first cluster as societies that should be given the greatest prominence. This is only to be expected, given the ethnic makeup of Singapore. The 'Western' countries of the U.S. and the U.K. were placed in the second cluster, together with Japan and Indonesia. Indeed, the U.S. was ranked above the two Asian countries in that cluster, while both the U.S. and U.K. were also ranked above Thailand and Korea. Despite the fact that these were 'Western' countries, the respondents felt that the U.S. and U.K. were important, and their customs relevant, to Singapore. In general the values that were held in high regard by the respondents were drawn from both East and West and similarly, the societies and customs deemed to be relevant to Singapore are both Eastern and Western. There is a view, commonly presented in Singapore, in which the country is seen as being an 'Asian' society, where 'ethnic' values should be drawn from traditional Chinese, Malay and 'Indian' sources. In contrast, the picture that emerges from the study is a complex one where the set of values that should be taught is drawn from diverse sources, with the unstated possibility that these might interact to produce further complexities.

Regional Values

Respondents were, as a whole, ambivalent with regard to whether there was a distinctive set of Asian values (mean = 3.36), and whether schools should make an effort to teach Asian values (mean = 3.36). In fact, the widest range of views was found for the latter (s.d. = 2.00). There was some disagreement as to whether Confucian and

Asian values were essentially the same (mean = 4.48), and there was also an appreciable range of views on the issue (s.d. = 1.98).

Looking more closely at the notion of Asian values, half the respondents (56 percent) thought that there was a distinctive set of Asian values, although a quarter (24 percent) gave a neutral rating of 4 on a scale of 1 to 7. Sixty percent agreed that schools should make an effort to teach Asian values, while 24 percent disagreed. Only a third (32 percent) of the respondents agreed with the proposition that Confucian and Asian values were essentially the same, while 52 percent disagreed.

A possible explanation for the ambivalent response to the question concerning whether there was a distinct set of Asian values was that the views with regard to 'Asian' values are too complex to be expressed within the constraints permitted by the question. One respondent wrote:

> Asians, particularly Singaporeans, tend to pitch Asian/Eastern values against Western values. Basically, the values are the same except for emphasis, and neither is superior.

In other words, the respondent was stating his dissatisfaction at the way 'Asian' and 'Western' values were expressed in polarized terms, and disagreeing with the inclination to make one appear superior to the other. Hence, given the perceived frequency with which 'Asian' values are pitted against 'Western' ones, and despite the support for 'Asian' values expressed earlier, respondents might have been wary about expressing a belief in a distinctive set of 'Asian' values, and for schools to teach these.

How Should Values Education be Conducted?

An overwhelming majority of respondents (76 percent) disagreed with the proposition that values education should only begin in secondary school after young people had had a clear idea of what they believed to be important. Three-quarters of respondents also indicated very strong agreement with the notion that values education should begin at an early age since the foundations of values were established in early childhood. There was, therefore, a high degree of support for the view that the school was an appropriate and important socialising agent, especially where relatively young children are concerned.

Almost two-thirds of respondents disagreed with the idea that students of different academic abilities should undergo different values education programs. Three-fifths of respondents agreed that values education should be integrated throughout the curriculum instead of being taught in separate subjects. In other words, more than half the respondents would disagree with the practice of teaching Civics and Moral Education as a separate subject.

With regard to perceptions of the most effective settings for religious education, there was—as has been noted—strong consensus that religious groups and institutions (52 percent), as well as home and family (40 percent), constituted the two most effective settings for religious education. Especially interesting was the fact that none of the respondents cited religious instruction within the classroom or school as the most effective setting.

Similarly, the two top choices for the second most effective setting for religious education were home and family (44 percent), and religious groups and institutions (32 percent). Once again, relatively low priority was given to school and classroom.

When asked which groups should receive the most exposure to religious education, there was no consensus of opinion. However, high school, secondary and primary groups received the highest total percentage ratings among the top three groups. The four top choices for the group that should receive the most exposure to religious education were: pre-schoolers (28 percent), primary (24 percent), university (24 percent), and secondary (16 percent).

With regard to the most effective settings for civic/national values, the school and classroom assumed a more important role compared to the teaching of religious values. However, it was clear that respondents thought that other institutions and means played an important role as well. The top ratings for the most effective setting for civic/national values were: school and classroom procedures (32 percent), classroom instruction (24 percent), home and family (20 percent), and the media (12 percent).

There was a lack of consensus as to which groups should receive the most exposure to civic/national values. High school, secondary, and primary groups, as in the case of religious education, were cited most often among the top three choices. The four top choices for the first ranked group were: primary (32 percent), secondary (20 percent), preschoolers (16 percent), and young children (12 percent).

The settings that received the highest rankings as being most effective for moral education were home and family, and the school. Most of the other settings were seen as irrelevant. The percentage ratings for the most effective setting were: home and family (64 percent), classroom instruction (24 percent), and school and classroom procedures (16 percent).

As in the case of religious education and civic/national values, there was no clear consensus as to which groups should receive the greatest exposure to moral education. Primary, secondary and high school received the highest overall percentages as groups that should receive the most exposure to moral education: primary (52 percent), young children (28 percent), and pre-schoolers (12 percent).

Discussion

While our intention was not to construct a picture of the 'product' of values education, a clear position emerges as a result of our survey and forms the basis on which the choices may be made with regard to values education. The position that emerges is that of citizens who may

- be capable of spiritual development,
- have a sense of individual responsibility,
- have respect for women,
- have civic consciousness,
- have a respect for democracy,
- be able to think critically, and
- have empathy for others, regardless of their background.

The important values that such an individual would hold include

- Moral Values,
- Civic Values,
- Family Values,
- Values of Diversity and Multiculturalism, and
- Values of Personal Autonomy and Reflection.

Among other things, such a person should also hold in a lesser degree values needed for economic development, such as hard work, creativity and individual competitiveness.

It could be said that the values that such 'modern' individuals would hold should constitute a blend of traditional of 'Asian' values, and 'Western' values, as well as the values needed specifically for living in a multicultural society like Singapore. It is uncertain whether such a blend is internally consistent, or how comfortably the elements sit beside each other. However, there is the hint of a notion of a diverse and rich set of values that might interact in complex ways.

With regard to the relative emphasis that schools should give to the different themes, moral and civic values were considered to be highly important, followed by family, diversity and multiculturalism, and personal autonomy and reflection related values. At the same time, the role of schools is seen as laying the ground for spiritual development, without fostering religious values. This could be because schools were considered ineffective for this purpose; alternatively, there could be concern that religious values might be divisive in a multicultural society and, hence, that universally held values would be more appropriate. Finally, it was felt that schools should place strong emphasis on teaching children the value of critical thinking, and of preparing them to live in a multicultural society, as well as in an 'Asian' society.

Respondents thought that slightly more curriculum time (10 percent to 16 percent, compared to the current figure of 7.5 percent) should specifically be set aside for values education. Interestingly, a majority (60 percent) felt that values education should be integrated throughout the curriculum instead of being taught in separate subjects. There was strong agreement that values education should begin at an early age, as is the practice in Singapore, and that students of different abilities should not undergo different values education programs. Finally, it was felt that the school was an effective setting for civic/national values and moral education, but not for religious education.

There is a degree of divergence between the goals for individuals and the role of schools emerging from our survey and that envisaged and promoted by the authorities regarding values education. For instance, the ranking of the values of personal autonomy and reflection above those of work, national identity and patriotism related values are contrary to the official position. Indeed, these responses may be an attempt to redress the current situation where there has been little emphasis on nurturing individuals' habits of personal autonomy and reflection. Similarly, the strong emphasis given to gender equality seems to run counter to current views and practice in a country where, despite the avowed position of ensuring equal opportunity, official policy enshrines the man as the head of the household.[4]

The overall goal for individuals is, to form a more autonomous, critical thinker perhaps beyond what official policy might support. Given the proposed emphasis on such values as gender equality, personal autonomy and reflection, the picture that emerges may be more 'Western' than the authorities might deem appropriate for an 'Asian' society.

Whatever the case may be, there appears to be a degree of tension between what members of the elite conceive to be the ideal product of values education, regarding the role of individuals and schools, and what the authorities might deem desirable.

References

Chew, J. (1997). "Schooling for Singaporeans: The Interaction of Singapore Culture and Values in the School". In J. Tan, S. Gopinathan and W. K. Ho (eds.), *Education in Singapore: A Book of Readings*. Singapore: Prentice Hall.

Chew, J. (1998). "Civics and Moral Education in Singapore: Lessons for Citizenship Education?" *Journal of Moral Education* 27: 335-354.

Kennedy, K. (ed.) (1997). *Citizenship Education and the Modern State*. London: The Falmer Press.

Lo, L.N.K., and Man, S. (eds.) (1996). *Research and Endeavours in Moral and Civic Education*. Hong Kong: Hong Kong Institute of Educational Research, The Chinese University of Hong Kong.

Ministry of Education (1997). *Launch of National Education* (May 16, Press release).

Ministry of Education (1998). *Developing Thinking Schools: A Strategic Perspective on Education for the 21st Century*. Singapore: Ministry of Education.

Tan, J. (1998). "The Marketisation of Education in Singapore: Policies and Implications", *International Review of Education* 44: 47-63.

---

[4] For instance, the policy gives employed men medical benefits for their children but denies similar benefits to employed women.

Conclusion

CHAPTER 14

THE FUTURE OF VALUES EDUCATION
IN THE PACIFIC BASIN

William K. Cummings

Introduction

The educational and social institutions of the Pacific Basin region have been exceptionally rich in developing an internalized inclination towards familial, social, and national responsibility. Thus, many of the Pacific Basin societies have benefited from an impressive stock of social capital manifested in social stability and the mobilization of communities in campaigns to promote sanitation, health and family planning, the resolution of labor disputes, and other social purposes. But in recent decades, there has been many indications that these social institutions are under stress: governments, facing increasing fiscal challenges, are less capable of looking after the welfare of their citizens; workplaces facing the uncertainties of global competition are less able to guarantee security to their employees; communities have become larger and more heterogeneous; families have become smaller and more vulnerable. Because these institutions, the pillars of modernization, are less capable today of looking after their members, the attachment of individuals to these institutions appears to be weakening. Social critics link the increasing incidence of divorce, juvenile delinquency, government corruption, and white-collar crime to these developments.

The elites sampled in the International Elite Sigma Survey of Values Education, carried out from 1996-1998, indicated a high level of concern about these developments. In virtually every corner of the region, these changes have led elites to question the efficacy of old values. The values of obedience, cooperation, and hard work are reputed to have enabled the Pacific Basin to make rapid progress over the past half century. But will these values provide the best direction for the future generations as they cope with these new developments? In all of the settings reviewed, the leaders have expressed their concerns about the limitations of the inherited values and the ways in which these values are being conveyed to the new generation. A vigorous search is thus underway for new values to guide the region through the next half century. This book has been about that search.

The New Values

What is surprising, in view of the diversity of the region, is the level of consensus on new values. The elites in virtually all of the settings indicate that their highest priority is new values that strengthen the individual. Based on a review of current debates in the Pacific Basis, the members of the research team developed a list of the major "arguments" for change as reported in Table 14.1 below. The elites in each setting were asked, "in your view, which are the most persuasive reasons for improving values education in your society today". As indicated in Table 14.1, the highest ranked concerns are to "help young persons develop reflective/autonomous person-

Table 14.1 Why Should There be Values Education? Elite Rankings by Settings

Why Values Education?	Russia	Japan	Taiwan	Mexico	US	Hawaii	Malaysia	Singapore	Thailand	Hong Kong	Korea	China
Develop reflective/ autonomous personalities	2	1	1	1	6	2	5	9	10	2	1	6
Provide foundation for spiritual development	1	3	3	7	15	16	2	7	4	1	2	2
Increase sense of individual responsibility	3	2	5	2	1	3	3	1	1	3	7	1
Guide for daily life	4	5	2	4	2	5	6	6	2	6	4	4
Encourage civic consciousness	7	11	9	5	5	10	14	4	2	3	3	14
Promote values of justice and equity	14	NA	6	3	4	6	14	4	14	5	3	NA
Strengthen families	8	4	11	6	8	7	4	5	7	10	15	12
Develop appreciation for heritage/ national identity	10	12	7	8	12	11	8	3	5	6	5	4
Foster economic development	13	15	16	13	11	8	9	8	9	11	8	3
Combat prejudice/promote tolerance	6	8	10	9	7	4	6	2	16	8	10	13
Promote orderly caring school communities	15	11	8	11	3	1	7	11	6	9	12	7
Combat juvenile delinquency	13	6	4	12	9	12	12	14	11	16	11	9
Help youth interpret values in media, internet	5	12	12	15	13	9	11	12	12	13	9	10
Combat ecological abuse	12	8	13	15	16	17	16	16	13	14	14	8
Promote world peace	9	7	17	13	17	15	16	16	15	15	13	11
Promote pride in local communities	17	NA	14	17	9	14	13	13	8	11	16	NA
Improve respect/opportunities for girls and women	16	10	15	10	13	13	17	17	17	17	15	15

Note: Only 15 items were ranked in China and Japan.

alities", "to provide a foundation for spiritual development", and "to increase the sense of individual responsibility".

The elites in most of the Pacific Basin countries seem to believe that a good society derives from the spiritual and intellectual strength of thoughtful and responsible individuals. As one leader indicated, it takes a strong and confident individual to make the right decisions in an age of uncertainty; fixed rules of behavior will no longer suffice. Another argued that innovations in science and business require individuals who can think for themselves. Similarly it was argued that new leadership is required in politics to break through old patterns and devise new goals and strategies that will help the nation to be more outward looking and adaptive. Even among leaders who expressed concern with the decline of nationalism has emerged the individualistic argument that the strength of nations starts with the love of one's self.

In the second tier of the elite rationales are more "collective" concerns such as "providing a guide for behavior in daily life", "encouraging civic consciousness", and "promoting values of justice and equality". Other collective concerns such as "fostering an appreciation for the heritage and strengthening national identity", and "fostering family values" tend to be less uniformly supported in the region; these values stand out in certain nations but are relegated to a low priority in others. For example, concerning "fostering an appreciation for the heritage and strengthening national identity", the U.S. elites (as well as those from Japan and Russia) are decidedly lukewarm. In contrast, the elites of the newly industrializing countries of Eastern Asia (Korea, mainland China, Hong Kong, Singapore, and to a lesser degree Taiwan and Thailand) are comparatively positive. While all of the values in this second tier make reference to social entities, the primary emphasis is on encouraging individuals to make wise choices in their associations with social entities as contrasted to blindly accepting societal prescriptions.[1]

There were some surprises in the relative emphases of particular settings. For example, while Russia under communism stressed secular and collective values, the top concerns of the contemporary Russian elites are spiritual development and an autonomous reflective personality. Both of these values are deeply imbedded in Russian history and the Russian philosophical tradition, and thus are re-emerging as core contemporary concerns. The elites of Japan, Korea, and Hong Kong also give high priority to spiritual development and an autonomous reflective personality, but in these cases their responses reflect a quest for a new direction rather than a resurrection of the past.

In contrast, despite (or perhaps because of) the U.S.'s strong individualist heritage, U.S. elites are more inclined to show concern for the strengthening of collective or control values such as a guide for behavior and individual responsibility. In terms of the stress on collective concerns, the American elites are close to the elites in Singapore, Thailand, Malaysia, and even mainland China. Mexico and Taiwan tend to

---

[1] A factor analysis was used to verify these tiers. For the full sample of elites, the rationales of reflective/autonomous personality and spiritual development were firmly in a common factor, with individual responsibility a borderline addition. Similarly, the several rationales noted for the second tier were also in a common factor. The factor analysis is reported in Appendix 14A. For another illustration of factor analysis, see the chapter on Russia.

straddle the gap between these two groups, expressing a mix of concerns with more individualistic and more collective concerns.

In indicating why they believe certain values to be important, the elites of the several Pacific Basin countries/settings tend to stress both areas they feel are of fundamental importance for maintaining the traditional strengths of their societies and areas they feel need strengthening in order to cope with the future. Thus while the mainland Chinese elites, being from one of the less economically developed settings in the study, stress the need for work values to foster economic development, most of the other elites tend to de-emphasize this value area (Korea, Singapore, and Thailand were among the settings giving work values moderate stress). Settings such as Korea and Hong Kong, which have only recently opened up their polities for popular voting are notable for their stress on the need to encourage civic consciousness; the U.S., Thailand, and Mexico also stress the need for these values.

While the elites in most of the countries give a moderately high ranking to "promoting values of justice and equity" (especially those from the U.S. and Mexico), they give low rankings to several other issues that have mobilized social activism in past decades—promoting world peace, combating social prejudice and promoting tolerance, and combating ecological abuse. Japanese elites stand out as promoters of world peace, Singapore elites are the strongest proponents of combating social prejudice, and Japanese and mainland Chinese elites express the most concern for ecological abuse.

In view of the prominent attention accorded by the media to the issue of combating juvenile delinquency, it is of considerable interest that the elites of most countries tend to accord this a relatively low priority; Japanese and Taiwanese elites are the major exceptions. Russian elites are notable for their concern for the dangers posed by the negative images and information provided by the media and the internet. Thai and U.S. elites express the greatest concern for promoting pride in local communities.

It might be said that the elites of these twenty settings agree that values education needs to place greater stress on helping individuals make ethical choices. But the elites have divergent views on the areas of choice that might need the greatest emphasis. The elites of each country focus on somewhat distinctive areas, reflecting the particular challenges their countries have and will be facing.

Patterns of Variation

Recognizing that there are differences between the settings, we next explored whether the thinking of the elites in certain settings are more similar to each other than to other settings. For example, Russians and Mexicans stand out for their stress on autonomy. But the Mexicans place more stress on civic consciousness than the Russians. So who are the Mexican elites most alike, the Russians, or the elites in another setting?

To gain an understanding of differences in emphasis for the different settings, the setting rank orders for each rationale were analyzed with multi-dimensional scaling.[2]

---

[2] Initially all 21 settings were included, but the positions of the several settings respectively in Mexico, Russia, and the U.S. were relatively proximate so these details were dropped in the MDS presented in Figure 14.1. On the other hand, the distances between the several settings

Figure 14.1 presents the relative position of each setting. Also on Figure 14.1 are listed, in different corners, phrases to identify the value rationales preferred by the elites in these settings. For example, elites in settings towards the top of the diagram stress civic consciousness and democracy, those to the right prefer individual responsibility and the need to provide guides for behavior.

Figure 14.1 Multidimensional Scaling of 15 Rationales for Values Education

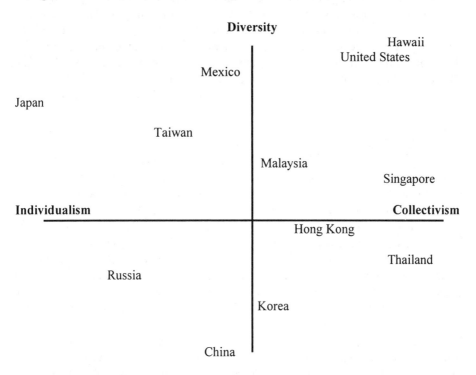

One way of interpreting the outcome is to distinguish four groupings of settings:

1) *Far West Liberals.* The topmost U.S-influenced grouping of Japan, Taiwan, Mexico, and the U.S. which stress the need for civic consciousness and democracy.
2) *Southeast Asian Moralists.* The rightmost group of Singapore, Thailand, Malaysia, and Hong Kong which shares a Southeast Asian affinity for morality and economic growth.
3) *Confucian Middle Way.* A lower quadrant Sinic grouping of Hong Kong, Korea, and mainland China, which stresses the strengthening of national identity and hard work.
4) *Former Socialist/Centrists.* Finally the distinctive group of Russia that stresses personal autonomy and spiritual development.

of China were substantial, hence they were entered in the diagram. Similarly, each was assigned a separate chapter.

Several other sets of country data were also analyzed with the multi-dimensional scaling technique, and the same basic pattern repeatedly emerged giving strength to the observation that the differences in the elite preferences of these groupings are firmly grounded.

What Should be Emphasized in Values Education?

Distinct from perceptions of the conditions values education is expected to improve, elites were asked which they believed should get a strong emphasis in contemporary educational institutions. Across the Pacific Basin, the value areas receiving the most support were personal autonomy, moral values, civic values, and democracy. In the second group were work, ecology, family, peace, national identity, and diversity. Gender equality, global awareness, and especially religion received the lowest priority for inclusion in the values education curriculum. But not all countries minimized these values. Malaysian elites ranked religion as the second highest priority (after moral values). Gender equality was ranked fourth in Mexico. And Japan and Hong Kong gave moderately high priority to global awareness.

The particular problem foci of the respective elites tended to shape their thinking about what should be emphasized in the values education curriculum. For example, those country elites who tended to express concern to help young persons develop reflective/autonomous personalities were more likely to rank autonomy a high priority in values education ($r = .69$) and to stress civic education ($r = .72$). Those who emphasized the need to strengthen civic consciousness tended to give high priority to civic education ($r = .59$) and democracy ($r = .66$). Those that stressed the need to combat ecological abuse gave high priority to ecology in the values curriculum ($r = .66$) and to global awareness ($r = .72$). Somewhat surprising was the pattern for those who gave high priority to improving the respect and opportunities for girls and women: they gave high priority to gender values in the curriculum ($r = .82$), but they de-emphasized both family values ($r = -.77$) and moral values ($r = -.75$). Because there was an overall pattern of strong correlations between the related why and what responses (both at the individual level and by setting), the figure for the multidimensional scaling of the what responses had an appearance similar to Figure 14.1. The same four groupings were evident, and essentially the same values were associated with each grouping.

Distinct from the particular values to be taught are the images the elites believe will be most helpful in conveying these values. In colonial times, the curriculum tended to draw on European images. One test of the emergence of the region from its earlier Eurocentric orientation is to consider the images that elites propose for the values curriculum. The Sigma Elite survey asked the elites of each country to list the countries that they felt should be given the greatest emphasis when choosing examples for the values education curriculum. Needless to say, the elites of each setting gave highest priority to examples from their own setting. After that, there was a certain tendency to stress examples from the leading Western nations such as the United States, the United Kingdom, and France. But four of the Pacific Basin settings gave Japan a higher ranking than these Western nations, and two gave China a higher ranking. The U.S. and Russia, which span both the Atlantic and Pacific Basins have tended in the past to see their origins in Europe, and thus the major tendency in their response was to stress Eurocentric examples. However, looking at the regional groupings within these two large nations, we find that the educational elites in these two countries who live closest to the Pacific Basin (Vladivostok in the Russian case and California and Hawaii for the U.S.) are far more likely than their Atlantic counterparts to stress Pacific Basin examples. Thus our study finds evidence of an emerging tendency of mutual respect and admiration among the Pacific Basin neighbors.

Some Outstanding Issues

Recognizing the complexity of several of the issues touched on in the Why and What sections of the survey, in a separate section we encouraged respondents to elaborate their thinking through probing their views on different sides of the same value. The following are the major examples.

Autonomy

The five questions relating to this value were among those receiving the strongest emphasis across the several countries. In every country the educational elites placed a strong emphasis on critical thinking (though the tendency was somewhat moderated in Korea, Japan, and mainland China). Assisting each child in developing his or her own values was also given exceptionally strong emphasis across the several countries, as was the importance of fostering personal pride and identity (though here the U.S. and Russia were the strongest dissenters). The elites of most countries also agreed that it was important to help children understand that they have individual rights, including the right to be happy; Mexico and Thailand were most supportive and Singapore least so.

Civic Values

The view of "understanding all political and social viewpoints" received much greater support than that of "teaching respect for hierarchy and support for the government". Singapore and Malaysia were two cases where elites tended to reverse the emphasis; similarly, the elites in these two countries stressed the noblesse oblige sentiment that it is "the duty of the fortunate to help those who encounter difficulties". Elites in all of the countries agreed it was important to "stress that all are equal before the law".

Nationalism

Elites of all nations, excepting Russia, agreed on the importance of "promoting understanding and love of the nation" but they expressed somewhat less enthusiasm for "venerating heroes and promoting national pride". The reluctance to venerate national heroes, in several instances, reflects important internal disputes concerning who should be considered a hero.

Religion

As noted in the discussion of why and what, the elites of most Pacific Basin countries were not very enthusiastic about including religion in the values education curriculum. More interest was expressed in "fostering an understanding of all religions" than in helping students to "gain a deeper understanding of their own religion". The elites of Malaysia and Thailand tended to take a contrary view.

Tolerance

Elites from countries with explicit multi-ethnic policies such as the U.S., Russia, Singapore, and Malaysia were more supportive of "common values to all without differentiating class, ethnicity, and race" while the elites of Korea, Beijing, Hong Kong, and Taiwan were more inclined to have "schools help the members of each group gain a clear understanding of their unique origins and heritage". A somewhat intermediate position strongly supported by most elites was that "schools should encourage empathy, for people of different ethnic, language, and social backgrounds;" Taiwanese, Singaporean, Beijing, Mexican and U.S. elites were most supportive of encouraging empathy and Russian and Korean elites least supportive.

Gender

Overall, the elites of most countries expressed very progressive views on gender issues—but this stands in marked contrast with the low priority they accorded this area in the values curriculum as such. For example, the view that "girls should be given equal opportunity and encouragement" and that "values education should encourage mutual respect between boys and girls" were strongly affirmed. In contrast, little enthusiasm was expressed for having schools teach that "it is the destiny of girls to have significant home-building responsibilities". Also, the elites of most countries agreed "values education should take up issues relating to human sexuality and health, such as chastity, preserving the integrity of the body against drugs and prostitution, and understanding the risks of promiscuity". On all these gender issues, Taiwanese, Korean, Malaysian, and Russian elites tended to be more traditional or family-oriented, and Mexican and American elites more progressive.

For Whom and How Should Values Education be Implemented?

Values education implementation is, in important respects, a more specialized matter than the "what" and "why", and, it was apparent that the educational elites were less confident about their preferences in these areas. For example, the "who" and "how" may vary depending on the curricular area. Some experts maintain that certain moral and religious precepts can be taught to very young children, whereas much that goes into civic education requires a minimal cognitive understanding of the nature of community organization and the key organs of government. Given the complexity of this question, the Sigma Survey restricted its coverage to three values areas: religion, morals, and civics. Overall, the responses across the several countries indicated a high level of agreement. Below, we will highlight a few differences.

First, concerning the "who" there was broad agreement that values education should begin at a relatively early age, and that all children should receive a common program (e.g., irrespective of their academic ability). The major exceptions to these propositions are mainland China, where the elites placed more stress on values education at the secondary level, and Hong Kong, Taiwan, and China, where the elites indicated that children of different ability levels might be taught different value curricula.

Also, as noted already, there is general agreement that civic education is better taught to somewhat more academically mature students, whereas the other value areas can just as easily begin at an early stage. While the elites stressed the early years as a good time to begin values education, there was a strong indication both from the survey and the country studies that the elites believed the value crisis to be endemic and thus deserving of a lifelong educational approach; for example, they accorded nearly as much importance to values education for teachers as to values education for students.

The Survey's "how" questions focused on two issues: 1) What is the best locus for values education? and 2) Should values be taught as a separate subject or woven into the curriculum and co-curriculum? Concerning locus, we identified several possibilities: home, school, summer camp, internships, religious institution, and national service. For all value areas the home and family are viewed as the critical settings by the elites in all of the Pacific Basin countries (though the Russians and Taiwanese expressed somewhat weaker faith in this locus). Without familial support, in the view of our elite sample, values education carried out in other settings is unlikely to have much impact. As a complement to the family, religious institutions are pointed to as critical agents for religious education; Malaysia is the one case where schools are also viewed as a vital setting for religious education. For moral education, along with the home and school, many elites also highlighted special camps as useful settings. And concerning civic education, many elites (especially the Russians) noted the potential of internships as well as community and national service. Malaysian (and, at least for some value areas, Hong Kong and Singapore) elites were most supportive of the media as effective means for values education.

Schools are but one among several settings where a coordinated program of values education can take place. For the values education that takes place in schools, the elites of most of the Pacific Basin countries are favorable to having values education integrated across the curriculum, while in Korea, Hong Kong, and Singapore there is greater stress on values education taught as a separate subject. For most of the other loci identified above, values education tends to be integrated across the curriculum.

Challenges for the Philosophy of Education

The several case studies go into considerable detail on selected features of pedagogical thinking. Among the many stimulating challenges to pedagogical thinking, the following deserve special attention:

What is Autonomy?

Autonomy has often been neglected in discussions of values education, though it is certainly a core concept in theories of human development (Loevinger, 1976). Autonomy was added to our list of value rationales at the suggestion of an educator familiar with the Russian tradition, where personal autonomy is associated with personal and moral development but not with political orientation (Bain in Chapter 2). This conceptualization goes back in Russian thought to at least the period of Tolstoy and has gained new life in post-Glasnost Russia. While elites from other settings also expressed a strong interest in autonomy, it is likely that the meaning attached to this concept varied. For example, in Mexico personal autonomy appears to have a strong association with civic values, and in Malaysia it is closely associated with religious values.

Individualism and Collectivism

The concepts of individualism and collectivism are sometimes portrayed as opposites and even as in opposition to each other. For example, Asian collectivism is often contrasted with Western individualism as in Ruth Benedict's (1969) contrast of shame versus guilt cultures or Lucian Pye's exploration of Asian Power. Wing On Lee (Chapter 10) observes that these same arguments have been discussed among Hong Kong educators, but that they have concluded that the two concepts are complementary rather than opposing. As Lee argues:

> Some societies place stronger emphasis on individualism, while others collectivism. However, the two are not necessarily dichotomized and mutually exclusive. On the contrary, there are subtle relationships between them. In societies where individualism is more obviously valued, the significance of common interests, common will and common good is also valued. Likewise, in societies where collectivism seems to be dominant, there are various extents of respect for individuality, and self-realization is seen as best achieved through collective realization. In the Chinese tradition, even though collectivism has been a dominant social value, self has been seen as the starting point of civic values… (CDC, 1996, p. 15).

Love of Country: A Foundation for Internationalism.

It is also sometimes argued that nationalism and internationalism are in opposition. But, in recent years as several Pacific Nations have sought to expand their international involvements and hence their outlook, they have taken the view that a strong sense of national identity is an essential foundation for nationalism. The argument often presented by Japanese educational philosophers builds on the Christian maxim that one has to love oneself before it is possible to love one's neighbor. While this position is sometimes criticized as a feeble excuse for perpetuating nationalism, it is persistently advocated by a number of leaders in the Pacific Basin.

The case studies of this volume identify many other instances where the concepts used in particular settings have distinctive meanings. The differences in the meanings attached to concepts, and the logic that educators use to linking concepts with each other and with action, are a rich area for deeper exploration.

Possible Lessons and Problems

The case studies reported in this volume suggest a number of lessons for the future of education in the Pacific Basis.

1. *Values education will be a high priority for the immediate future.* All of the leaders included in this study believe that values education requires more emphasis. They have a broad vision of values education as contributing to the development of the whole person. They see values providing guides not only for the way future citizens behave, which tends to the objective of character education in the U.S.,

but also for shaping the goals of behavior. In other words, they believe education should play a fundamental role in shaping the future.

2. *At the core of values education is the autonomous individual.* In the past in many parts of the Pacific Basin, values education tended to be directive—do this, do that. Individuals were taught social rules and expected to blindly and persistently follow these rules. But the new thinking in the Pacific Basin seems to be to move beyond rules towards a reliance on the judgement of the autonomous individual. Values educators do not assume, as in the case of Kohlberg's Values Clarification approach, that the young student has a coherent value system of his/her own. Rather the assumption is that the values perspective of the young person has to be nurtured in the home and school through a thoughtful and caring process. But the outcome of this process should be strong individuals who have a clear sense of what is important, so that those individuals can make sound decisions on their own.

3. *Schools should play an important role in values education.* Whereas homes and churches were once thought to be the most important locus for values education, it is now understood that the work of these settings needs to be complemented by a significant effort in the schools. After all, many children come from unstable homes and/or are not affiliated with formal religious organizations. Thus, in the case of many children, the school may play not just a complementary but an essential role in values education.

4. *Many pedagogies need to be considered.* There is a rich heritage of pedagogies in the Pacific Basin that encompasses virtually every values education option known to the modern educator. In view of this rich heritage, most school settings will be reluctant to commit themselves to any single approach, but rather will prefer to be eclectic, relying on approaches (direct approach, role models, tell stories, experiential, participatory) that are comfortable and appear to address the situation at hand. To enable this flexibility, teachers will need to be provided with rich and diverse backgrounds in values education.

5. *An integrated approach is preferred.* Most elites favor an integrated approach for values education that includes, along with classroom instruction, values throughout the curriculum and the co-curriculum. The comprehensive approach favored by Pacific Basin educators means that schools will have to devote considerable time each year to planning their values education approach.

6. *The pressure of exams may thwart the goals of values education.* A potential contradiction is between the cognitive content of the values education curriculum and the behavioral necessities associated with passing competitive examinations. The values education curriculum may emphasize such themes as honesty and helping other. However, the examinations require students to work alone without helping their peers, and some students resort to cheating on the exams in order to do well.

7. *The theme of multiculturalism is neglected.* While the values education philosophies of Pacific Basin elites seem to be thoughtful with respect to most contemporary challenges, in several of the settings there is an unusual level of dissonance with respect to the approach to racial and ethnic differences. More careful thought

needs to be devoted to the area of multiculturalism, as the next decades are certain to accelerate the level of interaction between people of different backgrounds.

8. *More time in the school day might be dedicated to values education.* In view of the above goals outlined for values education, more time may be needed for values education. The elite survey sought to obtain estimates on what might be required. Virtually every elite contacted for this study indicated that more time would be required—e.g., Singapore elites on average proposed an increase in the time allocation for values education from 10 to 16 percent. Alternately, the time for values education might be better utilized. And values education can be better integrated with other subjects.

Conclusion

Whereas past accounts of the Pacific Basin stressed the penchant for orderliness and control including the tendency to use values education to shape habits of national loyalty and obedience, the elite respondents of the twenty settings participating in the Sigma Survey suggest a new era may be emerging with an increased emphasis on personal autonomy and responsibility. Looking to the future in the Pacific Basin, the elites indicate values of nationalism are likely to be balanced with increased civic consciousness. Values of hard work are to be balanced with increased creativity and competitiveness. Values of unique national heritages are to be balanced with increased respect for the traditions and languages of others. And values of hierarchy and patrimony are to be balanced with the values of equity and respect for the rights of women as equal partners in the labor force. To the extent that elite thinking is translated into educational policy, it can be presumed that the nature of social capital in the Pacific Basin will undergo important changes in the coming decades.

Concerning each of these dimensions, current thinking varies widely across the region. But focusing on the major differences between countries, this variation can be divided into four groupings: the Far West Liberal group, Confucian Middle-Wayism, Southeast Asian Moralism, and the (former) Centralist/Socialist group. The Far West is notable for its concern with civic values and gender issues; the Southeast Asian Group is notable for its concern with moral education, orderly schools, patriotism, and religion; the former Socialist/Centralized countries are notable for their concern for personal autonomy and the need for spiritual development; and the East Asian countries tend to stand in the middle of these various tendencies.

While contextual developments and longstanding traditions may lead to divergence with respect to the "why" and "what" of values education, there is greater unanimity concerning the "who" and "how". The elites agree, for most areas, that it is important to start early, while recognizing that values education is a lifelong challenge. Thus in terms of who can benefit from lifelong education, they indicate that teachers and adults, as well as school children, should be the focus of values education. Most elites stress the home as the backbone of values education followed by the primary school. But here again there are some differences. Elites from the former Centralist/Socialist group are most inclined to rely on internships and adult institutions; the Southeast Asian Moralists are most inclined to stress schools and to prefer that values education be taught in specialized subjects (and even be evaluated by tests). The elites from the Far West tend to stress integrating civic and moral values education across the curriculum while assigning religious education to the church and family. And the Middle-Way Confucians tend to draw elements from the other groups.

Perhaps the major dilemma faced by Pacific Basin educators is that their current views, if put into practice, may foster increased personal autonomy, but at the cost of weakening past approaches to preserving and strengthening social capital. The educational and social tradition of this region have been exceptionally rich in developing an internalized inclination towards familial, social, and national responsibility; and these social institutions have tended to reinforce and reward this inclination. But in recent decades, there have been many indications that these social institutions are under stress: governments, facing increasing fiscal challenges, are less capable of looking after the welfare of their citizens; workplaces facing the uncertainties of global competition are less able to guarantee security to their employees; communities have become larger and more heterogeneous; families have become smaller and more vulnerable.

The values education now envisioned by Pacific Basin elites is adaptive in the sense of helping the new generation to individually cope with these new complexities, to help this new generation make decisions that maximize their needs. But the new values education may be weak in providing a vision of the broader social purpose, of the fabric that binds many individuals into broader social entities of common value. In other words, Pacific Basin educators are fashioning a new vision of heightened individualism, but they may be forgetting the need to complement this individualism with a complementary path towards the continued strengthening of the Pacific Basin's traditional reserve of social capital. Will future generations have a greater social consciousness, or will they be more concerned for their own private interests? Will they be more or less committed to resolving social conflicts, to strengthening community life, to correcting environmental injuries?

This warning does not apply equally across the region. As we have seen, the elite thinking tends to divide into four groupings. The Southeast Asian group is the most consistent follower of the nationalistic moral approach that has long characterized the Asian core of the Pacific Basin. The Far West, possibly having experienced the greatest excesses of individualism, evidences a new concern to introduce collective corrections. The former centrist group is most apprehensive of collective inhibitions, and thus may, at least in the short run, be neglecting its past practice of strengthening social capital. And the Middle Way Confucianists are seeking to strike a balance between these extremes. Of course, these projections are based primarily on our analysis of the thinking of educational elites. There are other components involved in the shaping of the respective country's emergent values—including popular movements, the military, and religious groups—which may point the values future in yet other directions. What is certain is that the Pacific Basin is undergoing a profound reconsideration of basic values, characterized by a new stress on personal autonomy and diversity.

Appendix 14.A. Clusters of Values

The common instrument used in this study specified a long list of rationales for value change that are being articulated in the different settings. Particular rationales may have special salience in particular settings. But distinct from these particular differences, it seemed useful to identify the core themes of the values debate. To guide our thinking on core themes, we both reviewed the case studies and carried out a factor analysis of the rankings of individual elites.

Several of the case studies, especially those of the larger nations with several settings, depicted dimensions of divergence in the ways elites think about values. For example, the Russian study highlighted three dimensions: (1) personal autonomy and reflection as contrasted to collectivism and conformity; (2) openness and tolerance versus isolation; and (3) progressiveness versus tradition. The Mexican study highlighted in the single dimension of modernity versus tradition some of the above elements and added the additional dimension of pluralism versus nationalism. In other settings there are variations on these distinctions.

Taking these dimensions as a guide for thinking, we conducted a factor analysis of the rankings on the rationales for change of the 800 elites from all of the regions. This analysis generated five major factors. As suggested in Table 14A, there is a close resemblance between these five factors and the dimension highlighted in the case studies.

Table 14A. A Comparison of the Major Values Dimensions Reported in the Case Studies and Revealed in Factor Analysis

Case Studies	Factor Analysis
Personal autonomy vs collective control	Individualism vs. collectivism (Factor 4)
Open vs. isolation	Open vs. orderly (Factor 2)
Progressive vs tradition	Liberal vs. traditional (Factors 1 & 2)
Pluralism vs. national	Civic vs. national (Factor 5)

References

Pye, L.W. (1985). *Asian Power and Politics.* Cambridge, MA: Harvard University Press.

Benedict, R. (1969). *The Chrysanthemum and the Sword.* Cleveland and New York: The World Publishing Co.

Curriculum Development Council [CDC], Hong Kong (1996). *Guidelines on Civic Education in Schools.* Hong Kong: Curriculum Development Council, Education Department.

Loevinger, J. (1976). *Ego Development.* San Francisco, CA: Jossey-Bass.

ABOUT THE AUTHORS

Olga Bain, a former Assistant Dean of Kemerovo State University, recently received a Ph.D. in Comparative Higher Education at the University at Buffalo, USA. She is a frequent consultant to the Council of Europe and other international organizations. Her current research focuses on educational finance, decentralization, and university governance.

Tsunenobu Ban is Professor of sociology of education at Naruto Educational University, Japan. He formerly was an official of the Ministry of Education.

Thomas N. Barone is an Assistant Professor in the Department of Educational and Psychological Foundations at Northern Illinois University, USA. He is interested in comparative values education research and its implications for educational policy. Other areas of interest include multicultural issues in education especially equal educational opportunity. A recent publication (with I.A. Bajunid) is "Elite Perceptions of Values Education in Malaysia and the Pacific Rim," *Educational Theory and Practice* 21(2).

Ibrahim Ahmad Bajunid is Director of Institut Aminuddin Baki, Ministry of Education, Malaysia. He is interested in educational research focusing on educational management and Islamic Education issues. A recent publication is "Reform Imperatives in Islamic Education in the Developing World," in W. Cummings & N. McGinn (eds.), *International Handbook of Education and Development: Preparing Schools, Students, and Nations for the Twenty-First Century* (New York: Pergamon Press).

William Cummings is Professor of International Education and Associate Dean for Research at the Graduate School of Education and Human Development of George Washington University, USA. He has recently published (with Noel McGinn) the *International Handbook of Education and Development: Preparing Schools, Students and Nations for the Twenty-First Century*.

Joy Chew is Associate Professor in the Division of Policy and Management Studies, Nanyang Technological University, Singapore. She has published articles on moral education and school leadership in Singapore

Sheena Choi is an Assistant Professor in the School of Education at Indiana-Purdue University Fort Wayne, USA. Her doctoral dissertation, which focuses on Korea's Chinese minority, is entitled *Invisible Minority: Factors Influencing the Educational Choices of the Ethnic Chinese in Korea* (1999).

M. Elizabeth Cranley is a former Peace Corps member in Thailand. She is currently pursuing a Ph.D. in Comparative Education at the University at Buffalo, USA.

Walter P. Dawson is a Ph.D. student in the Comparative and International Education Program at Teachers College, Columbia University, USA. His research interests include moral and political education in Japan. He has studied and worked in Japan.

Christine Han is Assistant Professor in the Division of Policy and Management Studies, Nanyang Technological University, Singapore. Her latest publication is "National Education in Singapore and 'Active Citizenship': The Implications for Citizenship and Citizenship Education in Singapore," *Asia Pacific Journal of Education* 20 (2000).

John N. Hawkins is Professor of Comparative Education at University of California, Los Angeles, Graduate School of Education, USA. His recent publications include *Development or Deterioration: Work in Rural Asia* (with Bruce Koppel), Lynn Reiner Press, 1994; "Recent higher education reform in China," a chapter in *The Transformation of Higher Education: A Comparative Perspective*, Sam Aroni (ed.) Paris: ESTP Press, 2000; and "Centralization, Decentralization, and Recentralization: Educational Reform in China," *Journal of Educational Administration*, 2000.

Hsin-ming Samuel Huang is pursuing a doctoral degree in Educational Leadership and Policy at SUNY-Buffalo, USA. His recent publication, "Educational Reform in Taiwan: A Brighter American Moon?" in *International Journal of Educational Reform* (1999), illustrates the administrative and social psychological aspects of the causes and new policies of Taiwan's contemporary educational reform.

Julie Lee is a Ph.D. candidate in Comparative Education at University of California, Los Angeles, USA. She has taught Asian American Studies at California State University, Fullerton and Scripps College in Claremont, California.

Wing On Lee, is a former Dean of School of Foundations in Education of the Hong Kong Institute of Education, is also the co-head of the Centre for Citizenship Education at the Institute. Professor Lee is currently the Principal-Investigator for the Hong Kong component of the IEA Study of Civic Education. He was the Principal Drafter of the conceptual and curriculum framework chapters of the 1996 Guidelines on Civic Education in Schools.

Ying Ying Joanne Lim is a Ph.D. candidate in the Measurement, Evaluation and Applied Statistics Program at Teachers College, Columbia University, USA. She is an instructor and evaluator in the International Center for Cooperation and Conflict Resolution (ICCCR) at Columbia University. She has lived and worked in Hawai'i.

Mayumi Nishino is Senior Researcher at the National Institute of Education in Tokyo. She is one of Japan's leading authorities on moral education.

Neon Pinpradit is an Associate Professor of social psychology at Khon Kaen University, Thailand. Her research includes studies of the psycho-social factors of behavioral and moral development. She is also an active consultant to the Kohn Kaen Provincial Police and the Northeastern Narcotic Control Office.

Gay Garland Reed is an Associate Professor and Graduate Chair in the Department of Educational Foundations at the University of Hawai'i at Manoa, USA. Her recent publications include a chapter on Chinese moral/political education in *Higher Education in Post-Mao China* (Hong Kong University Press, 1998) and an article on North Korean Education in *Compare* (June 1997).

Michael C. Rodriguez is Assistant Professor of Measurement and Evaluation in the Department of Educational Psychology in the University of Minnesota, USA. His areas of interest include educational and psychological measurement, educational statistics, survey research methods, large-scale test design, and classroom assessment methods. His current research focuses on multi-level modeling of mobility in school; choice policy; relationships between classroom assessment practices and large-scale test performance; and construct-equivalence of multiple-choice and constructed response items.

Kingfa Sintoovongse, Ph.D., is an Associate Professor of Science Education at Khon Kaen University, Thailand. Her areas of specialization are international academic collaboration and instructional development involving cognitive, affective and psychomotor learning and the related pedagogical approaches.

Gita Steiner-Khamsi is an Associate Professor of Comparative and International Education, Teachers College, Columbia University, New York, USA. Her research areas are civic education, multicultural education, educational transfer and methods of comparative education, European studies and Central Asian studies.

Maria Teresa Tatto is Associate Professor of Education at Michigan State University, USA. She has coordinated and participated in local and national level research studies in Latin America, the United States, and Asia. She has several publications on the effects of education reform on teachers' practice, the influence of teacher education on teachers' practices and beliefs, the effectiveness and costs of teacher education, and, more recently, on values education policy in Mexico. Her areas of specialization are the comparative study of teacher education and student learning, the relationship between educational policy and practice, and the comparative study of the contexts of policy formation in education.

Lilian Alvarez de Testa is associate researcher at the National Autonomous University of Mexico (UNAM), in Mexico. She has conducted research on the history of educational thought in the Hispanic and Pre-Hispanic periods in Mexico, as well as studies on higher education and human rights. She is an advisor to the Minister of Education in the field of ethics, values, sexual and civic education.

Jason Tan is Assistant Professor in the Division of Policy and Management Studies, Nanyang Technological University, Singapore. He is co-editor of *Education in Singapore: A Book of Readings* (Singapore: Prentice Hall, 1997).

Medardo Tapia Uribe has been associate researcher in the Regional Center of Multidisciplinary Research (CRIM) of Mexico's National Autonomous University (UNAM) since 1989. He has been recognized since 1992 as national researcher by the National Council of Science and Technology in Mexico. He has published five books, more than thirty articles in specialized journals and more than twelve book chapters in Mexico, the United States and the United Kingdom. His research focuses on regional and cultural educational issues regarding the individual's agency in the educational process.

Armando Loera Varela is a Lecturer at the Inter-American Institute for Social Development in the Inter-American Development Bank in Washington, DC, USA. His interests are related to innovative methodologies for policy evaluation, policies and good practices to enhance educational equity, and techniques to promote policy dialogue among educational stakeholders. He has publications on innovation and decentralization, qualitative studies of rural schools, values program evaluation, and qualitative evaluation methodology.

Zhou Nanzhao is Director of Special Projects for UNESCO Bangkok, Thailand. Zhou's work includes "Comparative Education in Asia and Its Prospects," *Prospects* 20 (1990). He has also played a leadership role in the Chinese Comparative Education Society.

APPENDIX

The International Values Education Sigma Survey

Societies, for their survival and renewal, seek both to understand prevailing values and promote new ones. To this end they look to various institutions including the family, the schools, the community, religious institutions and the media to educate the public. In recent years in a variety of settings, leaders concerned with education have expressed increasing interest in improving or modifying current approaches to values education.

Thus far, most of this discussion has been within particular settings, but it is our belief that the discussion can be vastly enriched through communication between settings. That is the purpose of this first-ever Sigma Elite Survey for which we, an international consortium of values educators, are asking your cooperation. Unique to the Sigma survey is the procedure for sharing results so participants can gain a better understanding of where they stand on various issues relative to their peers. To highlight critical differences, the Sigma survey has three stages.

a. First we seek your views on the 15 carefully selected questions that follow. Over the next two months, we will collect the responses from some 500 elites in varied settings around the world.

b. Then in April 1998 we will send you a report where your answers are compared with the average for your compatriots and for the full international panel. At that point you will be able to gain a clearer understanding of what is unique in your approach to values education. We will ask you at that time to help us to provide some insights on the unique aspects of your approach.

c. As a final stage in this project, we will prepare a report highlighting the major differences in the thoughts of the participants in this project. This report will be returned to you by September of 1998.

We respect your leadership role in shaping the debate on values education, and with this survey we wish to promote a process of mutual understanding, helping you understand what other leaders think and helping others to understand what you (and your compatriots) think. This survey is being distributed to elites in various parts of the world where values education is undergoing review.

The questions which are in a multiple choice format are divided into three sections, and it will take between 15-30 minutes for you to complete them. We welcome your thoughtful comments on any of these questions. We understand the delicacy of many of the questions we are asking, so unless you indicate otherwise, we will guarantee anonymity as we report the findings of this project. To complete the tabulations for the first phase and to send a report back to you, we will need to temporarily preserve your personal identity indicator. But on the completion of the study, that information will be destroyed.

Why Should There be Values Education?

1. Many arguments have been advanced for stressing values education. In your view, which are the most persuasive reasons for *improving values education in your society today*? Below we briefly summarize 17 arguments that prevail today. From these arguments, please in the left column place a check by all of the arguments that are prevalent today in your society.

Check Below if Prevalent in Your Society	Rank Those Checked in Terms of Their Importance
a. To help youth interpret the values transmitted by the mass media, the internet, and other information technologies	
b. To provide a foundation for spiritual development	
c. To promote more orderly and caring school communities and thus facilitate learning	
d. To help each young person develop a reflective and autonomous personality	
e. To develop an appreciation for our heritage and to strengthen national identity	
f. To provide a guide for behaviour in daily life	
g. To combat juvenile delinquency including bullying, gang violence, and drug abuse	
h. To combat juvenile delinquency including bullying, gang violence, and drug abuse	
i. To foster economic development by strengthening values such as hard work, creativity, and individual competitiveness	
j. To improve the respect and opportunities extended to girls and women	
k. To combat the recent trends of ecologial abuse	
l. To promote world peace	
m. To combat the tendency for social prejudice and to promote greater tolerance for ethnic, language, and racial groups	
n. To increase the sense of individual responsibility	
o. To strengthen families	
p. To enourage greater civic consciousness and thus strengthen democracy	
q. To promote pride in local communities and community life	
r. To promote the values of justice and equity	

Now in your view, which of these prevalent arguments is persuasive, and captures your support? Focusing on the arguments above that you have checked, please rank them in terms of their persuasive with 1 being the most important. Write the rank numbers in the right column above.

What Should be Taught in the Schools?

2. Recognizing that a school teaches many things, in your view about what percent of a school's time and effort should be devoted to values education?

   a. Percent in Specific Classes
      (e.g. moral education, civics, religion)   %

   b. Percent of Time/Effort in Values Education
      Integrated Across the Curriculum   %

3. Values Education tends to cluster around a number of themes. In your view, which of these themes requires the greatest emphasis in the schools, and which is best left for other institutions? Please indicate the relative emphasis you believe should be placed on each by schools:

	Very Strong Emphasis				Should be Left Out		
	1	2	3	4	5	6	7
a. Religious Values							
b. Values of Personal Autonomy & Reflection							
c. Moral Values							
d. National Identity & Patriotism							
e. Civic Values							
f. Gender Equality							
g. Values of Diversity & Multiculturalism							
h. Peace & Conflict Resolution							
i. Family Values							
j. Ecological Awareness							
k. Global Awareness							
l. Democracy							
m. Work Values							

4. Concerning each of the themes listed above, there are differences of opinion on content. What are your views with respect to the following controversial issues? Please indicate the relative emphasis you believe should be placed on each:

	Very Strong Emphasis				Should be Left Out		
	1	2	3	4	5	6	7
a. Schooling should first promote an understanding and love of nation and then teach about the rest of the world							
b. Schools should foster an understanding of all religions							
c. Schooling should assist each child in developing their own individual values as a foundation for their acceptance of broader social values c. Moral Values							
d. Schools should stress that all are equal before the law							
e. As sound preparation for the world of work, habits of loyalty, obedience, hard work and punctuality need to be stressed in school							
f. Schools should help young people gain an understanding of all political and social viewpoints from the most conservative to the most liberal							
g. Schools should teach young people to venerate their heroes and promote national pride							
h. Schools should help every child gain a deeper understanding of their own religion							
i. Schools should note social differences and stress the duty of the fortunate to help those who encounter difficulties							
j. It is important to highlight the role of individual competitiveness and creativity in realizing both social andeconomic success							
k. Girls are destined to have significant home-building responsibilities and the schools should prepare them for this future							
l. Schools should help young people appreciate the essential role of unions in guaranteeing safe work conditions and fair wages							
m. School should teach each child the value of critical thinking							
n. It is best for schools to teach common values to all children without differentiation on the basis of class, ethnicity, or religion							

o. Schools should teach children to respect hierarchy and to support the government							
p. Schools should encourage empathy for people of different ethnic, language, and social backgrounds and create opportunities for growth through shared experiences							
q. Recognizing the importance of a personal pride and identity, schools should help the members of each group gain a clear under-standing of their unique origins and heritage							
r. Girls have essentially the same talents as boys and should be given equal opportunities and encouragement in schools							
s. Schools should foster values supporting the family, such as respect for parents, fidelity, and taking care of children and elders							
t. Values education should take up issues relating to human sexuality and health, such as chastity, preserving the integrity of the body against drugs and prostitution, and understanding the risks of promiscuity							
u. Values education should encourage mutual respect between boys and girls							
v. Schools should promote a truly global view of the world							
w. Schools should promote values of solidarity within communities							
x. Schools should help children understand they have individual rights, and that they some-times must fight for these rights							
y. Schools should help children understand they have the right to be happy							

5. In informing children of your society about other societies and cultures, educators have to make choices about which societies to feature in examples (based on the importance of the societies, the relevance of their customs, and so on). Considering the following list of societies, which in you view should be given most prominence in the curriculum of your schools? And which should be given the least prominence?

	Much Prominence				Little Prominence		
	1	2	3	4	5	6	7
Egypt							
France							
Thailand							
USA							
China							
Malaysia							
Japan							
Russia							
Mexico							
Korea							
Singapore							
UK							
Indonesia							
Canada							

How Should Values Education be Conducted?

The following statements focus on options for the conduct of values education. Please indicate the extent to which you agree/disagree with each statement:

	Strongly Agree				Strongly Disagree		
	1	2	3	4	5	6	7
6. Values education should only begin in secondary school after young people have a clear idea of what they believe to be important.							
7. The foundations of values are established in early childhood so values education should begin at an early age.							
8. Pupils of different academic abilities should undergo different values education programs.							
9. Values education should not be taught in separate subjects; rather it should be integrated throughout the curriculum							

The next questions focus on settings for teaching different types of values and on target groups. For each we ask you to rank the options that seem most appropriate.

10. What settings do you believe are most effective for **religious education** (please rank up to three by indicating 1, 2, 3 in the left column):

	During school as a class
	During school through the rules of behavior and classroom procedures the school establishes
	Outside of school activities such as clubs, sports, arts
	Internships and community service
	Camps (e.g. during vacation)
	Religious groups and institutions
	Military training and national service
	Home and Family
	Media

11. Thinking exclusively of **religious education**, what groups should receive the most exposure (please rank up to three by indicating 1, 2, 3 in the left column):

	Inservice teachers
	Teacher learners
	Young children (3-4 yr. old)
	Pre-schoolers (5 yr. old)
	Primary (6-11 yr. old)
	Secondary level (11-14 yr. old)
	High school level (15-17 yr. old)
	University level (18 yr. old or older)

12. What settings do you believe are most effective for teaching **civic/national values** (please rank up to three by indicating 1, 2, 3 in the left column):

	During school as a class
	During school through the rules of behavior and classroom procedures the school establishes
	Outside of school activities such as clubs, sports, arts
	Internships and community service
	Camps (e.g. during vacation)
	Religious groups and institutions
	Military training and national service
	Home and Family
	Media

13. Thinking exclusively of **civic/national education**, what groups should receive the most exposure (please rank up to three by indicating 1, 2, 3 in the left column) :

	Inservice teachers
	Teacher learners
	Young children (3-4 yr. old)
	Pre-schoolers (5 yr. old)
	Primary (6-11 yr. old)
	Secondary level (11-14 yr. old)
	High school level (15-17 yr. old)
	University level (18 yr. old or older)

14. What settings do you believe are most effective for **moral education** (please rank up to three by indicating 1, 2, 3 in the left column):

	During school as a class
	During school through the rules of behavior and classroom procedures the school establishes
	Outside of school activities such as clubs, sports, arts
	Internships and community service
	Camps (e.g. during vacation)
	Religious groups and institutions
	Military training and national service
	Home and Family
	Media

15. Thinking exclusively of **moral education**, what groups should receive the most exposure (please rank up to three by indicating 1, 2, 3 in the left column):

	Inservice teachers
	Teacher learners
	Young children (3-4 yr. old)
	Pre-schoolers (5 yr. old)
	Primary (6-11 yr. old)
	Secondary level (11-14 yr. old)
	High school level (15-17 yr. old)
	University level (18 yr. old or older)

Your Thoughts on Values Education

We appreciate your patience in answering these questions, and as we indicated in the introduction we will be contacting you in the future to indicate the respects in which your thinking on these issues stands out from the thinking of other international educational elites. As a conclusion to this Sigma survey, would you have one or two thoughts on values education that you would like us to take special note of as we proceed to the second stage? Please share these with us below:

Thank you Kindly!

The International Consortium for the Understanding and Promotion of Values Education.

••

Optional Questions, recommended to be added after q.14 in a special section called Regional Values?

16. It is sometimes said that Asia has developed a distinctive value system that emphasizes group harmony, compared to the individualistic and competitive values of the West.

	Strongly Agree				Strongly Disagree		
	1	2	3	4	5	6	7
a. Would you agree that there is a distinctive set of Asian values?							
b. Would you agree that schools should make an effort to teach Asian values?							

(Confucian can be substituted for Asian)

17. It is sometimes said that socialist societies place exceptional stress on collective values and on equality of social status.

	Strongly Agree				Strongly Disagree		
	1	2	3	4	5	6	7
a. Would you agree that there is a distinctive set of socialist values?							
b. Would you agree that schools should make an effort to teach socialist values?							

18. It is sometimes said that Islamic societies place considerable stress on community values and on personal habits of abstinence and discipline.

	Strongly Agree				Strongly Disagree		
	1	2	3	4	5	6	7
a. Would you agree that there is a distinctive set of Islamic values?							
b. Would you agree that schools should make an effort to teach Islamic values?							

19. It is sometimes said that Latin American societies favor values of solidarity within communities and the family as the institution where most trust is placed.

	Strongly Agree				Strongly Disagree		
	1	2	3	4	5	6	7
a. Would you agree that there is a distinctive set of Latin American values?							
b. Would you agree that schools should make an effort to teach Latin American values?